The Meaning of Whitemen

The Meaning of Whitemen

RACE AND MODERNITY IN
THE OROKAIVA CULTURAL WORLD

Ira Bashkow

THE UNIVERSITY OF CHICAGO PRESS
CHICAGO AND LONDON

IRA BASHKOW is assistant professor of anthropology
at the University of Virginia.

The University of Chicago Press, Chicago 60637
The University of Chicago Press, Ltd., London
© 2006 by The University of Chicago
All rights reserved. Published 2006

Printed in the United States of America

15 14 13 12 11 10 09   2 3 4 5
ISBN: 0-226-03890-4   (cloth)
ISBN: 0-226-03891-2   (paper)

Library of Congress Cataloging-in-Publication Data

Bashkow, Ira

The meaning of whitemen : race and modernity in the Orokaiva cultural world / Ira Bashkow.
    p. cm.

Includes bibliographical references and index.

ISBN 0-226-03890-4 (cloth : alk. paper) — ISBN 0-226-03891-2 (pbk. : alk. paper)

1. Orokaiva (Papua New Guinea people)—Ethnic identity. 2. Orokaiva (Papua New Guinea
people)—Psychology. 3. Orokaiva (Papua New Guinea people)—Attitudes. 4. Blacks—Race
identity—Papua New Guinea—Oro Province. 5. First contact of aboriginal peoples with
Westerners—Papua New Guinea—Oro Province. 6. Ethnopsychology—Papua New Guinea—Oro
Province. 7. Race awareness—Papua New Guinea—Oro Province. 8. Oro Province (Papua New
Guinea)—Race relations. 9. Oro Province (Papua New Guinea)—Social conditions. I. Title.

DU740.42B375 2006
305.8009953′09045—dc22

                                                    2005031375

I DEDICATE THIS BOOK TO STEVEN SEAMBO
AND THE PEOPLE OF AGENEHAMBO:

Nau ajamama, epemane, nameikamei, duepone, hovapahu, meni hatira, na umo ere pekihena. Oro-ta puvuto ungota simba ue, pure donda indihe, ahepoekari umbuhe, jawotoho be ere mihahena. Mihima tao, avo toto egerembeto pambuto Amerika-ta puvuto ke iroja keto avo ijie hihi kaeto kito buku-ta ikihene pambei kijo. Amita jota amo hihi be mane-ra, ke jo be jo mane-ra, amo hamo ke pere-ra. Amo taupamane-ta hihi, enana-ta irari-umbari mo dainge, kaiva embomeni-ta tihi-ta. Aingeto kito amo pure isapa ra, amo kastom-ta ke pepeni-papeni mane-ra, te amita jota amo-re nau humota ari, nau tungambari, mine ari amita hajire kijo. Avora, ke evi kakane ere ua, pekihena jo aima-na kijo, na Aira Robert Bashkow avo erena.

What on earth is whiteness that one should so desire it?

W. E. B. DU BOIS, *Darkwater*

Contents

Photographs follow page 94.

Acknowledgments

Although these pages explain that Orokaiva typify whitemen as persons unencumbered by heavy social obligations who thus are said to be 'light,' I have become, in the course of years of research and writing of this book, extremely heavy with the substantial debts I owe to many who have contributed to the work and sustained me during its preparation.

Writing was supported by a National Endowment for the Humanities Fellowship and a Richard Carley Hunt Postdoctoral Fellowship from the Wenner-Gren Foundation for Anthropological Research. The main fieldwork and archival research on which the study is based was conducted from December 1992 to June 1994 and January to September 1995 with funding from a Wenner-Gren Dissertation Fieldwork Grant and a Fulbright-Hays Dissertation Research Abroad Fellowship. In Papua New Guinea (PNG), the National Research Institute extended the status of Research Associate. I am grateful to all these institutions for their critical help. Any views, findings, conclusions, or recommendations expressed in this book do not necessarily reflect those of the National Endowment for the Humanities, the U.S. Department of Education, or the PNG National Research Institute.

At the University of Virginia, I have enjoyed the intellectual friendship of wonderful colleagues in the Department of Anthropology, which has provided a supportive environment for developing this book and seeing it through to completion. In particular I would like to thank Fred Damon, Richard Handler, Susan McKinnon, Peter Metcalf, and Roy Wagner for reading and commenting on chapter drafts or the dissertation on which the book is based, as well as for their professional guidance and mentorship. I thank Jeff Hantman for his good-natured coaching through the final phases of writing and rewriting, and Dan Lefkowitz and Wende Marshall for helpful conversations about the book's arguments. I am grateful to the students in my courses "Whiteness" and "How Others See Us" in 2001, 2003, and 2004, in which key parts of the book's argument took shape. The University of Virginia's Vice President for Research and Graduate Studies provided funding for summer writing and, with the Dean of the College of Arts and Sciences, a grant to help support the cost of preparing the work for publication.

This book originated as my doctoral dissertation in anthropology at the University of Chicago. I feel an inexhaustible debt of gratitude to George Stocking for his consistent support of my growth as a scholar, for his encouragement of my interest in the history of western understandings of others, and his advice that I pursue it within the discipline of anthropology. His support for my research extended to the point of contributing financially to a feast I held in Agenehambo, and his confidence in the value of my work has been a lodestar helping me keep on course for all this long journey. I also thank Nancy Munn for my first and most rigorous training in ethnographic analysis, and for the example of her own New Guinea research, which has been formative for me. In numerous conversations, she pushed me to think beyond ordinary categories of ethnographic analysis and helped define my framework for understanding the role of whitemen in Orokaiva morality. To Marshall Sahlins I am grateful for establishing important ideas that I now take for granted, for recognizing the theoretical significance of parts of my project when they were as yet inchoate, and for asking deceptively simple questions that significantly advanced my understanding of my material. I am mindful too of my debt to other Chicago teachers and mentors, including Arjun Appadurai, the late Barney Cohn, Jean and John Comaroff, Jim Fernandez, Bill Hanks, John Kelly, Ralph Nicholas, Michael Silverstein, Terry Turner, and the late Valerio Valeri. I thank my dissertation group for much-needed encouragement when my writing was in the fledgling stages: Greg Downey, Anne Lorimer, Susan Seizer, Terry Silvio, Seung-Hoon Song, and Rupert Stasch. For their responses to an early draft of chapter 3, I additionally thank colleagues in the Pacific Ethnography Reading Group at Chicago: Alex Golub, Fred Henry, Don Kulick, Debra McDougall, Daniel Rosenblatt, Danilyn Rutherford, and Michael Scott. Special thanks go to Barney Bate, whose enthusiasm after reading two chapters in draft provided a crucial boost to my belief in the project at a critical stage. Certain basic ideas in this work emerged synergistically out of my conversations with Matti Bunzl, Greg Downey, Anne Lorimer, Daniel Rosenblatt, and Rupert Stasch, to all of whom I am grateful for their colleagueship and enduring friendship. For logistical support during my fieldwork, my thanks go to Anne Ch'ien.

At the University of Chicago Press, I am grateful to David Brent for his clear, early support of this project and to Elizabeth Branch Dyson for shepherding it through the production process with such grace and care. Insightful comments by the anonymous reviewers allowed me to strengthen the clarity of key arguments. Linda Berry of Designers Ink in Charlottesville cheerfully embraced the ins and outs of taro planting, feast piles, babies sleeping in string bags, and so on, in order to produce the book's fine illustrations and maps.

Robert Edgerton, Fred Errington, Michael Gottfried, Catarina Krizancic, and Joan Mathews read the entire book manuscript (or preceding dissertation) and offered encouragement and helpful suggestions. Others who have provided particularly useful responses to draft chapters include John Comaroff, Robert Foster, Ilana Gershon, Laura Lewis, Ali Aghazadeh Naini, Joel Robbins, Stuart Rockefeller, and Thomas Strong. Robert Proctor has been an important mentor since college and provided inspiring advice on the introduction. Versions of chapter 5 were presented at the Princeton Department of Anthropology where I am grateful for comments and questions I received from James Boon, Abdellah Hammoudi, Rena Lederman, and Lawrence Rosen. Bambi Schieffelin, Pamela Stewart, and Andrew Strathern wrote constructive reviews of parts of chapter 4, which appeared in an earlier form as " 'Whitemen' Are Good to Think With: How Orokaiva Morality Is Reflected on Whitemen's Skin" in *Identities: Global Studies in Culture and Power* 7 (3): 281–332; copyright 2000, reproduced by permission of Taylor & Francis, Inc., http://www.taylorandfrancis.com.

I owe a huge debt of thanks to my predecessors in Orokaiva ethnography, especially Eric Schwimmer and André Iteanu, whose wide-ranging scholarship introduced me to Orokaiva ethnography. Their encouragement and practical suggestions helped my fieldwork enormously. (To André Iteanu, I am also indebted, on top of collegial debts, for the gift of a pig.) John Barker, Andrew Chalk, Elin Johnston, Bud Larsen, Bill McKellin, Janice Newton, and Eric Schwimmer have all generously shared with me unpublished manuscripts, bibliographies, and other research materials on Orokaiva history, ethnography, and linguistics, for which I am grateful. I also think back with gratitude to those who helped with PNG contacts and practical advice about doing research there when I was first starting out: Eytan Bercovitch, James Carrier, Colin Filer, Robert Foster, Bud and Marlys Larsen, and Andrew Strathern.

Among the librarians and archivists who have assisted with my historical research are Martin Beckett of the Mitchell Library in Sydney, Kathy Creely of the Melanesian Archives at the University of California at San Diego Library, and Tukul Keiko formerly of the Papua New Guinea

National Archives in Port Moresby. The Australian Board of Missions kindly granted me permission to consult the Anglican Board of Missions Records held in the Mitchell Library, Sydney, and the Australian War Memorial in Canberra allowed me access to their war records collection. Terry Brown, Paul Heikkila, Robin Hide, Ryan Schramm, Nancy Sullivan, and Paige West helped me with up-to-date information on tinfish and rice brands for chapter 5, with Robin graciously producing a trove of PNG newspaper articles from his marvelous database. Jefferson Gray provided particularly helpful references and insights concerning the Middle East.

Over the course of the roughly three and a half years that (to my own surprise) I spent in PNG, the following people extended themselves over long periods as my hosts outside Agenehambo, and I owe them debts of friendship I will never be able to repay: Nick and Jill Araho, Mark Busse, John and Mary Dean, Ian and Lyn Fry, Allan Jones, Russell Mallyon, Laura and Lesley Martin, and Susan Turner. I also wish to express my gratitude for the hospitality or logistical help I received from Bryant Allen, Vere Augerega, Bob and JoAnn Conrad, Frank Coppock, Beth Harding, Bud and Marlys Larsen, Wendy Loi, Tony McKenna, Hope Mueller, Bernard Narokobi, Diny Naus, Lucy Palmer, Richard and Jeanie Teare, and Michael Walter. My research benefited from encouragement and information provided by Brian Deutrom, Bishop David Hand, Malcom Hiari, Wari Iamo, David Ivahupa, Arthur Jawodimbari, Willington Jojoga Opeba, Chris Owen, Bishop Walter Siba, Sylvenus Siembo, and John Waiko, as well as by Robin Atkins, Donald Munro, and Leo Ruki of the Oil Palm Industry Corporation in Popondetta. For their gracious hospitality during two long spells of rest-and-writing at their home in Pusahambo village, I am grateful especially to Angela and Willie Kumaina, David and Joyce Mary Gole, and Suckling and Matilda Asimba.

But my greatest debt in this research unquestionably goes to the Orokaiva people of Agenehambo who patiently taught me about their way of life. Most of all, I thank Steven Seambo for accepting me as his own brother, and for looking out for my well-being and safety over a long period of time. I thank his wife Stella for her patience and tolerance not only of me but also of the many additional people that my presence as a whiteman attracted regularly to her home. I owe a huge debt of gratitude as well to the other Seambo brothers—Mackenton, John Newman, Alphius, and Trophimus—and to their wives—Florence Oreka, Clarissa Tatara, Elna Huvivi, and Dorcas Jamota—and to their sisters Elsie Numari and Jill-Joyce Bage, with their husbands Saidom and John Stafford, for taking me into their family, feeding and caring for me, and helping me with virtually every aspect of my fieldwork, from learning the language to clearing a garden to plant taro, from accompanying me on journeys to helping me find the authoritative tellers of particular tales. I am grateful as well to their many children, particularly Montagill Kanga and Millicent Haunaja, Mary-Faith Indaite, Steven Baiho, Giorgina Noere, Elsie Numari, Arthur Garaina, Hilbert Honi, Bartimus Javoko, Selwyn Ogo, Maisel Diorina, and my saso Robert Joma.

I would like to thank the following other Agenehambo villagers, along with their families, who often hosted and fed me during my stay in their village: James and Theresa Hingopa; Crispin Kirevo and Julia Uraepa; Kingsford, Harriet, and Linda Penunu; Peddy and Joyce Orovo; Gertrude Jigari; Bornfree and Annie Emomo; Rodeny Mamoko and Emma Jajemo; Dorcas Luke Orebi; Neville and Tryposa Deiko; Lester Goira; Noel Goira; Noble Deiko and Lucy Sisiro; Walter Deiko; Cyprian and Millicent Ogo; Conrad Ogo; Lancelot and Cecilia Orovo; Lance Ere; and Gladys Haunaja and Montagill Joma. Perry Scot Orovo, Steven Alfred Penunu, Lina-Faith Penunu, Alphius Seambo, Trophimus Seambo, Steven Seambo, Anselm Monokopa, and Richard Urua assisted me diligently in conducting surveys and making maps. I also thank Dicksford, Jennifer, and Beatrice Penunu; Augustine Penunu; Kerry Penunu; Kevin Penunu; Stafford Ere; Copland Ere; Denzill and Daphen Savote; Stafford Ajame; Damen Auripa; Gretel Monokopa; Gabriel Monokopa; Brian Monokopa; Oscar Monokopa; Jeffrey Orovo; Solomon and Levi Deiko; Napoleon Sogiri; Godwin Senari; Dennis Javoko; Apolas Sohupa; Richard Urua; Wesley Komota; Gaiford Porusa; George Porusa; Dudley Porusa; Leon Porusa; Harry Kivaja; Clare Henika; Jeffrey Haveni; Immanuel Sasere; and Prudence Sumbiri of Peromba with her whole family. I would also like to thank Father Ireneus Baupo, Father Randolph Bipi, Father Jasper Orovari, and Father James Bodger Enuma. I remember too those villagers who have died since my fieldwork began: Abel Gaviro, who was the leader of my adoptive Paru clan, and the last of his generation; Petra Ogo, his daughter, who helped make my first garden; Theresa Deiko, who often brought me cooked food; Benjamin Joma; Ann-Dora Gombari; Augustine of Uhita; Enoch Porusa; Maisel Osiembo; Arthur Gaina; Bartimus Michael; and my dambori Lawrence Kanekari.

Those outside Agenehambo in Orokaiva country I wish to thank include Chris Poraripa, Hansford Baraha, Sailas Orovari, Septimus Evovo, Evatus and Rob-Roy of Timbeki, Frances of Hevapa, Wilson Boruga, Collin Baroi, Hayward Baroi, Dalton Dumai, Gilpin Egupa, Joseph Kimai, Taylor Kiove, Conway Koko, Barnabas Bongade, Benson Osirimbari, Dick

Polas, Gideon Pueka, MacNeil Pueka, Conway Sinahi, Chris Sohembo, Cyprian Soriembo, Arthur and Anastasia Ute, and Nathaniel Victor—and the people of the following villages I visited: Jungata, Pusahambo, Hojane, Mumuni Pe, Uhita, Handarituru, Soroputa, Barevaturu, Timbeki, Kiorota, Koropata, Awala, Isugahambo, Sarimbo, Waseda, Koipa, Jajau, Papaki, Hanjiri, Kokoda, Barisari, Sakita, Korisata, Bolugasusu, Petekiari, Poho, Koninida, Gaiari, Orobeari, Ioma, Kurereda, Iaudare, Barara, Bebewa, Sia, Mambatutu, Taotutu, Deboin, Gona, Kombesusu, Duve, Savarituru, Peretembari, Kogohambo, Kendata, Serembe, Ururu, Sivepe, Sasembata, Hevapa, and Urarituru.

A large part of the first draft of this text was written in Wautogik village, East Sepik Province, where my wife Lise Dobrin was conducting linguistic fieldwork. I thank the people of Wautogik—especially Bernard Narokobi, Jacob and Scola Suonin, the late Arnold Watiem, James Moutu, and the many children of "Red Ground," all of whom helped me in various ways from day to day. I also thank the village as a whole, for welcoming me as their *tambu* (Tok Pisin: in-law) and for their willingness to acknowledge that what I was doing alone in the house all that time was "working," not "sleeping."

I am particularly heavy with debt for the nurture and support I have received from my family. My parents David and Sylvia Bashkow have given me every benefit of love and steadfast encouragement, however long and distant were the paths I chose to tread. My brother Jack Bashkow assisted the fieldwork with long-distance errands like arranging to fix and return broken cameras and tape recorders. Among Orokaiva, a man is especially indebted to his parents-in-law for his spouse and thus his children, and my own in-laws, Philip Dobrin, Joan Mathews, and Emanuela Charlton, deserve this recognition amply. I am grateful for their support of my work in ways both practical and intellectual, and for their loving care of my children during their visits, which lightened our burdens and freed precious time for us to work. My children Elie and Hannah have grown up as this book took shape, and their own tremendous developmental achievements in this time have helped me keep the work in perspective, as does their love. I also wish to express my gratitude to the beloved babysitters, Waldorf School teachers, and family friends whose help and care provided me with needed time for writing this book, especially Sue Garfinkel and Jenny Mills, Chelsea Ralston, Lise Stoessel, Sue Horne, and Lauren Spivey.

Finally, in marrying Lise Dobrin, I learned how accepting the heaviness of obligation can lead to greater strength, well-being, and happiness.

Lise's contribution to the writing of this book has been enormous. Many of the ideas presented in it found their form through our conversations, and her resolute belief in the work emboldened me to simply say what I mean. At many points throughout my work on this project, and for the entire summer of 2004, she devoted herself to helping me with revisions, sitting beside me at the computer, refining the text and sharpening its arguments. It is because of her discernment that my arguments have their clarity and the text has its flow. We met and married when I was returning from my fieldwork and she was laying the groundwork for embarking on her own, allowing so much about PNG to become common sense shared between us. I am humbled to be able to share my life and work with such a person. My happiness only increases with my debt to her.

Note on Orthographic Conventions

Items in the Orokaiva vernacular are transcribed roughly phonemically, with the quality of the vowels as in Italian or Spanish. Stress is always word-initial.

Because so many Orokaiva utterances mix elements from different languages, especially Orokaiva, Tok Pisin, and English, I have needed to resort to an unconventional system for distinguishing literal speech from glosses in quotations. Single quotation marks always enclose glosses and translations from languages other than English (unless otherwise indicated, they are from the Orokaiva vernacular). Where glossed Orokaiva speech includes words or phrases borrowed from other languages such as English, I have generally reproduced the borrowed words as spoken, in italics, within the translated phrase. Apart from sparing use as "scare quotes" to mark problematic or unusual terms, double quotation marks are reserved for material quoted directly in the language of utterance or publication, such as direct quotations of statements made by Orokaiva people in English.

1. Introduction: The Cultural Construction of Whitemen

The Western study of the Third and Fourth World Other gives way to the unsettling confrontation of the West with itself as portrayed in the eyes and handiwork of its Others.

MICHAEL TAUSSIG, *Mimesis and Alterity*

Anglo-Americans, though rarely present in Apache homes, are never really absent from them either.

KEITH BASSO, *Portraits of "the Whiteman"*

This book is about how white people are viewed by black people in the postcolonial Pacific island nation of Papua New Guinea (PNG).[1] I have written the book as an experiment in reorienting the traditional ethnographic enterprise of coming to know others by turning it to the purpose of understanding how others have come to know us. What do others notice about us? How do they make sense of us in terms of their own culture's concepts and values? In what ways do they draw the comparison between themselves and us, and what do the differences they perceive mean to them? For us in the West, there can be great fascination in seeing ourselves from an alien cultural viewpoint. Such a fascination is expressed in literary works as old as Montesquieu's *Persian Letters* (1721), as well as in science fiction and films like *Koyaanisqatsi*. Indeed, one of anthropology's most cherished promises is to show us our lives afresh through the defamiliarizing insight afforded by cross-cultural comparison. Usually it is we who are doing the comparing, but in principle we should be open to the insight that is gained by the others when they are drawing the comparisons themselves.

Beyond helping us learn about ourselves, asking how others see us is also important for what it can teach us about the lives of others, and in particular those significant aspects of their lives that they in some sense attribute to us, as the legacy of our cultural influence. It is a truism of globalization studies that westerners' actions affect the lives of distant others materially, through the global economy, for example, when we buy what they make or when they are affected by our governments' policies. But along with this, we play a symbolic role simply in instantiating vernacular categories such as "European," "westerner," or "American," categories through which, whether we like it or not, we constitute an other that exerts a powerful force in far distant lives.

One such category that is of striking importance to people throughout the world is "the whiteman." It is no historical accident that the whiteman, as a perceived cultural presence, is a global phenomenon, and it is thus unsurprising to hear that the *blanco* or *gringo* in Mexico, the *laowai* in China, and the *obroni* in Ghana are all similarly archetypes of western modernity, wealth, and race privilege, personifying the legacy of imperialism, the ideal of development, and the force of globalization.[2] But what is astonishing is how otherwise varied are the whiteman stereotypes found in different societies: how culturally distinctive are the characteristics attributed to them, the failings and virtues they are thought to exemplify, the fantasies that surround them, the jokes that are told about them, and the conventional wisdom that explains what they are. In this book, I offer a portrait of a particular community's distinctive conception of whitemen, describing the part that this conception plays in people's lives as a cultural other representing the West.

The community I write about, a community of Orokaiva people in eastern Papua New Guinea, has had continued relations with white foreigners for more than a century, forming a history of entanglement with the West which, in its broad outlines, recalls that of other indigenous peoples in many parts of the world. The first Orokaiva encounters with whites were associated with the spread of administrative control by the colonial powers Britain and Australia, which opened the way for more extensive contacts with colonial officers, gold prospectors, plantation labor recruiters, traders, and missionaries. Colonial rule brought economic development projects that focused on cultivating commodity tree crops like cocoa and coffee for world markets, but these projects were largely failures, and in the postcolonial era since Papua New Guinea became an independent nation in 1975, little else has come along to enable Orokaiva to share in world prosperity. In comparison with many indigenous peoples, Orokaiva have been quite successful in maintaining the vitality of their vernacular culture and traditional economy, but over the last decade these have become increasingly imperiled by the large-scale loss of lands which were formerly used for subsistence gardening but are now being dedicated to commodity cash-cropping, an activity spurred on by people's increasing need for cash and by the expansion of a development project for the cultivation of oil palm funded by the World Bank (see chapter 6). In sum, white involvement has changed Orokaiva from a self-ruled people who were sovereign over their own lands and wealthy in their own traditional forms of wealth, to a politically marginalized people who recognize themselves as poor in the context of a global economy.

Given their history, I initially expected that Orokaiva views of whitemen would be predominantly critical. I had in mind previous works such as Julius Lips's 1937 compendium *The Savage Hits Back* and Keith Basso's landmark 1979 study of the jokes Western Apache Indians tell about whitemen, that confront us with primarily negative images of western subjects seen through others' eyes. But the images I encountered among Orokaiva were complex and ambivalent, providing no one-sided condemnation of whites for past wrongs, no comeuppance for colonialism. It is true that Orokaiva were critical of the greed and arrogance that drove whites to colonize foreign lands, and that they resented their material inequality with whites and the failure of white-planned development projects to bring them prosperity. But Orokaiva were also admiring of whites in certain fundamental respects, and they were grateful to whites for having instigated far-reaching changes in their society that Orokaiva do not doubt, as we might, were vastly for the better, morally and practically. As Orokaiva say, whites forced an end to cannibalism and warfare, reducing fear and enabling people to travel more freely. They introduced Christianity, reducing the menace of angry spirits of the dead. They established schools that teach reading and writing, they expanded medical care, and they brought new tools. They introduced many tasty new foods, fruits, and garden crops. With whites came money, cash-crops, and wage work; roads and vehicular transport; radio, post, and, in some places, phones; roofing iron, sawn timber, and other long-lasting building materials; and new techniques of construction. And with whites came batteries, flashlights, kerosene lanterns, and (in the towns) electricity, providing light on dark nights. All these aspects of the white legacy are welcomed.

I have no doubt that in the colonial era Orokaiva resented domination by whites. Some of this resentment is still evident; for example, I saw the ignorance and hauteur of white administrative patrol officers parodied in a clown's performance at a village feast. But today Orokaiva face different problems, like state authorities that are too weak and disorganized to control corruption, lawlessness, and violence. Today, lamenting the progressive degeneration of towns and infrastructure in the years since independence, Orokaiva tend to look back on colonial times with nostalgic fondness.[3] They are not inclined to think that their ancestors suffered indignities or that they were subjugated under colonial rule.[4] And, unlike in many other colonial situations around the world, Orokaiva emerged from colonialism still in control of their customary lands. Because colonial land expropriation was extremely minimal (only roughly 2 percent),[5] Orokaiva culture has maintained its grounding in a lived reality that is organized predominantly around an economic dependence on traditional lands. Today, Orokaiva clear lands for gardens, cut trees to build houses, forage for food and medicines, and hunt for game on the same forested mountain slopes and along the same rivers where their ancestors lived before them and where the events recounted in the myths of their past took place. They live still in many respects at the center of their own cultural universe. And it is from this perspective that their narratives of colonial experience are constructed. They do not see themselves as but one people in a vast global fraternity of colonial victims. In many of the stories they tell, it is as if their ancestors had been behind-the-scenes powers pulling the strings that enabled the colonial project to succeed.[6]

Such are the ambiguities in Orokaiva views of colonialism today. To some, the fact that these views are at all positive may be an embarrassment, flattering as they do certain western self-conceptions such as the metanarratives of civilizational and technological progress that whites used to justify colonialism in New Guinea and elsewhere. To others it may appear a kind of exoneration of the colonial project that positive views of whites are held by people who were among colonialism's victims. But even if Orokaiva views of their colonial history were unambiguously positive (which I emphasize they are not), it would by no means excuse whites for having taken on the "whiteman's burden" in colonial New Guinea, since present day Orokaiva views derive not in fact from colonialism but rather from their experience of the postcolonial situation. The trend in cultural studies fields like postcolonial criticism has been to treat the postcolonial situation as the recapitulation or perpetuation of colonial power relationships, albeit relationships we are encouraged to reconsider. But recent work in anthropology, history, and colonial studies is showing that even the original colonial power relationships were morally and politically complex, and that they were highly specific to particular ethnographic and historical situations.[7] They did not fit the Manichaean image of a morally unambiguous opposition between colonizing master and colonized victim, domination and powerlessness. In light of these new understandings, it is only appropriate to reconsider the postcolonial power relationship from the moral perspective of the people concerned.

I do not attempt here to reconcile Orokaiva evaluations of their colonial past with western moral frameworks concerned with the justice of past western interventions. Just as we in the West are primarily interested in what our history with others can reveal to us about ourselves, Orokaiva are primarily interested in what their shared history with the West can reveal to them about themselves. Thus, it is primarily their own concerns that we find reflected in the stories they tell about whitemen. To understand Orokaiva discourse about whitemen and the West, we need to understand it in its particular ethnographic and historical context. This book is therefore actually about Orokaiva people, and not about white people. It is about the ideas that Orokaiva have about whites, and the role of these ideas in their culture today.

The terms for 'the whiteman' in Orokaiva are mostly foreign loan words. The most commonly used are "whiteman" and "whiteskin," from English by way of the Papua New Guinea lingua franca Tok Pisin, and *taupa* or *taupada* (plural: *taupamane*), which are assimilations of the word *taubada* ('big man,' 'whiteman') from Police Motu, the lingua franca used in Papua during colonial times. Other loan words include the Anglo-Australian term "European" and Tok Pisin *masta* ('master'), though the latter is increasingly rare. Orokaiva also use some interesting vernacular expressions with specialized connotations. Two which are considered archaic and poetic are *ijo hujo*, meaning 'those who go and come' or 'moving haphazardly hither and yon,' and, in the Aeka dialect, *sisiki popoki*, which means 'wanderers' (Williams 1930, 152). Orokaiva explain these terms through stories of their early experiences of the whites who traveled in colonial administrative patrols. Orokaiva, like Melanesians elsewhere, marveled that these white men walked anywhere they pleased, respecting neither boundaries of lands nor fences nor privacy of gardens; they crossed indiscriminately through the lands of friends and enemies, remaining in transit, and always in a hurry. A further set of expressions are metaphors for the skin color of whites and are used primarily in humorous or indirect speech, for examples, 'white cockatoo skin,' 'shafts of sunlight skin,' 'bright flaring torch skin,' and 'wheat-flour white skin'—the last using an adaptation (*parara*) of the English word "flour" (Tok Pisin: *plaua*). All of these terms are glossed here as 'whiteman' or 'whitemen.' But I retain the term *taupa* in the important Orokaiva phrase, *taupa kastom*, meaning the 'customs' or 'ways' of whitemen, or Orokaiva perceptions of western culture.

From this point on, I will attempt to maintain a consistent distinction between 'whiteman' or 'whitemen' on the one hand, and English phrases like "white men," "white people," and "whites" on the other. The latter are meant to refer to actual white people; the former refer to Orokaiva constructions of whites. The gender bias inherent in these terms is not merely linguistic; Orokaiva conceive of whitemen stereotypically as men. Historically, their interactions with whites have been most frequently with men, and many of the attributes they associate with whitemen, such as great mobility, are culturally masculine qualities. Because the gender bias is itself culturally significant, I do not take the usual tack of trying to neutralize it in my terminology.[8] Similarly, I maintain the racially oversimplified terminological opposition between "white" and "black" because it is in fact the central organizing principle of Orokaiva vernacular racial categorization.

Even so, the application of Orokaiva racial categories is complex, and it is often manipulated in creative and counterintuitive ways. Like other Papua New Guineans, Orokaiva are intensely interested in racial ambiguities such as those they perceive in black Americans, in other wealthy black foreigners, and in individuals whose racial appearance or ancestry is mixed. The category of whitemen sometimes, but not always, includes Asians from China, the Philippines, and Japan along with Caucasians from England, America, and Australia. When discussing particular whites Orokaiva are often concerned to identify the person's nationality (e.g., Australian, German, American), and, as we will see, they liberally bend and revise racial boundaries to suit their aims in particular contexts, often as a means to overcome social boundaries and strengthen relationships with individual expatriates and Papua New Guineans of other ethnic groups. This kind of malleability belies the fact that, at bottom, racial categories reflect only one way of dividing a complex human reality that could be conceptually divided in other ways just as well, and that their seeming naturalness, which is so important a part of their meaning, is illusory, a reflection of our general human tendency to mistake convention for necessity (Boas 1965 [1938]).

But while it is important to recognize the arbitrariness, flexibility, and context dependence of racial categories, we must not underestimate the ideological power of the basic opposition between black and white skin to color people's imaginings of their social universe. Among Orokaiva, as throughout Papua New Guinea, this opposition shapes people's thoughts on such diverse matters as education, time use, diet, architecture, morality, religion, and economics, and it does so in ways that tend to place the ambiguity and complexity of race in the background. In this book, rather than looking past the black/white opposition to focus on the complexities into which it breaks down, I try to understand the basis for its powerful force. As W. E. B. Du Bois asked long ago in America, why is the cunning division of humanity into black and white so compelling to people? Why, despite evidence to the contrary, does it continue to seem to people so definite, natural, and well founded?[9]

There are many works that deal with indigenous people's perceptions of whites in the earliest phases of their historical contact with them. This book, in contrast, is about the present-day postcolonial situation when whitemen are hardly new and have become quite familiar. A hundred years ago when Orokaiva had their initial contacts with whites, they had only the resources of their traditional culture with which to make sense of them, and so it was to concepts such as spirit versus human and to vernacular ideas about power and travel that Orokaiva assimilated their first impressions. This is not to say that the arrival of white men caught them entirely unaware; in all likelihood they had some foreknowledge of whitemen from neighbors' reports. But these too would surely have been understood in the terms of an essentially precontact traditional culture. Now that whites have participated in the Orokaiva world for several generations, those initial impressions have not been perpetuated unchanged, nor, however, have they completely disappeared. Rather, they have been elaborated into a much more complex specialized area of knowledge about whitemen, their ways, and their things, an area that Orokaiva refer to as taupa kastom.

Readers sometimes seek to understand the Orokaiva construction of whitemen by evaluating its similarity to qualities they perceive in themselves, or by attempting to derive its features from particular white individuals with whom Orokaiva had historical contact, such as missionaries, traders, and colonial administrative patrol officers. But we must appreciate that for some five generations now Orokaiva children have been introduced to whitemen by hearing about them from other Orokaiva. They have grown up in communities in which Orokaiva themselves increasingly take the part of whitemen in 'whitemen's activities' like church and business. They have grown up eating 'whitemen's foods' that they have been fed by their own mothers and aunts. Orokaiva do have dealings with actual white people both in the villages and outside them, and some Orokaiva have even stayed with whites in their overseas homes. But for the most part Orokaiva interpret these experiences with white people from the reference point of their far more intimate acquaintance with the construction of whitemen they learned about first at home.

It is not that this Orokaiva construction of whitemen bears no correspondence to white men whatsoever. To the contrary, it is a sedimentation of historical experiences in culturally transmitted knowledge. It conventionalizes attributes of whites that are noticeable and indeed striking to Orokaiva in comparison with themselves and their vernacular culture. Some aspects of this construction, like Orokaiva impressions that whitemen are highly mobile and enjoy relative wealth, reflect the realities of the particular circumstances in which Orokaiva encounter whites. Others, like ideas that whitemen regulate their activities by calendrical and clock time; that they live on money, using money to obtain even their basic needs of housing and food; that they bear only relatively light material obligations to most of their kinsmen; and that they are little afflicted by sorceries worked by others jealous of their successes—all of these might well be considered real cultural generalities in much of the West, though they emerge for Orokaiva only through contrasts they draw with their vernacular culture. That Orokaiva essentialize these typifications—considering them broadly characteristic of whitemen even though they do not in fact apply to all white people in all "western" countries—should not lead us to the absurd conclusion that their construction of whitemen is merely fanciful. Instead, Orokaiva selectively draw from, transform, and reinterpret their experience of whitemen and the West within a contemporary indigenous framework of ideas and moral economy.

In important respects, the Orokaiva construction of whitemen is similar to western constructions of "primitives" and "orientals," such as Jean Jacques Rousseau's "noble savage" who knew no false bodily needs; Denis Diderot's invented Tahitians, free of artificial sexual inhibitions; the primitives of Victorian evolutionist anthropology who were constructed as morally inferior and intellectually confounded, unable to interpose reason between impulse and act; the primitives of early modernist art who were celebrated for their aesthetic vitality; and the ecologically sensitive primitives of recent western counterculture, who provide the West with alternative models for authentic ritual, balance in social relations, and harmony with nature (Ellingson 2001; Bartra 1994; Stocking 1968, 1987; Clifford 1988; Torgovnick 1990; Rosenblatt 1997; Diderot 1964 [1772]). In all of these examples, as in "orientalist" constructions of "the East" as timeless, mystical, corrupt, sexually exotic, and despotic (Said 1978), we find discourses organized around an antinomy of self versus other. Westerners know such "primitives" predominantly by virtue of these discourses, and not from direct experience and encounters with the peoples that the discourses purport to represent. Indeed, when they do come into contact with the actual "primitives," their perceptions are mediated by what they already "know" from the discourse, and they may find themselves explaining away the experience as an aberration given what they "knew" (see, e.g., Deloria 1998).

Our western notions of primitives are charged—compelling to us—because they respond to the moral concerns of our own society at a particular time. Material needs and desires, sexuality, artistic creativity, rationality, authenticity; these are among the major themes in western self-consciousness that the primitivist discourses have provided an arena for us to explore. And just as we do with our primitives, the Orokaiva project onto their whitemen, from their own evaluative viewpoint, their most pressing moral concerns. So just as the western "primitive" may say more about the culture of the West than it does about the supposed primitives, the Orokaiva construction of whitemen ultimately leads us to a greater understanding of the world of the Orokaiva.

Modernity and Race

One of the central arguments of this book is that, for Orokaiva, modernity and race are understood in terms of each other: the Orokaiva construction of whitemen reflects people's experience of modernity and social and economic change—development, as they conceive it—and conversely, Orokaiva notions of modernity and development are personified in their construction of whitemen. When I first set out to do research among Orokaiva, my aim was to understand the ways they thought about development. Given that the impetus for their development activity so often originated with foreign agencies with their own interests and aims based in a global political economy, what might development mean to people whose participation in those projects was shaped by their own political economy and cultural assumptions? But what I quickly realized was that my Orokaiva informants thought it quite odd that *I* should be asking *them* about development. From their perspective, I must myself be an expert on development; after all, I was white. Development was something they were eager to learn about from *me*, and they brushed aside my questions with the answer, "Look, our skin is black. Development means living like you whitemen." With gestures to my bare arm they made it plain that I myself represented the state of development about which I was asking. Eventually I began to take seriously that this *was* the answer, that skin color was the predominant idiom through which Orokaiva contrasted their traditional lives with modernity. Indeed, it proved impossible to separate people's ideas of race from their ideas of modernity. Modernity, among Orokaiva, is so deeply "raced" that it is a racial concept itself.

There have been few ideas as compellingly criticized as the natural connection of modernity with race. Such a connection was central to theories of social evolution in nineteenth-century scholarly thought,[10] as well as to European imperialist ideology, according to which whites brought progress to colonized peoples who were incapable of bringing it about themselves. The arguments against this quintessentially modern Eurocentric idea are manifold. For one thing, European modernity, beginning in the Enlightenment, itself drew frequent inspiration from racially diverse peoples in China, North Africa, and elsewhere outside Europe; for another, the crucial context in which Europeans came to understand themselves as modern was in the experience of self-comparison with non-Europeans.[11] And any idea of an intrinsic connection between modernity and Europe or between modernity and whiteness is utterly confounded by the existence of non-European modernities, such as the one that linked together black artists and intellectuals on both sides of the Atlantic in the nineteenth and twentieth centuries (Gilroy 1993), and the culturally distinctive "development miracles" that are well known to us in Japan, Korea, and other parts of contemporary East Asia.[12] Given that Europe has held no monopoly on such hallmarks of modernity as progress and rationality, postmodernist scholars have successfully challenged the Eurocentric notion of a singular western modernity. But their critiques, which have sought to fragment it into a plurality of histories and discourses that reflect differences in positions of power, do not lead us to a deeper understanding of modernity as itself a racialized discourse. Instead, the whole connection is critically dismissed as a problematic consequence of western power.

From the perspective of such critiques, the Orokaiva premise that development is a natural characteristic of whitemen can only reflect the Eurocentric hegemony of race that was imposed on them in colonial times. Not that this is wrong; it was under colonialism, after all, that Orokaiva confronted race as a social barrier creating unequal access to imported wealth, and it was under colonialism that they suffered the humiliation of being told they were "backward" in contrast to whites' "advancement." Under colonialism, whites' persistent efforts to change Orokaiva habits, economy, religion, and so on incorporated Orokaiva into the western paradigm of inequality in which whites, as instigators of progress, were the active makers of history, while blacks were passive subjects: at best, they were followers who could attain a second-hand civilization by imitating the whites. But colonial origins are an insufficient explanation for the Orokaiva association of modernity with whiteness, since as we shall see, such origins hardly exhaust the current significance of whiteness for Orokaiva. The Orokaiva co-construction of race and modernity is today perpetuated by Orokaiva in a formulation that is distinctive to Orokaiva vernacular culture and that interacts with global frameworks of development and with western ideas of race and power in complex ways. Although modern forms of racism in PNG have colonial origins, knowing this is not enough to specify the complexities of local racial dynamics or the particularities of how race is constructed. As Franz Boas showed long ago, the meaning of a thing in its culture of origin does not determine the meanings that it takes on in new cultural settings; when we emphasize derivation from western sources, it directs our attention away from those aspects of the Orokaiva co-construction of race and modernity that are essentially the most important ones from the perspective of the people themselves. Moreover, the racially charged Orokaiva conception of modernity raises a question that hardly receives a second thought in western contexts where it is obvious that associating modernity with race reproduces a self-interested western dominance in the global status quo: why should Orokaiva continue to accept a premise that for them is so disempowering? There would seem to be little for Orokaiva to gain from treating modernity as the essential property of the white other. And much like the old Eurocentric ideas that western scholars have so vehemently criticized, the Orokaiva raced construction of modernity is inadequate for depicting reality inasmuch as it presupposes clear social lines that are in fact contradicted by the complex distribution of key symbols of modernity across varied subclasses of whites, as well as among Asians, nonwhites such as Africans, urban Papua New Guineans, and even Orokaiva villagers themselves. Why, then, should Orokaiva continue to accept such a disempowering and descriptively inadequate artifact of an outmoded colonial racial hegemony? To answer this question requires us to appreciate the Orokaiva folk conception of race in its own terms, and to recognize the uses to which racialized views of modernity are put by Orokaiva within the contemporary discursive practices of their own society.

In order to do this, I have found it useful to reconsider what racial stereotypes and cultural constructions of race actually consist of. While critical studies of race long ago established that popular racial stereotypes are misleading in that they do not in fact correspond to definable groups, scholars have nonetheless for the most accepted that, in one critical sense, stereotypes are indeed what they purport to be, namely representations (albeit false ones) of persons or groups of persons. But what we shall see by looking at the construction of race in the unfamiliar context of Orokaiva society is a folk conception of race that is more complicated than this: in the Orokaiva construction of whitemen, it is not only—and not even primarily—persons that anchor the key symbolic components of the racial stereotype. To the contrary, the most salient characteristics attributed to whitemen are substantiated in areas other than persons: in objects like store-bought foodstuffs, in institutions like business and church, in places like town (as opposed to the village), and in styles of activity like clock-based patterns of time use, all of which are identified with whitemen symbolically yet exist independently of actual white persons and are typically experienced outside their presence. My observation that racial stereotypes consist not only of ideas about persons but also crucially involve objects, institutions, places, and styles of activity helps us understand why racial stereotypes remain so robust even when contravened by the facts and people's experience, and it is surely relevant to the study of race in other ethnographic contexts. For example, it helps explain why U.S. whites' stereotypes of African Americans have remained so robust notwithstanding a century of scientific criticism which has established their falsity as representations of persons. These stereotypes are highly resilient because they are built from elements that include not only imputed personality characteristics and typified demeanors of African American persons, but also perceptions of objects like hip-hop clothing and certain styles of cars, of institutions like gangs and one-parent families, of places like inner-city churches and neighborhoods, and of activities like street hustling and gangsta youth style. The point is that because such elements, which form a protean set, exist outside of persons, they are appropriable and can become meaningful within the life experience of people who hold the stereotype, substantiating the stereotype in ways that do not depend on, and cannot be contravened by, knowledge of actual persons who may fail to make sense in terms of it. It is in just this way that the racialized construction of modernity is robust for Orokaiva even in the face of its ambiguous distribution in the populations they encounter.

Another issue I have found it helpful to reconsider is the uses to which people put cultural otherness and oppositions of "us" versus "them." Us/them antinomies are regarded with suspicion because we assume they are inherently prejudicial to the other. Such an assumption is foundational to Edward Said's important critique of *Orientalism* (1978), which suggests that *any* division of humankind into an "us" and a "them" is necessarily suffused with cultural self-conceit and expresses "hostility" to the other (Said 1978, 45; see also Said 1993; Clifford 1988, 261). In the work of postcolonial critics who have elaborated Said's ideas, the us/them distinction is often repudiated as part of a "binary (self/other) logic of colonial power" that is associated with Eurocentrism, imperialist expansionism, and racial discrimination—it is treated, in short, as something that in the worlds we study is bad, and that our work should strive to transcend (Prakash 1995, 3; see also Carrier 1995). But as Xiaomei Chen has compellingly argued in her study of Chinese portrayals of the West that are unremittingly positive and that thus directly oppose the Maoist government's official anti-western propaganda, the cultural discourse of otherness is not intrinsically invidious, and it is not necessarily prejudicial toward the other; indeed, its very moral neutrality (or flexibility) makes it possible for symbolic constructions that take the same form, self versus other, to be "manipulated for very different ideological ends" (Chen 1992, 693; see also Sax 1998; Scott 1999).

Among Orokaiva, whitemen are not objects of the kind of hostility so often associated with "us" versus "them" divisions of humanity. Rather, as we shall see, whitemen are morally ambiguous figures which are evaluated differently depending on people's purposes in the context of speaking. In some circumstances Orokaiva inferiorize them, constructing them in opposition to indigenous virtues like generous gift-giving and hospitality, hard work, and compassion for unfortunates. In other circumstances they project onto whitemen superior values, endowing them with desired qualities of self-control and social harmony. Ambiguity characterizes not only the *evaluation* of whitemen as good or bad, attractive or repulsive, better or worse than Orokaiva themselves, but also the very *otherness* of whitemen, their difference and distance from Orokaiva (see also Todorov 1984, 185). As the following chapters show, the salient qualities of whitemen that mark them as exotic or alien emerge against a background of shared characteristics that Orokaiva take for granted in themselves. For example, in being attributed a morally charged freedom from material obligations to kin, whitemen are striking exceptions to the human condition as Orokaiva experience it. Yet at the same time Orokaiva assume that whitemen depend for their wealth on maintaining the favor of their deceased ancestors, a dependence that Orokaiva project onto whitemen on the implicit presupposition that whitemen are similar to themselves and that they inhabit essentially the same world of causality and morality. A background of similarity is not in contradiction with the perception of meaningful difference; to the contrary, it is necessary for the differences between Orokaiva and whitemen to constitute a stark contrast. In effect, then, there is "a perpetual tension" in the Orokaiva construction of whitemen between separation or difference, on the one hand, and closeness, similarity, or affinity, on the other (Tambiah 1985, 208). Whitemen are a cultural other for Orokaiva, but this does not put them in a decisively different ontological realm. Rather, Orokaiva draw whitemen into a shared moral universe with them as part of the very process by which they distinguish whitemen from themselves.

These two dimensions of ambiguity in terms of moral inferiority versus superiority and alienness versus affinity come together in the Orokaiva use of whitemen as a foil for cultural self-critique. In a common genre of rhetoric, Orokaiva criticize themselves and their society for failings such as fractiousness, sorcery, and lawlessness that are held to be absent in the idealized world of the other. Although the failings are ones that concern Orokaiva as problems they seek to solve for their own reasons, the virtues like social harmony and lawfulness that correspond to them as their inversions are attributed to whitemen because Orokaiva tend to identify material wealth and power with moral virtue, and whitemen are the consummately wealthy and powerful beings in their contemporary cosmology. As a result, whitemen come to be identified with a higher morality characterized by an absence of precisely those problems that most preoccupy Orokaiva in their own society. Through this projective process, the discourse of whitemen serves as a medium through which Orokaiva blame themselves and their race for their subordinate position in the world economy. Yet it is not a discourse of abjection in which everything connected to the self is degraded. In constructing whitemen in terms of indigenous virtues that invert their own moral failings, Orokaiva assert the primacy of local categories and moral concerns, thereby effectively projecting onto the wider world the essential dimensions of their own noncapitalist ethos.

If what Ashis Nandy (1983) has called the "intimate enemy"—the West internalized by its non-western others—has become an ambiguous, morally complex, and culturally creative "intimate alter" for Orokaiva, then this has implications for our understanding of globalization. For one thing, it shows how the West and "the global" actually exist in distinctive cultural versions, so that people, as they construct their particular versions, help shape the western influences they feel. This perspective, which is consonant with the recent literature on "vernacular modernities" and the "indigenization of modernity" (Knauft 2002a; Sahlins 1992, 1997; Sivaramakrishnan and Agrawal 2003), does not make the particularization of modernity an unequivocally positive or even redemptive form of globalization. A modernity constructed as an answer to the self's problems is highly effective at insinuating itself into local cultural processes and tapping into the dynamics of the local moral order, exploiting its weaknesses and leading people to devalue the traditional culture to which it seems antithetical. In this way, the inevitable problems that beset life in any society become central motivations driving people's desire to reforge their society in the image of the modern other.

Whiteness and Method

As a white person myself, should it not be awkward to conduct research among black people in PNG about their ideas of modernity and race, issues that would surely be central to their perceptions of who I was? Would the fact that I was white not influence the responses they gave to my questions and the actions they took in my presence, distorting my findings? To this fair question I offer two answers. One is the classic Malinowskian premise of fieldwork, in which, despite all the controversy that surrounds it, I believe strongly: learn the language and stick around long enough, sharing in people's everyday lives and listening carefully, and at some point or another, it all comes out in the open.

But there is a second, more challenging answer, which requires a perhaps uncomfortable adjustment of the importance we attribute to objectivity in producing knowledge in the human sciences. Rather than assuming that I needed to minimize the distortions that inevitably arise in participant observation, I instead embraced my own whiteness as a research tool in studying the views of whiteness held by my black informants, to whom I was most definitely saliently white, developed, and western. Through our interactions I was able to learn what my whiteness represented for them (in the same way that minorities in America get to know how they are represented by the mainstream)—through countless revelations, large and small, of people's assumptions about my life, through the questions they asked me, and through the roles they expected of—and indeed foisted on—me, their white friend. What I thus attempt here is a self-reflective ethnography that is not autobiographical or confessional, nor oriented to the critique of representational strategies as in familiar "reflexivisms" that seek to hedge or deny the authorial power ethnographers have. Instead, I attempt a reflexivism that is empirically and ethnographically focused. Following George Devereux, I have tried to discover how my own world was perceived by my Orokaiva research subjects and to learn from the complementary roles and ascribed statuses they projected onto me (1967, 27–28, 234, 243; see also Englund and Leach 2000). In short, I found that my own whiteness, far from being a hindrance to my project, actually provided me with a powerful methodology that allowed it to succeed.

My interest in this methodology grew out of a previous study in which I examined the anthropologist David Schneider's fieldwork on the

Micronesian islands of Yap in the 1940s; in that study I focused on the relation between ethnographic knowledge and the colonial situation of ethnographic research (Bashkow 1991). As I read through nearly two thousand pages of Schneider's field notes and correspondence, I discovered a side of his research and, indeed, sensibility, that one would not have expected from reading the relatively technical and theoretical kinship studies for which he is best known. In his field notes, Schneider offers extensive introspective reflections on his evolving relationships with particular Yapese informants, describing the ways in which their responses to him were affected by the colonial context, despite all his efforts to distance himself from the islands' colonial administration. Although he himself was American, Schneider was disturbed that his informants associated him with the U.S. naval administration of the islands, with which he felt ethically at odds. But nothing he did or told the Yapese could change their views. Instead, when Yapese saw Schneider break Navy rules with impunity, they concluded, to his exasperation, that he represented an authority that must be "higher than the Navy" within the same basic category of American whites.

Schneider's insight into Yapese culture turned out to be most penetrating where he grasped that his own colonial power distorted the ways in which the Yapese represented their culture to him. Yapese patterns of accommodation to colonial rule colored the motivations of his Yapese hosts and informants and biased the things they told him about their politics, kinship, and lands. In part because he thought that these distortions invalidated his data, he ultimately "pulled" this contextually sensitive material from his ethnography, and instead specialized in kinship, which seemed to him an area of culture where the colonial situation of his research on Yap would not affect his results. But this impression turned out to be wrong. Because he had discounted the effects of the colonial situation on his data, Schneider came to an interpretation of Yapese kinship that he was later forced to repudiate (Schneider 1984). It was not in the material he published, but in the material he "pulled" that Schneider achieved some of his most enduringly valuable insights into Yapese culture. It was here that he understood the ultimately political reasons why his data were distorted in the particular ways they were.

The methodological implication I draw from Schneider's experience on Yap goes against a tradition, perpetuated in anthropologists' oral lore and published memoirs, that idealizes the notion of "rapport" in ethnographic fieldwork. This tradition holds that authentic relationships between fieldworker and subjects are essential if the researcher is to achieve the empathetic insight that is the cornerstone of humanistic anthropological understanding. Such authenticity requires that the anthropologist break through the ascribed identities based on colonial power, race privilege, and superior wealth that informants initially project onto him or her in the field. Thus, in his famous introduction to *Argonauts*, Bronislaw Malinowski explains that he had to set himself apart from colonial officials, missionaries, and traders, so that the natives would accept him, unlike these others, in their daily lives (Malinowski 1984 [1922], 6). In his essay on the Balinese cockfight, Clifford Geertz tells us that his perceived complicity with the Balinese when he fled with them in a police raid had the effect of breaking down barriers of artificiality and distrust that had previously prevented him from achieving rapport (Geertz 1973, 415–16). Indirectly, this idealization of rapport is also reflected in writing since the 1960s' "crisis in anthropology" that criticizes anthropology's institutional ties with colonialism as invalidating the moral integrity of the field and thus its scientific value (Leclerc 1972; Asad 1973; de L'Estoile 1997; Pels and Salemink 1999; see also Hymes 1972).

But as I saw in Schneider's experience on Yap, and as I found in my own field experience, this romantic egalitarian ideal of rapport is fundamentally flawed. For one thing, it is based on an overly simplistic and ethnocentric model of power. For another, it is at best possible to achieve only partially, and at worst the effort to shed power itself intensifies the asymmetry. And finally, by denying that power asymmetries can themselves constitute an authentic part of fieldwork relationships, the ideal of rapport denies us a useful tool for understanding the real processes that perpetuate inequality and domination.

Power has long been a focus of interest in the human sciences. Centuries of reflection have produced models of power that are dialogic and complex. We understand well that power is always an interdependent relationship involving complicity and indeed reciprocity between superiors and subordinates (Hegel 1977 [1807]; Kojève 1969). We have learned how exercising power itself produces knowledge, so that those linked in hierarchical relationships come to have an intimate familiarity with one another through their roles (Foucault 1979). And yet we consistently shy away from the power that we ourselves hold in many ethnographic relationships, assuming that this power is inherently exploitative and antithetical to empathetic anthropological insight (Buckley 1987). But not only is this inconsistent with what we know to be true of power relationships more generally, it is also a culturally (and probably class) specific view of power. For their part, Orokaiva, like Yapese, do not view power as inherently bad; far from it, they see power as a sign of virtue and ancestral favor. Thus, anthropologists' impulse to deny their power is fundamentally ethnocentric.[13]

Nor, as Schneider found and my own fieldwork experience confirmed, is denying this power actually feasible. From the point of view of my Orokaiva informants, the power implied by my whiteness was a central aspect of our relationships, while my social identity in my own culture was irrelevant. Social distinctions that were basic and important to me, such as the contrast between my goals in New Guinea and those of missionaries, were simply not meaningful to most Orokaiva villagers in the way they were to me. Moreover, I recognized that the actions I could take in the field in order to lower my status, minimize expressions of my power, and decline the special privilege that people gave me because of my whiteness—such as refusing to sit in the one available chair—would often have been ungrateful and arrogant. Such actions would themselves have been an exercise of power over them, because they would have forced people to behave in ways that they themselves considered inappropriate and that contradicted their sense of proper hospitality and respect. Paradoxically, it is only by accepting the power and privilege that our informants extend to us that we empower them by allowing them to structure the encounter in ways that reflect and respond to their own values and interests. It would of course be immoral to take this acceptance of power to an extreme.[14] But it is also a false egalitarianism that refuses to accept the few things that the people genuinely want to give us and are in fact able to give while not materially depriving themselves.

The power that anthropologists have in the field should not be rejected as merely an obstruction to good ethnography. Rather, it can be an important tool for understanding the real processes that perpetuate inequality and domination in the culturally and historically specific situations in which they occur. In Papua New Guinea, as in much of the world, power is specifically associated with whiteness. What I came to understand through my fieldwork experience is that the meaning whiteness holds for others is not coextensive with the meanings we ourselves imbue it with—race privilege, power, and so on. The meanings of whiteness for Orokaiva reflect their own historical experience, are substantiated in their own present-day activities, and are lent coherence and supported even in their contradictions by their place within their own scheme of ideas. The meaning of whiteness for Orokaiva was something I could only learn about through first-hand experiences of the way it colored their relationships with me, a white man, while I lived among them during my fieldwork.

During my fieldwork, my whiteness was something Orokaiva were very interested in and often wanted to talk about, and initially I feared that my own actions and talk would affect people's ideas about whitemen, the West, and modernity that were the focus of my research, so that I would be unable to know what these "really were" apart from my presence (cf. Kulick 1992, 271–72). But I quickly learned that Orokaiva notions about whitemen and the West were highly resilient. In instances where I contradicted them, it was not the case that people would immediately revise their views in light of what I had said; they were more likely to explain my information away as an anomaly. For one close informant the proper understanding of the whiteman's capacities was a matter of intense intellectual concern and practical exploration. From me he wanted new understandings, though he only seemed to fully assimilate what I said when it made sense in the familiar terms of his culture. When I gave him an answer that did not fit his prior knowledge and assumptions, he often ignored it; perhaps he would nod politely, as if in agreement, then change the topic, or else rephrase his question from a new angle, as I so often did with him. On reflection, it seems an odd conceit to think that anything I would say would radically transform his patterns of thought. Even had I wanted to, it would have been hard to reconfigure his basic conceptions about whitemen and their ways; after all, whitemen were a part of his world and had been so since before the time of his grandfathers, and his views were not mere speculations, lightly held or lightly considered, unmirrored and untested in his own experience and ongoing life projects. I was a white man, but I was just one small part of his world of experience, and it is only reasonable that I should have been constructed in his terms, rather than able to change those terms with a few of my utterances.

In any case, my situation and body revealed more to Orokaiva than anything I said. Could I have denied that I had traveled there from a faraway place and that I had ample access to money? Could I deny that my hands and feet, unlike theirs, were soft and uncalloused, and that because of my whiteness I attracted attention and special treatment wherever I went? No, I could not deny these salient aspects of my presence in their world. But I could try to understand, from the point of view of Orokaiva, what they meant.

Chapter Outline

The chapters that follow develop varied perspectives on the meaning of whitemen in the Orokaiva cultural world. Chapter 2 lays out the *ethnographic and historical background* which is necessary for understanding contemporary Orokaiva constructions of whitemen. I introduce the reader to the basic dimensions of cultural life in Agenehambo village, the location where my research was concentrated, and I situate Agenehambo in the wider regional context of Orokaiva peoples known from the classic studies by F. E. Williams, Eric Schwimmer, and André Iteanu. Whites were increasingly involved in the world of Orokaiva peoples through the 1960s, but after the local white population peaked in the years before independence, whites began to recede from the scene, moving back overseas or retreating to air-conditioned head offices in Papua New Guinea's cities and towns. But even as whites' physical presence among Orokaiva has decreased, the importance of whitemen and taupa kastom in the local culture has continued undiminished, as an elaborate complex of ideas about whitemen and their customs, institutions, and things has developed in the vernacular culture. Although the moral status of whitemen has long been ambiguous for Orokaiva, positive evaluations of whitemen have become especially plausible and compelling to Orokaiva in the postcolonial context. National independence and the ongoing trend of postcolonial white flight have changed local race relations and made possible nostalgic reassessments of colonialism, while distancing whites from contemporary social problems and political power. By virtue of these structural changes, the construction of whitemen has been divested of many of the negative features historically associated with whites, allowing the whiteman to become a compelling cultural and moral other that Orokaiva use as a foil for evaluating and objectifying their own moral strengths and failings.

The next three chapters examine the characteristic attributes of whitemen as Orokaiva construct them. We will see that similar attributes emerge as significant in diverse contexts such as whitemen's social habits, travel, sexuality, exchange, bodies, and foods, a redundancy that makes them appear all the more self-evident and natural to Orokaiva. Chapter 3, on *whitemen's lightness*, introduces a quality that Orokaiva associate with whitemen and whitemen's things as an essential and ubiquitous attribute. Whitemen are seen as possessing several special powers, the most important of which is their impressive—and desirable—ability to extend themselves and their influence across spatial distance. This ability to travel represents a moral condition of 'lightness' (*ejeha*) that in Orokaiva culture stands for lack of encumbrance by social obligations or troubles. Since for Orokaiva, normal moral existence also includes times when a person is 'heavy' (*boka*) with debt, obligation, or grief, restricting his movements and limiting his ability to act in ways that extend his influence over space, the apparent ease with which whitemen regularly travel, and the vast distances they cover, suggest for Orokaiva an extreme condition of lightness that is unbalanced by its natural moral complement, the inevitable heaviness of human life. Orokaiva are struck by this unnatural and uncanny quality of lightness in whitemen, and I often saw their ambivalence about it reflected in laughter and jokes.

In chapter 4, I discuss Orokaiva ideas about *whitemen's bodies*, particularly the skin. The chapter is organized into six sections. The first introduces basic Orokaiva conceptions of the person, body, and skin. For Orokaiva, the person has both an invisible 'inside' (*jo*) that others cannot know directly and that is the seat of the will, and a quintessentially social outer body or 'skin' (*hamo*), which is the medium of social relationships and of a person's visible social characteristics like possessions and wealth. Orokaiva do not generalize about whitemen's inner wills, but rather about the qualities that are apparent on their outer skin. The five sections that follow focus on two highly charged qualities that are held to characterize whitemen's skin, 'softness' (*suruha*) and 'brightness' (*usasa*). The softness of whitemen's skin is understood to result from three things: that they use expensive commodities such as shoes, mattresses, and imported medicines to care for their skin; that they do not regularly enter harsh environments such as the dense jungle where Orokaiva by necessity go to produce their food; and that they do not perform the kinds of heavy outdoor work that cause Orokaiva bodies— especially men's bodies—to become hard and callused. Since it is only by means of such work that Orokaiva can themselves create wealth, a morally charged question arises for Orokaiva: how do whitemen obtain their elaborate wealth without doing any hard physical work? The second quality, brightness, associates the light color of whitemen's skin with visibility, the arousal of desire in others, and the interpersonal economy of attracting, displaying, and maintaining wealth. In certain contexts, like traditional dancing and the debut feasts held for adolescent girls, Orokaiva intentionally make themselves bright by decorating the skin and displaying wealth openly. But in ordinary day-to-day life, Orokaiva deliberately avoid being bright, instead keeping their outward appearances drab so as not to draw others' eyes, arouse their desire, and create jealousy. For Orokaiva, jealousy is an acute problem that prevents individuals from developing and maintaining wealth at a level that exceeds their peers, but uncannily, whitemen seem always to be 'bright,' attracting attention to themselves and their wealth without being undermined by the jealousy of others. Thus, both the softness and the brightness of whitemen entail a contradiction with the wealth Orokaiva see 'on whitemen's skins.' To resolve these contradictions, which are deeply rooted in their own moral concerns and experience, Orokaiva construct explanations for whitemen's ability to create and preserve wealth that project onto whitemen moral qualities that Orokaiva desire for themselves but are unable to attain, qualities they see as essential preconditions for achieving the prosperity they associate with development and western modernity.

Chapter 5, on *whitemen's foods*, examines Orokaiva ideas about the production, use, and exchange of foods, comparing the properties of indigenous garden crops with those of the commodity foods that Orokaiva identify with whitemen. Like other Melanesians, Orokaiva have a complex set of ideas surrounding foods and eating. They personify their key foods, taro and pork, and see themselves as embodying the qualities of the foods that they eat. Orokaiva taro is heavy food grown on ancestral lands, and when eaten it produces sleep, which makes those who consume it grow. By contrast, whitemen's foods are 'light.' Instead of being rooted in heavy Orokaiva lands, whitemen's foods, which are easily preserved and transported, are imported from afar and are bought with money. When eaten, they do not make the body feel full or 'heavy' with tiredness, yet they are thought to produce even greater growth than do Orokaiva indigenous foods. Thus whitemen's foods embody another aspect of the unnatural lightness of whitemen. But through these foods, Orokaiva can harness this potent quality and redirect it to their own ends using their own ritual forms. For example, whitemen's foods are increasingly prominent in hospitality and feasting, where they represent the power associated with modernity and create a whitemanlike heightened capacity for extending influence across distance by expanding the giver's social influence and renown in ways that I will explain. What is especially interesting about the Orokaiva construction of foods is what it teaches us about the folk conception of race, in which, as with the construction of persons, the real complexity inherent in a domain is resolved into an opposition between ideal types that are ideologically foregrounded and highly conventionalized in everyday talk and actions, while anomalous and ambiguous examples recede into the background.

The concluding chapter deals with the significance of whitemen beyond the village. Orokaiva individuals, notwithstanding their differences, do not differ greatly in the kinds of subjects they raise and the basic moral stances they take in their talk about whitemen, and individuals enjoy in this talk a powerful experience of mutual intelligibility and shared morality. This participation in a shared discourse about whitemen-as-other is also found in urban environments, where Papua New Guineans of diverse regional and ethnic groups share in the experience of being unable to fully realize whitemen's ease of life. In such settings Papua New Guineans from different areas emphasize the commonalities in their respective cultural discourses about whitemen in order to strengthen their relationships with one another. The construction of whitemen is thus a national phenomenon. The national discourse about whitemen, which is predominantly in Tok Pisin and English, centers on three themes that differentiate Papua New Guineans from whitemen: Papua New Guineans' system of kinlike exchanges of favors and obligations (the "wantok system"), their strong ties to their lands, and their inherent moral failings that stand in the way of development. Finally, this chapter draws implications of the study for Orokaiva culture, for anthropology, for race studies, and for the place of the West in the world.

The Meaning of the Orokaiva Whiteman in *Our* World

At terrible cost we have learned that others' views of us can dramatically affect our own lives. Since I began work on this project, international terrorism and other manifestations of anti-Americanism in many parts of the world have directed unprecedented attention to the question of how others see us. But our responses in the West have been marked by an arrogance that is possible only because of our continued ignorance of others and their concerns. Specialized terms for whites recur in language after language around the world, and a survey of ethnographic reports, works of postcolonial literature, and anthologies of native voices confirms that such terms are invariably charged with meanings that reflect those people's own particular experiences of economic, political, and racial domination by the West.[15] But we are systematically inattentive to such meanings, and our ignorance is publicized in pronouncements by western politicians and pundits who fail to take seriously the motivations of those who oppose us while asserting patriotically that the rest of the world looks up to us and our "civilization" as an exalted model of enviable qualities such as freedom, democracy, opportunity, and prosperity. One seeks in vain for the basis of such claims. Was there a worldwide opinion poll (e.g., Pew Global Attitudes Project 2005)? Were international newspaper editorials surveyed?[16] Or do we just make it up, secure in the presumption that we can imaginatively intuit what others think? The real truth is that we do not really care what the rest of the world actually thinks. A placard seen at an antiwar rally sums up the risks entailed by this kind of arrogance: "They hate us because we don't know why they hate us."

Scholarly critiques of the patriotic public discourse about "our enemies" have emphasized how it reactivates the unfavorable stereotypes of earlier Orientalist discourse (e.g., the Arab religious fanatic) which represent enemy others in ways that make them easy to dismiss out of hand. While such critiques provide an important voice of dissent in our society, they share with the mainstream public discourse the fundamental failing of focusing the attention back on ourselves. In this they perpetuate one of postcolonial criticism's frequent shortcomings, which is to reduce western writers and artists to "retailers of exoticist and racist stereotypes, without in any obvious way thereby empowering" those stereotyped and without even attempting to make their views accessible to us (Thomas 1999, 2). Thus, the critiques unwittingly collude with the politicians and pundits in insulating us from the diverse others with whom we share the planet. It would be difficult to overstate the scale of the imbalance that exists between the vast number of works devoted to what white western observers have thought and written about other peoples, and the mere handful of works that express what these peoples have thought and written about whites and the West—even though whites have of course long been objects of scrutiny and discussion in all the varied corners of the world that they have explored and exploited.[17]

To remedy our ignorance we need to strive for what Chinua Achebe has called a "balance of stories": we need to begin to hear and retell the stories that others in the world tell about us (Achebe 2000, 78). And when we do so, we should be prepared to listen beyond simple polar evaluations such as love for us versus hate for us, with us versus against us. In any case, when simple assessments of us *are* expressed they are unlikely to mean what they at first blush appear to, since they may be vitiated by unfamiliar discursive norms, people's immediate purposes in the context of speaking, and the reality of human ambivalence. But in order to appreciate the complex meanings we as whitemen have for people, we also need an understanding of the cultures within which their stories make sense. For this there is no shortcut for ethnography.[18]

It is just such an ethnography that I present in this book. As we will see, a central theme in Orokaiva stories about whites is their invulnerability to the reactions that their enormous wealth produces in others—their imperviousness to the consequences of their own vast wealth. While this theme does reflect real admiration for what Orokaiva perceive as a society that countenances prosperity without discord, it should nevertheless give us pause, for it simultaneously represents what Claude Lévi-Strauss called "our own filth, thrown into the face of mankind": the seemingly limitless consequences of our own greed (Lévi-Strauss 1974, 43). Of course, the Orokaiva story bespeaks in part the frustration that Orokaiva, like others the world over, feel at their powerlessness to achieve equality with whites given their marginal position in the global economy that supports whites' vast wealth. But it is more than this. Although we often think of our own society as premised on equality, for Orokaiva equality is such a deeply held cultural value that there are simply no terms in which inequality between peers can be justified, and it is felt to be only natural that those who have little should be made so indignant by the sight of others' wealth that it provokes them to destroy it. Thus, looking at ourselves from an Orokaiva cultural perspective invites us to acknowledge the cultural peculiarity of our own *lack* of outrage at the vast inequalities our capitalist culture produces within our society and throughout the world. These inequalities are perpetuated by our own system of cultural morality, which places high value on achievement within a competitive framework and which legitimates our acquisitive impulses—indeed, proliferates them—while encouraging us to indulge them virtually without limit.

Although to Orokaiva it may appear that whitemen are invulnerable to others' jealousy, recent events suggest otherwise.[19] While one response to those events is to attempt to further shield ourselves from others whom we do not know, who do not share in our prosperity, and who may wish us harm, the fact is that we remain vulnerable. But a more effective response to those same events would surely be to begin to address the alienating effects of our power. And as a necessary first step, we might try taking seriously the concerns of the many others who are continually confronted with us through the cultural presence of the West in their own lives, through the actions we take as a world power, and through the institutions of the modern nation state and global economy. Perhaps, if we can overcome our arrogance and learn "to see ourselves as others see us," we can begin to act in the world in a way that might truly secure lasting peace and well-being.

"To a Louse"
O would that some Power were to give us the small gift
Of seeing ourselves as others see us
It would save us from many a blunder.[20]
ROBERT BURNS (1789)

2. Cultural World, Postcolonial Situation

The wind came and set me thinking:
I'll live in America
I'll become the son of Rambo!

The wind came and set me thinking:
I'll live in Australia
I'll become the son of Crocodile Dundee!

White man! You came from your home
And you brought money to me.
You created the town life.
And the time came for running away.

> "LIFE TODAY: A POEM BY PERRY SCOT OROVO FOR IRA BASHKOW,"
> JULY 1993

PNG is a land of many cultures and values with about 750 languages. We ask of understanding and respect for the values and norms of their respective environment [*sic*]. We encourage mutual understanding of different behaviours and ideas from the indigenous peoples and visitors alike. Please refrain from prejudging these values and customs of the people, and you will appreciate the courtesy you will receive during your stay in PNG. We advise common sense in dressing, night travel and use of language. We also advise that you ask for a local guide if travelling outside urban areas. These basic principles, if followed, should ensure a pleasant stay in Papua New Guinea.

> PNG IMMIGRATION ARRIVAL CARD (INTRODUCED 1993)

Orokaiva Peoples of Papua New Guinea: An Orientation

The places Orokaiva call home are villages in Oro Province, Papua New Guinea. Oro Province, until recently called Northern Province, is located on the north coast of the New Guinea mainland near its east end, across the central mountain ranges from Port Moresby, the national capital (see fig. 2.1). The land area of the province is as large as Massachusetts, but its population, according to census figures, is only about 100,000 (NSO 1994a). Within this culturally and linguistically diverse population, Orokaiva are the largest group, numbering an estimated 60,000.[1] Their lands, which vary in character from rugged mountains, through gentle hills, to low-lying plains and swamp, occupy the better part of the northern half of the province, including much of the more densely populated country around Popondetta, the province's only town (see fig. 2.2).

Language

Orokaiva speak several languages of the non-Austronesian Binandere language family. The largest of these languages, which has some 35,000 speakers, is also called Orokaiva; the others are its neighbors Notu, Hunjara, Aeka, and Binandere.[2] These languages are not wholly discrete but instead merge into and overlap with one another. In other words, the regional linguistic situation is characterized by dialect chaining, in which dialects spoken in communities that are located closer to one another tend to be more similar, while those spoken in communities farther apart differ more in their phonology, vocabulary, and grammar.[3]

The people themselves use linguistic criteria to express differences of identity, and they name languages (or dialects) for groups of people and vice versa. For example, people at Agenehambo speak an Orokaiva dialect they call Ehija, in contrast with the neighboring Etija dialect spoken a few miles to the west. Speakers of Etija systematically substitute *t* for Ehija *h*, and these differences in pronunciation are used as shibboleths, that is, as tests for identifying a speaker with one of the two groups. However, all Orokaiva do not draw a given linguistic boundary the same way. So for people living to the east of Agenehambo where *t* is rarer still, Agenehambo speakers (who in their own eyes are Ehija) are felt to use so many Etija-like features that they classify them as Etija. Such ambiguity, construing things differently from different standpoints, is intrinsic to virtually all distinctions that bear upon identity questions among Orokaiva. This is true generally throughout Papua New Guinea.

In addition to their vernaculars, the main languages spoken by Orokaiva are English and Tok Pisin, an English-based creole. As languages of wider communication these have almost completely supplanted the colonial era lingua franca Police Motu, which was the pidgin used in the southern colonial terri-

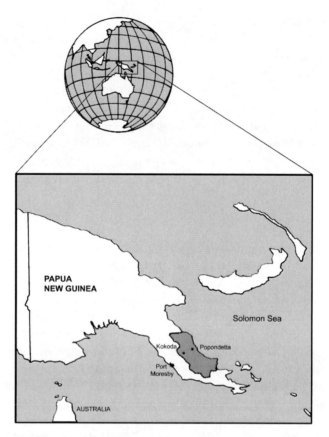

FIGURE 2.1 · Oro Province in Papua New Guinea

tory, then called Papua. Notwithstanding some resistance to Tok Pisin by a Papuan nationalist movement committed to Motu in principle, in practice Tok Pisin is emerging as the national language of Papua New Guinea. It has become the main language spoken in towns and cities and in plantation and settlement areas, like those around Popondetta, which bring together people from different parts of the country. Tok Pisin, along with English, is the main language of commerce and government business, while English is remarkably the sole language of instruction in schools.[4] In Orokaiva villages, even older, unschooled people know English phrases such as greetings and development jargon like "feasibility study" and "implementation"; greater fluency in English usually indicates education or experience in town or with wage employment. There is no doubt that Orokaiva children, who learn Tok Pisin from other children outside of school, are by and large more fluent in that language

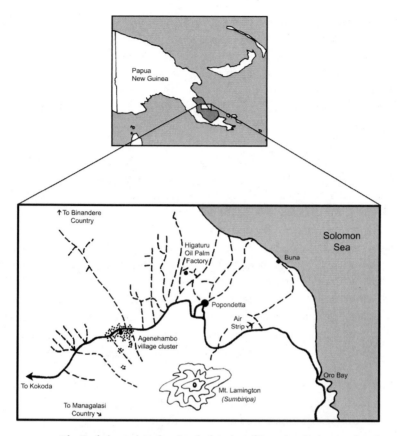

FIGURE 2.2 · The Orokaiva region, showing the location of Agenehambo (centered on the site of the Anglican church and the village elementary school) along the main road connecting Popondetta and Kokoda (Important feeder roads are shown as dashed lines.)

than are village adults. But at least for the time being, the vernacular remains vital. It is the first language acquired by virtually all village children, it is used for ordinary communication in most settings, and it is the major medium of public speech at village meetings, where lofty rhetoric in the vernacular is an important political skill and a form of art in its own right.

The Name "Orokaiva": Ethnography and Ethnogenesis

The name "Orokaiva" was first used as a cultural designation and classification of people by white colonial officers. In 1894, when the colonial administrator Sir William MacGregor explored the Mambare River, people living along it cried out in greeting, "Orokaiva!" and apparently MacGregor appropriately returned the greeting, shouting back the same word to them. "On the Mambare," he wrote, "the password is 'Orokaiva,' which seems to mean 'man of peace.' It, at all events, puts one on a friendly footing" (MacGregor 1894, 32–33).

In the earliest colonial reports, the term "Orokaiva" does not yet appear as a designation of native peoples. It emerged as such some time around 1908–11, as officers grew confident in their knowledge of the numerous, newly pacified "tribes" under their jurisdiction, mapping their territories and working out similarities and genetic relationships among them (Northern District Patrol Reports [NDPR]: Kokoda patrol reports 1911–12; PAR 1908, 79). In other words, the cultural classification "Orokaiva" arose as part of a colonial process that generated ethnographic knowledge, including racial classifications and maps, in order to facilitate colonial administration. Wilfred Beaver, who, with his fellow Resident Magistrate E. W. P. Chinnery, did as much as anyone to popularize the name, wrote in 1918: "[W]e are at a loss to find a generic term to describe all that group of tribes who are considered to belong to one stock and who speak affiliated languages. It seems to me cumbersome to be continually referring to geographical boundaries or to places which are less than mere place names to most people, and consequently I have been in the habit of using 'Orokaiva' as a general term. . . . I would welcome a more correct general term, could one be found" (PAR 1918–19, 96–97, quoted in Williams 1930, 2; see also NDPR: Kokoda patrol reports 1911–12 [by Chinnery]; PAR 1914–15, 48, 50 [report by Beaver]). In the mid-1920s, this use of Orokaiva as a "general term" for a "group of tribes" was adopted by the colonial Government Anthropologist F. E. Williams, who in his ethnographic monographs on *Orokaiva Magic* (1928) and *Orokaiva Society* (1930) wrote of "the Orokaiva" as "a people" who transcended local political divisions. The name Orokaiva has since become conventional in the ethnographic literature.

Because the concept of "Orokaiva culture" bears the stamp of a "colonial form of knowledge" (see Cohn 1996), it should not be accepted uncritically. But it remains appropriate as a frame for discussion, especially inasmuch as the category is now widely taken for granted by the people themselves. As in numerous cases of "ethnogenesis" documented in other parts of the world, where lines etched by colonial authority have defined new peoples and ethnicities (see Hill 1996; Whitten 1996), the colonial classification *Orokaiva* has itself shaped the reality of the people, producing a category of identity that has become perfectly real in politics and everyday life. To the people, *Orokaiva* is a 'big name' (*javo peni*) that supplements both the various smaller names that express a person's identity in terms of dialect, region, village locality, hamlet, clan, subclan, and so on, and the bigger (i.e., more encompassing) names associated with the province, region, and nation (see chapter 6).

Orokaiva stories of the origin of the name recognize the role of white colonial power, portraying whitemen as eliciting the name from its Orokaiva inventors, as well as disseminating it. (This power to disseminate information and extend control across distance is a salient attribute of whitemen discussed in chapters 3 and 5.) However, the name is never depicted as an unwelcome foreign imposition. For example, according to the stories told in many villages around Agenehambo, the name was invented by a local man while greeting white patrol officers, who wrote it down and publicized it. To understand the stories, it is important to appreciate that people throughout the region welcome visitors and acknowledge the gifts they are bringing with exuberant cries of greeting like "Orokaiva! Orokaiva!" and "Oro! Oro! Orokaiva!"[5] The stories portray the origin of this greeting cry, the origin of its use as a name for a people, and the initial encounter with whitemen; all of these are represented as aspects of a single event. In telling the story, people often commented that a different greeting cry had been used formerly (some said that it was "Jau-oro!"), but that the new cry supplanted this old one. According to the story, a man's nephew was captured by whitemen, presumably in order to kill and eat him. But when the man learned that the whitemen had come not to make war but to bring peace and so would spare the boy, the man, overwhelmed with joy, was inspired to shout "Orokaiva!"[6]

Existing studies do not represent "the Orokaiva" as a homogenous group, but instead, to the contrary, they have highlighted the wide variation that exists among local communities in details of social organization, ritual, diet, arts, and traditional knowledge. This variation, as André Iteanu observes, "is not simply due either to the disparity in the methodologies used by the different ethnographers or to their specific personalities. It is a matter of the facts themselves" (1991, 347n2). Without the standardizing influence of a unified polity and centralized institutions, idiosyncratic cultural forms are free to develop and become conventionalized, resulting in relatively stable patterns of variation among localities. At the same time, however, there are basic similarities in morality and culture throughout the Orokaiva regional world, similarities that are often recognized by the people themselves (Iteanu 1983a, viv; 1991, 346; see also Williams 1928, 1930). Orokaiva societies are characterized by a distinctive set of variations on common Melanesian cultural themes, such as the centrality of gift exchange in sociality, the spirit of "eclecticism" and "opportunism" (Douglas 1982, 187), the fluidity of leadership and land tenure, a subsistence economy based on shifting agriculture, and highly autonomistic notions of the person.[7] Orokaiva values exhibit the familiar Melanesian contradictions of egalitarianism versus a stress on competitive achievement, and individual autonomy and willfulness versus a valued sociality that is premised on conformity and obedience. And as in other Melanesian societies the focus of Orokaiva community life moves back and forth dialectically between locally grounded activities like gardening and village-building, and socially expansive activities like public speaking, gift exchange, travel, and feasting, all of which are associated with the extension of influence, control, and fame across distance (see Munn 1986).

Throughout the Orokaiva region, a primary focus of community life is the cultivation of taro, a root crop grown in swidden gardens that are invested with great social, ritual, and spiritual significance. Along with pigs and other garden produce, taro is also a major object of exchange (see chapter 5). The fact that people grow their own food (and can use their own forest materials to build their houses) means that in practice they enjoy a remarkable independence from the cash economy, and over time individual households tend to move in and out of participation in it. Apart from payment of school fees, and the purchase of the three near-necessities, salt, soap, and kerosene, money is used primarily to buy commodity luxury foods, especially for use in feasting. Orokaiva feasts, which are occasioned by brideprice payments, deaths, the debuts of young girls, and church and community events, center on the display and distribution of huge quantities of garden produce, store foods, pigs, and above all, taro.

Negotiating Orokaiva Identity within a Regional World

Popular images of New Guinea frequently emphasize the theme of insularity; the name New Guinea conjures up images of remote fastnesses sheltered by mountain walls from nearly all outside influence, and islands shrouded in the obscurity of old ways and self-sufficiency. We think of cultural isolates, backwaters where the native people imagined themselves until recently to be at the center of a world that was populated by few apart from themselves. Such images sustain the idea that the impact of whitemen has been a massive decentering for Papua New Guinea peoples (see, e.g., Osborne 2005; National Geographic Television and Film 2005).

In this view, the advent of whitemen showed people that they were not, in fact, at the world's center, but rather highly peripheral to it, in effect displacing them.

But the Orokaiva world is not such a place, and according to the evidence, it never was. Contrary to the images, Orokaiva have long been and still are culturally adept at negotiating their identities within the world beyond the hamlet or village-cluster, a world they themselves actively construct by travel and exchange relationships throughout the region.[8] Thus while the impact of whitemen has significantly changed the world of Orokaiva culture, the changes have not been as radical or unambiguous as might be presumed. Indeed, the global order associated with whitemen has in many ways become for Orokaiva another arena of self-definition coexisting with their traditional vernacular ones.

As I use it here, the name Orokaiva identifies people with the regional world within which substantial connections of trade, migration, and warfare were maintained since precolonial times (Chinnery and Beaver 1915a; Jojoga Opeba 1982; Waiko 1972, 1982; see also Barker 1996). Around the turn of the century, pacification led to a dramatic increase in travel and exchange between previously distant "tribes," promoting the regional spread of art forms, rituals, and social movements such as the Baigona and Taro cults in the 1910s (Williams 1928). Still today, travel remains an important part of Orokaiva life, and there is a well-developed ethos of hospitality and reciprocal visiting. It is considered a pleasure to stay with others, eating their food, hearing new stories, creating and strengthening relations, and receiving gifts to bring home. People enjoy travel and will readily set off on the spur of the moment to visit friends or relatives living the better part of a day's walk away. Even unplanned visits can wind up lasting for days. Indeed, Orokaiva use a specific term, *jomo*, to describe the exhaustion normally felt by hosts once guests have departed.

Indigenous norms allow every community to identify itself as 'the center' of the regional complex for some reason or another. And indeed, every locality I visited boasted of some claim to special status within the region. *Why* people would claim centrality for themselves is not hard to understand; after all, it reflects their experience, which centers of course on their own lives and thus the places where they dwell. But it is perhaps less obvious *how* people could sustain such claims in the face of comparable claims made by others. Part of the answer lies in Orokaiva discursive etiquette, whereby speakers diplomatically calibrate representations of social position to avoid offending, or indeed to flatter, others within the speech situation.

Orokaiva are also used to constructing regional status and identity in ways that are relational and dynamic, entailing reciprocities and reversals of position over time.[9] Traditionally Orokaiva had no fixed hierarchical relationships between villages. This is clearly illustrated by precolonial cannibal warfare, in which success in a raid made a village a center of valor—until they suffered a revenge attack (Beaver 1919; Williams 1928). Reciprocity and reversal of status is similarly exhibited by the hierarchical relationships created through feasting. The recipients of a feast gift are 'pushed down' (*kikira*) by the giver's superiority at that moment. But when they later return the gift at a feast of their own, it is they who will have the superiority, reversing their earlier roles. Such cycling of status has histori- cally characterized Orokaiva intervillage relationships, even from the point of a village's founding. As Iteanu (1983b) has shown, a group of disparate family settlements traditionally achieved recognition as a village by to- gether holding a feast. At any feast, the guests accede to the host village's status in attending. Thus, the recognition itself becomes part of a series of longer-term intervillage reciprocities, which will continue when the guests of today later hold feasts of their own and invite former hosts.

As a rule, guests do not contradict their hosts' claims of centrality during a visit, but when they later receive their erstwhile hosts at *their* village, the roles will normally be exchanged. I often saw this etiquette observed by guests in the face of hosts' claims that their village was the 'center' of the Orokaiva world and the 'root' of its culture, notwithstanding that the guests claimed as much for themselves while on their own ground. In addi- tion, hosts would sometimes flatter guests by praising their villages as the 'root' of culture, history, traditional knowledge, or particular arts. Even within a single visit, praise and forbearance of others' claims were them- selves exchanged between guests and hosts, and it was on the basis of such exchanges that the relative status of villages was negotiated. It was never unambiguously fixed.[10]

Unlike these traditional relationships among people and localities, the hierarchical relationships that were introduced as part of whitemen's custom are permanent and relatively unambiguous. Modern western-style institutions and infrastructure tend to be organized hierarchically around a superordinate central position (see Scott 1998). This is especially true of government, which people understand is successively subdivided into provinces, districts, and wards. Similarly, Orokaiva are keenly aware that the Anglican Church is organized on a pattern of radiating authority, with a "mother church" in England and the Papua New Guinea daughter church divided into dioceses, parishes, and chapels: when I asked Agenehambo women about their 3-kina (about U.S. $3) annual dues for the Anglican "Mothers Union," they explained that 1 kina was kept by the parish of Agenehambo, 1 kina went to the Mothers Union of the whole diocese, and 1 kina was sent all the way to London.[11] The hierarchical system of place names familiar from the West is also conventionally used by Orokaiva when identifying themselves to others, so that around the village they are known as residents of particular subhamlets; in the larger region they are known as residents of the village cluster that encompasses their hamlet; when in town, they identify themselves as hailing from the nearest government station whose jurisdiction includes their village; and outside the province they identify themselves as coming from "Popondetta," the name of the provincial capital. This system of "bigger" and "smaller" places is roughly congruous with the hub-and-spoke road network that radiates out from Popondetta town into the surrounding countryside. In most modern contexts, Orokaiva see themselves as existing within these permanent, hierarchical systems, so that their hamlet, which in traditional contexts they might claim to be a big important place, is reduced to one that is 'small' and 'backwater.' As a result, Orokaiva have developed a consciousness of themselves as low, remote, and marginal with respect to a wider world (see also Robbins 1996; Knauft 2002b).

Orokaiva villagers acknowledge the centrality of town in many of the activities that they consider whitemen's. They travel to town to use the bank, the post office, the police station, the health center, and so on; they stock their village tradestores with goods that are brought from town; they appeal in town for government assistance; and they treat official visitors from town—such as agricultural extension officers, development advisors, school inspectors, and bishops—like VIPs to whom they must defer. The town axis is a long, dusty road lined with government offices, the hospital, and the high school. At one end is the town market, where villagers come to sell garden produce and betel nut. At the other end is one city-type block where five wholesale stores are set amid vacant lots (see plate 23). The population is less than 8,000. There are no bright lights and no forms of entertainment at night, apart from drinking and Christianity. People throughout the province like to disparage the town for being small and rundown. They sometimes call it "four corners," meaning that it has *only* four corners, just one city block. But the town does serve as a gateway between the region as a whole and other centers. There are no vehicular roads that connect Oro Province with other centers due to the rugged terrain. Instead, people travel to cities like Port Moresby and Lae mainly on boats or planes, both of which are normally accessed by traveling through Popondetta.

The centrality of town implies a marginalization of village life in a way that is a familiar concomitant of globalization throughout the world, and Orokaiva perceptions of their regional world have changed as a result. But it should not be supposed that people's perceptions of their place in the world have been completely transformed. Far from being brittle, Orokaiva identity reflects a high tolerance for contradiction, ambiguity, and multiple bases of claims, within relationships that are premised on give and take, exchange and alternation. People were not able to construct themselves as absolutely central in the traditional world, and they do not perceive themselves today as absolutely marginal in the globalizing world.

Indeed, despite the central position of town in the modern global framework, the regional world of intervillage relationships is still the one within which issues of centrality versus peripherality are actively worked out in people's lives. In part, it is the very permanence and objectivity of town's centrality that makes it uninteresting to villagers as a reference point for self-definition. Even in modern activities identified with taupa kastom—including activities like Christian worship and modern forms of travel identified with whitemen—villagers focus on intervillage relationships. An impressive amount of visiting goes on between villages for Christian purposes, including "outreach" missions in which groups of villagers travel to a different area and visit one or more villages there in succession, staying overnight at each village and receiving elaborate hospitality as ambassadors of the spirit. Such outreach missions and other village-hosted Christian events, like "bible courses" and "workshops," create hospitality debts and complex assertions of relative centrality by both guests and hosts, while serving as occasions for individuals of different villages to forge and strengthen their exchange relationships. Similarly, modern forms of transport do not merely inflate the importance of town by drawing people's travel along the network of roads that converge on it. They also make it faster and generally easier to travel between villages, and they increase the prestige of the villages where motor vehicles are based, making them transport hubs in their own local areas. Orokaiva frequently use trucks to increase the scale of their traditional feasts, hiring them during preparatory phases to transport large loads of firewood, taro, and pigs, and on the climactic day to bring guests by the truckload from distant places. In sum, the regional world of Orokaiva today is not the world of precolonial times. It has been shaped by pacification, colonization, centralization, and modern transportation. It has been moved by globalization into larger frameworks of the nation and globe. But it is still very much an indigenous world, in which villagers construct their own village's position in relation to other villages and indigenous groups.

In Agenehambo village, where my research was focused, people identified themselves as "Middle Orokaiva" or "Central Kaiva," names that were often spoken in English and that may be taken as relatively new designations, arising since the 1970s.[12] People explained their use of these names in many different ways, and all of them positioned Agenehambo and the villages near it as central to the Orokaiva regional world I have been discussing; they did not refer to the nation, the Pacific, or the globe, nor to smaller units. Some of their explanations amounted to artful claims that we were at the center of the world, between east, north, south, and west. People also liked to point out that we were midway between the mountain ranges rising to the west and the sea in the east; that we were midway (actually a third of the way) along the main road from Popondetta to Kokoda; and that on the map of the province we were located very nearly at the central spot. Other claims, which were expressed through origin myths and narratives about the colonial era and World War II, asserted that their own ancestors had played the central role in formative historical events. There were claims to centrality based on superiority to other Orokaiva in language, dance and music, body decoration, feasting, and fame. And there were claims based on the confirmation afforded by the arrival of prestigious visitors from outside, like Prince Charles (in 1967), the Archbishop of Canterbury (in 1991), and numerous foreign missionaries, local public servants and politicians, and me.

My research was carried out throughout the 1990s in village communities around Agenehambo, as well as in Port Moresby and Popondetta where I spent several months doing archival research and fieldwork on Orokaiva migrants.[13] During my fieldwork, I gained comparative insight by traveling widely in the Orokaiva region and by a two months' residence in a second village, Pusahambo. But my perceptions of the Orokaiva world are largely centered on Agenehambo, and it is about the people of Agenehambo that I principally write.

Agenehambo in the 1990s

Agenehambo is a large village-cluster about one hour's drive west of Popondetta along the main road to Kokoda (see fig. 2.2). The landscape is anchored in the south by Mt. Lamington (called in Orokaiva Sumbiripa), an active volcano whose long northern slopes form a piedmont area of rugged mountains cut by fast-flowing rivers. Moving farther north, the terrain becomes gentler until the hills disappear in a vast expanse of low-lying plains and, eventually, swamp. It is in the intermediate band between the mountainous piedmont and the low-lying plains that Agenehambo is situated. Formerly, this area was a no man's land between enemy groups living on the plains and on the volcano's footslopes, and the name Agenehambo recalls this time. The noun *hahambo* (in suffixal form *-hambo*) denotes a place where warriors gather to ready themselves for raids. Here they did so in the shelter of a legendary silver gray *agene* tree.

In 1904, colonial government-drafted work parties constructed a broad walking trail from the seacoast to an inland gold mine. This trail, which followed the contours of the terrain, passed through the heart of this no man's land separating warring tribes which had not yet been pacified (PAR 1903—4, 39; Schwimmer 1973, 34). (Along this trail—now an unpaved vehicle road—there is in fact a string of villages whose names end in *-hambo*: Agenehambo, Isugahambo, Pusahambo, and so on.) A colonial rest house, for the benefit of patrol officers and their carriers, was built at the site around 1909 (PAR 1908—9, 19; NDPR: Buna report no. 4 of 1919—20), and by 1924, there is mention of a village growing up beside it (NDPR: Kokoda reports no. 3 of 1924—25, no. 7 of 1925—26). The settlers who created this village were people from the volcano's footslopes, and they were led by an exceptional man named Pahuva who had claimed three cannibal victims before the whites arrived and appointed him a guardian of their new peace, giving him the badge and the uniform of a native Village Constable, or "VC" (NDPR; Williams 1930, 161—62). Pahuva had been assigned to organize the building of the first rest house. Patrol reports throughout Pahuva's three-decades-long tenure as village constable have, remarkably, nothing but praise for his conscientiousness in fulfilling his duties. He was considered extremely loyal, reliable, able, and hospitable, and he was unfailingly generous in provisioning visiting officers with garden produce and pigs (NDPR). In retrospect it is clear that his generosity was amply repaid. His custodianship of the rest house gave him the de facto right to settle his own people on the great tract of no man's land the whites' peace made available. In effect, then, his alliance with the whites allowed his mountain people to expand their land rights, while shutting his enemies, the plainsmen, within the boundaries of the lands they had occupied historically.

Today where the old colonial rest house once stood is a field, used for soccer and feasts, that is surrounded by the village primary school and Anglican parish church. This area is called Agenehambo "station," as it has served as a government station and then as a mission station. The main part of Agenehambo consists of several named hamlets that are clustered around the station near the road, as well as individual family compounds set amid the forested spaces between them. There are also a half dozen satellite hamlets located farther away (see fig. 2.2). The farthest of these, Hojane, is located well off the road, to the southwest, and to get there from the station is a walk of three hours, on a forest trail that crosses two major rivers and numerous streams. Hojane occupies a ridgetop in the mountainous area that most of the rest of the people left when they migrated down to Agenehambo's current location. It is a place where many families living along the road still own traditional lands, which they continue to use, notwithstanding the distance, for planting the cash-crops cocoa and coffee and for making gardens for food crops.

Although the hamlets that make up Agenehambo have distinct identities and are not contiguous, people understand them to be 'inside' the 'big name' of Agenehambo for many purposes. One of these purposes is the census, whose units reflect the colonial policy of consolidating people into large villages to facilitate administration and the provision of services. The census unit used by many government agencies today for purposes connected to health services, cash-cropping, development allocations, politics, police, and education, is the village of Agenehambo. For purposes of the census, the individual hamlets within Agenehambo have no official existence; they are not shown on maps, and their names have no status for budgetary allocations. Thus, during elections and at the decennial census, people know that Agenehambo (misspelled as Agenahembo) is their official village of residence. In the 1990 census, the population of Agenehambo was 571, which compares with my own 1995 estimate of 700.

Another factor in unifying Agenehambo is the Anglican Church, which initiated missionization in this inland region in the 1920s. Here, for half a century, the Anglican mission had a virtual monopoly on Christian influence and education, though its dominance has since been challenged by competition from a host of charismatic and Pentecostal denominations like the Christian Revival Crusade (CRC), the South Seas Evangelical Church (SSEC), the Christian Outreach Centre (COC), the New Life Centre (NLC), the Assemblies of God (AOG), the Four Square Gospel Church, and the locally based Renewal Church, as well as by the Seventh Day Adventist Church (SDA), the New Apostolic Church, and the Mormons. Today in Agenehambo there are church buildings for the SSEC, the COC, and the New Apostolic Church. However, the Anglican Church still commands the majority of adherents, and it remains a powerful presence in the community. Agenehambo's spacious church, St. Michael's and All Angels, with its high, tiered roof, is the seat of the parish. The parish applies its own set of divisions to the population, incorporating additional nearby hamlets within the "church village" of Agenehambo. Today, Anglican functions and festivals like holidays, chapel openings, and ordinations occasion the largest and most spectacular Orokaiva feasts, so that the church village of Agenehambo is substantiated in the system of feasting that defines people's position in the wider regional sphere of intervillage competition.

Apart from issues of scale, Orokaiva draw no categorical difference between a large village, a hamlet, and a single-family compound. In Orokaiva, all are classified as settlements, or *da*. What distinguishes a da from a mere place (*degi*) is an open space of cleared ground. Traditionally, this is an area of hard-packed earth maintained by women (it has to be frequently weeded, stamped down, and swept), though modern alternatives include cut grass and concrete, which are maintained by men. The aesthetic is to site most buildings around open spaces, creating clear sightlines, order, and control. To beautify these spaces, people plant flowering bushes, crotons, hedgerows, and fruit trees, though usually only around the periphery, leaving the central areas clear.

People use a variety of materials to build their houses, and many enjoy experimenting with new architectural styles such as corner gables or wraparound verandas associated with the houses of whitemen. The most common types of house-building materials are those that can be obtained locally for free: local timber for posts, the bark of blackpalm for flooring, sago frond thatch for roofing, and tree products for walls. Corrugated iron roofing is desirable but expensive, and so it is found on less than a tenth of the village's houses. All houses are built on posts, with the floor raised a few feet above ground. Most houses are cramped, peak-roofed wooden boxes, and people spend little time in them, entering them primarily to sleep. The main type of building in which people spend time socializing, cooking, doing handiwork, hosting guests, and holding meetings is the *arara* or sitting platform, which is like a living room without walls. Araras are comfortable and adaptable all-purpose spaces in which most village social life takes place. The absence of walls—most have just a low banister—lets breezes enter, while allowing people to see out and to be seen by others. Since araras are used in the heat of the day, they are always built with frond thatch roofing, which stays cooler than roofs made of iron. Further description of araras and houses is given in chapter 4.

Hamlets change a great deal over time, as houses made of untreated timbers slowly deteriorate and are torn down and rebuilt. I saw many changes in the layout and composition of hamlets over just seven years, and I came to know many hamlet sites that had been abandoned entirely. Periodically, hamlets are disbanded and new ones built elsewhere, usually in the aftermath of a dispute or a big man's death (see Iteanu 1983b). As road access becomes increasingly important and roadside space increasingly scarce, one might predict that hamlet locations along the roads will stabilize. But for the meanwhile, residential patterns continue to have considerable fluidity (see also Wagner 1974).

Land tenure arrangements are similarly fluid. They are negotiated on ad hoc customary bases, with limited intervention by formal authorities. Paradoxically, the fluidity of land tenure has a powerfully stabilizing effect on the community, since it encourages people to remain on or near the lands they claim in order to maintain de facto possession, lest their lands be lost to others with competing claims. Thus, for example, my five village brothers divided themselves among three hamlets so as to maintain their hold on nearby family lands. When asked to justify their ownership of lands, people tend to give explanations in terms of the norm of patrilineal inheritance within clan and subclan groupings. But as prior ethnographic studies of other Orokaiva communities have found, frequent irregularities occur with respect to this pattern. Indeed, clan affiliations are sometimes adjusted so as to reflect desired land arrangements. Moreover, it is not unusual for men to give lands to their sisters and daughters, effectively transferring the lands to other clans via the women's husbands and children.[14] But such land transfers do not represent an absolute alienation of land from the original clan. They remain contingent upon the continued good will of the parties involved, and the way this is ensured is through active relations of exchange.[15] The set of clans that own lands around Agenehambo have been intermarrying for as long as anyone can remember, and they are thus knit together by generations of ambiguous land transactions and the continual series of exchanges that these entail.

My fieldsite home was a "community hall" in one of Agenehambo's smallest hamlets, Homa, a very short way from Agenehambo station. The hall was a long, low, iron-roofed rectangle on a concrete foundation with small rooms at each corner and a large, open-air area in the center that was used as a large arara, and it served as a rest stop, a space where people who walked down to the road from distant hamlets, like Hojane, rested and refreshed themselves, sometimes spending the night, before proceeding along the road to town, the government clinic, or other destinations. The hall was also a favorite venue for various types of community meetings and functions, so that I found myself attending many meetings simply because they were held on my doorstep. But most of the time, the community hall was simply a part of the household of my main Orokaiva host, Steven Seambo, his wife, Stella, and an ever-changing group of children and relatives. (I introduce Steven properly in the next chapter, together with several of the other Orokaiva individuals who were important in my research.) Living as part of this household, participating in the family's work, exchange relationships, rituals, crises, and cares, I shared in the everyday experiences that people cope with and that their ideas interpret.

A Century of Whitemen in the Orokaiva World

To understand the construction of whitemen in contemporary Orokaiva culture, it is important to know something about the history of the presence of whites in this region, which was colonized more than a century ago.

Early Colonialism on a Shoestring, 1890s to 1963

In 1884, when Germany and Great Britain partitioned the eastern half of the immense island of New Guinea, a line on a map was drawn dividing territories that Europeans had never seen. The lands that were north of the line were taken by Germany, while the area south of it, which became known as Papua, became a British Protectorate, and four years later, a colony. The first administrator, Sir William MacGregor, faced with the task of exploring the territory, "spent 85 percent of his time as head of government on exploratory expeditions and tours of inspection in the Papuan hinterland" (Schieffelin and Crittenden 1991, 21–22). Exploring the Mambare River near Orokaiva country in 1894, he found "colours of gold" in the water above the confluence of Tamata Creek, sparking a gold rush (MacGregor 1894, 32; Nelson 1976). The prospectors and miners passed through what is today the Orokaiva region to reach the mines in the Yodda and Gira valleys, leading to a period of violent encounters and bloodshed between Orokaiva and whites, which has been chronicled by John Waiko (1970, 1972, 1989).

The dominant white figure in this period of initial contacts was the infamously brutal Resident Magistrate C. A. W. Monckton, who was known for his "shoot and loot" tactics in punitive raids (Monckton, quoted in Lutton 1978, 71; see also Nelson 1976). It was Monckton who organized the building of an overland trail (the Yodda "road") through present-day Agenehambo, at a time when the "tribes" of this area "were fighting like Kilkenny cats, and war parties of one or other of them were sweeping the country" (Monckton 1922b, 141–42; 1922a, 304). Although at first this road "could only be traversed by strong forces of police, and with almost incessant fighting," Monckton soon pacified the tribes, uncharacteristically "nearly bloodlessly" (although his sanguinary reputation must have been known by them) by appointing natives as village constables, to act as "intermediaries between white men and the villagers in trading relations ... as interpreters for white men and their native employés and as guides, or to obtain men for transporting a European party from one village to another [i.e., as carriers]" (Monckton, in BNG 1903-4, 39, and in BNG 1904-5, 36).

Although a few years later, "small periodical raids" by "strong tribes" uphill were still being made on "weaker ones" in the plains, "excellent relations" prevailed between the natives and the government, and the road became institutionalized as a place of sanctuary and barter (PAR 1906-7, 15, 56). Reports by several observers remark on the absence of thefts or violence along it, and on the formation of roadside markets at which local people supplied carriers with taro and other produce in exchange for tobacco and glass, which they used to make razors (PAR 1906-7, 15; Murray 1912b, 105). According to Monckton, "the Yodda road is a sanctuary for any and everyone; the wildest tribes only visit it in peace to trade food and goods to passing travellers. They rather like it, as small parties of hostile tribes can move freely about on it in safety with their women and children" (Monckton, quoted in Schwimmer 1973, 34).

After the 1905 transfer of Papua to Australia, Monckton was dismissed when J. H. P. Murray, the new lieutenant-governor of the Territory, curtailed officers' use of violence and their reliance on collective punishments, and instead sought to extend the influence of the government through peaceful means (PAR 1912-28). Initially, Murray's priority was to enlarge the plantation economy by increasing the supply of Papuan labor (Murray 1912a; 1912b, 344-65). But the plantation economy never took off in Papua as it did in German New Guinea, and when the influx of settlers and capital ceased with the outbreak of World War I, Murray shifted the emphasis in Papua from plantation agriculture to an approach to economic development that did not require the investment of outside capital, namely village-based cash-cropping by natives on their own lands (PAR 1921-22, 6; Legge 1971; Denoon and Snowden 1981; Lewis 1996). Orokaiva villagers were compelled to plant coconuts, rubber, and other "economic trees" from 1914—when a prophetic movement called the Taro Cult spread throughout the region, expressing local anxieties over the redirection of their resources away from traditional gardening (PAR 1914-15, 49; Williams 1928).

Low cost was the hallmark of Australian policy throughout the first period. The administration, constantly balancing the forces for greater exploitation of the colony against its responsibility to protect the native populations, never took the kind of truly bold, merciless steps, like widespread expropriation of lands and toleration of long-term indentured servitude, that probably would have been necessary for the colony to generate a fat profit.[16] The administration built little infrastructure, its presence in the hinterlands consisting of little more than the native-built rest houses and walking trails—the "roads"—that connected remote, inland stations like Agenehambo to the coast. The main business of administering the population was done by patrol. A village would receive a visit from an Australian patrol officer once every year or two, at which time he would take a census, give a speech urging adherence to government regulations, hear complaints, and inspect roads, village hygiene, and villagers' plantings of cash-crops. Education was left to the missions, which by a "gentleman's agreement" divided Papua into spheres of influence—Methodist, London Missionary Society, Anglican, Catholic, and later Seventh Day Adventist (Murray 1920, 23; Dickson 1971; Langmore 1989). The country of the Orokaiva came under the Anglicans. Anglican missionaries had been active along the northern coast since the turn of the century, but it was not until 1921 that the first Australian mission station was established inland near the Central Kaiva region, followed eight years later by a second (PAR 1921-22, 68; Chittleborough 1976; Wetherell 1977). By 1936, six hundred children from the area were sporadically attending Anglican grade schools (Bishop Philip Strong Papers: Bishop's Report 1937; Anglican Archives).

During World War II, the area was crisscrossed by tens of thousands of foreign troops. The first were Japanese who landed at Buna in 1942 and, misinterpreting the term "road" on Australian maps to imply "suitable for vehicular travel," attempted to assault Port Moresby via the Kokoda Road, a torturous footpath that winds overland across fantastically steep mountains. Within a year, the Japanese were turned back by Australian and American forces in battles that killed 8,000 Allied troops and 13,000 Japanese (McCarthy 1959, 531; McAulay 1991; Taaffe 1998, 11). The violence led most Orokaiva to flee to forest hiding places, but many were recruited to serve the foreign forces as carriers or scouts, or as members of the Papuan Infantry Battalion which had been newly formed under Australian command (Chalk 1986; Byrnes 1989). The Australians called their Papuan helpers "little fuzzy wuzzy angels," a phrase (still famous in Australia) which suggests that racist condescension was part of even the best of wartime relations. But in general, the troops saw natives as important strategic allies and dealt with them far more equitably and generously than most whites Orokaiva had encountered before (Pike, Nelson, and Daws 1982). To Orokaiva, the troops, with their generous gifts of foods, tobacco, and discarded clothing, tools, and equipment, were expressing an extraordinary and intensely gratifying regard for them, and this, together with amazement at the enormous resources the troops controlled, aroused people's hopes that a prosperous new era of egalitarian relations with whites was soon to arrive (Schwimmer 1973, 35-36; Baxter 1973, 40-43).

In the immediate postwar years, a cooperative rice-growing project that was started on the coast by an Anglican priest was copied in several inland Orokaiva villages, reportedly in the belief that participation "would—magically or mystically—in short time raise the native to the status of the European in all respects" (Kleekham memo, quoted in Schwimmer 1969, 86; see also Anglican Archives; Keesing 1952, 7; Dakeyne 1966; Crocombe 1964, 29-30; Jojoga Opeba 1993). But the projects were abruptly halted by the devastating peléan eruption of Mt. Lamington in 1951. The eruption killed almost 4,000 Orokaiva people, decimating the formerly large and powerful Sangara group. After the eruption, foreign aid workers assisted thousands of displaced Orokaiva survivors with food, tools, medicines, and blankets, settling them in camps by the road until after a year or so many of them returned to rebuild villages on their traditional lands on the volcano's slopes (NDPR; Belshaw 1951; Keesing 1952; Schwimmer 1969).

The postwar period is notable chiefly as a time of disappointment, as both government promises and Orokaiva hopes for increased development failed to be fulfilled. Following a string of failed economic experiments, including more cooperatives and an elaborate scheme to settle a group of about a hundred Australian and native war veterans on new plantations near Popondetta (the scheme collapsed and the Australians abandoned it after an infestation ruined the cocoa crops), colonial policy in the region resumed prewar patterns and returned to promoting village-based cash-cropping as the major form of rural development (Crocombe 1964, 31; Howlett 1965; Dick and McKillop 1976, 26). Education was still limited to the most rudimentary training in mission primary schools. As late as 1963 less than half a percent of the appropriate aged population of the entire colony received any post-primary schooling, and it was not until 1965 that the first indigenous person from anywhere in the territory received a bachelors degree (Spate 1966, 124-25; Mair 1970 [1948], 227; Dickson 1971).

The main form in which native people received education in whitemen's ways, *taupa kastom*, was labor. Since the 1920s, Central Kaiva men had been "signing on" in large numbers for work as policemen and indentured laborers; it has been estimated that as many as two-thirds of the young men of the prewar period labored outside the district at some point in their lives (PAR; NDPR; Baxter 1977, 64; Dakeyne 1977, 158; Waiko 1990; Kituai 1998). Policemen in particular traveled widely throughout the colony, but other workers for the government and plantations passed through colonial towns like Port Moresby and Samarai for training or transfer. From the

1960s, Orokaiva traveled in increasing numbers to the urban centers of Port Moresby and Lae, where large Orokaiva workers' communities and squatter settlements began to develop (Oram 1976; Rew 1974, 102-16; Norwood 1984, 87; NSO 1994a, 81).

Accelerated Education, Development, and Independence, 1963 to 1983

The boom years of Orokaiva contact with whites, as well as with education and development generally, were the two decades surrounding Papua New Guinean independence from Australia in 1975. Unlike many former colonies that were granted independence as the outcome of a long anti-colonial struggle, Papua New Guinea was rushed to independence largely at the initiative of the colonial power itself. In fact, the small nationalist movement that took shape shortly before PNG independence was assiduously cultivated by Australia, which hurried PNG to independence over significant local opposition so as to divest itself of a growing political, moral, and financial burden.

For Papua together with the former German colony of New Guinea, which had come under Australian rule in the course of World War I, the turning point was the United Nations Visiting Mission of 1962, which set in motion a new policy regarding independence. Previously, independence for the colony was assumed to be "so far in the future as to be irrelevant" (Turner 1990, 12). It was widely believed within the government that indigenous political progress not only would be slow, but also that it "*should* be slow, that virtually the entire indigenous community should be prepared for each step forward before that step was taken, [and] that policy should be such as to discourage the emergence of an *élite* based on educational privilege and political experience" (Hudson and Daven 1971, 158; see also Hasluck 1976; Johnson 1983, 185). Criticizing this policy of gradualism, the Visiting Mission's report urged the government to take immediate steps to accelerate economic development, create a parliament, train indigenous leaders, and expand education. Educational opportunities were to be increased at every level, but particularly at the higher levels, where the report proposed creating a university in the territory (United Nations Trusteeship Council 1962, 16).

The pace of change quickened at the national level over the following years as Australian policy shifted to pursue early independence. The university was opened, and the government vastly increased education spending, creating almost from scratch a system of secondary education, and greatly expanding the system of primary schools, in part through subsidies to the missions.[17] Huge investments were also made in health services, infrastructure like bridges and roads, and agricultural development. The public service grew fivefold, an increase in part accounted for by the recruitment of Papua New Guineans to trainee positions, and in part accounted for by a great increase in the number of white officials. In 1964, elections were held for the first House of Assembly—the forerunner of the PNG parliament. Now the government was racing to build an indigenous elite, the emergence of which it had formerly tried to suppress (Nelson 1974; Turner 1990; Waiko 1993). Soon there were stirrings of nationalism within the university and the ranks of New Guinea's first political party, the Pangu Pati.

The impact of these changes was felt in the Orokaiva region where villagers' contact with whites increased as education, economic development, and scientific research by foreign scholars intensified. An influx of foreign experts and capital from international agencies such as the World Bank supported large-scale development projects for the cultivation of the commodity crops cocoa, coffee, and palm oil. Alongside these development projects, the government upgraded vehicular roads and constructed new health facilities, vocational training schools, and agricultural extension centers, all of which were staffed by white expatriates. Villages received regular visits from white agricultural officers, patrol officers, advisers to local government councils, and coffee buyers. They also received visits from whites conducting all manner of surveys: of cocoa trees, coffee trees, livestock, land allocation, native people's time use, health, indigenous trade stores, soils, facilities, development prospects, geology, flora, fauna, and more (NDPR). During this boom period, more than forty white scholars conducted field research in Orokaiva areas. Within anthropology, nearly all of the studies of Orokaiva published since 1930 are based on ethnographic fieldwork conducted in these years.[18]

During this period, a small community of whites existed in Agenehambo. Most were teachers at the Martyrs Memorial School, an Anglican boarding school for boys that had opened on the outskirts of the village in the 1950s. The school, which began to change from an upper primary school to a high school in 1963, had a small staff of white expatriate missionaries and foreign volunteers from Australia, Britain, and Canada (Roberts 1986). In many ways it stood a world apart from the village, but villagers were welcome at festivals and at an early morning produce market three days a week. There were also several white missionaries at Agenehambo station: the parish priest and his wife, two primary school teachers, and sometimes a nurse. The mission station had rainwater storage tanks, an electrical generator, and a small dispensary. Mission carpenters had constructed a beautiful, high-ceilinged rectory with a polished wood floor, and the priest maintained a car and a motorcycle that were used for patrols to the surrounding villages, four outstation schools, and the town (Anglican Board of Missions Records: Martin Chittleborough circular letter 1971, Box ML MSS 4503/20).

The town of Popondetta was by now substantially larger than the bare-bones colonial station of the 1950s, when it consisted of only the government office, a trade store, and a few houses. Popondetta in the 1970s boasted a golf course, a cinema, a hotel (with bar), a rugby oval, two banks, a post office, a hospital, several churches and several primary schools, a government high school, an agricultural college, a bakery, a soft drinks and ice cream factory, eight stores with freezers, four trade store wholesalers, a hardware store, two second-hand clothing shops, a weekend market, and four auto mechanic shops (Oro Province 1978; Waddell and Krinks 1968, 30n1; Dakeyne 1969, 29; Baxter 1973, 53—55). To expatriates who knew it then, Popondetta was one of the more attractive and comfortable New Guinea small towns. In its heyday it served the province's fairly large resident expatriate population of government workers, planters, tradesmen, missionaries, and storekeepers, whose numbers reached as high as some six hundred in 1966, in addition to many foreign visitors affiliated with the government, development agencies, research organizations, and missions (NSO 1994a, 71–72).

The Postcolonial Weak State, "White Flight," and Localization, 1983 to the Present

The third period, which dates from circa 1983 to the present, continues the situation of the previous period with increased educational opportunities and an increasingly local workforce, but now with the white population sharply decreasing. The departure of white expatriates from Papua New Guinea began around independence, and it has continued since then due to rising crime rates, the unsuitability of the country for most types of investment, and the deterioration of infrastructure, services, and governmental authority in the context of a weak and largely ineffective postcolonial state. Census figures document this trend of postcolonial "white flight." The 1990 Oro Province census shows a foreign population of only 173, roughly a quarter of what it was in the previous period. The number of Australians fell from a high of 379 to a mere 32. The number of English dropped from 78 to 38, and New Zealanders from 17 to 4.[19] Although the number of Americans and Canadians rose from 3 in 1966 to 11 in 1990, this total apparently includes several Summer Institute of Linguistics missionaries who left shortly thereafter. The only expatriate group that has grown substantially is Malaysians, of whom there were 35 in 1990, most of them loggers. Otherwise, the main nationalities represented in the province in 1990 according to the census were Filipinos (8), Solomon Islanders (8), Japanese (6), Central American or Caribbean (6), Irish (3), Burmese (2), Fijian (2), Vanuatuan (2), and Singaporean (2) (NSO 1994a, 72, 178).[20] The foreign population, once so clearly dominated by Australia, was now far more diverse as well as much smaller.

But census figures tell only part of the story of the decreased presence of whites in the region. Also significant are changes in the lifestyles expatriates lead and the jobs they perform, changes that are being driven not only by the politics of localization but also by the rise of crime, which in PNG has become a growing problem whose seriousness is ill-conveyed by the local term, "rascalism."[21] Expatriates today fear robbery, carjacking, gang rape, armed assault, and murder. Such crimes have become much more prevalent throughout PNG since independence, and they have begun to victimize whites, who had formerly enjoyed relative immunity from serious crime. It does not appear that whites are disproportionately targeted, relative to wealthy black Papua New Guineans, but whites know that their skin alone makes them attractive targets for crime inasmuch as all whites are assumed to be rich. Oro Province is reputed to be one of the worst parts of the country for crime. It is well known among resident expatriates that a white Australian teacher from the Martyrs School was murdered during a robbery in 1990, and a white New Zealand road engineer was the victim of a targeted killing in 1995. The "rascal problem" is a common topic of conversation among expatriates, who share a well-developed discourse on how to maintain personal safety by avoiding certain areas and types of situations that make one vulnerable when among the natives. Most whites in Oro today, including all expatriate businessmen, live behind high, razor-wire-topped fences that are guarded at night by fierce dogs or watchmen, and they avoid unnecessary travel in rural areas where highwaymen may lay in wait. The exceptions are a handful of teachers, volunteers, and missionaries who cannot afford such precautions or who oppose them on principle. Because of Oro Province's reputation as lawless "cowboy country," the U.S. Peace Corps stopped placing volunteers there, as did the other main international volunteer service organizations Australian Volunteers Abroad, Voluntary Service Overseas (UK), and Canadian Universities Service Overseas.

Indirectly, rascalism has increased the expense of hiring white and other first-world expatriates, because employers, except for the missions, must pay high-risk allowances and provide costly security. As a result, many first world expatriate employees have been replaced by people from the third world, especially in development organizations and the government, where an "expatriate-level" wage that is too low for Australians may nonetheless be quite attractive to applicants from Africa, Asia, and the Pacific.[22] In 1995, the expatriate doctors at Popondetta hospital were Burmese, Indian, and Filipino; the expatriate director of the province's agricultural development branch office was a Filipino; and the two expatriate teacher slots at Popondetta high school were both filled by West Africans. Because foreigners tend to adapt themselves to the local norms of expatriate culture, these differences in the racial composition of the expatriate population have not brought about a significant change in the tone of local race relations, as one might have hoped.[23] However, they have significantly reduced native Papua New Guineans' contact with white expatriates.

More important has been the tendency, in view of the huge expense of hiring whites, to hire them only for jobs at the highest level of directive control. In the mid-1990s, this was the case in several of the largest businesses in Popondetta, including the large Steamships wholesale and retail store, the Papua New Guinea Banking Corporation bank branch, the Oro Guest House, and the main auto dealership, each of which had a single white employee, the general manager. It is no longer true that all such modern institutions have white (or Chinese) men at the helm. Indeed, the last white person to hold a public service position in the Oro provincial government left in the early 1990s. But if there is any white person employed in an organization, people can safely assume it will be a white man at the center of power—or at least near to it. (When I asked about the job a certain white man did in the oil palm company, my informants looked surprised that I was even asking, and replied, 'He is the whiteman!') A similar situation is found in the Anglican mission, where whites are not paid high salaries and there is a strong ideological commitment to localization, resulting in a largely indigenous clergy led by a black bishop, Bishop Walter Siba, from the Solomon Islands. However, whites have retained an important role as the principal teachers at the theological seminary outside Popondetta and as the comptroller of administration and finances in the diocesan head office in Popondetta. The Anglican Martyrs School near Agenehambo had an Orokaiva headmaster for a time, but the bursar has always been white, and the head of facilities has usually been so.

Thus, unlike in the two prior colonial periods, when whites occupied rural outstations and went on frequent patrols through villages for purposes of inspection, information collection, or education, it is now rare for whites to appear in the villages in the normal course of their duties. Today, whites work as a rule in air-conditioned back offices, usually in the town, while virtually all rural outstation jobs, as well as jobs that involve rural patrolling and inspection work, are done by Papua New Guineans.[24] At Agenehambo station, the staff of both the mission and the school has been completely indigenous since the 1980s. This includes the Anglican priest, the assistant priest, the deacon, the school headmaster, and all teachers. The school inspectors and auditors who periodically visit the school are also Papua New Guineans. Except for the National Court in Popondetta, where both white and Papua New Guinean visiting circuit judges hear high-level cases for one or two weeks each quarter, all police and magistrate services that villagers call upon are nationalized, as are agricultural extension services for cocoa, coffee, and oil palm cash-cropping, livestock-raising, and so on. When in town, villagers visiting shops, the bank, the post office, and government offices are served almost exclusively by PNG nationals. This is in stark contrast to the situation of just thirty years ago, when "practically no Papua New Guineans were employed by the larger trading firms, private banks and business houses in their offices or behind their counters" (Latukefu 1985, 39).

This rapid localization is widely seen to have resulted in a severe deterioration of government services, especially in rural areas:

> There has been a progressive withdrawal of government services from rural areas. Extension officers frequently fail to practise their appointed trade, and remain in their offices rather than go out into the field. Too much paperwork, too little transport, no budget, poor equipment, law-and-order problems, and inadequate skills, are typical explanations of this sad state of affairs. In some places government housing has deteriorated so much that field officers have physically withdrawn from the rural posting, and commute from provincial headquarters—transport permitting. Rural populations have come to expect less and less from government employees....
>
> The typical impression of a public servant is somebody who comes in a vehicle once in a while, stays a very short time, and then disappears in a cloud of dust. If the village is not on a road, then visits by government officials will be less frequent or non-existent.... [T]he general situation is one of poor and declining services. (Turner 1990, 137–38)

During my fieldwork, there were times when the entire provincial police force had no working vehicle; times when the rural health center had no medicines, even for treating malaria, or was closed because of staff complaints of being harassed by villagers and neglected by superiors; and times when the village primary school was closed when the facilities failed to meet minimal standards. Even in the best of times, the quality of instruction at the school is appallingly low, and Agenehambo school attendance rates, after dramatic increases between 1963 and 1980, have begun to decrease, as in other rural areas, with only about half the school-aged children now attending school (NSO 1994a, 117; 1994b, 117). Although there are undoubtedly many teachers and public servants who are dedicated and able, it is hard to disagree with the assessment that, in general, the exercise of rapid localization has proven "disastrous" (Latukefu 1985, 45).[25] Villagers often complain that the government is not helping them develop. As one hears frequently in the villages, as well as in political discourse and the PNG news media generally, the government is not "delivering the goods and services to the people"; it is not "bringing us development."

But while postcolonial white flight and localization have reduced the physical presence of whites, this has not diminished the importance of whitemen and their culture in people's lives. Although actual encounters with white expatriates are increasingly rare, such encounters are no longer central to villagers' knowledge of whitemen or development. Today people's ideas of whitemen's culture are also formed through experiences in the town and in PNG cities; through encounters with the modern black elite who are regarded as "heirs" to the former colonial masters (Latukefu 1985, 49); through books, newspapers, videos, and advertisements (Foster 2002; Gewertz and Errington 1996); through schooling and Christianity; and through people's own experiences of 'turning whitemen' in government, missions, businesses, education, and town life, as well as in village activities, rituals, and discourse concerned with development (Gewertz and Errington 1999).

Orokaiva villagers today seek development for themselves and their households by starting village businesses like tradestores, chicken farms, truck services, and gardens for produce to sell; by planting their own mini-plantations of cocoa, coffee, and oil palm; and by investing in the education of their children and other young relatives. Because most village businesses fizzle out within a year or two, men often try their hand at several different kinds of business ventures in the course of their lives. (Such business activity is virtually always on top of rather than in place of gardening for subsistence.) People also invest enormous hope for development in Christian religious activities, with the majority devoting a substantial share of scarce resources to the endless project of reinvigorating the Anglican church, while a growing minority work to build new charismatic and Pentecostal churches associated with youthfulness and progress (see Bashkow 2000b; Robbins 2004b, 2004c). People are adept at organizing themselves into village development associations like money saving circles ("money-go-rounds") (see Ardener and Burman 1995); cooperative work groups; and women's, youth, and church groups. These kinds of development activities have now become an integral part of Orokaiva village life. In order to support them, Orokaiva put significant effort into representing themselves in whitemen's terms in the applications they make to government and other agencies in pursuit of cash grants (see also Tvedt 1998, 227). In such ways people's construction of whitemen has come to be grounded in their own experiential world centered on the village, where it is perpetuated independently of whites' actual presence.

Whitemen as Enemies, Allies, and Returned Ancestors

Having outlined the main events and trends of the century of Orokaiva relations with whites, it remains to consider how indigenous conceptions of whitemen have changed during this time, and how they reflect the particular circumstances of colonization and postcolonial change. These are questions that can be answered only roughly. Few sources shed significant light on Orokaiva conceptions of whitemen in earlier periods, and those that do are generally equivocal, hard to contextualize, and hard to interpret. This is particularly true of the documentation that exists for the Orokaiva Taro Cult of the 1910s to 1930s. Although a degree of "anti-White feeling" in the cult has long been evident to scholars, in general the cult is best characterized as an "avoidance protest," in Michael Adas's terms, that did not so much confront or resist whites as it did avoid certain forms of engagement with them (Worsley 1968 [1957], 67; Adas 1981). The discourse of the Taro prophets, like other vernacular high oratorical forms, was polysemic, indirect, and ambiguous: a tissue of allusions and "veiled" hidden meanings (A. Strathern 1975; Schwimmer 1986). Moreover, there was no unified cult, but only diverse local sects, so that what was recorded at one location might not apply to Orokaiva in other areas. Problems in interpreting attitudes to whitemen in the Taro Cult, which is relatively well documented, indicate the challenges involved in reconstructing historical Orokaiva perspectives in everyday race relations.

It is useful to draw a distinction between two approaches to understanding Orokaiva relations with whites, one focusing on particular relationships, and the other, more revealing approach focusing on the conventionalization of racial differences in Orokaiva views. The former approach is concerned with particular Orokaiva-white interactions, which are conceptualized by Orokaiva as exchanges and evaluated in terms of reciprocities. Orokaiva regard exchange as the driving force of social relations; indeed, it is hard for people to "envisage any significant social relations in the absence of exchange relations" (Schwimmer 1973, 49). John Waiko's work on the early history of colonialism among Binandere Orokaiva illustrates how attitudes toward whites were governed by considerations of exchange. For example, in the "Green bloodbath" of 1897, Binandere warriors killed a white colonial officer, John Green, and his native policemen, to pay back earlier killings of Binandere people by whites (Waiko 1970, 1972; Nelson 1976).

It is in the nature of exchange relations to be changeable and perspectival. They are changeable in that they allow bad relations to be transformed into good ones; thus, people were able to make peace with whites by engaging in material exchanges with them (e.g., offering gifts of pigs and taro and accepting village constables' gowns, medallions, and sashes), so that periods of worse relations alternated with periods of better ones (see Schwimmer 1973, 218). Exchange relations are also perspectival in that one group may be troubled by an alliance that empowers another; thus, during Monckton's time whitemen were judged differently by different Orokaiva communities, depending on whether the whites were their allies or their enemies in terms of regional conflicts that the colonial police had been manipulated into joining (Waiko 1982, 1989).

For these reasons, the numerous stories of particular exchanges between Orokaiva and whites do not in the end add up to a coherent point of view. Many show whites in a negative light, as engendering negative exchange relations. In 1943-44 the Australian military administration punished thirty Orokaiva who were accused of having collaborated with the Japanese in 1942 by publicly hanging them—an atrocity by any cultural yardstick (Chalk 1986, 58-64). But there are also many stories of whites acting positively, participating in exchange relations with Orokaiva that created a lasting positive impression in Orokaiva memory. I already mentioned the generosity of Allied troops in the World War II years, and after the Lamington eruption the heroic efforts of foreign aid workers were warmly remembered by thousands of Orokaiva survivors. It would be possible to select from among such stories and use them to paint an overall picture of good relations or bad ones; indeed, this is what Orokaiva themselves tend to do in particular narratives, presenting the history as either good or bad depending on circumstances of the telling. But this possibility of representing whites in diametrically opposed moral terms shows that as an ensemble, Orokaiva stories about particular Orokaiva-white relationships are fundamentally ambiguous.

It is the second type of approach, dealing with broad, cumulative effects and structural aspects of the history of Orokaiva relations with whites, that is more revealing for the contemporary Orokaiva construction of white-men. Orokaiva knowledge of whitemen ultimately owes less to face-to-face interactions with particular whites than it does to the ongoing Orokaiva experience of wage labor, a cash economy, Christianity, government, schooling, and modern transport, all of which are identified as 'whitemen's things.' In the course of the century in which whites have been actively involved in the Orokaiva world, Orokaiva have built up an elaborate com-plex of specialized knowledge about whitemen's customs, institutions, and material culture, a complex that has become conventionalized in contem-porary Orokaiva vernacular culture and that is today transmitted largely within it. This complex incorporates knowledge of categories of whitemen like missionaries, government officials, and traders; it emphasizes typified images such as the colonial officer barking commands and moving hur-riedly from one village to the next on patrol; and it reflects the predomi-nance of contact with unmarried white males, who were specifically recruited into a colonial field service that had an ethos of extreme inde-pendence and unflinching masculinity.

The single most important feature of whitemen is their moral ambiguity. At any one time, people may focus on either the good or the bad in them, but both are always potential themes. In the early years of colonization, this ambiguity was manifested perspectivally depending on whites' alignments in warfare and politics. Whites were judged differently depending on whether people saw them as attackers or allies, whether they were burning down their houses or allowing them to plunder the houses of their enemies. Here the framework of evaluation was basically the Orokaiva morality of exchange; there was not yet a rich fund of knowledge and experience of whitemen and their customs, and there was not yet a symbolically elaborate construction of whitemen as a cultural other. Inevitably, people assimilated whitemen to existing categories, such as friends versus foes and men versus spirits. But there is every indication that people's interpretations were dif-ferent at different times and locations.

A pan-Orokaiva discourse about whitemen began as part of the Taro Cult (1910s–30s), which together with its predecessor, the Baigona Cult, bridged local divisions and stressed unity and community. In these move-ments, the symbolism of whitemen was basically negative, but there were also some positive elements that certain Taro prophets sought to appropriate, such as whitemen's powers to extend control over distance, by, for example, letter writing, telegraphy, and shipping (Williams 1928). In this pre–World War II period, Orokaiva contact with whites was mostly restricted to situations like plantation labor, police service and carrying, mission schooling, and administrative patrol visits, situations controlled largely by whites in accord with their own ideals of racial distance and hierarchy. Period patrol reports and mission documents show that whites engaged in what to them were intensive exchange relationships with the natives, but given that there were so few whites interacting with a great many Orokaiva, such exchange relations could never have been as intense or open-ended as Orokaiva would have wished. Indeed, a key feature of the construction of whitemen through present times is a frustrating tendency to refuse relationships in the forms and intensities that Orokaiva desired.

Because of the generosity of the Australian and American troops with whom they had contact then, World War II is widely felt by Orokaiva to have been a time of legendarily intense and positive exchange with whites. But when Eric Schwimmer surveyed Sivepe villagers in the 1960s, asking them to name all the *taupa* (whitemen) they knew, the results were interesting: respondents generally named only those whites with whom they had personal exchange relations. They omitted the white patrol officers, magistrates, traders, teachers, doctors, and missionaries with whom they had occasional contact without exchanging or sharing food. The whites they mentioned were anthropologists who had worked in the same village previously, past employers if the job they had held had been "in the employer's home or if both employer and employee lived on the premises (e.g., in a hospital)," and aid workers at the resettlement camp where villagers had stayed after the eruption. All such whites, with whom respondents had enjoyed positive exchange relations, were felt by the villagers to be unusual whitemen (Schwimmer 1969, 62–66; see also Belshaw 1951, 249). The nameless whitemen, those who Schwimmer's respondents knew but failed to list, were the typical whitemen, the background against which these extraordinary individuals stood out. In short, although World War II and its aftermath provided Orokaiva with many positive particular experiences with whitemen, it is clear that by this point whitemen were widely viewed as unengaged in material reciprocities. Thus they were defined in terms of their exchange behaviors in a way that differentiated them from others with whom Orokaiva had bad relationships in their own communities, such as their enemies in cannibal warfare with whom exchanges were active and reciprocal but negative, or with lazy, ungenerous exchange partners, with whom exchanges were active and positive but one-sided.[26]

This pattern of discounting those whites who maintain good exchange relations with Orokaiva as exceptional cases is also evident in the many stories of whites who are believed to be returned Orokaiva ancestors. In each of the cases with which I am familiar, a specific Orokaiva identity was attributed to a white individual as a way of interpreting the fact that the individual had been engaged with Orokaiva in culturally appropriate, positive exchange relations. In Sivepe village, the anthropologist Eric Schwimmer and his wife were regarded as returned ancestors within the Jegase clan, and in Agenehambo, the well-liked Anglican missionary Martin Chittleborough was taken to be a man named Urepa who had died two years before his arrival (Schwimmer 1969, 68; Anglican Board of Missions: M. Chittleborough circular letter 3/28/68).[27] In my own fieldwork, it was a recurring question (never fully resolved) whether I was a reincarnation of Garaina, one of the Seambo brothers into whose family I was adopted. (Garaina had died as a child, I was told, around the time I was born.) When I asked one of the Seambo brothers why they thought I was Garaina even though they knew I had my own family and home in the United States, he responded by listing gifts I had given him and said, 'Why else would you be doing all these things for us?' Such stories show just how powerful is the idea that it is not the nature of whitemen to participate in exchange and that they therefore stand aloof from normal social relations. A white who engages generously in exchange is not "really" a whiteman; it makes more sense to interpret such a person as Orokaiva in disguise.[28]

Despite the existence of such stories, whitemen are by no means identified with returned ancestors categorically. Although Schwimmer reports that during his fieldwork in the 1960s, "Americans were placed definitely in the category of returned ancestors," it was precisely because of the generosity of American troops during World War II:

> I was told that they were very different from other *taupa* (or rather, they were not really *taupa* at all). The American forces . . . and the Australian troops accompanying them, maintained friendly relations with the Orokaiva who helped them in various ways, supplied them with whatever food they had in return, [and made other] generous gifts. The American soldiers ate with the Orokaiva, which Australian officials hardly ever do, and fraternised with them. . . . A great proportion of the cooking pots, adzes and other steel tools found in the villages today were gifts from the Americans. (Schwimmer 1969, 68–69)

In the 1990s, thirty years after Schwimmer's fieldwork, my middle-aged informants confirmed that their fathers had thought the American troops must be returned ancestors, and there is no doubt that the war improved people's evaluations of whitemen on the whole. Moreover, the presence of black American troops suggested to Orokaiva that people with black skin could be whitemen, just as whites could be reincarnated Orokaiva, both ideas that fit with the Orokaiva assumption that the skin is changeable (Bashkow 2000b, 135). (On African American soldiers in New Guinea, see Hall 1995.) But it would be wrong to conclude that these Americans who are taken for returned ancestors serve thereby as the basis for a more general typification of whitemen for Orokaiva, as might be suggested by some of the literature on "first contact" and "cargo cults" elsewhere in New Guinea and the Pacific. To the contrary, the exceptional status they are attributed as covert Orokaiva reaffirms that such unusual cases are interpreted against a background view of whitemen as strangely unreachable through exchange.

Postcolonial Evaluations of Whitemen

Just as Orokaiva views of whitemen in earlier periods reflected people's experience of race relations under the colonialism of those times, the present-day Orokaiva construction of whitemen reflects circumstances of the current postcolonial situation. National independence and the ongoing trend of postcolonial white flight have changed local race relations, made possible nostalgic reassessments of colonialism, and distanced whites from contemporary social problems and political power, allowing whitemen to serve in many ways as a cultural other of a purely moral sort. Today, the Orokaiva construction of whitemen is charged with ambiguities that invert the virtues and vices that Orokaiva see in themselves. From the western perspective, it might be hard to square whites' historical role as colonial oppressors with the fact that Orokaiva attribute virtuous qualities to them. We might expect whites to be reviled and resented by people whom they had subordinated and exploited under colonial rule. But Orokaiva have not consistently regarded colonialism as evil, and they actually tend to view positively some of the very aspects of colonialism that western scholars have most criticized (this is not to justify colonialism; indeed, such a thing can be said in good conscience only now that it's over). Pacification, for example, although it was forced on the people, in many places with bloodshed, and although it ruined a highly developed traditional culture of warriors, cannibalism, and male initiation, is invariably recalled by Orokaiva today as being one of the best things that ever happened to them, and there are many indications that even at the time of pacification people were relieved to be free of the constant fear of raids and the pressure to battle, and that they were understandably glad of the peace, which allowed them greater freedom to travel (BNG 1900-1901, 55; 1902-3, 12, 34; 1903-4, 38-39; 1904-5, 14, 36; PAR 1906-7, 56; 1907-8, 9; Monckton 1922a, 270-71; Francis Edgar Williams Papers). Similarly, the paternalistic spirit of colonialism, particularly under the Murray administration, is not regarded as disdainfully by Orokaiva as it is by some scholars. To the contrary, paternalism is seen by Orokaiva as a kind of ideal relationship, entailing long-term solicitude and substantial reciprocal obligations that have the potential to improve their material conditions.[29]

These attitudes are not simply a matter of victimized people loving their chains. Nor are they to be discounted as purely an imposition on the people of colonialism's own paternalistic idioms. As Stephen Leavitt writes, interpreting colonial experience "within the orbit of personal and deeply felt relations with intimates" allows people to reconstruct their relation to colonial power in terms of the kind of moral exchange that they themselves value (1995, 179). Moreover, the attitudes reflect a cultural worldview in which power is not necessarily bad. For Orokaiva, as for people elsewhere in New Guinea, the concentration of power is its own legitimization. Power is seen as bad primarily when it is ineffective; its goodness is manifest in the fact of its productivity. Indeed, things that are powerful cannot possibly be altogether bad; otherwise they would be diminished by the operation of superior powers wielded by still others. The western notion of power as suffused with potential evil is one that Papua New Guineans do worry about today, particularly with respect to issues surrounding an uncertain future (Bashkow 2000b; Robbins 1997a, 1997b), but it is not one they apply in interpreting their colonial past.

None of this is to say that Orokaiva and other New Guinea peoples did not suffer under colonialism. Andrew Lattas has written movingly of the humiliations experienced by Kaliai in New Britain as the result of the racial prejudice institutionalized in their lives by colonialism. Colonialism brought suffering, pain, dislocation, and profound forms of alienation. Along with the hard labor and the racial insults that they endured under white rule, people suffered the disempowerment of a kind of double alienation: an alienation first from the traditional world of their ancestors and their ancestral power, and then from the new, more powerful other, the whiteman, who exploited the energy of their traditional societies in order to achieve their own ends, only to ultimately reject these societies as inferior

(Lattas 1991, 1992a, 1992b, 1998; Maclean 1998, 89; Waiko 1982, 1990; Knauft 2002b).

But alienation and pain are only one side of the people's understanding of their colonial past. And the significance of their former colonial experience has changed dramatically for people since independence. One reason for this, which scholars have tended to discount but which should be acknowledged, is that the past four decades have actually seen substantial improvements in race relations, so that we cannot simply summarize people's colonial experience solely in terms of the worst discrimination of which we have evidence in archives and oral historical sources. Most discriminatory colonial legislation was repealed by the 1960s.[30] And throughout the postwar decades, there was a gradual shift away from the early colonial style of race relations characterized by what John Black calls the "master-servant, yes sir no sir, *taubada* business" (*taubada* is cognate for *taupa* in Police Motu; Black is quoted by Nelson 1982, 165). Whereas formerly whites assumed the right to inflict corporal punishment on their wayward servants ("boong-bashing"), white people now know that even verbal mistreatment of "nationals"—the new term for "natives"—could lead to subsequent revenge attacks against themselves, their families, or their property. Discriminatory practices have diminished alongside changes in the local racial balance of power.

Further, national independence and postcolonial white flight have themselves created a condition in which it is possible for Papua New Guineans to be nostalgic about white colonial rule.[31] Now that exploitation and humiliation are rarely felt to be the direct result of whites' actions, Papua New Guineans "do not appear overtly interested in being told about the horrors of colonialism, as such accounts potentially belittle today's descendants of yesterday's victims" (Neumann 1994, 122). People are not inclined to think of their ancestors as having been compromised by the power of others, and they certainly do not like to see themselves as but one people in a vast global fraternity of colonial victims. To the contrary, consistent with colonialism's nostalgic revaluation, many indigenous stories appropriate it, representing it in terms of relationships that the ancestors *elicited* from whitemen by virtue of their worthiness (see also Schwimmer 1969; Strathern 1992; Gewertz and Errington 1991). From this perspective, PNG independence, rather than being seen as a nationalist triumph, is often construed as the rash repudiation of a positive relationship, and the whites' departure, rather than being seen as a means to ending a period of colonial exploitation, is often construed as symptomatic of the lawlessness and poor moral condition of Papua New Guineans today. Papua New Guineans' own iniquity (or that of their government) seems to have driven their white benefactors back to their own lands.

Another element vital to nostalgia is that now people face different problems. Instead of being subjected to intrusive colonial administrative patrols, Papua New Guineans are now passed over in the assignment of government services and are troubled by their government's neglect. They suffer from the severe degeneration of town infrastructure since independence. And they are victimized by the new forms of crime common since independence, including gang violence, armed hold-ups of buses, break-ins of homes, and terrifying "pack rapes," all of which the police are powerless to prevent, much less effectively investigate and punish. Today, Papua New Guineans are generally far less concerned with being discriminated against by whites on racial grounds than with being discriminated against by other Papua New Guineans on ethnic or regional grounds. They complain that corrupt state authorities practice family and ethnic group partisanship. They worry that other "blackskins" with whom they compete will surpass or exploit them. In this context, people look back nostalgically to an earlier time of control by white outsiders. The whites, people say, were better at managing modern state institutions since these originated in the whites' own culture, and they ran things more impartially since they lacked kinship ties obligating them to local people. Whitemen's lack of kinship and exchange obligations, which in other contexts is regretted, is here construed as an asset that puts whitemen largely outside the current, generally intraracial, competitive fray.

But however much race relations have changed in the postcolonial situation, race is still important in Papua New Guineans' lives. For Orokaiva as for other Papua New Guinea peoples, "the opposition of black and white skin is now as important in organizing thought as are those other classically Melanesian dichotomies of male and female, kin and affine, and friend and enemy" (Robbins 2004a, 171). There is a kind of sorting process that people engage in as a normal part of interpreting life, that codes institutions, activities, objects, talk—any type of sign—by identifying it either with black skin or with white skin: with Orokaiva culture ('our ancestors' customs') or with whitemen's culture (*taupa kastom*). Indeed, much of what is categorized in terms of the opposition between "traditional" and "modern" (*ari mahu* 'old ways,' *ari eha* 'new ways'), or the opposition between 'custom' and 'business' (*kastam/bisnis*)—the latter an opposition described for many Pacific societies (Jolly and Thomas 1992; Foster 1992, 1995; Akin and Robbins 1999)—is assimilated to a fundamental racial dichotomy between black indigenes and white foreigners.

Thus, the importance of race is not to be explained by the continuing presence of a few white faces, even if the positions held by whites in the missions and business are powerful ones. Rather, it is a colonial legacy that the people themselves have internalized as a part of their culture in the course of their history. For some four generations now, Orokaiva children have been introduced to 'whitemen' by hearing about them from their parents, relatives, and friends as they are growing up. When they encounter whites, their experiences are not written to a tabula rasa of racial knowledge, but are instead interpreted from the reference point of a symbolically rich complex of culturally transmitted knowledge of whitemen and whitemen's culture—in short, the Orokaiva cultural construction of whitemen that they learn about at home.

This construction of whitemen has in the course of the past century become an important part of the Orokaiva moral world. Its symbolism is intertwined with that of development: an important part of what development means is that the people will come to be more like whitemen. This is their own conception, but we should not overlook that it is hardly an idea foreign to us. On the face of it, the vernacular construction of whitemen is what western development proponents have always supposed that development should be: an internalization of aspects of western culture by the people, willingly, without rancor. They are aspects that the people themselves have played a role in selecting, in accord with their values, and that they interpret as improving their lives—not absolutely, of course, but on balance. While from the western perspective successful development would of course be largely propelled from inside and no longer require the constant motivating and monitoring presence of westerners, if anything, Orokaiva would prefer that foreigners played a more active role in their world. From their perspective, it is a misfortune that they are located in an area that the whitemen's world has mostly ignored.

But it should also be recognized that the Orokaiva construction of whitemen is also deeply subversive of western ideas of development, because it is centered not in the western world that sees the concept of development as its own, but rather has been adapted into the Orokaiva cultural world that operates on very different principles. Orokaiva know that the aspects of whitemen's culture they institute in their own development activities look different from what whites do in their countries overseas. To some extent, they are proud of the differences: 'we change it around,' I was told. 'If you do it this way, we turn it that way, to make it fit.' But they are also haunted by a sense that they are just not as good at doing what whites do, and this suggests to them some failing in themselves. As we will see, Orokaiva characteristically interpret this failing in moral terms. They identify it with the moral problems that they see in their own society, and conclude that these must be solved if they are ever to successfully bridge the gap between themselves and whitemen. In other words, their development activities, which they understand to be a part of whitemen's culture, paradoxically lead them back to the moral concerns of their own culture.

3. The Lightness of Whitemen

The heavier the burden, the closer our lives come to the earth, the more real and truthful they become. Conversely, the absolute absence of a burden causes man to be lighter than air, to soar into the heights, take leave of the earth and his earthly being, and become only half real, his movements as free as they are insignificant. What then shall we choose? Weight or lightness? ... Which one is positive, weight or lightness? The only certainty is: the lightness/weight opposition is the most mysterious, most ambiguous of all.

MILAN KUNDERA, *The Unbearable Lightness of Being*

On the *Southern Cross*, on the voyage to Eddystone, [the anthropologist W. H. R. Rivers] stood on deck, watching the pale green wake furrow the dark sea, reluctant to exchange the slight breeze for the stuffy heat below deck. At one of the stops a group of natives got on, the men wearing cast-off European suits, the women floral-print dresses....

[Rivers] squatted down beside them, and, as he expected, found enough knowledge of pidgin to make conversation possible. He'd devised a questionnaire that he used on occasions when it was necessary to extract the maximum amount of information quickly. The first question was always: Suppose you were lucky enough to find a guinea, with whom would you share it? This produced a list of names, names which he would then ask them to translate into kinship terms. And from there one could move to virtually any aspect of their society.

When he sensed they were getting tired he paid them their tobacco sticks and stood up to go, but then one of the women caught his arm and pulled him down again. Poking him playfully in the chest, she retrieved two words of English from her small store: "Your turn."

The questions were posed again and in the same order. When he told them that, since he was unmarried and had no children, he would not necessarily feel obliged to share his guinea with anybody, they at first refused to believe him. Had he no parents living? Yes, a father. Brothers and sisters? One brother, two sisters. Same mother, same father? Yes. But he would not *automatically* share the guinea with them, though he might *choose* to do so.

The woman who'd pulled his arm looked amused at first, then, when she was sure she'd understood, horrified. And so it went on. Because the questions were very carefully chosen, they gradually formed an impression—and not a vague impression either, in some respects quite precise—of the life of a bachelor don in a Cambridge college. Hilarity was the main response.

PAT BARKER, *The Ghost Road*

Kingsford Penunu of Agenehambo village was delivering feast taro in a procession of drummers and men shouldering poles hung with bundles of taro plants tied up at the stems. The large taro roots were black with earth. As his men set down the heavy taro bundles on the ground, Kingsford called out to me. 'Our large taro,' he joked, 'is what prevents us from going to the moon.' Others burst into laughter. I asked Kingsford what his joke meant. Becoming serious, he explained that Orokaiva 'bear the heaviness of earth, unlike whitemen who are light and so travel freely to the moon.'

On the surface, his joke was a complaint about the weight of the taro that he and the men had been carrying. It was humorous because Orokaiva men regularly carry around heavy loads of taro, and indeed it weighs them down. But the complaint was also disingenuous because Kingsford was actually proud to be giving me such a large load of taro in preparation for the next day's feast. His complaint in effect drew attention to the taro's impressive size.

But at a deeper level, the joke was a play on ideas about whitemen that to Orokaiva are truisms. In his explanation of the joke, Kingsford made these explicit in a remarkably concise synthesis. His explanation suggested that whitemen differed from Orokaiva in being untied to lands; that they differed further in being unburdened by the heavy reciprocities and obligations of kinship; and finally, that this lack of encumbrance, this uncanny quality of 'lightness,' enabled whitemen to project themselves and their influence across vast distances, so that they reached even so far as the moon—and Orokaiva country as well. The significance of these ideas is encapsulated in the important Orokaiva notion of the lightness of whitemen, about which they have a deep moral ambivalence. This moral ambivalence is charged by two fundamental tensions in Orokaiva society, between the autonomy of individuals and their obligations to others, and between their egalitarian ideals and the inequalities that are continually created among Orokaiva in competition for status.

The lightness of whitemen is not a quality of skin color (which Orokaiva construe as 'brightness'; see chapter 4), but a quality revealed for Orokaiva in whitemen's social habits and powers. Here I illustrate these with the example of Kingsford himself. In showing how Kingsford embodies characteristic attributes of whitemen, however, I do not mean to suggest that he was a "typical" Orokaiva man. To the contrary, Kingsford is a good illustration precisely because he was extraordinarily comprehensive in his cultural experimentation. He had considerable energies and talents that supported his inclination to leave no stone unturned in his attempt to bring development to himself and his household; at one time or another, he had tried his hand at nearly every type of development project from which village men selected. Indeed, this comprehensiveness contributed to his undeniable status as 'big man': there was no arena of value in the Orokaiva world in which he had not participated.

'Unto them are the rocket ships, unto us the root crops.' Kingsford had a talent for drawing sweeping visionary generalizations. He was a masterful orator, a prolific feast-giver, a community leader, and a keen entrepreneur. A man true to his time, he was at once a staunch traditionalist and an assiduous innovator. It was his special gift to meld the two roles skillfully to synergistic effect. Three years earlier, on my first visit to the place, I was brought to meet him by my Orokaiva friend Steven Seambo (see plate 1). We found him alone in his taro gardens, an elfin man, balding and bearded, wearing ragged shorts and working in his bare feet (see plate 2). That day he told me he had thirty-six pigs—most middle-aged men kept about half a dozen—and he showed me the impressive yam house he had filled one week earlier with his family's harvest. Unlike traditional Orokaiva yam houses, which are little more than thatch-roofed cupboards raised up on stilts, this was a roomy, walk-in log cabin built on the ground, with a floor of gravel from the riverbed. It was a "new technique," Kingsford told me, proudly—this was the kind of English phrase he was adept at using. He had imported the cabin's design from the Managalasi people who lived on the other side of the Lamington volcano.

That Managalasi yam house revealed a great deal about Kingsford's selectivity in innovation. The Managalasi had been warring enemies of the Orokaiva before pacification, and prejudices against them were nursed in battle tales and ethnic jokes about their stupidity. But no Orokaiva would deny Managalasi superiority in the cultivation of yams. And yams were accorded great ritual value by Orokaiva. On several occasions, after I had harvested my own yams, people urged me to decorate one and carry it conspicuously to feasts and Sunday church services: 'others will respect you when they see your beautiful yam.' However, the yams that Orokaiva displayed at feasts were at most two feet long, whereas the Managalasi, like people from the Sepik region who are famed for the great size of their yams, harvested yams that were quite literally as long as men. So when Kingsford visited the Managalasi plateau, he made sure to learn about their yam culture, and he brought back an identifying mark of his new expertise. He adopted a recognizable piece of their special capacity to produce a form of value that was meaningful in his culture.

The Special Powers of Whitemen

Just as he did with the Managalasi yam house, Kingsford selectively appropriated those powers that Orokaiva especially identify with whitemen. These are of four kinds, reflecting four basic forms and ends of power (*ivo*) in their traditional culture. The first of these is fecundity and the production of wealth, and it is paralleled by whitemen's special capacity for making money. The second form is suasion, bringing the intentions and actions of other people into line with one's own, and this corresponds to the special capacity that whitemen are seen to have for creating social harmony by 'lining up' things and people. The third form of power is perpetuating one's influence, renown, or name in time, and this corresponds to whitemen's special capacity for creating lasting objects and knowledge that endure in time. Finally, the fourth form of power—one closely identified with the lightness of whitemen in Kingsford's joke—is extending one's influence or control across spatial distance, a power that is realized in whitemen's modern means of transportation and communication. These four capacities—for making money, creating social harmony, making things last in time, and extending control across distance—are all qualities that Orokaiva admire in whitemen and that they seek for themselves through development. I will discuss them each in turn.

Money Making

Money originated with whitemen, and they live on it, just as Orokaiva live on taro. As Orokaiva are the 'fathers' and masters of taro, whitemen are the 'fathers' and masters of cash.[1] But whereas whitemen have no need for taro, money is essential for many purposes in Orokaiva life. It is needed to buy store foods, tools, roofing iron, transportation, and other such 'whitemen's things.' And not only is it a means to other ends; it has also become a new medium of traditional gift exchange in its own right (see also Simmel 1990 [1900], 232). Orokaiva now give money gifts to relatives and make cash "sorry payments" in order to end disputes. They give money as a central gift in brideprice payments and mortuary feasts. They give it in donations at church. They use it to pay children's school tuition. It draws the eye as a body decoration, especially during initiation ceremonies and dances, and it is used as an ingredient in magic (as well as to pay the magician). Big men like Kingsford save money to support election campaigns for local or national government offices. There can be no doubt that money is a meaningful form of value in contemporary Orokaiva vernacular culture. It was one Kingsford had seen increase dramatically in importance in the course of his lifetime.

As Kingsford saw it, there were three main ways, or 'roads' (*embere*), by which money was made. The first was to 'plant it' (*kovari*), and Kingsford had made himself expert in this. He cultivated all three of the major local cash-crops—coffee, cocoa, and oil palm. Most Orokaiva households cultivated only one or two of these, with uneven results, but Kingsford was considered by development extension workers a "model farmer" of all three. Indeed, his oil palm miniplantation won a "model farmer" award from the oil palm company for high yield per hectare.

The second road was "business," in which one started with some money and made it increase. Nearly all Orokaiva men try their hand at business, but Kingsford was one of only a handful of village men who had gained access to bank credit, having paid off several bank loans in the past. For a time, he ran a tradestore and a passenger bus. Later, he built a cocoa fermenting shed, and he bought wet bean cocoa from other villagers for drying and resale. He also middle-manned coffee. Kingsford understood many aspects of business by analogy to vernacular customs. For example, he likened bank loans to competitive gift exchange at feasts: 'you pay it back later with more on top.' Similarly, "investment," which Kingsford saw as the "key" to business, had parallels in taro cultivation: you eat only a part of the fruit and reinvest the rest as seed in new gardens. The whitemen's techniques may have been different, but they were not wholly unfamiliar.

The third road was wage labor, which Kingsford had done for a time as a young man. Although Kingsford himself had only completed six grades of village primary school, he invested heavily in secondary education for his children and several adoptees in the hope that one or two would go on to earn salaries and return a remittance. But Kingsford was unusual in being able to appreciate the institution of wages from the employer's perspective as well. Visiting his house one morning just before Christmas, I was greeted by an unusual sight. Kingsford had set up a table inside his house (furniture is rarely used in Orokaiva village houses). Standing across the table from him were five women, his two wives and three daughters-in-law, who were waiting to receive the 568 kinas (approximately U.S. $650) in cash laid out in neat piles on the table. This money represented their share of proceeds from the year's coffee harvest, and they were eager to receive it so they could go shopping for presents in town. In a short speech, Kingsford apologized for not being able to distribute more, which he blamed on a fall in the market price of coffee during the year. He then called up each woman in turn and gave her a share, as his son made a tick beside her name in a notebook. Watching this, I was surprised by the hyperbolic formality of Kingsford's performance. Dressed in a khaki uniform shirt with an official-looking boy scouts insignia patch, he was acting for all the world like the paymaster on a plantation. But through this annual household ritual, Kingsford was carefully managing the domestic peace by distributing payments openly, discouraging the growth of resentment due to the suspicion that others were getting more than was fair. By acknowledging the women's labor formally, he was maintaining their cooperation, which was so vital for his cash-cropping success—unlike most men, who take for granted the work contributed by their dependents, resulting in bad will and desertions at critical times. By recompensing his household with this whitemen's form of wage-paying, Kingsford was carefully cultivating the harmony of his household labor force, which allowed him to successfully navigate all three roads of planting, business, and wage labor, indeed, simultaneously.

Social Harmony

Creating social harmony is a second special capacity that Orokaiva attribute to whitemen. From their perspective, social harmony is evident in whitemen's ability to maintain large organizations like companies, and it is a decisive factor in allowing them to create their extensive wealth. Orokaiva often complain that 'we all want to be boss,' whereas whitemen can obey one another and accept subordinate positions. Whitemen seem able to undertake group projects without jealousy and personal resentment, allowing their individual wills to be constrained within external structures. By contrast, Orokaiva see themselves as highly autonomist and destructively competitive. Whenever they cooperate well with one another, such as when greeting outsiders or making feasts, they feel it to be an extraordinary achievement, requiring feats of great material sacrifice, impressive speechmaking, and shrewd interpersonal diplomacy.

This notion of social harmony is not, as implied by the English term, a "harmonizing" of different parts, as in a choir or orchestra. Living in a cultural world in which everyone has more or less the same kinds of resources—land, garden crops, pigs—Orokaiva conceptualize social harmony as a 'oneness' of orientation or will. It is a "mechanical solidarity" (Durkheim 1933 [1893]) that Orokaiva describe using images of 'unification' (*wahai ari*) and 'alignment' (*dehembari*): lining things up— above all, people's intentions. This value placed on unity suffuses their aesthetics; for example, they dance in lines, trying to move in concert as a single body. From the Orokaiva perspective, whitemen excel at this valued straight-line aesthetic, which is assumed to be somehow inherently productive of harmony and thus prosperity, and it is not only in lining people up (like Kingsford did with the women) that Orokaiva apply the technique. They create "program schedules" and use "agendas" to 'line up' villagers' activities at public events. They draw up "organizational charts" that visually 'line up' village leadership positions. In Kingsford's compound the houses are 'lined up' behind neatly trimmed hedgerows surrounding a large grassy rectangle. Unmistakable as an Orokaiva version of *Better Homes and Gardens*, this rectilinear environment, so different from most Orokaiva compounds, communicates Kingsford's understanding of the straight line as the specific form of whitemen's material well-being (see Errington 1974). Kingsford explained to me that the reason we whitemen are so developed is that we have successfully 'lined up' our ancestors so that they give us strength and increase our yields, their spirits gratified by our following their lead. Development was harder for Orokaiva because they had not 'lined up' their ancestors. They cannot even agree among themselves on their own genealogies: they cannot get the story 'straight' (*dehekari*). Kingsford was trying to resolve this once and for all by 'lining up' his ancestors in a chart.

Making Things Last in Time

The third special capacity of whitemen is to make things last in time. One important tool that enables them to do so is writing. Paper and books preserve information in time, and although physically soft, they are categorized with other enduring 'marks' (*hajire*) of the past as 'hard' things (*gaiha*). Enduring physical marks of the events in a narrative are taken as evidence that corroborates oral testimony, differentiating 'true histories' (*hihi be*) from 'mere stories' (*hihi teho*). A valuable ornament, a certain tree: any such hard, perduring item might be cited as proof of a story's veracity. Some of the most important Orokaiva 'true histories' were evidenced by particular boulders. Four such boulders were famous throughout the region, and Kingsford had a dream that had led him to a fifth one, indeed on his own property, supporting his claim to the legacy of the village's founder, Pahuva, the former war leader who rejected cannibalism to become a kind of colonial chief under the whites' new regime (see chapter 2). Although Kingsford excavated and named the stone, other villagers denied its significance. The problem was that while Kingsford was entitled to a share of Pahuva's inheritance as his classificatory grandson, Pahuva, who was childless, had transferred his possessions to a foster son before his death, and it was the descendants of this foster son who held the established marks of relationship to Pahuva in the form of a bronze Village Constable ("VC") medallion that had been the old man's insignia of colonial office. The VC medallion was hard evidence of their competing claim. But now Kingsford was energetically claiming Pahuva's legacy, appending his name to his own and his father's, calling himself "Kingsford Penunu Pahuva." He held feasts to commemorate Pahuva, and he represented himself as the perpetuator of the shining example Pahuva had set in converting whitemen's powers into his own in indigenous contexts, and vice versa. Irked that he did not hold the medal, Kingsford created substitutes, such as a concrete memorial to Pahuva that he built by the roadside. He also bought an old photograph, said to be of Pahuva, from descendants of another village constable to the west, investing the photo with value by performing the transaction in a visit made with great pomp in an entourage, and by paying for it the equivalent of $400 plus pigs. Like the stone on his property, these evidentiary objects made of cement and photographic paper may not have been convincing to all, but they were nonetheless reasonable justifications for Kingsford's claim, in that they, like the bronze, were 'hard.'

Traditional Orokaiva valuables are made out of hard materials like pig tusk, black palm, bone, and shell. The permanence of such materials is striking in the tropical environment, where most things are manufactured of plant products that decay in a short time. For example, traditional houses are built of forest materials that last only a few years. The sago frond thatch roofing tatters and leaks, the supporting posts rot, and the untreated woods composing the frame and walls lose strength. Whitemen's materials like roofing iron, steel piles, and treated lumber, by contrast, can last as long as decades, and Orokaiva, appreciating this, call houses built of them "permanent."

Orokaiva admire whitemen's ability to preserve their own histories in books and records stored in offices and libraries. When telling stories in which whitemen figured in virtually any way, Orokaiva would often assume that evidentiary records of the story had been made by the whitemen. A historical story, they would say, 'is there' (*miha*), meaning that written traces of it existed somewhere. People even sometimes asked me where those records might be held. I never heard Kingsford claim as much for his stories of Pahuva, though he did volunteer explanations of why government records might be mistaken about the identity of Pahuva's successor. To address this problem, Kingsford had his high school educated sons write down his own account, make photocopies in town, and mail and fax them to government officials in the provincial and national capitals, in order to ensure that his own story would also be represented in the archives.

Extending Control over Distance

This fourth special capacity of whitemen is reflected in two main ways: their ability to travel and the ease with which they communicate with one another across distance. For Orokaiva, spatial distance is not a neutral dimension, but rather a real obstacle that takes great effort to overcome. The greater the distance, the greater the value attached to overcoming it, whether by physically traversing it, or by extending the force of one's words or name across it.

In the Orokaiva world, many of the places to which people want to travel are accessible only by foot. In order to see their relatives in other villages, people walk for hours and sometimes days along narrow, overgrown forest trails that descend in places to cross rivers and even merge with riverbeds for long stretches so that the traveling party must walk through the water. Even a routine walk to a food garden can take a half-hour or more. If there has been rain, the trails will be muddy and slippery. Walking in the morning, it is cool, but the dew too makes the trail slippery, and people think it is unhealthy to get the cold dew on their legs. Walking in the daytime, discomfort comes from the heat of the equatorial sun. Thus Orokaiva assume (usually correctly) that a person arriving after travel will be sweaty and hot, and will need to rest and cool off before the visit proper can begin.

It is even more of a challenge to communicate over long distances. Without being physically present, one can never be sure that one's message will be received and acted upon as intended. People often use children as messengers, but children's talk carries little authority, and children rarely do a good job of transmitting messages fully and accurately. But involving another adult in your chain of communication introduces that person's own motivations and interests into your business; at the very least an adult messenger will need to be compensated in some way for his or her effort, and there is still no way to be sure that the message will be conveyed with fidelity. As a result, the problem of communication over distance often reduces to having to deliver the message yourself, that is, by traveling to say it in person. Even then, there can be no assurance that the people you are visiting will be there when you arrive. They may have left for their gardens or themselves gone off traveling, perhaps to another village where a relative has died: it is simply impossible to know what is going on at a distant place. Finally, even if you do go yourself, find the people, and succeed in conveying your message, when you have returned home afterward you will have to worry that your message may be reinterpreted by its recipients in a way that undermines your intent, that other people are manipulating it for their own purposes, or that attention has simply drifted away from your concern.

Given these difficulties, whitemen's techniques of communication and transportation have long impressed Orokaiva as an important manifestation of whitemen's power. From the early colonial messenger mails to today's satellite and cellular phones, whites have had special mechanisms to transmit their talk, so that their words travel in place of them, exerting the force of their persons in faraway places.[2] Not only do their communication mechanisms reduce their need to travel, but also when whitemen do have to travel, they do so with apparent ease on account of their well-developed means of transportation. Since colonial times, Orokaiva have seen the emphasis whitemen place on improving transportation infrastructure: widening foot trails, constructing vehicular roads, clearing airstrips, and bringing in motorized vehicles such as motorbikes and trucks. Whereas Orokaiva rarely had a choice but to go on foot, I was frequently told that whitemen traveled whenever and wherever they wished in cars, trucks, boats, helicopters, and airplanes. These great powers of mobility and great spatial reach extended even as far as the moon, as Kingsford recognized.

For many Orokaiva men, being able to afford their own truck is the ultimate goal of their business activities. Although it is hard work driving a truck on the region's pitted, unpaved roads, to control a truck is to wield a particularly valued ability to carry great loads of people, produce, feast gifts, firewood, and building materials that would be all but impossible to transport over long distances by hand. Truck owners always name their trucks, painting the names on the trucks' fronts and backs, to be broadcast across the region for all to see (see plate 13). So widely and visibly do trucks extend their influence and names that their owners feel especially concerned that they might be arousing others' jealousies, thus making themselves vulnerable to hold-ups and sorcery-induced mishaps (see chapter 4).

As Kingsford clearly implied in his joke, this capacity to extend control and influence across distance manifests an underlying quality of lightness, one that Orokaiva see as an essential characteristic of whitemen. Of the whitemen's four special capacities, lightness is most closely associated with the extension of control over distance; indeed, the term 'lightness' is often used virtually synonymously with "the ability to travel." But in order to fully understand why whitemen are held to be so light, we must first appreciate the moral significance of the lightness/heaviness opposition in Orokaiva culture.

'Lightness' and 'Heaviness' in Orokaiva Morality and Culture

In Orokaiva culture, there are times when one is 'light' (*ejeha*) and times when one is 'heavy' (*boka*). When Kingsford made his joke about white people traveling to the moon, part of what made the joke funny was that it played on my exhaustion and burden at the time; I was in a physical, emotional, and moral state that Orokaiva call 'heavy body' (*hamo boka*). Given that we were preparing a feast, the state of being heavy was appropriate and expected. For some weeks, we had been working hard, building feast houses and food display platforms, collecting firewood, and harvesting crops. We were awake through the nights, dancing on the feasting ground until the first light of dawn. And when we were not actively laboring in preparation for the feast, our days were spent extending hospitality to the other participants and managing the complicated arrangements that would ensure the feast's success in its multiple social purposes. Among the most salient of these purposes were that the postpubescent daughter of one of the Seambo brothers was being released from seclusion, and a long delayed brideprice was finally being paid. But for my Orokaiva friends, the most novel and exciting purpose of the feast was for me to gain, as they put it, "practical training" in this basic activity of their culture. They called it my feast, as I was its 'trunk' or 'root' (*susu*). I was using it to repay certain debts I had incurred as part of my fieldwork, for example to Kingsford, who had given me the seed yams and taro offsets (the transplantable shoots) that allowed me to start my own garden. Even though my exertions in service of the feast many times exceeded what I felt was the normal call of ethnographic duty, I could hardly have extricated myself from it gracefully, and given my investment in and identification with the feast, I felt enormous pressure to do whatever I could to make sure it came off well.[3] Kingsford, the practiced feast-giver, saw that I was worn down and anxious. His joke expressed empathy for my evident heaviness while gently making the point that the heavy burden of custom was an ineluctable part of the Orokaiva human condition.

Kingsford's joke was thus pointing out that feast-making was taking a toll on me, making me heavy and therefore more like Orokaiva. This implication was conveyed in Kingsford's phrase 'large taros.' Literally, 'large taros' are heavy ones like those Kingsford was carrying at the time, and their large size indicates that the ancestors have been pleased by the gardener's moral conduct. Since what most pleases the ancestors, in turn ensuring the yield of large taros, is feast-making, the phrase 'large taros' also implies the entire complex of traditional taro horticulture and feasting. In explaining the joke, Kingsford emphasized this by using an even stronger expression, 'heaviness of earth' (*enda ta boka*). This was a conventional formula referring to the ritual obligations surrounding death and burial. 'Heaviness of earth' thus again evokes the traditional complex through which the living repay the dead for the productivity of their bodies and their lands (see Iteanu 1983a).[4]

In Orokaiva, 'heaviness' (*boka*) is a quality both of physical weight and of moral burdens of obligation and care. A thing is 'heavy' (*boka*) when it is hard to carry. A person feels heavy after eating a heavy meal, as well as when encumbered by obligations or debts. The term *osaga* is used similarly to denote a worry, problem, or concern. As in English, these terms are applied to both the object of concern and the feeling itself. When a man is concerned over a debt he owes to his friend, he will feel 'heavy' because of the debt, and the debt itself is his 'heaviness.'

'Lightness' (*ejeha*), by contrast, implies a relative lack of encumbrance. In English, we say that heavy obligations are like a ball and chain that keep a person down. Lightness conversely implies freedom of action and mobility: He who travels light travels far. A dancer should be light on his feet. Such expressions translate readily into Orokaiva. In both cases, lightness is associated with movement and mobility. However, in Orokaiva, lightness implies less of an emphasis on the gravitational dimension of motion than is suggested by the English term, which brings to mind things that rise, bubble up, or float (vs. heavy things that fall or sink). The Orokaiva term, *osa*, which is the opposite of *osaga*, denotes pleasure or happiness and is conceptualized as a kind of inner lightness or buoyancy. But Orokaiva conceive of weight less in terms of lifting or weighing on a scale than they do in terms of walking or carrying. Light things, being less exhausting to move, can be carried farther than heavy things, which impede motion or are impossible to move altogether. What is really emphasized in the Orokaiva concept of lightness is the overcoming of distance. It is lightness and heaviness in this sense that Orokaiva extend to human morality and social interactions.

For Orokaiva, the human condition is to be bound to others by numerous reciprocal obligations of exchange. People only live by virtue of the things that have been given to them by others: feeding and care, knowledge and skills, lands, material possessions, their very bodies themselves. All such things entail the obligation that they will be 'reciprocated' (*mine ari*) in time. In a few certain highly formalized gift exchanges that are made during feasts, the reciprocation given is equivalent to what had earlier been received and so counts as full "pay back," ending that phase of the exchange relationship. But in all other cases, the expectation is not that reciprocation will cancel the debt or end the relationship; rather, people normally expect their gestures of reciprocation to acknowledge, maintain, and extend their relationships. Indeed, such invaluable gifts as the nurture and care that allow one to grow to maturity cannot ever be fully repaid, inasmuch as they result in an open-ended capacity to produce new value of one's own: In producing the child, the parents also produce the child's own future productivity, so that when the child matures and plants taro of his or her own (or earns wages at a job in town), the child is indebted to the parents for that as well. Thus, gifts and reciprocations build on one another in expanding cycles or, as André Iteanu (1983a) calls them, 'rounds' that are closed only with the final mortuary feast after death—and even then not entirely, as spirits of the deceased continue to repay the living.

At any given moment, of course, a person is not consciously concerned with every debt he or she owes. The debts are latent, as are the claims that can be potentially exerted upon others. It is usually a particular circumstance that brings a debt back into awareness. For example, an old man's death will prompt me to recall the ways he cared for me as a child—by feeding me, admonishing me to be careful, taking me hunting, giving me gifts, and so on—and it is these recollections of my indebtedness to him that will move me to join other mourners in grieving for him and to contribute to the exchanges following his burial. Similarly, the visit of a friend will bring to mind the hospitality I had received in the past when I had visited her, so that when she mentions now that her food gardens are withered, I will be moved to generosity in recognition of my indebtedness to her, and send her home with a load of taro and sweet potatoes. It is through such specific events and encounters that Orokaiva people are reminded of their debts, feeling them as a kind of heaviness.[5]

Heaviness is often felt to be negative inasmuch as it diminishes one's abilities to do as one pleases. If a man owes a debt of pigs to a clan relative, it means that he has that many fewer pigs to dispose of at will, for example by contributing them to the feast of another friend to whom he is also indebted. It also means he must act with caution generally, for should he harm or offend someone, his pigs will be needed to pay compensation—a familiar double-bind for villagers throughout Papua New Guinea. This example illustrates how feelings of heaviness correspond to a reduction in the person's capacities to extend influence in new endeavors. The simpler forms of heaviness, like that felt after eating heavy foods, dissipate by themselves. But the more morally significant forms of heaviness can only be relieved by giving something of value to others. It may take the man years before he has enough pigs to be able to reciprocate his friend and lighten his debt. And until he does, he will remain heavy for the many purposes in Orokaiva life in which pigs are required.

But even though heaviness is felt to be negative, it is also understood from the Orokaiva perspective to be an inherent aspect of the human condition. What is truly immoral is to refuse to acknowledge one's debts. To do so is to act 'falsely light' (*ejeha arako*), which Orokaiva see as cause for shame. For example, I heard it said of a certain man that he did not care for his parents though they were old and infirm and could no longer plant food, collect firewood, or repair their roof thatch. People said: 'He should help them, but instead he goes around falsely light, feeling no osaga.' The point was that in his situation, heaviness was proper, 'because when he was small his parents did hard work to feed and care for him, but now he turns away and acts as if he does not see them.' Were he to see them, he would presumably feel the appropriate heaviness and osaga, moving him to help the old couple with their chores. Thus Orokaiva do not identify moral virtue with an absence of heaviness, but rather with a lightness that has been properly earned by acknowledging the heavinesses that are a part of life and by making the appropriate material sacrifices to relieve them.

I once asked Kingsford why it had fallen to his brother Augustine to organize the mortuary feast for Augustine's brother-in-law two years after the death. It had cost Augustine dearly to pay off all the debts that had been created by the funeral: to the mourners, to those who had fed them, and to those who buried the body. Why had it fallen to *him*? Why not to someone closer, someone in the same clan as the deceased? But Kingsford took issue with the point of view of my question. 'You should ask instead,' he said, 'how did [Augustine] *seize* the burden? How did he *succeed* in taking it for himself? It wasn't pushed on him. He *stole* it! He stole the *blessing* that otherwise would have gone to [the dead man's children].' By "blessing" Kingsford meant the dead man's future gifts of protection, strength, and fecundity, which would now go to Augustine, so that when Augustine planted, his crops would grow large; when he ran a tradestore, his money would grow similarly. Augustine's wealth and well-being would now wax, while that of the dead man's children would wane, because Augustine had taken on the dead man's 'heaviness of earth.'

Although mine was not a mortuary feast, the deceased ancestors of the group of brothers I had joined with in giving my feast were there. Our nightly dancing served to invite them, and as the feast day approached, there were more and more reports of dreams and visions attesting their presence and support. What seems to please the ancestors most are the very things that are hardest to do, such as maintaining amity within a community. In making a feast, men recreate themselves as paragons of Orokaiva virtue, promoting amity—that is, social harmony—by praising others and providing generous hospitality, and by committing themselves to creating and distributing abundant wealth. Amity is not only an outcome but also a necessary precondition for a feast to progress to culmination, since any angry word or perceived slight can bring the preparations to a grinding halt. That one must carefully balance the needs to maintain amity, arrange hospitality, and provide food on such a large scale is precisely what burdens Orokaiva in their preparations for a feast. As the feast day approaches, the feast-givers become increasingly heavy with exhaustion from the work and dancing, and heavy with care from the stress of managing and supplicating those who contribute food and labor. Feast-givers' heaviness is also associated symbolically with the huge quantities of food they amass. In the logic of Orokaiva feasting, they identify with the heaviness of these foods that they then cast off in the feast's culmination, when they give it away.

Indeed, the main quality transacted in a feast is heaviness itself. People who receive feast gifts always bring countergifts called *tihanga*, but though these may be as large as the feast gifts they receive, they almost never contain raw pork, the greatest medium of 'heaviness.' The heaviness of the pork is made salient in various ways, such as in the songs that are sung when the pigs are being carried in, which liken them to heavy stones. It is above all from eating the pork that the recipients of feast gifts become 'heavy-bodied' (*hamo boka*), or tired. They are said to be 'pressed down' (*kikira ari*) and humbled by the feast gifts they receive. When they eat of these gifts the heaviness is transferred to their bodies, and it is expected that they will need a few days afterward to rest. The feast-givers, conversely, are left light at the feast's end, because they have paid off debts that had been weighing them down, and also because they have given away all they had.

And so, with the Orokaiva notion of heaviness, we can understand why Kingsford's joke is so funny. In asserting that it was their 'large taro' that precluded Orokaiva from going to the moon, Kingsford seemed to be lamenting that taro culture and feasting dissipated energies that could instead have been better put toward lunar exploration. Certainly, at one level this was true. But in the context of feasting the statement was ironic, an inverted figure of the kind Orokaiva call 'upside down talk' (*haperekari ke*). Kingsford was not so much criticizing as hyperbolizing and celebrating the heavy work of feasting, measured by the sacrifice it represented for me. Kingsford knew that, as an American, I was likely to hold lunar exploration to be a greater achievement than the production of large loads of root crops. This American, however, had taken on the heavy burden of feasting and now embodied the weight of pigs and taro, and in so doing had become more like Orokaiva. I had sacrificed the kind of lightness that allowed whitemen to go to the moon.

The Unnatural Lightness of Whitemen

The moon was never a subject about which I could collect much native exegesis, in part because my Orokaiva friends were sure that I knew more about it than they did. There were certain obvious things, like the connection to menstruation, which was called *hariga*, 'moon,' which I will talk about below. But for the most part, I learned about Orokaiva ideas about the moon, as with many other things, through the questions they asked me.

The first time the subject arose was on my very first night in the area. I had arranged to stay at the nearby Martyrs Memorial High School, where I stayed alone in a small second-floor room in a house that was undergoing renovations. After dark, a flashlight beam waved on my window screen, and I heard a man call out: "Nuboi! Nuboi! Udeh! Oi! Oi! Nuboi!" ('New boy! New boy! You there! Heh! Heh! New boy!'). I went downstairs and opened the door to meet the night watchman, Rodney Mamoko, a village man I later came to know well. Rodney acted of his own accord as a one-man Orokaiva welcoming committee for foreign visitors to the high school. That night, after a long introductory session of visiting and storytelling on the school grounds, Rodney walked me back to the house where I was staying, and before letting me go, he gestured to the moon with his flashlight and a nod of his head. He looked at me knowingly: 'You American people,' he said, 'very, very clever, going *there*.'

During the few days that followed, I met many of the people who became important figures in my fieldwork. It was then that I met Kingsford as well as Steven Seambo, who was to become my closest Orokaiva host, mentor, and friend. Steven was a villager in his thirties, about the same age as me, who, being childless, was freer than most village men to travel around with me when I was scouting for field sites. For several years previously, Steven had traveled around the region organizing youth activities for a government program that had paid him a small allowance. But like other villagers, he made his basic living cultivating garden crops to support his wife and himself. Steven's youth work gave him contacts in many villages, and he had political and rhetorical skills beyond his years. I enjoyed his intelligent company and appreciated his resourceful English, and after a week at the school, I moved into his house in nearby Agenehambo village. When I began the actual fieldwork nearly two years later, I returned to Agenehambo and stayed with Steven as his brother, and it was through that tie of kinship that I established the primary relationships essential to my fieldwork. My inner circle was Steven and his four brothers, Mackenton, John Newman, Alphius, and Trophimus. Mackenton, the eldest, spoke no English and was a great craftsman of traditional ornaments (see plate 14) and also an oral poet skilled in the fading art of composing allusive and moving dirges to draw mourners' tears. John Newman, the next brother, was a master of traditional dance. For a time he had worked as a truck driver for the oil palm company, later participating in the oil palm project as a village smallholder. Steven was the middle brother. Alphius and Trophimus, the youngest two, both spoke fairly good English, having worked at odd jobs (Alphius) or attended some high school (Trophimus) before marrying and settling down in the village. The Seambo brothers also had two married sisters who had converted from Anglicanism to the 'newer' denominations of their husbands. The elder, Elsie, had married a charismatic Christian preacher from the Eastern Highlands and lived at the time with his clansmen in a squatter settlement on the outskirts of Port Moresby. The youngest sibling, Jill-Joyce, who was quick-witted and raucously funny, had married into an Orokaiva hamlet of Seventh Day Adventists a few hours' walk away. I now appreciate how the Seambo siblings with their diverse experiences of tradition and modernity represent in microcosm the true situation of contemporary Orokaiva society. But this was still for me to discover when, late the last night of my initial visit, Trophimus found a moment to pose a question that had been weighing on him: "Why do Americans go up to the moon?"

For Trophimus this was a question that was connected to economic development. He said that Papua New Guineans are "underdeveloped," so they have to learn from people from other countries, like Americans, who are developed and go to the moon. When Trophimus had asked this same ques-

tion of another American visitor six years before, he recalled the man reply-
ing, "We went to the moon to get new ideas, to develop the whole world." The
American had been in the village for some weeks with an American missionary group specializing in Bible translation, the Summer Institute of
Linguistics, to help the villagers build the Agenehambo community hall—a
project instigated by Steven to support his youth work. According to Steven,
the American had described himself as a retired rocket engineer who had
worked on three American moon launches, and he had reported to villagers
about staged rocket firings, moon orbiting, moon walking, moon rock collecting, and the U.S. government's well-funded quest for humanly inhabita-
ble worlds in the sky. Steven often hooted with laughter as he recounted these
wondrous things. He also credited the man with having spoken of multilane
highways, elevated train lines, tunnels under rivers, and submarines. "Ah
America!" Steven slapped his knees then gestured an airplane's flight with
one hand and travel underground with the other. He said, 'Whether high in
the sky, deep in the water, deep underground, or over the land, you want to
go, you just go' (pambari perera).

So for Orokaiva, moon travel was not primarily a story of the triumph of
technological ingenuity, can-do spirit, or national will. Nor was it specifically about levitation and the conquering of the heavens. The story of
moon travel for Orokaiva is about traversing the greatest distance imagina-
ble, achieving the ultimate mobility and spatial reach. Since it is the moral
and social condition of lightness that allows for mobility, the great extent of
the distance traveled is a symbol of the moon-going Americans' incredible
lightness.

Orokaiva love traveling. Travel refreshes the eyes, they say, with the
sight of new surroundings. Through traveling, people learn new designs
and techniques, as Kingsford did from the Managalasi yam house. They
create new relationships with people who may give them valuable parting
gifts. They taste new kinds of foods and see new types of plants. Orokaiva
often return from travels with cuttings of fruit trees, flower bushes, or food
plants to plant in their own villages and gardens. Whatever the NASA engineer had actually said to Trophimus, the notion that visiting the moon
might yield new knowledge to develop the world resonates strongly with
indigenous notions of innovation as importation. Diffusionists to a fault,
Orokaiva see most of their domesticated food crops, and much of their
material culture, as imported. Other people are taken to have valuable
things that Orokaiva want. Good things come from afar.

But just as lightness is only one side of a two-sided moral coin, so too is
travel. While travel is in many ways positively valued, it is also full of

danger, uncertainty, and risk—heaviness—that is felt to increase in rough proportion to the distance from home. When Orokaiva travel far, they fear ambush by robbers and the many types of sorcery that are practiced by strangers. Women fear rape. By traveling around, a person makes him- or herself conspicuous, and while it enlarges the traveler's field of influence, it also has the potential to draw unwelcome attention. This has a way of generating unforeseeable problems that the traveler might not even learn of until far into the future. Perhaps, after a visit, a man in the visited place would become sick, and the visitor would be blamed for ensorcelling him. Or if a holdup were to take place near the visited location, the visitor might be suspected (during my fieldwork one of Steven's brothers-in-law was blamed and murdered for such a reason).

Even short of inviting trouble, traveling raises a further concern that applies particularly to men of means, like Kingsford. Such men have many reasons to travel, and they generally have the most far-flung networks of connections. But they rarely travel far from their homes for long periods of time. They know that when they visit others, they will receive elaborate hospitality and often large food gifts, thereby incurring debts they must repay generously in accord with their own wealth and status. And they fear that if they leave their gardens, homes, and dependents long unprotected, others may target them, perhaps out of jealousy. Such big men experience the heaviness of travel most acutely of all.

When Kingsford said that whitemen are 'light,' what he meant was that they are uncannily 'light.' Notwithstanding their wealth, they travel everywhere, as if without the heaviness of obligations at home, and they appear to do so effortlessly, without becoming encumbered by the heaviness that normally affects Orokaiva when they travel such as incurring debts or attracting unwanted attention. For Orokaiva this ability of whitemen to travel exceedingly freely reflects a condition of lightness that is unnatural and uncanny, in that it is unbalanced by the normal burdens of human moral existence.

Villagers often asked me questions about my own travel to reach them: How long was the airplane ride? How much money had the tickets cost? These and other such questions were not just about the mechanics of travel or my own personal experience. They were really efforts to figure out where whitemen's extreme lightness really comes from, and how whitemen maintain it: how do they remain so uncannily free of social encumbrance?

Wherever I went during my fieldwork, people would ask me a remarkable question: when I visited my brother at home, and ate and slept at his house, did I pay him at the time in cash as they know is required of guests at whitemen's establishments like restaurants and hotels? The moral concerns expressed in this question were complex and highly charged. Extending hospitality to others with generosity and graciousness is one of the most important values in Orokaiva society, and open-handedness with visitors is a conventional way of praising someone as a good person. When people are away from home, they are of course dependent upon others' hospitality, since it is impossible to carry one's own food, shelter, and firewood on a long journey. But it is the height of shame to demand immediate payment for hospitality from anyone, least of all from a brother. Between brothers, who for many purposes constitute a single social entity and so share with one another rather than exchange, possessions are ideally held jointly, and it is inappropriate for brothers even to keep track of the food, work, and so on that is transferred between them. Nevertheless, the scenario of brother-charging-brother holds a sort of horrible fascination for Orokaiva, since imbalances often do develop between brothers, causing tensions and con-flicts that can be hard to resolve and sometimes even to acknowledge. (Thus as in many PNG societies, discord between brothers is an important theme in Orokaiva myths.) The whitemen's putative use of immediate money pay-ments might offer a way of preventing such problems. Unlike food and fire-wood, money is easily carried while traveling, so in principle one could pay off all debts incurred on the spot. Travel would not result in heaviness under such circumstances, since there would be no intervening period during which the debts were latent and subject to recall.

The hospitality question expressed Orokaiva people's fascination with yet another morally ambivalent possibility: that whitemen use money to repay debts of every kind on the spot, so that in effect no debts persist at all, and everyone always goes around feeling light. For Orokaiva, this would be a highly ambivalent scenario. On the one hand, free from the possibility that at any moment a latent debt could be recalled, people would be free of the anxiety that their possessions could be pulled away from them at any time by those to whom they are indebted. On the other hand, such a scenario would imply an absence of even inexhaustible debts, such as those to one's parents, without which the perpetuation of generations of people would be incon-ceivable. It would also imply a radically individualistic world in which peo-ple do not help one another simply out of affection or kinship, but always and only for payment in money. Usually, when people asked me whether whitemen have to pay for hospitality, their immediate goal in the context of speaking was to express their hope that I would 'remember' them once I returned home to the United States. There I should think back warmly on the generous gifts that they had given me freely, simply out of affection, without asking me for any repayment at all. The question implied that once I was plunged back into my own world that was ruled by money, I would value the spontaneous generosity of my Orokaiva friends all the more—prompting me to send them money out of my own affection at that later time. The Orokaiva verb, to 'remember' (*hotembari*), is indeed synonymous with an aim to reciprocate. Their questions about whitemen's lack of persisting debt were thus ironically pre-scripting for me a heaviness of debt I was supposed to feel later.

Another common theme in the questions villagers asked me was whitemen's mourning customs. Was it true that we gathered only for a short service to bury the body, and then returned to our work? To Orokaiva, this was possibly the height of amorality. Orokaiva are 'heaviest' when they are in mourning. They do not travel at all. They do not play games, they do not make plans, they do not work. Those who are closest to the deceased are rendered helpless and immobile by their grief, requiring neighbors and relatives to come feed them and bury the body, taking on the 'heaviness of earth.' This phase of intense mourning lasts about three weeks until a small feast distribution (see plate 3) releases the mourners to bathe and return to their work. But it is not until the *pondo dopa* feast a year or more afterward (see plate 4) that people travel freely again. And they will still voluntarily abstain from visiting certain places, eating certain foods, and doing other things that they associate with the deceased until a third feast takes place several years later still. For Orokaiva, to return to normal rhythms of life soon after a death is highly unnatural. And that whitemen might do so, as Orokaiva suspect, implies that whitemen's attachments to their deceased, and to one another more generally, are uncannily insubstantial. Whitemen's lightness in grief is another manifestation of their lack of encumbrance by the natural consequences of social relations.

I was questioned in a similar vein about whitemen's lack of substantial food exchanges. Many Orokaiva told me that the whites they had spoken to in the past denied that they gave others food gifts; they did not even give food gifts in payment to their in-laws when taking a bride. Orokaiva infer from this that whitemen feel no special obligation to the people to whom they are indebted for the birth of their children. Indeed, whitemen seemed to have no rituals at all that make them truly heavy. They have no feasts, but only "parties" where the food served is insubstantial: "cake." 'What is the meaning of cake?' I was asked. To Orokaiva it is a mere 'light food' (*donda ejeha*) that does not make one feel full and imposes no obligation to reciprocate on those who eat it. Moreover, just as whitemen serve light fare at their own functions, they eat lightly when attending Orokaiva feasts or when visiting native friends in the villages. Rodney, who occasionally invited home white volunteers and teachers from the Anglican high school, would imitate how his foreign guests carefully examined his food trays, suspiciously poking at a banana or a piece of taro before finally selecting the smallest sweet potato or taro root they could find. Alphius often recounted to uproarious laughter how once at a feast he had seen eight white people share one banana, each accepting only "a taste." I heard many such stories about whitemen's light eating habits, and when I attended Orokaiva feasts with other white guests, my own observations confirmed them. For the whites, the food seemed unappetizing, probably dirty, and certainly unfamiliar. Moreover, some whites felt it was wrong for them to "take food away" from people who were so poor. Many whites also recognized that in extending hospitality, Orokaiva were trying to pull them into more substantial relationships that would call for gifts from the whites in reciprocation—an aim that most white visitors found manipulative, exploitative, and unwelcome. For their part, Orokaiva were perplexed and hurt that the whites wouldn't eat their food, since to refuse a gift of food is tantamount to a refusal of the relationship. This was one more way in which whitemen keep themselves aloof, light. When they heard that I was living as a part of Steven's household, other Orokaiva would often ask him what it was they fed me—did I, a whiteman, really eat their taro?—and Steven would proudly describe my heaping platefuls, to the others' amazement. When another anthropologist visited me and also ate local garden foods copiously, Orokaiva were delighted. Here were two whites with whom they could have a relationship.

A final topic people wonder about, though they were never so impolite as to ask me about directly, is whitemen's imperviousness to the effects of women. I mentioned above that the moon is associated with menstruation, which is called simply 'moon' (*hariga*). This association is part of a larger scheme of gendered contrasts by which men and the sun are attributed qualities of vigorous activity, lightness, dryness, and heat, while women and the moon are attributed their negative counterparts: slowness, heaviness, wetness, and cool. To Orokaiva, the sun does not shine passively but actively 'spears' the earth, penetrating and drying. The moon, by contrast, simply 'gives off' its cool light, and under it the leaves grow wet at night with dew. Within this scheme of gender, whitemen's masculinity may be contradicted by their association with the moon as a feminine object, as well as by certain other qualities such as softness and sedentariness, discussed in chapter 4 (see also Biersack 1987). However, whitemen's quality of lightness is distinctly masculine. Insofar it relates to the moon through the imagery of travel (there and back again), the question it raises is not whether whitemen might be moonlike and thus feminine, but rather how they sustain contact with the moon without losing their masculine potency.

The Orokaiva division of labor between the sexes is remarkably fluid in practice, particularly in ordinary everyday contexts where men and women work singly or as married couples. But there are normative differences which are followed in formal ceremonial contexts where work parties are large. Then men tend to do the most vigorous work, like cutting down trees, clearing brush, and digging, whereas women perform the relatively sedentary and ultimately harder repetitive tasks like weeding. Men build fences and talk, which is considered an active pursuit, connected to planning. Men also hunt and travel more than women (the two activities are closely connected). The notion that women are generally heavier than men is so taken for granted that when a woman works exceptionally quickly and vigorously, it may be remarked upon and the woman called 'light' as a term of praise. Such a 'light woman' is one who completes tasks with dispatch, causes few problems, and makes little fuss—these traits standing out as extraordinary against the background assumption of women's relative languidness. Whereas women see no shame in succumbing to the heaviness of sleep, men think it unmanly. While some men sleep beside their wives (an adoption of 'whitemen's custom'), the traditional way was not to, and it is still considered mildly contradictory to the ideal of masculine vigor.

It is contact with menstrual blood that is the focus of men's fears about contact with women. Menstrual blood is considered 'dirty' (*hatikari*), 'stinky' (*masa*), cooling, and emphatically 'heavy.' While their wives are menstruating, men do not go hunting, since the 'stink' is thought to scare away animals; nor do they enter taro and yam gardens, since it would cause these sensitive plants to wilt and die. Individual men vary in the precautions they take. Some are careful to avoid physical proximity with their menstruating wives if they are going to gardens; others merely insist that foods cooked by a menstruating woman must be eaten while still hot, which is thought to disable the blood's contagious 'cooling' effect. But at rivers everyone takes scrupulous care to ensure that men bathe upstream from women, lest the men be contaminated by any menstrual blood flowing in the water downstream. People similarly avoid sexual intercourse until the period is completely 'dried up' (*evekari*), since it is through intercourse that blood communicates its greatest weakening, disabling, stinkifying, cooling, and heavy-making potentials.

Many people had heard it rumored that whitemen have sex during menstruation, and I once confirmed for someone that this was true. But the question this raises is troubling, for how could white men do this without thereby being weakened? How do they remain so light notwithstanding such contact? It is as unnatural and uncanny as flying up to the moon. Indeed, when Steven told me the NASA engineer's story, he made a point of noting that precautions were taken to prevent contamination from the astronauts when they returned: they wore special sealed suits from the time they were fished out of the ocean in their space capsule until they had arrived in the building where they were temporarily quarantined. Just as whitemen are unnaturally impervious to the dangers of menstrual blood, they can even prevent their contact with the moon itself from making them heavy.

Thus, the image of going to the moon and back condenses many meanings that share one essential implication: the lightness of whitemen is unnatural and therefore impossible for Orokaiva themselves to attain. Whitemen seem to be able to move freely about the world however they wish, without being subject to the consequences their actions would entail if they were Orokaiva (bearing obligations to relatives, incurring risks in travel, becoming indebted to hosts, being confined by grief, being weakened by the contamination of menstrual blood, etc.). For an Orokaiva person to become this light would mean ceasing to be Orokaiva—or more precisely, ceasing to be human at all. Although Orokaiva value the state of lightness as generally superior to that of heaviness, the facts of life for them are that they must be heavy in many situations. In the world as they know it, lightness and heaviness each have their place and are dynamically linked.

Now we can understand how Kingsford's joke about whitemen's travel to the moon is ultimately a reversal of the western romantic trope of lucky savages living carefree amid plenty, eating fruit ripening naturally on the trees. For Orokaiva, it is the whitemen who are the carefree ones, the ones who reap without having to sow. After all, they do none of the work of preparing difficult rituals, maintaining reciprocities, and bearing up the deeply moral heaviness that is demanded by the ancestors to make the earth bear its fruits. What are Orokaiva to make of it that whitemen defy the basic terms of moral existence, that they are light in ways that are amazing yet exasperating, enviable yet pitiable? What are Orokaiva to do in the face of such a profoundly troubling contradiction but laugh uproariously? Those jokes are best, it is said, that we laugh at until we weep. Such a joke was Kingsford's.

The Orokaiva Construction of Whitemen

Many of the qualities that Orokaiva attributed to whitemen in the questions they asked me did not seem to very fittingly characterize my own life or the lives of the other white people I knew. After all, many whites feel their family obligations acutely, experience profound grief at the loss of their loved ones, and observe reciprocities in gift-giving and hospitality. And at that time in particular, I was certainly highly alert to the dangers to which I was subjecting myself in traveling so far afield. But when I would try to set the record straight, for example, by answering no, I do not pay my brother for meals we share at his house, my answers were not taken as definitive; they did not stick. The questions would recur as if my replies had made no impression. At best, my responses were taken to mark me as an exception to the rules, which were thereby preserved. Or it was speculated that it was not me as an individual but rather some subcategory I represented (American, Jewish, anthropologist, etc.) that made me different from a more prototypical whiteman: you Americans are unlike Australians, you know how to be generous and love your brothers as do we Orokaiva.

One reason my replies had so little impact on people is because their questions were not actually meant to elicit authoritative information from a whiteman. In the situation of speaking with me, Orokaivas' questioning about whitemen really constituted a kind of moral tutorial, a way of teaching me what I should do to have good rapport with them on their terms: If I ate their taro, accepted their hospitality, became heavy and indebted to them, and reciprocated generously in my turn, my relationship with them would be genuine and I would find favor in their eyes. In effect, in the contexts in which they were raised, people's questions were intended to draw my attention to Orokaivas' own moral virtues, which were expressed succinctly and compellingly through the ready device of the implicit contrasts with the nature of whitemen. It was presumed that, although a whiteman myself, I would be able to recognize their practices as virtuous, since their moral yardstick was taken to be natural, projected as it was as an element of their own cultural worldview onto humanity as a whole.

But the most important reason why my answers did not conclusively satisfy anyone's curiosity about whitemen is that the questions did not arise in the first place from isolated impressions; people were not just looking to confirm stray bits of information that were open to revision independently of one another as a merely empirical matter. Instead, the questions were motivated by an integrated constellation of ideas deeply entrenched in Orokaiva vernacular culture: the Orokaiva construction of whitemen, a highly redundant set of indigenous ideas which is organized according to the indigenous moral logic that Orokaiva naturalize as objectively governing human relations. The questions Orokaiva entertain about whitemen are so compelling to them because they raise the possibility that these exotic

beings are unaffected by the natural concomitants of their social interdependencies and so somehow defy one or another of the principles governing the moral universe. In this way, the Orokaiva construction of whitemen
is similar to the western construction of "primitives": westerners are insa-
tiably curious about these others' putative irrationality, promiscuity, and
cannibalism, since these represent dramatic inversions of morally significant aspects of our conception of ourselves.

Clearly, many aspects of the Orokaiva construction of whitemen are
inadequate to represent the complexity of the current racial reality. But we
must recognize that its basic categorical distinctions reflect Orokaiva
experiences with whites during earlier phases of their colonial history.
For example, notwithstanding that people now encounter white women
as well as white men, the gender connotation of the Orokaiva construction of whitemen is distinctly masculine. Thus, the white moongoers in
Kingsford's joke are presumed to be masculine, and Orokaiva interest in
whitemen's imperviousness to menstrual contamination focuses on the
men's immunity to the blood, rather on the alternative possibility that the
blood itself has no debilitating effects.

But historically, the whites Orokaiva have seen have been predominantly men, particularly in the earliest years of contact with gold prospectors, labor recruiters, traders, missionaries, and colonial officers. In later
years, especially during the decades between World War II and independence, a number of white women came to live on Anglican mission stations
as nurses and teachers. But until then white women were so rarely seen in
Orokaiva areas that the arrival of an Australian colonial official's wife in
1922 attracted crowds of Orokaiva spectators. It so impressed the colonial
official that he wrote in his patrol report that it was "as if half the population" of natives had turned out to get a glimpse of her (Liston Blyth 1922).
(A few years later crowds similarly gathered to catch sight of a white infant
[Flint 1924].)

Such are the historical facts. But what rendered them so salient to
Orokaiva that they became sedimented in the whitemen category is surely
the place they assume within the indigenous scheme of expectations about
gender and the life cycle. In Orokaiva culture, men are the light ones, and
lightest of all are young bachelors. Such young men do not yet have wives
or children to house, feed, and protect; they do not yet have a wife's family
regularly calling on them to work in the name of their affinal obligations;
their parents are not yet so old that they have become dependent upon them
for food and firewood; and they do not yet have the weighty responsibility
of being sole custodian of their lands. Young men are not expected to

remain in the parents' household as are their sisters; they instead enjoy an almost nomadic lifestyle, staying for periods in friends and relatives' homes while they work for them in bursts on short-term projects like preparing feasts, building houses, and clearing new gardens. The houses that young bachelors often do build for themselves in their parents' compounds have even evolved a characteristic style that betrays their occupants' lightness architecturally: raised dramatically high off the ground, these houses put young men on a symbolically distinct plane from the one on which ordinary social life takes place.[6] Thus, when I returned to Agenehambo as a newly-wed a few years after my fieldwork, all my older Orokaiva friends commented that alas, I was no longer light, as I had been when I had lived among them as a young bachelor. I had made the bittersweet transition to maturity, and through their comments they empathized with the heaviness this condition entailed.

Throughout the history of Orokaiva engagement with whites, even though the whites themselves were not necessarily objectively young, salient aspects of their behavior conformed closely to Orokaiva expectations of young men. Hence, the Orokaiva construction of whitemen has come not only to be gendered but also to be associated with the social independence of male young adulthood. In the colonial period, white administrative officers, traders, and labor recruiters would invariably come from afar, stay only for a short time, and then leave again to some other faraway place. To Orokaiva it seemed as though even these adult white men of relatively high rank traveled with the lack of social encumbrance characteristic of young men. (Indeed, the original vernacular term that Orokaiva used to describe whitemen was *ijo-hujo*, literally 'those who go and come.') Moreover, there was a connotation of carefree youth in whites' aloofness from Orokaiva-style reciprocities. For Orokaiva, maturation involves a broadening and deepening of one's exchange relations with others, yet the whites they encountered in their villages seemed never to become indebted, since they systematically minimized their dependence on villagers during their travels. To the maximum extent possible, visiting whites carried their own food; for the sake of efficiency, reliability, and comfort, they aimed to keep practical arrangements under their own control. What village food they did eat they paid for on the spot, in which case they would purchase it raw and have it prepared within their own party. They virtually never allowed themselves to be hosted by accepting cooked meals or staying with villagers in their homes.

These early experiences with whites must have suggested to Orokaiva an orderly world in which everyone is self-sufficient, a feature that is significant in the present-day construction of whitemen. Whitemen seem to

Orokaiva to be free of the need to call on one another the way they themselves do; as Orokaiva would tell me, 'among you whitemen every man has all the money and goods he needs to look out for himself.' Similarly, while Orokaiva take a keen interest in the kin relations of individual whites they get to know, in their construction of whitemen society is reproduced almost magically, without anyone actually having to raise children, care for the elderly, or tend the sick. It is as if in the whitemen's alien world, generations are not bound to each other by ties of dependence and nurture. Whitemen, like Orokaiva young men, simply do not seem to be deeply engaged in the hard work of social reproduction. They live as if in a state of perpetual autonomy and youthfulness, somehow achieving an Orokaiva version of the recurrent western male fantasy of living free of all obligations, like the cowboy romance hero who can just ride off into the sunset.

Whatever its historical origins, the Orokaiva construction of whitemen finds present-day confirmation in Orokaiva people's experiences of taking on whitemen's roles in various domains of their own lives. Orokaiva now know firsthand that in business, generously giving away one's goods and services will lead inexorably to failure; that in town, one must work for money in order to survive; and that in wage work, dropping everything to attend to family obligations for lengthy periods will lead to losing the job. They know through modern travel that one can move great distances without physical effort and without relying on the hospitality of friends and relatives along the way, and through Christianity that salvation is a matter of purely individual belief in stories that endure and spread throughout the world through the power of the written word (see Robbins 2004a). Even schoolchildren are exposed to whitemen's special techniques for creating social harmony, rigidified in their classrooms in row seating, scheduled activities, and disciplined behavior. This kind of knowledge of whitemen through direct personal experience was something that Kingsford had in spades. He knew the special powers of whitemen not only through the culturally mediated perceptions of an external other observed outside his society but also from actually trying them out himself in the service of his own interests and plans. Kingsford may have been exceptionally broad in the range of his cultural experimentation, but he was not qualitatively different from others in his community who have similarly gained a working knowledge of what it is like to live in the whitemen's world through a kind of participant observation in which they experience the actual causes and effects of whitemen's customs within their own social and moral environment.

In short, while the Orokaiva construction of whitemen in many ways reflects local historical realities, those realities are interpreted through the

lens of Orokaiva culture and present-day experiences. Like all constructions of cultural others, the Orokaiva construction of whitemen is in-
controvertibly ethnocentric; the complex realities are selectively given
significance and are even distorted by the ideas and values Orokaiva bring
to them. But the fact that the construction of whitemen is ethnocentric does
not justify our dismissing it as a merely fictive cultural projection that fails
to embody real cross-cultural understanding. As we have seen, the Orokaiva
construction of whitemen constitutes a reasonable interpretation of whites
in Orokaiva terms, and the appropriate response for us is not to criticize it as
an Orokaiva distortion of reality (as if we are in a better position than they
to perceive reality without cultural mediation!). Rather, we need to work to
explicate their cultural worldview, without which we can neither make
their ethnocentric ideas intelligible nor come to any kind of informed and
therefore legitimate evaluation of them.

Nor is the ethnocentric Orokaiva construction of whitemen a merely
self-congratulatory device for reifying cultural differences in a way that
only distances and denigrates the other. Ethnocentrism is not a purely evaluative process for chauvinistically constructing an other in negative terms
relative to oneself (Swartz 1961). The phenomenon of ethnocentrism consists more broadly in interpreting the other by bringing to bear moral issues
and conceptual frameworks of understanding that are founded in the self's
own cultural world. To that extent, it does not in itself imply any particular
evaluative position. Indeed, in contrast to the usual assumption that ethnocentric evaluations must of course be inherently negative, there is a tendency for ethnocentric constructions of others to in fact be ambivalent,
involving attraction as well as repulsion.[7] In some contexts the views people express may be critical; in others they may be admiring. But in both
cases the other is portrayed in ways that selectively draw upon a loosely
structured repertoire of images, tropes, typifications, and evaluations of the
other, a Foucauldian "discourse," through which the individual statements
resonate meaningfully in the culture in which they are produced.

Orokaiva ambivalence about whitemen should not be confused with an
uneven distribution of opinions across individuals and sociological categories. It is not the case that people of one social category hold primarily
admiring views, while those of another tend to be critical. Indeed, I often
heard diametrically opposed evaluations expressed by the same person on
different occasions. For example, a young man I knew who in one context
expressed a longing for a whitemanlike freedom from burdensome relatives spoke disparagingly to me in another context of whitemen's aloofness
from their kin, as shown by their failure to make the material sacrifices that

would betoken a real love for them. By no means is this an isolated example; all Orokaiva I knew—men as well as women, illiterate villagers as
well as university professors, the young as well as the old—made these
kinds of context-dependent contradictory evaluations. The Orokaiva construction of whitemen is irreducibly ambivalent; the ambivalence is culturally shared.

The reason for this ambivalence is that the indigenous moral qualities in
terms of which whitemen are understood are, as we have seen, themselves
ambivalent. Orokaivas' own moral category of lightness has both good and
bad dimensions (as do others, as we will see in the next chapter): it can
mean autonomy and rising over restrictions, but it can also mean a failure
to live up to one's responsibilities. This multivalent evaluative potential is
what gives the construction of whitemen such broad utility: people can
foreground differently evaluated aspects of the whiteman construct depending on what they are trying to do. Thus, on the one hand, when
Orokaiva want to criticize problems in their own society, whitemen can be
portrayed admiringly, as a model for Orokaiva to emulate. When Orokaiva
wish to bemoan the pressures they feel from their obligations at home, the
lightness of whitemen offers a ready foil connoting an appealing unfettered
freedom. When Orokaiva feel their intentions thwarted by the inconven-
ience of travel and unreliability of communication across distance, the
lightness of whitemen can be used to represent the contrasting possibilities
of frictionless mobility and messages transmitted effortlessly and without
degradation over even the greatest distances. On the other hand, in contexts
where Orokaiva wish to highlight their own virtue, they can call upon negative images of whitemen to cast it into relief. So when hosting visitors, they
can draw attention to their own generosity by speaking of whitemen's pecu-
niary insistence on immediate payment for everything given out. When
buttering up distant relatives as a prelude to asking for a favor, Orokaiva can
indirectly remind them of the importance of material sacrifice by speaking
contrastively of whitemen's callous neglect of their kin. And when strate-
gizing about how to get outside help with development projects or grant
aid, Orokaiva often express frustration at their exclusion from whitemen's
prosperity, a problem that is a challenge for them to overcome given whitemen's morally incomprehensible unwillingness to participate in exchange
with them.

There are also contexts where the evaluation of whitemen one way or
another is not crucial to achieving any proximate social goal. People often
talk and joke about whitemen to entertain themselves in leisurely conversation, as well as out of an eager curiosity about them. It is in this kind of

Orokaiva recreational ethnography that we find whitemen to be most morally ambiguous, fluid, and elusive. Is immediate payment for all things with money a brilliant institution, a genius solution to the problem of maintaining social harmony? Or is it a social nightmare, an abhorrent debasing of human relations? It was undecidable; the whole idea was only meaningful in the form of a question. Recall Kingsford's joke: whitemen's moon travel was no doubt an impressive feat, but it was also an absurd distraction from the consequential human matters of life and death and the fertility of the earth. The lightness it implies is both an alluring fantasy of escape and a terrifying vision of disconnection. How could one resolve such a question? Only one thing is certain: to Orokaiva the moral issues whitemen present are not indifferent. Whitemen and their special powers have become an important part of their lives, and they call for some understanding. Yet in so many ways, the lightness of whitemen seems to represent an absurdity, violating the principles that actually govern Orokaiva moral life. Perhaps this is why Orokaiva so often laugh when they raise the questions of whitemen.

PLATE 1 · Steven Seambo in his market vegetable garden, 1993.

PLATE 2 · Kingsford Penunu in his taro garden, 1991. At his feet are newly planted taro setts. The long poles on the ground mark garden plots planted for different purposes and recipients.

PLATE 3 · Small feast distribution (*umo kuhari*) held several weeks after a death to release the deceased's family from mourning seclusion. On the ground is a row of food piles, each intended for a different recipient. Cyprian Ogo is showing Alquin Pinoko his pile. Jungata hamlet, 1993.

PLATE 4 · For two or more years after a death, survivors exhibit their grief by not cutting their hair, by wearing plaited mourning bands, and by avoiding certain places or foods that are connected to the memory of the deceased. To mark the end of this prolonged period of mourning, a large feast (*pondo dopa*) is held. At this feast for the memory of his teenage daughter, Petra Ogo, Abel Gaviro is making a speech (being tape recorded by Steven Seambo) while holding a ceremonial staff (*kani*) and walking along the line of pigs laid out before the feasting platform. Hojane hamlet, 1995.

PLATE 5 · Brideprice feast, Agenehambo, 1994. Standing beside a pile of wedding gifts and the impressive feasting platform with its central tower of taro, Rob-Roy of Timbeki, the bride's father's brother, exhorts her on the importance of hospitality to her husband's relations. The string bags hanging from the forked stick at the left are *tihanga* gifts (see chapter 5) brought by the brideprice recipients as a reciprocal payment for the feast-givers.

PLATE 6 · Orokaiva must do hard physical work to get food (see chapter 4). Here Steven Seambo is cutting a tree down with an ax in order to make a new garden. Agenehambo, 1993.

PLATE 7 · Gardens newly cleared by the work of Orokaiva men's hands. For scale, note the two men standing on the tree trunk near the center of the photograph. Near Jungata, 1993.

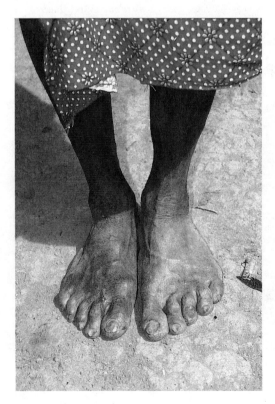

PLATE 8 · Papua New Guinean villagers' feet are callused, leathery, and tough, in marked contrast to the soft, shoe-protected feet of whitemen (see chapter 4). Wautogik, 1999.

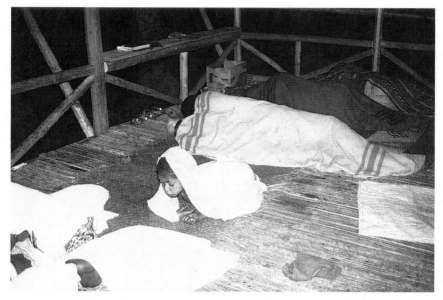

PLATE 9 · People sleeping in an *arara*, Agenehambo, 1994. Unlike whitemen, who enjoy the luxury of sleeping on soft mattresses, most Orokaiva sleep on mats on the floor, under just a thin sheet or blanket (see chapter 4).

PLATE 10 · Sunday morning church service in Jungata, 1995. Note the drab appearance of the village (see chapter 4).

PLATE 11 · Seambo family women: from left, Jill-Joyce Paingo, Elsie Saidom (standing), Clarissa Joma, Stella Baiho, and Gertrude Jigari, along with children. When guests visit, the cooking hearth is moved onto the ground, so that the guests won't see the food before it is presented to them (see chapter 4). Agenehambo, 1995.

PLATE 12 · Example of a village tradestore, Pusahambo, 1995, with its owner Suckling Asimba. To see the attractive trade goods ranged sparsely on the shelves, customers must peer through the wire mesh window into the dark interior (see chapter 4).

PLATE 13 · A small village bus on the main (unpaved) road from Popondetta to Kokoda. The name on the front (see chapters 3 and 4) is one belonging to the family of the bus's owner, Noel Goira (standing).

PLATE 14 · Sitting in an arara, Mackenton Seambo puts the finishing touches on a dancer's belt ornament. Agenehambo, 1994.

PLATE 15 · Orokaiva dancers beautify themselves with paints, feathers, flowers, and traditional ornaments to create an impression of brightness, exciting motion, and color (see chapter 4). Here Conrad Ogo decorates his face with bright spots of White-Out in preparation for a dance at a feast in Jungata hamlet, 1994.

PLATE 16 · Conrad Ogo later on in his full dance regalia, standing with Trophimus Seambo.

PLATE 17 · Alongside traditional body decoration, Orokaiva also make use of whitemen's ornaments like neckties, wristwatches, and cameras to represent their power in the whitemen's world (see chapter 5).

PLATE 18 · The debutante Elsie Joma, newly emerged from seclusion, seated behind a display of feast foods prior to being decorated for her debut feast (see chapter 4). Agenehambo, 1994.

PLATE 19 · Orokaiva dancers of the Paru clan rehearse before performing at a feast in Kiorota village, 1993.

PLATE 20 · Young men storm down from the feast platform (seen in back) to hurl chunks of raw pork at a group of beautifully decorated dancers (the women wearing painted barkcloth). This kind of dramatic mock attack is called *o taiha* 'pelting with meat' (see chapter 4). Hojane hamlet, 1995.

PLATE 21 · Along with sorcery, Orokaiva see the incidence of armed holdups and other violent crimes as one of the most pressing moral concerns in their society (see chapter 4). Here Cyprian Ogo holds up an increasingly popular type of weapon, a "homemade" rifle. Agenehambo, 1993.

PLATE 22 · Along with the gifts of pork he distributes, a feast-giver's name is carried to distant places. This quality of expansiveness is dramatized when feast-givers throw joints of pork down from the feasting platform to the recipients waiting below (see chapter 5), as Mackenton Seambo does in Agenehambo village, 1994.

PLATE 23 · Oro Province's capital and main town, Popondetta, is often derided as dilapidated and lusterless. This view shows its central shopping district, 1994.

PLATE 24 · The Higaturu Oil Palms factory mill with its waste tanks and smoke-belching stacks, 1994 (see chapter 6). The heavy oil palm fruit is trucked here from surrounding plantations for its first partial processing after which it is exported for further refinement.

4. The Bodies of Whitemen

With a white skin, no matter how frail one was, one could easily become master [in colonial Africa], and be served instead of serve. One could also be rich, live in a good house, ... and be driven around in a coach. ... One could challenge the local author-ities, and delegitimate kings in the territories where one chose to show that one had authority. Thus, [the people] wanted the white skin for the power, the authority, and the good life that the white skin symbolized. And whether as slaves in the planta-tions, or as toiling peasants in the colonies, the white skin represented such power and authority to them.

While the white man admired the black skin for being physically resistant (for physical power, if you prefer), the black man admired the white skin, because with such a skin one could afford to be in control and authority, and to live in luxury without having to make a lot of physical sacrifices. Thus from the outset, the black man was there to make the good life possible, while the white man was there to enjoy it. It's a situation which continues today. The black man does the physically demanding activities, while the white man earns money on him.

FRANCIS NYAMNJOH, *The Disillusioned African*

We want to develop like people have already done in the European countries. Here we die from spears and sorcery, but you, no. In the European countries, there's no fighting, and everyone lives well, in agreement, without conflict. And so you've got all kinds of factories to make cars, boats, airplanes—whatever. There aren't any factories here among us in Papua New Guinea. Also, in the European countries the way of life is good: there's no work. It's not like here where we must carry heavy loads on our backs and walk around in the forest like wild pigs. No. In the European countries you all just sit and [when you need to go somewhere] drive in a car.

OLD KRUNI OF GAPUN VILLAGE, PNG[1]

Orokaiva Categories of the Person, Body, and Skin

In this chapter, we consider Orokaiva ideas about whitemen's bodies. Underlying Orokaiva ideas about whitemen's bodies are basic vernacular

95

categories of the person, body, and skin. These categories reflect cultural assumptions about the nature of persons that to Orokaiva are so self-evident that Orokaiva apply them universally to all social persons, including white-men (and even some types of animals).

For Orokaiva, the 'person' (*embo*) is divided into two parts, the *jo* and the *hamo*. Literally, *jo* refers to anything's 'inside' or 'interior.' The word *jo* can be used to designate the inside of a house (*bande jo*), the interior of the forest (*ariri jo*), or the inside of a string bag or suitcase (*ehi jo, sutkeisi jo*). When describing the jo belonging to a person, people gesture toward the inside of the chest or trunk of the body. People speak of the jo as a real location within the body, identifying it with the guts or the inner organs, especially the liver. But idiomatically, the jo of the person is like the English "heart" as a seat of emotion: it refers not to the physical entity that can be revealed by the sur-geon's knife, but rather to an intensely personal, inner locus of motivation and feelings. In Orokaiva, the jo specifically connotes volition, intention, and will. Newborn infants are thought not to have a jo, since they do not yet have intentions that can be revealed. From the age when the child can move around on its own and express wishes that are more than physiological, it is assumed to have a jo of its own. It is the jo that explains why a person chooses one course of action over another; it is the state of a person's jo that determines how he or she will respond to a request. The Orokaiva jo is autonomous, beyond the control of others, invisible to them, and unknow-able by them. As André Iteanu has observed, the notion of jo "implies above all that something is concealed, and that what is concealed cannot accurately be described or accounted for. . . . [I]ts very nature is to be hidden" (Iteanu 1990, 41). It is axiomatic that one cannot know the true will or intentions found in another's jo. As the common saying puts it: 'We do not know [what will happen]; it is up to his[, her, or their] jo.' The Orokaiva jo is volatile, unpredictable, and inconstant, with no definite roots in the past. It is identi-fied with the future, as the cause that generates future events and ac-tion. Indeed, the future itself is called jo: the future (*iji jo-ta*) is the as-yet-unrevealed, hidden 'inside' of time. When people talk about the jo of a person, the only states they attribute to it are simple positive or negative dis-positions like 'good'/'bad,' 'cool'/'hot,' 'joyous'/'troubled,' or 'buoyant' (favor-ably disposed and receptive)/'hard' (displeased or angry). The jo is never spoken of as having internal differentiation or structure.

By contrast, the hamo or 'body' is that part of the person which other peo-ple can see. The term *hamo* literally means 'skin,' the exterior surface of any-thing with depth. In certain contexts, hamo has the negative connotation of superficiality. It might be said of a story that the teller revealed only the hamo—the 'skin' or surface details—while withholding the story's jo: its inner meaning, the heart of the tale. With regard to a person, hamo can refer either to the skin alone or to the entire body; it is also used to refer to the inner parts of a body that have been cut open and thus revealed. The hamo is the aspect of a person's body that was formed and nurtured by others. So whereas the jo is autonomous and associated with future action, the hamo reflects a person's social interdependencies and obligations that carry over from the past. (When I was getting ready to end my fieldwork, neighbors and friends began bringing me large quantities of cooked food with the intent that I should go home fat—indeed, so enormous that, as my friends pantomimed, I would lumber down the steps of the airplane, the size of my body reflecting to my waiting relatives the care I had been shown by my Orokaiva friends during my stay with them.) When a person is in mind of his debt, as discussed in chapter 3, it is the hamo that feels heavy. A person's family connections are apparent in the hamo from physical similarities of face, height, and build, and they are also evidenced in the hamo's sympathetic response to actions exerted upon close relatives. For example, it is believed that a person can be affected by sorcery worked against a sibling, and that sorcery committed by one man can be retracted by his sibling when the sorcerer cannot be summoned. Close relatives are moreover thought to enjoy certain forms of telepathy, like *segisese*, in which one's knuckle itches when an absent sibling utters one's name (the knuckle that itches depends on the sibling that spoke: if it was the eldest sibling, the thumb will itch, if it was the second eldest, the forefinger will itch, and so on, following birth order). Thus, whereas the jo is almost asocial, the hamo is the locus of everything that an individual is or has by virtue of others, and it represents everything about the person that others can influence, know, and see. It is the quintessentially social body, embodying the physically constituted social relationships in which the person takes part (Iteanu 1990; see also Strathern 1988).[2]

It is thought that the physical features of the hamo should reflect qualities of the person. When people speak of someone who is old or socially important, they often gesture that the person's body is of great physical size, even though in reality the person may be small or slight. Whereas the jo is invisible and people are hesitant to speak about the contents of another's jo, the hamo is by definition open to view and public discussion. Among Orokaiva it is not impolite to discuss people's physical characteristics that are associated with their hamo or skin, and people speak of the hamo in complex, socially significant and value-laden terms.

In what follows, I gloss the term hamo as either 'body' or 'skin,' depending on context. In English, "body" is the unmarked term, including the "skin." In Orokaiva, the markedness relationship is reversed. The hamo ('skin') includes the body: 'skin' is unmarked, while a separate, marked term, *hamo visi*, is needed to specify the body along with its inner 'flesh' (*visi*). While in English we distinguish between the body itself and adorning appurtenances like clothing and jewelry that are not actually a part of it, this is not a distinction that the Orokaiva language encourages people to make. In Orokaiva, the important distinction is between the visible and the invisible, the hidden and the revealed. As in other Melanesian societies, a person's wealth objects, animals, crops, and descendants are often treated as parts, attributes, or extensions of the body (Strathern 1988, 1992). As such, they are divided into things that can be seen on a person's 'skin' or hamo, and things that are unseen in a person's 'inside' or jo. The latter are possessions hidden from others, like pigs that hide themselves in the forest, growing taro hidden underground in a garden, traditional ornaments that are kept hidden in a suitcase in a person's house, and money kept hidden in the bank in town. Such things that others cannot gain control of, be sure of, describe accurately, or give a definite count of are identified with their owner's jo: they are his or her secrets, to be revealed at his or her will. It is only when they are revealed that they become part of the visible person; it is then that they are seen on a person's 'skin.' When a man makes a feast, the taro hidden in his jo (i.e., in his garden) is harvested and brought to the open village space for display, where it becomes identified with his hamo, his 'body,' so that the feast-giver is said to have 'taro on his skin.' Similarly, the owner of a truck has the truck 'on his skin'; everyone in the region can see his truck along the roads, and they identify it with him.[3] If a person works at a job, spends money conspicuously, or wears expensive clothing, he or she is said to have 'money on the skin,' meaning money that others know about and so can ask for (see also M. Strathern 1975). And when a person wears mourning bands, or leaves the hair to grow uncombed into dreadlocks, he or she is said to have 'grief on the skin,' since these signs make the inner grief that the person feels socially visible.

The ability to influence another person's jo is an essential political and practical skill, and its methods are given considerable thought. Since another's jo is a fully autonomous entity that cannot be directly controlled or coerced, Orokaiva seek to influence it by means of objects that can cross the hamo's surface and penetrate inside it. Such objects include food, betel nut, and tobacco, which others can ingest, satisfying or 'cooling' their desires, and thereby placating their jos. Persuasive talk, too, can influence the jo, although it is considered less effective. People characterize such talk as a material substance that enters the addressee's body and settles into his or her jo.

One must influence others' jos not only to gain their cooperation and resources but also to neutralize lurking ill-will by transforming it into positive feelings. Orokaiva people are anxious lest others harbor negative feelings in their jo that could lead them to attack them, undermine their projects, initiate sorcery against them, or provoke disputes. Such anxieties are sustained by the essential mystery of the jo, and they cause people to behave toward one another with a kind of fearful circumspection. One can never be certain about another's true intentions, since these are ineluctably hidden within the jo, and it can never be safely assumed that a person's overt words and deeds are not really dissimulation. It is only the hamo that one can see and know, act upon, satisfy, and directly control. But the hamo is susceptible not only to positive influences, like presents of food, betel nut, and tobacco, but also to negative ones, like sorcery, violence, ill-will, and community discord, all of which can affect the hamo by producing sickness, mishaps, and physical and mental infirmities.

The concepts of hamo and jo are so natural in Orokaiva thought and experience that Orokaiva apply them universally, including to whitemen. They take it for granted that each individual whiteman has an autonomous and unknowable jo that is of the same essential nature as the jos of Orokaiva. Just as it is hard for Orokaiva to know or speak about the state of the jo of an Orokaiva person, it is hard for them to know or speak about the jo of a whiteman. The only generalization I heard people draw about the jo of whitemen was its propensity toward getting 'hot,' toward getting angry—a topic discussed in the section on 'brightness' below.

By contrast, Orokaiva remark upon the many general differences they see between themselves and whitemen that are manifest on the skin, in the hamo and bodily habits. For example, unlike their own hair, which they consider bristly and strong, whitemen's hair is slippery, flimsy, and soft; once Steven likened my hair to the slippery, wet fur of water rats. Whereas most Orokaiva adults' teeth are 'hardened,' stained black or dark red, from frequent betel-nut chewing, whitemen's teeth look white and clean and are held to be comparatively 'soft.' And since it is the chewing of betel nut that leaves the mouths of Orokaiva feeling refreshed and fragrant, Orokaiva say that whitemen, who do not chew betel nut, usually have breath that stinks. Ingrained habits, too, are attributed to the hamo. So whereas Orokaivas' hamos are accustomed to sitting on the ground and sleeping on mats, whitemen's hamos are accustomed to sitting on chairs and sleeping on mattresses. Whereas Orokaiva are accustomed to bathing outdoors in cold streams that flow down from the mountains, whitemen are said to bathe 'up in raised houses' in special small rooms. Orokaiva are accustomed to urinating and defecating in the forest; whitemen are accustomed to using the toilet. I often heard Orokaiva contrast themselves with whitemen in their habits of drinking and sexual jealousy using terms that recall colonial discourse about undisciplined natives. Whereas Orokaiva said they would 'go crazy' when drinking beer and guzzle lots of it quickly, whitemen were said to take it easy, sipping their beer slowly over the course of a meal. Whitemen were also said to exhibit self-restraint with women, making it acceptable for white wives and daughters to be alone with strange men, a situation that Orokaiva equate with adultery— 'since we blackskins go crazy'—leading to jealousy, recrimination, and ultimately revenge.

All such contrasts that Orokaiva draw between themselves and whitemen have moral connotations. But they are not all equally central to the moral concerns of Orokaiva today. The issues that people find most compelling reflect particularities of history and of culture. Thus, for westerners, the contrasts in degrees of restraint in drinking and sex are morally very troubling, since they resonate to the longstanding western emphasis on the restraint of "base" impulses, and they appear to reproduce colonial justifications for prohibiting natives from drinking alcohol and being alone with white women (Inglis 1975; Marshall 1982). For most Orokaiva today, however, these are not the contrasts that engage the greatest moral concern.[4] The contrasts that are most significant and given the greatest elaboration surround two qualities, the softness and brightness of whitemen's skin, the first of which is associated with the production of wealth, and the second with its preservation. In what follows, I examine the meanings of whitemen's 'softness' and 'brightness' in turn.

The Softness of Whitemen

During my fieldwork, I was often told by Orokaiva that my skin, especially on my hands and legs, was 'soft' (*suruha*) and 'weak' (*ivo-ambu*), and they contrasted it with their own skin, which was 'hard' (*gaiha*) and 'strong' (*ivo-te*). Orokaiva considered my 'soft skin' (*hamo suruha*) typical of whitemen, so that they sometimes pointed to it and spoke of it as a mere instance of the general category, 'you whitemen's soft skin.' The softness of whitemen's skin is associated with ideas about foods that are discussed in the following chapter, where we will see that the whitemen's presumed diet includes primarily 'soft' foods, and "you are what you eat." But Orokaiva also connect whitemen's softness to three notable features of whitemen's lives. First, whitemen protect and care for their skin using expensive commodities that Orokaiva cannot afford. Second, they spend little time in harsh environments like the rainforests and gardens where Orokaiva go to find and grow food. Third, whitemen do not perform the kinds of hard physical work that Orokaiva must perform in order to survive.

Orokaiva many times observed to me that whitemen use expensive commodities to protect and care for their bodies. They would tell me things like, 'We Orokaiva just say *maski* [Tok Pisin: 'never mind'] and walk barefoot while you whitemen wear shoes.' 'We Papua New Guineans just sleep on the floor, while you whitemen sleep on soft mattresses.' 'We blackskins just say maski when we get sores on our skin; you whitemen put on medicines and bandage your sores.'

Wearing shoes is crucial to maintaining whitemen's soft skin. My feet were one of the main things Orokaiva pointed at when discussing the softness of my skin. My feet were 'soft,' they said, because I had kept them in shoes my entire life. The soles of my feet were thus thin and tender, unlike their own soles, which were thick, hard, and tough because they walk barefoot on muddy forest trails, through rivers where they step on sharp stones, and on gravel roads blistering hot under the midday sun (see plate 8). The only footwear most Orokaiva own are cheap rubber flip-flops, but rarely do they wear them into the forest or to work in the gardens. Walking in flip-flops on difficult terrain can be slippery and dangerous, and they are especially ill suited for walking in mud, which tends to suck them in so strongly that the thong rips out, ruining them. So people often go barefoot and carry their flip-flops in their hands. Those who own boots or shoes tend to save them for church, for special dress-up occasions like greeting visitors and attending village court, and for wearing in town.

Another way in which whitemen are seen to maintain the softness of their bodies and skin is by sleeping on soft foam mattresses, protected by bed sheets and blankets, in well-sealed houses built of expensive materials like milled lumber, weatherboard, and manufactured metal roofing sheets. For Orokaiva, mattresses and whiteman-style building materials are highly desirable symbols of development, and villagers' use of both is becoming increasingly common. Even so, by far the majority of villagers sleep on thin woven mats, still wearing their daytime clothing, and on cold nights they cover themselves with only a threadbare length of cotton sarong (see plate 9).

The cramped huts they sleep in are made of forest materials with often-leaky frond thatch roofs. When sleeping at others' homes, which Orokaiva do frequently, sometimes for days or weeks at a stretch, they sleep directly on the floorboards around a smoldering fire in their host's arara (the raised open-walled sitting platform), exposed to night winds. When they congregate at feasts, people sleep beside one another in lines that cover the length of the araras, 'like pigs,' lined up as part of the feast display. I was often told that, when I was back in my soft bed at home in America, I should think back on how I had slept when I was with them: 'Then you will feel sorry for us. Our sleeping is hard, as our living is hard.' To Orokaiva, only people with hard bodies that were accustomed to it could sleep the way they did. Everywhere I went, people assumed that, as a soft white person, I needed a soft mattress to sleep on, and in many villages where I spent the night my hosts went to great lengths, notwithstanding my protests, to borrow a slab of mattress foam, usually old and crumbling and infested with bedbugs, from a neighbor for me to use.

Orokaiva recognize that whitemen's soft beds are part of a larger pattern of using commodities to comfort, care for, and protect their bodies. Orokaiva often travel for days or weeks without packing so much as one small bag; they are more likely to leave on a long journey with a stalk of bananas or a large sack of sweet potatoes than they are to bring along bedding or toiletries. When Orokaiva people do pack a travel bag, they include at most a change of clothes and a towel. Men often take a bushknife (machete) when traveling, women a cooking knife, and both will be sure to carry their paraphernalia for chewing betel nut. But it is uncommon for people to carry much more than this, assuming that they can borrow whatever else they need at their destination. In fact, all they consider absolutely essential is food. It is thus quite striking to them that whitemen pack large suitcases, trunks, and backpacks whenever they travel, in order to ensure that they will have on hand the many things they need to be comfortable. 'You are a whiteman,' Orokaiva would say while waiting for me to ready my backpack for an overnight trip, 'so you need to take this and that, or you won't stay well.'

One reason whitemen's bodies are soft is that from the time they are tiny babies, they have been accustomed to pampering and protection. It is the custom of whitemen to wrap their babies in diapers (instead of leaving them mostly naked), to dress them in baby clothes, and to give them pills and vaccinations to protect them from sickness. Since Orokaiva recognize their own babies to be soft as well, these customs seem to them very sensible, and they practice them as their money allows. Baby powder is a particularly valued form of whitemen's skin protection that Orokaiva try to provide for their babies; Orokaiva mothers sometimes dust it on their babies' foreheads in minute quantities, suggesting that the protection it affords is seen as more magical than physical (see also Liep 1990). When Orokaiva children grow older and get sores and skin diseases like scabies and grille (a fungal infection), their parents rarely treat them, unlike whitemen, who are known to treat even minor cuts and scrapes by applying medicine and bandages. My own regular use of 'medicines' to protect my skin from the sun and to repel the mosquitoes, which they themselves are resigned to, was entirely consistent with Orokaiva expectations of whitemen. "Ah taupa, taupa!" ('Oh whiteman!'), my friends would exclaim, greatly amused, as I would smear myself with repellent. They themselves have native medicines that make the skin fragrant and attractive, cure certain sicknesses, or protect them from harm. But there are none that are intended to resolve minor discomforts. As one man explained:

> When we Orokaiva see that mosquitoes are biting us, we say, 'nevermind, it's just something small.' Our skin is strong, you see. But you whitemen have soft skin, and when you are bitten by the mosquito, it makes a big bump. So to you it's a *problem*, that's what you call it, and then you get your knowledgeable people together and you do *research studies*. You look very carefully at the mosquito, and you try to find a medicine that will keep it away. You keep on trying until you find it. And then, wherever you go, you paint yourself with that medicine to protect your skin. Ah taupa, taupa! That's not how we are. We blackmen just say maski, and we leave our skin alone.

Orokaiva are hardened to discomfort. They can walk in the hot sun for miles without water and not complain of thirst. They can ride for hours on bumpy roads, cramped in the back of crowded flatbed trucks. They stoically bear wounds like deep cuts from slipped ax blows, boils, and other infected sores, never complaining about the pain. Against their norm of hardness, I felt embarrassed by the lengths I would go to in order to alleviate or prevent small discomforts like bedbug sores and blisters that the villagers do not feel acutely. But while they are often amused by the great attention whitemen pay to 'looking after the skin,' Orokaiva were surprisingly uncritical of the effort I put into maintaining my body's 'softness.' Indeed, they seemed if anything solicitous of my 'good' skin, making a fuss over my small scratches or blisters, reminding me to cover myself with sun block when we would set off on a sunny day to the garden, worrying on rainy days that my 'good shoes' would become covered with mud—even urging me at one point to buy hip-boots to protect my entire leg.

In part, Orokaiva understand the care whitemen give their skin as a manifestation of their high level of wealth and development. Few Orokaiva have
any idea just how vast a range of products are available to care for the skin in
developed countries like Australia and America: the central heating and air-
conditioning systems, wall-to-wall carpeting, and thick luxurious mattresses;
the huge variety of shoes and clothing, fashion accessories, drugs, lotions, and
cosmetics; the massages, manicures, and hairstyling treatments at spas and
salons; the Jacuzzis, acupuncture, and aromatherapy. All most Orokaiva
know are the few basic types of commodities, such as roofing iron, blankets,
foam mattresses, shoes and boots, and medicines, that are sold in PNG's
towns and used by people around them. But even these rudimentary
comfort-goods are associated with a life of wealth and ease. The small variety
of western products that are available in the fancy goods sections of the trade
stores in Popondetta are ordinarily beyond the means of village people, who
often go shopping with just enough money to buy a bag of salt and a liter of
kerosene. So in Orokaivas' eyes, it is whitemen's seemingly limitless access to
comfort-goods that helps them keep their skin soft. Whitemen's wealth and
development is indeed visible on their skin.

In Orokaiva morality, it is good to look after others and buy things to care
for them, but selfish to look after and buy things for oneself. Hence, the
ideal way to acquire things is to receive them from others as gifts that reflect
the giver's favor and make visible the worthiness of the recipient. This ideal
of receiving one's possessions from others and the converse devaluation of
self-initiated consumption is reflected in the sources of most of the
comfort-goods villagers have. Individuals only rarely buy comfort-goods (a
category that includes medicines) for their own benefit. Instead, they
receive them from others, and buy them to give away—if the goods are not
'pulled away' by others first. With the exception of boots and sneakers,
which many young men save up for in order to buy for themselves, most of
the footwear and clothes that people wear are gifts they received from others. Most people's mattresses were originally purchased by parents or
namesakes for high school boarding students (per school requirement),
were gifts to brides, or had been left as gifts by relatives living in town who
had brought them along on a visit. Most sheets of roofing iron were not
bought specifically for the homes on which they are found; rather, they
were usually bought with grants to build infrastructure for development
projects, like tradestores and cocoa fermenting sheds, which were disman-
tled once the project had failed.[5]

Thus, soft skin is a potentially ambivalent quality. It can indicate that
others have lavished expensive care upon someone, showing his or her

worthiness. Alternatively, soft skin can indicate selfish consumption of comfort-goods that could have been used more generously to care for others' skins. In effect, what Orokaiva evaluate is not the softness of skin itself, but rather its positive or negative meaning in terms of the exchange relationships connecting a person to others. The soft skin of whitemen is particularly open to moral interpretation in accord with people's aims and interests in the context of speaking, since the exchange relationships assumed to be behind it are generally invisible to Orokaiva, a fait accompli. Either whitemen have received enormous gifts of comfort-goods reflecting a commensurate worthiness, or they have been unbelievably selfish, greedily buying comfort-goods and keeping them all to themselves. So when Orokaiva people were solicitous of my skin, it was not because whitemen are felt categorically to have an unqualified birthright to enjoy physical protection and comfort; instead, it expressed the value my interlocutors placed on our relationship. I was being enjoined not to act more conscientiously to ensure my self-care, as it might appear, but really to reciprocally demonstrate *my* care for *their* skin, ideally by giving gifts of food, medical care, and comfort-goods to *them*.

A second contrast between their own and whitemen's lives that Orokaiva see evidenced in the softness of whitemen's skin is that whitemen rarely enter harsh environments like the rainforest and gardens where Orokaiva spend much of their time. The rainforest is where Orokaiva go to clear gardens for food, to forage and hunt, to collect native medicines, and to get materials like wood, vines, and sago fronds that they use to build houses and fences. Orokaiva are highly dependent on the forest, which they conceive as the prototype of a 'wild' place where good and bad things grow together in disordered profusion. The forest is full of hazards like sinkholes and pits, biting and stinging insects, thorny or irritating plants, poisonous snakes, and wild animals, not to mention many kinds of bad spirits. Orokaiva see their bodies as hardened by regular exposure to this harsh environment. Their muscles are developed by the exertion of moving through jungle, which they often have to cut paths through as they walk. Their skin is scarred from a lifetime of insect bites, wounds, and scratches. If whitemen routinely exposed themselves to such harsh environments, their skin, too, would be hardened, and the fact that it is not indicates to Orokaiva that the environments whitemen inhabit are less harsh than their own.

The idea that whitemen rarely enter the rainforest is reinforced by Orokaiva experiences with white people, who are primarily seen in towns and cities, and in cars on the roads, but of course almost never in subsistence gardens cut from the forest or on forest trails. Only exceptionally do white village guests go with their Orokaiva hosts into the forest and gardens, and their behavior when they do generally reveals that they are unused to these environments. Indeed, in contrast to Orokaiva, most whites tend to be clumsy bushwalkers. In descending steep muddy slopes, they easily lose their footing, not knowing where to plant their feet or how to grasp vines and branches for balance. When whites feel themselves about to fall, they tend to cast about wildly, grabbing at anything within reach, even vines with barbed thorns and weak rotted trees, and they are liable to harm themselves by reaching for the ground, plunging their hands through the tangled undergrowth where biting ants and stinging centipedes hide in rotting leaves. When facing the single-log bridges, which Orokaiva zip across easily, they have to muster their confidence, and they stumble when walking through flowing rivers where the rocky bottoms are slippery and hard to see.

White visitors generally know little useful bushcraft. They cannot build shelters, or hunt or track game. They cannot spot where trails go or keep track of their orientation, so they are vulnerable to getting lost. They do not know useful plants from useless ones, or how to handle common plants that are spiny, such as sago palm and rattan. It is rare and memorable to Orokaiva when white visitors go with them to the forest, but it also makes them anxious. Even though vehicular roads may be circuitous, hot, and unshaded, Orokaiva frequently urge white visitors to walk on them, rather than on forest trails, which are often more pleasant, since they know that most whites are not in their element in the rainforest environment and are likely to get hurt there.[6]

The notion that whitemen are not exposed to wild environments is further reinforced by Orokaiva images of the places where whitemen live. Orokaiva used to ask me, 'Is your country all *city*?' This notion of city does not imply the western distinction between urban skyscrapers, high-rise housing, and street grids on the one hand, and rural homesteads, small towns, and farmlands on the other. Rather it is based on the indigenous distinction between wild lands and domesticated spaces that are humanly ordered and built upon. Nearly all the media images Orokaiva see of whitemen's countries show lands that have in some way been developed—if with no more than a road. When villagers found an anomalous photograph of a wild forest scene in a coffee-table book about America, they lingered long over the image, asking me incredulous questions like, 'Is this picture really of America?' I found it hard to convince people that there were forests in my country, some of them huge, until I mentioned that forests were maintained by the government as parks and preserves where people from the city went "on holiday" specifically in order to see wilds from which they were normally distant. Such forests then made sense to people as cherished remnants, the exception that proved their rule.

What Orokaiva find particularly hard to make sense of is the presence of whitemen in deserts. To Orokaiva, deserts are like wilds in that they are harsh, undeveloped, dangerous, and untamed (though they also have qualities of dryness and openness to the sun that Orokaiva associate with humanly ordered spaces such as villages and gardens). Orokaiva are interested in deserts primarily because they were the setting of events in the Bible, a connection emphasized by the photographs of deserts included in the Orokaiva-language bibles produced by American missionaries from the Summer Institute of Linguistics (Larsen 1988). The photographs, which depict present-day Bedouins living in tents and tending camels, were intended to illustrate life-ways of the Biblical Jews, Jesus's people. Orokaiva find the pictures confusing because the desert environment, which looks wild and inhospitable, is out of keeping with Orokaiva notions that the whiteman's country of Israel, as the place of origin of such a supremely powerful ancestor as Jesus, should be highly prosperous and developed, and also because the Bedouins, who look swarthy and hardened, do not resemble the Jesus of conventional iconography, with his delicate features and thin, almost translucent, soft white skin. When Orokaiva speak of deserts as open and clean, as traversed by roads, or as the location of cities (e.g., Salt Lake City, Las Vegas), the desert is not wholly 'wild' and therefore makes sense as an environment for whitemen to occupy. But when Orokaiva speak of deserts that are truly wild, they are presumed to be inhabited not by ordinary whitemen, but instead by Indians and an exceptional type of whitemen, "cowboys"—in both cases people who are hard-skinned, strong, and rugged, like Orokaiva themselves.[7]

But even more important than whitemen's use of comfort-goods to care for their skin and their lack of exposure to harsh environments, Orokaiva see the softness of whitemen's skin as a sign that whitemen do no hard physical work. It was in connection with work that Orokaiva most often spoke to me of my softness, and here what they pointed to was my hands. 'Your hands are soft,' Kingsford's son once told me in his father's yam garden while we were harvesting yams. There are thorns on some yams, and he was saying that I should leave these to him, to avoid hurting my hands. 'My hands are hard,' he explained. 'They are used to the thorns. I was born to this work, it cannot hurt me. . . . The work in your country is easy [*ejeha* 'light']. Ours is very hard [*boka* 'heavy'].'

The hard work of Orokaiva villagers hardens their bodies in any number of ways. Their hands are toughened by handling coarse plant materials like vines and tree trunks, and by pulling out irritating plants when weeding their gardens. They are callused from swinging bushknives and axes, and from pounding the ground repeatedly with digging sticks and shovels. When working with tools, for example, when swinging a bushknife, the body's own repetitive motion is considered hardening, reflecting a general Orokaiva principle that things become hardened through the sedimentation of vigorous, wide-ranging, or repetitive motion. Hard coral and shell are formed by the sea's incessant churning where waves break on reefs; the pig's flesh becomes 'tight' and its valuable tusks hard when it roams far in the forest. Similarly, while working vigorously in gardens, the skin is subjected to the drying effects of the sun, which Orokaiva say 'spears' (*kajari*) the earth with a penetrating motion that extracts water and is hardening. Working under the hot sun, people sweat out moisture and feel their muscles stiffen and tighten with strain.

Many terse aphorisms express the truth that hard work is the basis of villagers' existence: 'Only if you sweat will you eat.' 'We live by hard work alone.' 'If your hands are still, you will die of hunger.' Orokaiva villagers' days are filled with hard work. Men do the most strenuous work like felling huge trees with axes to clear land for new gardens (see plates 6 and 7), or cutting large grassy areas around the village by hand using long scythelike grassknives. Women make long trips to the river to scour pots and wash plates, launder their families' clothes, and fetch water, which they carry home in pots on their heads. The bulk of most days are spent in the gardens, where people plant and weed crops, harvest tubers and greens, and chop and bundle firewood. Women carry home large string bags filled with heavy taro roots and other foods. Some days are given to 'money work,' like planting, harvesting, and processing the cash-crops coffee, cocoa, and oil palm. Coffee and cocoa require a great deal of labor-intensive processing before they can be sold. After coffee cherries are picked from the trees, they must be carried to streams and crushed to remove the outer pulp; then the hard inner beans are washed in the water, carried to the village, and dried for days in the sun. Cocoa pods must be broken, the wet beans scooped out, and large sacks containing up to 170 pounds of the sticky, wet beans carried out to the roads. Carrying heavy loads is essential to most work. When building houses, men carry load after load of logs for the posts and frame; sago frond midribs, bamboo, and heavy palm bark for the flooring and walls; and huge sago palm fronds for the roofing thatch. Building fences is the same: each load of posts and rails must be carried on someone's back from the forest. To cook a meal, women must first carry water from the stream; when the meal is done, they carry basinfuls of plates and pots to the stream to wash them. Some days are devoted to community work maintaining footpaths, the village church, and the village school buildings and grounds. People also give days to ritual work in preparation for feasts. The hard work of villagers' days leaves them feeling achy and exhausted at night. If the day's work was felling trees, the pain at night will be in the shoulders and back. If the day's work was digging or planting posts, it will be in the chest. If carrying, the neck. Aspirin has become popular among Orokaiva; even small village tradestores sell the drug, which people welcome as a palliative to their hard-earned aches and pains.

The softness of whitemen's bodies has a connotation of femininity. Although the bodies of Orokaiva women, like those of the men, are hardened by the work they do, men's work is understood by Orokaiva to harden the body more than women's work does. Prototypical men's work, like chopping trees, clearing bush, and building houses and fences, converts the disordered, 'wild' (*ariri*) spaces of the rainforest, where things grow uncontrolled, into ordered, domesticated spaces like gardens and villages, where the growth of valued things is cultivated and nurtured. The work usually done by women, like weeding, harvesting, cooking, washing, and caring for pigs and babies, generally focuses on the constant, repetitive needs of daily life and is relatively sedentary, being performed for the most part within the spaces that men's work creates. In essence, men's work carves out the spaces in which life is nurtured and wealth is created. As men freely acknowledge, the work done by women is more consistent and heavier than the work done by men. But the men's work is distinguished by requiring particularly vigorous motion—such as swinging the bushknife or throwing the ax—necessarily in harsh forest environments that the work itself (by its dynamism) transforms, so that this work is the most body-hardening kind of work that Orokaiva do. It is not that women are actually too soft to perform such work, or that they do not sometimes do it in practice. But the hardness of men's bodies is associated so clearly for Orokaiva with the vigorous work of transforming the forest into gardens that it made sense for one middle-aged woman to tell me, as she returned from garden clearing with an ax on her shoulder, 'I am a woman, but I chop down big trees. I swing the ax like a man, and my body is hard.' This statement shows not only that she regarded such work as exceptional for a woman, but also that she understood the masculine gendering of bodily hardness specifically through its association with the vigorous motion of masculine work.

Because of the conditions of gardening, there is a powerful connection between the masculine body hardened by motion and the creation of wealth. Paradigmatically, the production of wealth begins with men's clearing of forests to make gardens, whether for food or for cash-crops. A garden's yield is thought to be greater when the initial work of garden clearing is done vigorously and quickly. Men boast of their dynamism in blasting down trees by likening themselves to typhoons and by taking on nicknames like "Cyclone." With a swing of the arm, men gesture "sweeping" away forest before them, quickly clearing large tracts of land for planting crops that will grow large in return. Yields are also thought to be greatest in gardens that are cut from the darkest, densest, most forbidding areas, like old-growth forests and thickets, patches of dense, thorny growth that present a great challenge to clear. To overcome and balance the forest's qualities of still, wet, dark, and cool, men's activity must embody the opposite qualities of heat and kinetic dynamism; the logic seems to be that a balance of intense forces has more generative potential than a balance of weak ones. The men's work of clearing the land then ushers in a series of steps which echo it in bringing vigorous heat to the previously cool lands: first admitting the sunlight, which dries out the land and forest debris, then burning it, the final step before planting.

In contrast with their own lives, Orokaiva see whitemen's softness as due to the ease of life in town. From the perspective of villagers, the basic work of maintaining life is much lighter in town than in the village. People in town do not need to work as hard as villagers do in order to get their food, fuel, water, and light. When they need food they simply walk into a store and buy it; instead of gathering, drying, hauling, chopping, and stacking firewood, they simply turn on the flame of a propane or kerosene stove. They get water by opening a tap, and light by merely flipping a switch. People in town do not need to haul heavy loads on their backs, but instead transport their loads by truck. Nor are they constantly walking long distances in the forest and doing hard outdoor work. Because of all this, their bodies are soft. Not only whitemen, but also Papua New Guineans who live and work in town grow soft from the ease of their lives.

But whitemen are especially prone to being soft because they rarely make their living working at jobs that involve hard physical labor. To Orokaiva, whitemen's jobs are typified by managers, teachers, missionaries, government functionaries, consultants, doctors, and researchers, which are ordinarily performed indoors, often while comfortably seated. Such jobs do not deeply callus the hands or strain the muscles. They do not harden the skin, or require hard skin to do them. While Orokaiva recognize that such jobs are important and require special knowledge and skills, they result in no tangible products like garden foods or cash-crops; they do not transform the raw potential of forested lands into any material wealth. For Orokaiva, this is the most obvious implication of the whitemen's soft skin: that white-men do not exert themselves in the ways necessary to produce wealth.

The Meaning of Whitemen's Softness in the Moral Economy of Producing Wealth

Given the three notable features of whitemen's lives that Orokaiva associate with softness—using expensive comfort-goods to care for and protect the skin, not regularly entering harsh forest environments, and not having to do vigorous physical work—the softness of whitemen's skin entails a con-tradiction: while it implies that they have wealth, it also implies that they do not engage in the kinds of activities which are necessary to create wealth, namely those forms of physical labor that convert land into food and cash-crops, hardening the body in the process.

This contradiction between the wealth whitemen have 'on the skin' and their nonperformance of productive physical work has an analog in Orokaiva traditional culture in the deliberately softened skin of young girls secluded at puberty. In this ritual, which is commonly practiced today for a small number of an extended family's daughters in each gener-ation, a girl, upon the onset of menses, is secluded in a house until her rel-atives have amassed the large amounts of money, taro, and pigs needed to hold a spectacular feast at which she is beautifully decorated and makes her debut with this wealth displayed all around her.[8] The seclusion itself is called 'putting the girl up [in a house]' (*kakara i ta ikari*), and the name of the debut feast is 'decoration of the girl' (*kakara kogombari*). In cases I know of, the seclusion lasted for between two months (conveniently dur-ing school holidays) to well over two years (because the girl's father was unable to raise a pig for the debut feast).[9] It is considered reasonable for a girl to remain secluded for a full taro-planting cycle of several months to a year. The seclusion is intended to fatten the girls and to make their skin soft and 'bright,' so that when they make their debut decorated with the finest traditional ornaments, they exemplify the Orokaiva ideal of youthful feminine beauty. (We will discuss those aspects of seclusion that are thought to make the girls' skin 'bright' later on.) In seclusion, the girl's skin is softened by frequently wetting it with coconut oil and milk, and by pre-venting the girl from moving very much, a sort of traditional version of an enforced "couch potato." It is this lack of movement that is the primary factor leading to the girl's becoming soft: she sits inside the house for months on end, without performing any hard work or vigorous exertion.

When the girl needs to leave the house to relieve herself, she covers herself with a cape so that her skin is not exposed to the sun's drying action. Sometimes the girl may leave the house to walk around with her friends at night, but she is not allowed to cross the village periphery into forested spaces. In effect, the girl's skin is softened because she does none of the things that would harden it. Orokaiva liken the soft skin of the secluded girls to the soft skin of whitemen. When explaining to me the ritual's purpose, people often joked that 'it will make her skin just like yours.' They did not thereby mean that the ritual is intended to make the girls' skin like whitemen's; rather, they were noting that the body qualities traditionally sought in pubescent girls were also characteristic of whitemen. Indeed, people find it hilarious that mature whitemen exhibiting the ultimate powers of mobility should so resemble pubescent girls when they are confined within the four walls of a house.[10]

At their debut feasts girls are conspicuously soft, and they also have great wealth on their skin. However, this conjuncture of wealth and soft skin in debutantes does not represent a contradiction for Orokaiva, since it is an effect produced only temporarily, in a few individuals, through collective efforts that are publicly acknowledged through reciprocal food prestations at the debut feast. The girl's softness objectifies the surplus produced by her parents and kin, who fed and cared for her notwithstanding the loss of her work during her seclusion. Similarly, the food wealth that surrounds her at her debut feast represents pooled contributions brought by relatives and friends. Even the body decorations she wears are borrowed, to be returned at the day's end to their owners with "interest" paid in food. Indeed, part of the point of the seclusion-debut complex is to create an occasion for conspicuous reciprocities that solidify relationships between families and clans. After the debut, the girl is heavy with the many debts that were created by her seclusion and debut feast. Thus, the Orokaiva debutante is soft and associated with wealth, but in the logic of Orokaiva culture, that wealth is appropriately heavy on her skin; it was given by others and will need to be repaid. The wealth of whitemen, by contrast, burdens them with no apparent social debts. Whitemen are soft, yet as we saw in chapter 3, they somehow manage to keep themselves perpetually light.

To Orokaiva, the softness of whitemen's skin should imply a similar state of dependence on others who feed them and provide them with wealth. But it is hard for Orokaiva to identify who these others might be, since unlike the debutantes of Orokaiva society, who are few and secluded for just a short time, whitemen seem to have soft skin always. Orokaiva do encounter some relatively hard-skinned whites, like builders and carpenters who come from Australia on short-term programs organized by their Rotary Clubs to volunteer their work to the Anglican high school near Agenehambo. But meeting such whites does not lead Orokaiva to revise their basic conception that whitemen have soft skin, since they treat the tradesmen as exceptions, and ambiguous exceptions at that: Orokaiva note that, while they may have hard callused hands, the rest of their bodies are soft and fat. And in any case, a few exceptional hard-skinned whitemen could not account for all the great wealth whitemen enjoy.

The problem, then, is the image of whole countries populated by whitemen who do no hard physical work. How is their wealth produced? Who grows all the food that feeds them if whitemen themselves grow nothing? The very first day I met Kingsford, he asked if there were people in my country who 'worked hard cultivating the ground' like he did. During my fieldwork many other people asked me variations on the question, 'Are there people in your country who grow food?' To Orokaiva, food is the most basic form of wealth, and vast amounts of food must clearly be needed to support all the whitemen sitting in offices and factories. Steven asked me on several occasions to explain who grows the food that is sold in whitemen's stores. The law of his own life was that he had to work hard to get food; he could not just rely on others to feed him. 'And if I want money, I have to *sweat my gut* and plant cocoa or coffee. No one will just give it to me.'

Because the contradiction implicit in the softness of whitemen's skin is so deeply rooted in their own lived experience, Orokaiva are led again and again to try to resolve it by constructing explanations for whitemen's mysterious ability to create elaborate wealth. One such explanation is that whitemen produce their wealth by using machines like power tools and tractors that run on gasoline, diesel fuel, or electricity. These machines, which are classified as 'hard things' (*donda gaiha*), take the place of whitemen's bodies in doing the hard work of production. As Orokaiva say, machines have power of their own, and so enable whitemen to exceed the limitations of bodily strength. During my fieldwork there were three lawn mowers, a chainsaw, and an old tractor in Agenehambo, and bulldozers, backhoes, and graders were seen around the area, if infrequently, maintaining roads and culverts. Villagers also have seen or heard reports about industrial machinery, power hand tools, forklifts, machine shops, and so on. It is obvious to Orokaiva that such machines increase productivity and reduce the physical exertion certain types of work require. Tractors in particular are known to enable farmers to increase yields by tilling and planting areas that are much larger than they could dig by hand, and by transporting harvested produce relatively easily even on rough roads and trails.

But while the idea that whitemen's wealth is produced with the help of machines might be thought to adequately resolve the contradiction inherent in the softness of their skin, Orokaiva do not find it entirely sufficient, and even men experienced in using machines would continue to seek other explanations. To some extent, this reflects their knowledge that it really is physically demanding to operate many machines like chainsaws and lawn mowers, and that the physical exertion and vibrating motion of such work calluses the skin and hardens the muscles of the body in much the same way as work done by hand. Moreover, while Orokaiva also understand that white farmers benefit in their work from the use of large tractors, their use is enigmatic in its own right. As we will discuss further in the next chapter, many Orokaiva have seen pictures or video images of western farms show- ing broad, open fields, and they assume that white farmers, who do not have rainforest to cut for new gardens each season, cultivate the same land repeat- edly. In the experience of Orokaiva horticulturalists, this should lead to poor yields. High yields come from gardens cut from old forests where the soil is heavy and dark, since all lands (whether planted or not) gradually deteriorate when exposed to the sun, which dries and lightens the soil, so that after at most two plantings it must be allowed to stand fallow and return to the cover of trees under which it rejuvenates. So when I confirmed vil- lagers' impression that few Americans were farmers, but that with the use of specialized machines like tractor-combines their farms produce enough to feed the rest of the population, people were unconvinced. Many Orokaiva know that whitemen use fertilizer to compensate for the deterioration of the land when it is repeatedly replanted, but they themselves are skeptical about the benefits of chemical fertilizer, since they consider the salts dangerously 'hot' and liable to 'burn' the roots of crops.[11]

Whitemen's use of machines merely pushes back a step the most trou- bling question implied by the softness of whitemen's skin: why is it that whitemen have such elaborate wealth, including machines that enable them to make more wealth, and Orokaiva do not? It is obvious to Orokaiva that individual whitemen do not make their own machines, but receive them as part of a cultural inheritance. The objects Orokaiva see as forming their own livelihood and material culture are produced using raw materials and techniques that have been passed down to them from earlier generations. The ways in which they garden, build houses, hunt and forage, construct valuables and tools, and carry out rituals are understood by Orokaiva as their inheritance from their forebears. In the same way, they understand the wealth of whitemen—the electronic equipment, motorized vehicles, manu- factured clothing, and above all the machines, together with all the specialized materials and techniques used to produce them—to be the cultural inheritance whitemen receive from *their* forebears. But compared to the cultural inheritance enjoyed by whitemen, Orokaiva feel their own to be vastly inferior. Why should whitemen's ancestors have left them such a rich legacy, but their own ancestors left them so little?[12]

This is the question answered by the most important contemporary Orokaiva historical origin myth. According to the story, Orokaiva share a common lineage with whitemen that should entitle them to the same level of inherited wealth. In its briefest outlines, the first Orokaiva children were abandoned when their two white fathers saw that their skin was black, and when they subsequently attempted to secure the unambiguous blessing of their mother, they began to quarrel among themselves, ruining that relationship as well. In the story we see Orokaiva projecting onto events of the mythic past the same moral cause that they use to explain their lack of prosperity today: fractiousness and lack of social harmony.[13] This failing, which Orokaiva see as endemic in their own cultural character, is one of the most compelling moral concerns of Orokaiva today.

The connection between social harmony and wealth is part of an Orokaiva moral economy in which material prosperity is a sign of moral worthiness, in particular generosity and obedience. Hard physical work alone is never enough to ensure a harvest of plenty; sometimes the crops wilt despite people's best efforts. For Orokaiva, the difference between hunger and plenty is always assumed to have an underlying cause in the moral state of society, which is in turn a result of human actions. For Orokaiva, all of nature belongs to a common moral community in that all entities—humans and spirits, as well as plants, animals, and lands—are assumed to be responsive to people's moral states. When a person's pig runs away, it might be explained by the pig's owner having shamed or become angry with someone else. When crops fail, explanations are sought in bad feelings and discord within the community: perhaps the garden's owner speared another man's pig, making him angry, which in itself is enough to cause a garden to fail, or perhaps others are jealous of the gardener for owning his own truck or for his child's success in high school or in wage work. If there is a latent dispute over the ownership of the land on which the garden was made, that too could explain why the crops in the garden wilted.[14] Conversely, when harvests are rich, it is taken to be a sign of harmonious relations within the community and the favor of the gardener's dead forefathers, who are believed to be the ultimate arbiters of their descendants' productivity. Ancestral favor is procured through obedience to them during their lifetimes, and by pleasing the ancestors through acts of generosity to one's fellow men in the form of gift-giving, hospitality, and feasting that create social harmony (see also Iteanu 1983b, 2004).

Thus, the Orokaiva indigenous moral economy posits specific causal relationships between individual human actions, social conditions, and material wealth. These are diagrammed in figure 4.1.

Unlike individual human actions and their material results, which are visible, the underlying condition of social relationships is invisible and must be inferred. Social harmony involves people's inner states—their jos—being positively oriented and aligned with one another. Similarly, ancestral favor is associated with gardens, where a man's ancestors worked before him, and which are identified with the gardener's jo. The ancestral knowledge and inheritance that a man obtains by obedience to his father—serving him, listening to his stories, learning the boundaries of the family's lands, helping him in his work, and imitating his craftsmanship—this, too, is hidden in a man's jo. These three states of the underlying social condition become visible only in the fruits of a man's work and his standing in the community.[15]

Two examples may help make the causal links in the figure clearer. The first concerns obligations in feasting. In addition to being generous at the feast itself, a feast giver is under a serious obligation to provide generous hospitality to all who visit him in the weeks leading up to it. He is supposed

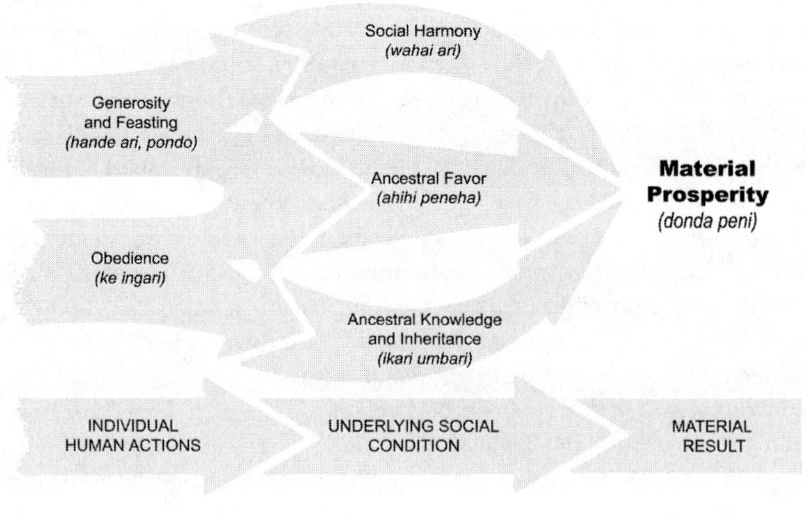

Social Harmony
(wahai ari)

Generosity
and Feasting
(hande ari, pondo)

Ancestral Favor
(ahihi peneha)

**Material
Prosperity**
(donda peni)

Obedience
(ke ingari)

Ancestral Knowledge
and Inheritance
(ikari umbari)

INDIVIDUAL
HUMAN ACTIONS

UNDERLYING SOCIAL
CONDITION

MATERIAL
RESULT

FIGURE 4.1 · The moral economy of wealth

to greet visitors with loud and exuberant cries that flatter their ancestral and clan names. He is supposed to welcome each visitor warmly with offers of food, betel nut, and tobacco. These expressions of generosity are made with the intent that any ill will possibly lurking in the visitor's jo will be dispelled and converted into positive feelings, which are required for cooperation and social harmony. Once the feast is over and the feast-giver's wealth has been dissipated, it is believed that the social harmony his generous actions fostered will result in an increased productivity and fecundity of his food gardens, family, and business. It is also believed that this social harmony will bring positive material benefits by pleasing the feast-giver's ancestors. Before the feast food is piled on the feasting platform for public display it is stored for several days in piles in the feast-giver's arara (open-walled sitting-platform). The spirits of deceased ancestors are believed to congregate in a feast-giver's arara before a feast, and if they are pleased with the feast-giver, the food will be magically increased while it is stored there. But should any harsh words or violent quarrels take place on or near the feasting ground in the weeks leading up to a feast, the injured parties must be formally compensated with payments to dissipate the ill will, if feast preparations are to continue. This rule is observed rigorously. Were the feast to be held in the shadow of any ill will, people would feel the disapproval of the ancestors, as well as the direct effects of their social discord: the dance would lose its luster, the food would prove insufficient to feed all the guests, and the desired subsequent increase in the feast-giver's productivity and fecundity would not occur.

Another example that shows how the creation of wealth is associated with ancestral favor involves the way people perceived my winning a grant to come study them. To Orokaiva, the distance I had traveled to reach Papua New Guinea from America implied abundant fortune and wealth, which can only have come through the favor or "blessing" of my father and deceased ancestors. I was many times told elaborate narratives describing how I must have attracted the good fortune of my fellowship: I must have sat at my father's feet and heard his stories when I was young, thus obtaining his knowledge; I must have diligently obeyed his commands as I was growing up; I must have helped him in his old age by bringing food and relieving him of hard labor (e.g., by fixing his house). In some of these accounts, I must also have held a *jo vivi*, a feast honoring an important elderly person in order to supplicate his or her spirit and formally obtain his or her inheritance and "blessing." It could only be because I had done these things that I 'held my father's bone,' ensuring my success and fruitfulness in all endeavors. Orokaiva would also say that I must have pleased my father with the generosity I had shown my other relatives and friends. By this they meant to point to the material assistance that I was habitually giving at the time to *them*, suggesting that because of it I would reap further rewards. Such ascriptions were intended to reinforce my acquiescence and generosity in the present, as well as to make of my success an instructive example for the other young men within earshot. People interpreted my grant, an example of extreme abundance and good fortune, as resulting from the same kinds of causal moral relationships that Orokaiva see obtaining among themselves.

Orokaiva use this same moral framework to interpret the extreme wealth they see on whitemen's skin. However, such wealth is difficult to reconcile with what they also see as whitemen's lack of generous hospitality, gift-giving, and feasting, which are necessary preconditions for Orokaiva themselves to achieve social harmony and ancestral favor. Orokaiva are thus led to speculate that perhaps whitemen achieve the effect of social harmony and ancestral favor by being highly obedient to their ancestors, parents, elders, and peers. Or perhaps they immediately reciprocate all social debts and material favors with payments of money, something Orokaiva often see whites do. In this way, the reasoning goes, whitemen would never feel shortchanged or disadvantaged, social harmony would never be disrupted, and they would be perpetually blessed with ancestral favor, and so enjoy abundant good fortune and vast wealth. As Kingsford had phrased it, 'you whitemen have your ancestors already lined up to support you' (see also Iteanu 2004, 110). In effect, Orokaiva start from the visible fact of whitemen's abundant wealth and reason backward to conclude that whitemen's society must be characterized by the ideal moral conditions that Orokaiva themselves continually strive to achieve.

The lack of social harmony is seen by Orokaiva to be the most pressing and intractable moral problem they face in their society. Countless hours are devoted in community meetings, church gatherings, and everyday conversation to exhorting one another to be unified and detailing the ways their lack of social harmony is preventing their undertakings from being successful. If people would only obey one another, coordinate their activities, and accept the leadership of knowledgeable elders; if they would only be more generous in helping one another and would exert self-control to avoid giving cause for offense; if they could only cleanse their hearts of competitive aspirations, grudges, and other forms of ill will; then, it is believed, their undertakings would all bear rich fruit, and their lives would be transformed by prosperity. Indeed, it is just this indigenous cultural ideal of social harmony that Orokaiva seek through Christianity (Bashkow

2000b; Robbins 2004a). Unfortunately, latent quarrels, jealousy, and obstinacy continually undermine the social harmony that Orokaiva so wish to attain, and indeed, in some cases, the intense focus on the need to create social harmony can itself lead people to become disaffected by the constant pressure of implied blame for failed projects (Brison 1991; Leavitt 2001). Whitemen's superior material wealth is taken as evidence of whitemen's ability to overcome these problems, which Orokaiva feel so acutely in their own society (see also Kulick 1992). To Orokaiva, the wealth of whitemen thus objectifies their own moral inferiority in being unable to create social harmony, and therefore in being unable to create and maintain abundance and wealth.

The contradiction of whitemen's softness—the fact that whitemen enjoy elaborate wealth without doing any hard, physical work—might be best resolved to a western sensibility by recognizing the legacy of colonialism in capitalist institutions that exploit cheap third-world labor and natural resources. If Orokaiva were inclined to see themselves as exploited, this might be a compelling explanation to them as well. However, while they surely did feel exploited during the colonial era, with the departure of whites in the decades since independence, Orokaiva today are more inclined to view colonial times with nostalgia, and to view whitemen positively, as potential sources of (rather than sinks for) power and development. The exploiters Orokaiva are most concerned about today are one another and other Papua New Guineans. For example, in 1993, when an "Oro for Oro" secessionist movement arose among Orokaiva participants in the World Bank–funded Higaturu oil palm project, the focus of resistance was not the white managers, the project itself, or the international economic interests it represented; rather, it aimed to expel Papua New Guineans from elsewhere in the country who had settled in the region to work on the project and who were being blamed for the robberies, gang violence, disputes, and other social ills affecting the province (see Koczberski and Curry 2004, 362–64).

So for Orokaiva, the contrast between the hardness of their own skin and the softness of whitemen's skin represents a difference in moral standing. The comparison with whitemen leaves them feeling like they are in something of a fallen state, though they themselves do not apply this biblical metaphor. By contrast, whitemen seem to be living in a blessed Edenic state in which wealth comes without difficult toil. As Steven once put it, expressing his annoyance at the national tourist-promotion slogan that likens Papua New Guinea to paradise: "They always say about PNG, '*paradise, paradise.*' But who are the ones who have good houses high in the air and paved roadways that run everywhere, even underground? Who are the ones who travel at great speeds on the sea and in the sky? Who are the ones with big factories that produce fax machines, handwatches, anything you can name? We in Papua New Guinea are all just *bullshit*. The only big thing we have is talk, and nothing ever comes of it because each man's head is too strong and he goes his own way."

The 'Brightness' of Whitemen's Skin

The "white" color of whitemen's skin is interpreted by Orokaiva primarily as a kind of 'brightness.' The several commonly used Orokaiva terms for whitemen's skin metaphorically express a variety of colors, ranging from the bright, almost pure white of the feathers of the white cockatoo ('white cockatoo skin man'), through the mottled tan-yellow color of the bark of the *oinga* tree ('light mottled tree bark skin man'), to the reddish pink of red coral ('red coral skin man') and reddish brown of red clay ('red clay skin man'). But Orokaiva attach little significance to these specific metaphorical references or the colors they indicate. Indeed, color symbolism is little elaborated in general in Orokaiva language and culture. What Orokaiva do systematically invest with symbolic significance is the light/dark contrast, which has clear moral connotations and is construed in terms of brightness or luminosity. All the colors that Orokaiva associate with whitemen's skin are light, bright colors. In certain playful, humorous expressions, luminous brightness is the foregrounded quality; I myself was sometimes jokingly called 'bright flaring torch skin' and 'bright Coleman pressure lamp skin.' Often Orokaiva follow the PNG national usage of calling whites by the Tok Pisin and English terms "white" and "whiteskin" and calling themselves "black" and "blackskin" in contrast. Orokaiva vernacular terms for black skin are *hamo pekuma*, denoting the color 'true black,' and *hamo mume*, meaning 'dark' (mume is also the term for 'night'). Orokaiva freely and often compare gradations of hue in their own and others' skin color, saying things like, 'My skin is lighter than hers,' 'He is black completely,' and 'He is like you; he has red coral skin.' I also frequently heard relatively light-skinned Orokaiva being greeted good-humoredly with epithets for 'whiteskin' like 'Hey there, red-pink coral skin man!' and 'Light-mottled tree bark skin woman!'

Brightness or darkness of skin color is an important way Orokaiva categorize people of different races. This is particularly true when the countries they come from are unfamiliar. Some Orokaiva recognize subtle variations in race and nationality, and it is considered a sign of worldliness

to be able to do so. During the time of my fieldwork, the expatriate population in Oro Province included Malaysians, Koreans, Filipinos, Burmese,
Indians, Chinese, Ghanaians, Australians, New Zealanders, Americans, and
Europeans. Orokaiva are interested in the different countries and places
these people come from, but they are not inclined to stereotype them in
terms of the kinds of morally charged personality traits (crafty, passionate,
inscrutable, etc.) that one often finds elsewhere (e.g., in Cameroon: "an
Englishman is tricky, . . . tight, but an American is loose . . . flexible"
[Nyamnjoh and Page 2002, 620]) and that are a staple of Euro-American
constructions of generalized national, racial, and ethnic groups.[16] Instead,
consistent with Orokaivas' general tendency not to venture generalizations
about hidden inner states—the jos—of people or classes of people, they
morally evaluate foreigners in terms of the foods they eat (discussed in the
next chapter), the kinds of work they do, the things they make, their ritual
customs, their characteristic behavior in exchange, and the qualities of their
skin.

Of the socially relevant characteristics that are visible on the surface of
the skin, brightness is among the most meaningful. Things that are bright
attract people's attention, giving brightness an essential social dimension.
Anything that is beautiful or that betrays wealth is bright, in the sense that
it draws or 'pulls' the eyes of those who see it. Foreigners in rural Papua
New Guinea *do* pull people's eyes. Resident expatriates often talk about
being treated like celebrities when they mix among local people, drawing
attention wherever they go. As an Orokaiva once told me, 'When we
blacks walk in the market, it's no big deal. But when you go in, every man
and woman looks at you, and everybody wants to talk to you.' Orokaiva
friends who accompanied me in public were constantly asked who I was,
what my purpose was in being there, and how they had acquired my
friendship. Simply because I was a whiteman, I regularly enjoyed special
treatment, such as being seated with the VIPs at feasts and public events,
being specially greeted whenever I visited a new family or village, and
being served first at meals, where I was always encouraged to take the best
portions.

Indeed, because they attract attention and are socially bright, foreigners
are still usually referred to as 'whitemen' even when their skin is objectively
dark in color. Hence, the two Ghanaian teachers at the provincial high
school were sometimes referred to as 'those black whitemen' (*taupamane
mume*), and they were treated like whitemen, for example being seated with
the VIPs at special events and being served first at communal meals.
Similarly, when two swarthy Spaniards passed through Agenehambo on

their way to the Kokoda Trail (a bush-walking destination popular for its significance in World War II), Orokaiva described the visitors as 'whitemen with dark skin.' This general categorization of foreigners as whitemen is sometimes found odd by those so categorized. As I was told by a female Malaysian researcher visiting PNG from Australia where she taught at a university, "Papua New Guinea was the first place that I was ever called a 'whiteman.' In Australia, I am called 'ethnic.' But here I am 'white.'"[17]

In being a whiteman in Papua New Guinea, I discovered the racially inverted counterpart to Ralph Ellison's "invisible man" (Ellison 1952): I was a consummately conspicuous and valued presence wherever I went. Having experienced my whiteness as unmarked or "normal" in the American contexts in which I had been socialized, the overtness of the attention and preferential treatment I received in Papua New Guinea felt to me unwarranted, inappropriate, and in some ways, burdensome. But to Orokaiva, there was nothing inappropriate about the special attention I was given; indeed, it was a necessary consequence and constitutive feature of my brightness. Orokaiva consider light skin to be beautiful, on themselves as well as on others. Foreigners, however, are bright not only because they are light skinned and thus beautiful, but also because they are exceptional, and, above all, presumed to have great wealth, a topic we will explore at length below. As with other bright things, whitemen's skin is understood by Orokaiva within a vernacular moral framework that associates beauty, through sight, with the arousal of desire in others and the social consequences of unequal wealth.

Beauty, Desire, and Jealousy in the Interpersonal Economy of Sight

Orokaiva conceive of seeing as a type of social transaction that requires reciprocation. The transactional nature of sight (*kiari*) is emphasized in Orokaiva linguistic expressions for looking and seeing that recall Aristotelian notions of sight as a moving principle that proceeds outward from the subject's eye to the object seen: for example, '[He] threw his eyes, [their seeing] traveled [to the object of sight], [he] saw it' (*tihi gosukenu pambunu avo kena*). In the act of seeing, the seer creates a relationship with the object seen that has the potential to extend beyond the moment of beholding. When a person dies, for example, close friends and relatives observe a prohibition on consuming produce that the deceased person had once laid eyes upon. The ban, called *isaki*, applies to all gardens that the deceased person had worked in or even had merely visited while still alive. It also applies to betel nuts and coconuts on the palms within sight of his or her home, until the fruits that these trees were bearing when the death occurred fall, and the trees bear new fruit.

In the act of seeing another person, an Orokaiva seeing subject identifies, if only momentarily, with the seen other. As a result of this identification, sight often creates situations where inequality between people is perceived. To adapt Ruth Benedict's phrase, the Orokaiva seeing eye is the organ of egalitarian values. When you see someone who is worse off than yourself, a person who is poor, disfigured, or weakened by old age, the appropriate moral response is to feel pity (*osaga*) toward the person and a pull to give him or her something that belongs to you in order to diminish the imbalance (see Schieffelin 1990, 124ff). Alternatively, when you see someone who is better off than yourself, someone who is wealthier or more beautiful, you are confronted with your own inferiority and relative poverty, and the morally appropriate response is for the other to give something to you as a gesture toward equalizing the difference. In a sense, the seer who is relatively worse off than the one seen is overcome (*umbari*) by the attractiveness of the other, which 'pulls' the excited interest (*hanahana*) and desire of the seer. As a result, the seer should be compensated for the breach of autonomy he or she has experienced, and the ideal way of doing so is for the superior seen person to give the inferior seer a share of that which attracted his or her eye in the first place. The way Orokaiva speak of such visually instigated 'desire' (*uje*) is as a kind of agitated 'heat' (*bevere*) that is provoked within the seer that the person who is responsible for it should 'cool' or satisfy (*jamo aja*) with a material gift. The gift reestablishes positive reciprocity by showing the seer that he or she, too, is attractive, since the gift is itself wealth that the seer has 'attracted' or 'pulled' from the other. Until the heat of desire is cooled and the feeling of imbalance counteracted, the perception of imbalance has the potential to assume a negative form, jealousy (*si*), that may lead to destructive actions.

Once again, feasting provides an example of Orokaiva ideals. At most feasts, the center of attention is the food display, which is usually set up on a platform about the width of a house. Feast-givers devote a great deal of effort to beautifying the food display with towers of taro and artful arrangements of yams, bananas, sugar cane, coconuts, and branches of betel nut (see plate 5). Sometimes feast-givers tie yams to the tops of long poles so that the guests' eyes are drawn high above the platform; sometimes the traditional decorations are brightened with colorful packages of store-bought crackers, cheese pops, sugar, rice, and cans of fish. Pigs are displayed around the base of the feast platform or else in a single line extending outward toward the guests from the foot of the platform steps (see plate 4). The feasting platform is thus an attractive display of abundance that externalizes the jo of the feast-giver. In feasting, Orokaiva say, the feast-giver 'becomes an outside man' (*embo araha aisuja*); that is, the man's essential social qualities are revealed for all to see.

Often feast-givers beautify themselves for their feasts with traditional body decorations designed to display brightness, beauty, exciting motion, and color. Headdresses are constructed with red and green parrot feathers, or springy black cassowary quills tied at the tips with bright white plumes that bob about as the wearer moves. The barkcloth loincloths that men wear are painted with bold geometric designs and have flowing aprons in the front and back. Sometimes feast-givers paint their faces in vivid red and yellow, accenting them with spots of bright white (see plates 15 and 16). They wear shell and seed necklaces, and elaborate pendants of boar's tusks, shells, and red coral disks, which are oiled before important occasions by rubbing them with coconut scrapings so that they shine. Flower sprays and branches of colorful croton leaves are slipped into bands on the feast-giver's arms, legs, and waist, and they flutter and shake attractively with every movement of the body. At many feasts, traditional dancers are invited to perform on the feasting ground in front of the food display. The dancers, who wear decorations similar to those worn by the feast-giver, amplify the feast's beauty; they are sometimes jokingly referred to using the English term "flowers." The ensemble of dancers, moving in unison, creates a powerful image of agility, grace, and colorful movement (see plate 19).

The beauty of a feast is identified with the feast-givers, so they will be at pains to ensure that all those who see their feast will leave having received at least a small share of it. Ordinarily, the majority of people present at a feast will receive payments in any case, either as part of the ritual work the feast is meant to accomplish, or in reciprocation for material help they contributed to the feast. But the question of reciprocation for simply having seen the feast arises for a category of guests called *ugo meni*, 'onlookers': people who come simply to watch. Feast-givers always reserve a part of their feast food for distribution to ugo meni. If there is an important person among the ugo meni, they will be singled out for a particularly substantial food gift, since the will that was 'overcome' and pulled in by the feast's attractiveness was more substantial, and the potential consequence of leaving it uncompensated and 'uncooled' is correspondingly more threatening. (As a whiteman, venturing onto a feasting ground to observe the proceedings was tantamount to compelling the feast-giver to make me a present of taro, pork, or bananas.) Ordinary ugo meni always receive cooked food to eat, and should they leave the feast without eating, it is a sign of trouble.

The ideal represented in feasting is that a thing of great beauty—the feast—should be decomposed and distributed in reciprocation for the attraction that it exerts upon those who see it (Strathern 1992). Those others, who each get a part of it (indeed, who each consume part of it, incorporating it into their persons), identify themselves in a positive way with their memory of the feast that they saw. This positive identification transforms the beauty of the thing seen into words of praise: they speak well of the feast, publicizing the feast-giver's name and increasing his or her status as the name is spread far and wide (Munn 1986).

Once it has been revealed, a thing of beauty must be dispersed for it to retain positive value, because it engenders in others who have seen it desire that must be counteracted. Either those who behold the thing must be given a share of it, or else their thwarted desire will lead (if only by the very fact of their ill will) to its diminishment. The converse of this notion that beauty is diminished as it is seen is the assumption that for things to grow and increase in beauty, they must be hidden. Orokaiva conceive of growth as a process that generally takes place out of sight. After all, the growth of children, plants, and animals is never directly perceived; it is only after growth has occurred that people become aware of it. Children are thought to grow at night while sleeping, when they are for the most part unwatched. Orokaivas' most crucial subsistence crops are not like wheat, rice, and corn, which ripen in the open air; rather they are root crops like taro, yams, and sweet potatoes, which grow unseen underground. The above-ground portions of plants are believed to grow particularly at night, when they are watered by dew. My informants insisted that our pigs, if kept penned in the village where they were visible, would never grow very big; pigs must be allowed to roam in the dark forest, which is where living things are known to grow most profusely.[18]

The invisibility that fosters growth in the darkness of night and the forest interior is created artificially in the practice of seclusion.[19] When secluded within a house, or even simply restricted from traveling beyond the village periphery, an individual in effect becomes socially invisible, since he or she is seen by only few others. Seclusion is used as a basic technique for inducing growth or restoring the vitality of individuals who have been weakened or compromised; the very old, the sick, people in mourning, and parents in the days after the birth of an infant all observe, as a matter of course, forms of seclusion in their houses. In addition, certain objects, like *kani* ceremonial staves that have the ritual status of persons, are secluded when their status is compromised, for example, upon the death of their owner. The seclusion of girls, as described above, begins when they first menstruate, as menstruation is considered a type of infirmity.[20] The anthropologist F. E. Williams, who observed seclusions of adolescent initiates in the 1920s, wrote, "If one asks either the elders or the initiates themselves for the reasons of seclusion, one will almost invariably receive the same answer: boys and girls are secluded to make them grow big" (Williams 1930, 198).

Orokaiva seclude girls in order to make them grow big and beautiful, so that they leave the seclusion not only soft, but also bright. In order for a girl's skin to become bright, Orokaiva believe that she should be hidden both from daylight and from other people's eyes. On rare occasions a girl is allowed to walk around in the village to punctuate the boredom, but only if she is completely concealed. It is not that some force of seeing will directly proceed from others' eyes and affect her skin. It is rather that her skin, as it becomes more beautiful, will increasingly affect those who see it, possibly moving them to employ magic, out of spite, to dull her beauty. Even if they merely harbor bad feelings, this can have destructive consequences; at minimum the premature seeing of a secluded girl will ruin the dramatic effect of the revelation at her debut. While I was twice asked to photograph girls in seclusion so that their families could preserve a memento, I was admonished not to let the developed pictures be seen by others until after the debut feast.

At the debut feasts I attended, the brightness of the debutantes was magnified by a food display and other wealth that was all given away as part of the feast. The girls themselves were draped with traditional ornaments and crowned with headdresses made from arrays of valuable hornbill beaks or bird of paradise plumes. All of the girls were dressed in fine barkcloth skirts; one had a long barkcloth "train." At two of the feasts, money notes were affixed to the girls' skirts in order to 'pull people's eyes.' The organizers of debut feasts strive to enhance the impression of beauty by artifice and drama. Steven's family considered placing its debutante on a platform hidden behind curtains of young palm fronds, which would be suddenly dropped, revealing the girl, to the eyes of all, amid a splendor of dancers. Debutantes ordinarily dance alongside the traditional dancers, to show off their beauty, and when possible pose by the food display to be photographed by relatives in an image intended to sum up the event (see plate 18). Often the debutante is actually seated atop the wealth, on a 'bed' (besi) of foods or piles of rice sacks. This food is said to 'uphold' (jigibe) the good impression that the debutante's beauty makes in the eyes of the guests: it becomes part of the tableau of her beauty, and is then distributed to the guests at the climax of the feast in compensation for their having seen it.

People inadequately compensated at a feast are bound to leave it with a 'bad impression' (*kiari sapura*) that will spread when they subsequently speak of the event to others in negative terms. During my first visit to the region, I once coincidentally arrived in a village as a girl's debut feast was winding up, and since it was the first such feast I had seen, I stopped to take photographs and ask what the feast was for. Later, whenever my Agenehambo escorts recalled the occasion, they were severely critical, indignantly complaining that I had not been offered so much as a single taro or hand of bananas, though I had come all the way from America 'to see the sight.' In time I came to understand that guests who are not in the feast-givers' group are inclined to find fault with particularities of the feast arrangements, food display, or dancers' performance, and will speak in a way that diminishes its luster (*usasa* 'light') by casting over it the 'shadow' (*uhumo*) and 'darkness' (*mume*) of their aspersions. At such moments, Orokaiva delight in recalling evil magic that their fathers, when alive, had used to spoil others' dances by robbing the dancers' costumes of beauty, making them heavy-footed, dulling the sound of their drums, or upsetting their throats so that the songs they sang came out sounding confused or so that they forgot them entirely. The power of their fathers' dance-destroying magic was so fearsome, people said, that feast-givers would hurry to give them taro and pork to secure their goodwill before they could do any harm. Such stories are thinly veiled allegories that depict in putative past events the alternatives people face in the present: spectators will either receive food gifts, which will incline them to evaluate the feast sympathetically, or else they will undermine the feast, defaming the feast-givers with their words (see also Iteanu 2004, 108). The food gifts mollify the competitive emotions aroused in those who see the great wealth and beauty displayed at a feast, and compensate the viewers for the inferiority they thereby experience.[21]

In accepting food gifts at a feast, guests also accept the 'reason' (*be*) for which the feast has been held; indeed, should any guests have reservations about the ritual work taking place at a feast, they will be sure to duck out before the food is distributed. At least some of the food people receive at a feast is taken away to be later shared with others, at which time it will be explained where the food came from, so that the reason for the feast travels out along with the food. A guest will say, for example, "So-and-so's daughter was decorated, I saw it, and so this food was given to me" (see also Iteanu 1990). Far into the future, a feast guest will be able to certify that the feast's ritual work was accomplished: because he or she ate of it, the guest's own body is proof that it took place.

Because the dancers at a feast are beautiful, those who see them require compensation. For the majority of guests, responsibility for this compensation lies with the feast-givers, since the dancers are really a part of the decorations that ornament the feast. There remains, however, a problem with respect to the feast-givers themselves: they too should require compensation, because they too are moved by the dancers' beauty. At the same time, however, it is the feast-givers who are obligated to pay the dancers, since dancing is hard work, and since the dancers have come at the feast-givers' behest. In fact, the feast-givers always pay the dancers, satisfying the latter of these two obligations. Sometimes this payment is made in the course of the normal distribution of food, once the dancing has already ceased. But oftentimes there is a special payment of pork that is given to the dancers while they are in the act of dancing. In this case, the payment is made in a very unusual, aggressive way: the feast-givers run down from the feasting platform and feign a dramatic attack on the dancers, literally pelting them with pork projectiles (see plate 20). When I asked about this strange custom, *o taiha* 'pelting with meat,' my Orokaiva informants always explained that the dancers had affronted the feast-givers by inappropriately asking to be paid for their work (they had made *pero* 'an insouciant request'). This explanation was given even when the dancers had never actually asked for payment at all. (In some cases I knew this because I was myself among the dancers or in the feast-giving party.) But the idea that the dancers had been somehow offensive to the feast-givers makes sense in terms of the interpersonal economy of sight: o taiha is a response to the conflict the feast-givers experience in witnessing the beauty of the dance. While the feast-givers are under obligation to pay the dancers for their work, their beauty arouses a desire in them that itself demands reciprocation. But the feast-givers know they will not receive any positive reciprocation from the dancers, so they reciprocate negatively. Their payment for the dancers' work takes a violent form, as unreciprocated desire is known to do: in this case, an attack against the object that had aroused the desire, albeit in the form of a theatricality that does no real harm.

The principle that desire aroused by the sight of wealth or beauty must be reciprocated does not only govern transactions in the special context of feasting; it also governs people's behavior in everyday situations. When a man wears a nice new shirt, for example, he risks arousing the desire of those who see him wearing it. He is in fact likely to be asked for it by relatives such as his in-laws, and he will find it hard to refuse giving the shirt away, lest the desire his shirt aroused in them be transformed into their ill will that may have negative consequences for him in the future. Whenever people have things that others might covet, whether a new shirt, an iron-roofed house, a package of crackers, or a handsome new coffee pulper, the principle of sight arousing desires that need to be cooled applies.

In everyday life, Orokaiva people avoid being bright with wealth that is visible to others, and they deliberately keep their outward appearances drab so as not to draw others' eyes toward them, arouse desire, and create jealousy. One way they do this is by keeping desirable objects out of sight. Ordinarily Orokaiva wear ragged clothes and allow only their old, undesirable possessions to remain out in plain sight. The emphasis Orokaiva place on keeping desirable objects hidden is also reflected architecturally in the design of their houses. The two basic types of houses they construct are the *bande* and the *arara*. The bande, the sleeping house, is raised on stilts, with a locking door and with windows (if it has any) that shutter closed. It is used almost exclusively for sleeping and for storing, that is, hiding, possessions. Except when in seclusion, people spend very little time awake inside the bande, and an individual would not ordinarily presume to enter the bande of others, except the closest of relatives, without being specially invited to do so—quite like Americans rarely look inside another person's wallet or purse. Instead, people spend most of their time and receive guests in their all-purpose "living room," the open-air arara, which has a raised floor and a roof but no walls. The virtue of the arara is that it is entirely open to sight, though there is little inside it for people to see. The only desirable objects one generally finds in an arara are those in use at the moment. Plates and cups, for example, will be brought out when food is served, then afterward put away out of sight. Even the location of cooking shifts in accordance with the principle that people should be prevented from seeing desirable things they will not get a share of. Most Orokaiva do not have a permanent clay or stone fire pit, but make their cooking fires atop an iron sheet (like the round lid of a 55-gallon drum), in effect creating a movable hearth. When the family is alone, this hearth may be set up in the arara. But when a household has guests, the hearth is picked up and moved out of sight, perhaps to a spot on the ground near the arara but out of the guests' line of vision (see plate 11). (If need be, to prevent guests from seeing it, it will even be moved inside a bande.) When hosts are preparing to feed their guests, they avoid letting them see the food until the moment of serving, when it is revealed all at once. In part this is done to keep guests' expectations low, so that the food, when revealed, will not disappoint them. But hosts are also worried about contingencies, like the arrival of still more guests, which might prevent the food (which would then be inadequate) from being served at all, leaving the first guests with bad feelings: having already seen the food in the pot, they would have a thwarted desire to eat it.

With the things of their indigenous material culture, Orokaiva are easily able to keep appearances drab. The forest materials like logs, sago midribs, and frond thatch that they use to build houses quickly turn to a brown gray, ashen color in the sun and so begin to look old. There are only a few types of materials like feathers, tusks, coral, and shells that remain bright permanently, and these are used almost exclusively to make valuable ornaments that are displayed only at feasts, where those who see them are formally compensated. The rest of the time such valuables are kept hidden away in the bande. The greatest part of indigenous wealth is food, like garden produce and pigs, which under normal circumstances remains out of sight in the gardens and forest. The only time a family will concentrate large amounts of food wealth visibly in the village is in preparation for a feast, when the wealth will soon be distributed. And as discussed above, people are especially concerned at such times to show elaborate hospitality to all who approach their houses, in order to forestall potential ill will. The hardest form of indigenous wealth to keep hidden from others is pigs. In the heat of the day, pigs like to hide themselves in the forest where it is cool. But in the evenings and on cooler days, pigs are often seen sleeping under their owners' houses or in places close by. 'Pig jealousy,' which is to say, the jealousy aroused by the sight of another man's pigs, is considered by Orokaiva to be the root cause of many conflicts. To prevent becoming the object of others' pig jealousy, people try whenever possible to publicly earmark their pigs for specific recipients in advance of their maturity. Because such earmarking diffuses ownership of the pig, it can attenuate some of others' potential jealousy.

Perhaps the brightest things visible in a village are colorful croton bushes and flowers. But these present little problem, because cuttings can be freely given to anyone expressing a desirous interest in the plants. Orokaiva often return from visits to new places with flower cuttings to plant near their own houses. Flowers and shrubbery are in fact the main form of beautification in Orokaiva villages, which otherwise appear remarkably drab (see plate 10). Lining up houses in rows and maintaining whitemen-style cut grass lawns are additional ways of beautifying the village that do not cause jealousy, presumably because they do not introduce a detachable thing for others to want. As mentioned in chapter 3, Kingsford built his family compound on a rectilinear plan around a spacious grass field, cleverly conveying an impression of order and modern prosperity without actually introducing desirable objects into view.

The problem with a lawn is that it requires maintenance, for which it helps greatly to own a lawnmower. But lawnmowers, along with roofing iron, household amenities, vehicles, clothing, and other such desirable modern commodities are problematic, because they are especially likely to create jealousy in others. First, they remain bright, and thus desirable, for a long time. Vehicles and machines, for example, remain attractive for as long as they continue to function; roofing iron remains serviceable for twenty years or more. Second, western commodity wealth objects abound in their kinds and varieties, making innumerable the dimensions along which people can compare their own wealth with that of others. So for example, although a man might exceed his cousin in owning many sheets of roofing iron, he might nonetheless feel jealous of a new hat, wristwatch, or sunglasses the cousin is seen sporting. Third, unlike most traditional valuables, many modern wealth objects are difficult to hide, either because they are too big, or because being hidden conflicts with their use, as with roofing iron, vehicles, and machines.

Modern commodity wealth is also associated with business and development activities, which create particularly acute problems of desirability and jealousy. Businesses like tradestores, trucking, livestock-raising, and cash-cropping are not only bright and desirable in themselves, but they are also seen as means for potentially generating new value over time, so that their brightness at any moment is magnified by expectations of future increase. Moreover, people typically start business and development projects once they have amassed large amounts of start-up money, often from outside sources like government grants, brideprice payments, and wage-earning kin. Although money as cash normally can be secreted in hiding places and bank accounts, such windfalls are virtually always matters of public knowledge. The high visibility of project start-up money is further exacerbated by the tendency to spend all the money at once on expensive supplies like seedlings, day-old chicks, feed, work boots, and tools, and on western-style building materials to construct special new buildings to be used in the project.

In village tradestores, the problem of the desire aroused by western commodity wealth is particularly salient. Even the design of village tradestores reflects a compromise between the storeowner's need to display the goods in stock so that people can see and buy them, and the need to control people's sight of the goods to ameliorate jealousy and prevent stealing. Unlike the large, supermarket-style stores in Popondetta, which have aisles along which customers can walk, village tradestores are built on the model of a service counter in which only the storekeeper has direct access to the goods.

Customers stand outside the small building and peer through a small window or wire grate at the goods displayed on shelves behind the store-keeper (see plate 12). Orokaiva speak of stocking a store as 'decorating' it (*kogombari*), since the goods themselves are attractive things that will pull people's eyes. Often, when a new tradestore is decorated for the first time, the owner contributes a part of the stock of store foods to a meal shared with extended family members and neighbors in a straightforward attempt to prevent the desire they feel upon seeing the goods from creating feelings of jealousy. Newton (1985) reports that in the late 1970s clan-based Orokaiva business groups launched their tradestores with feasts that were quite elaborate. But it is impossible to resolve the problem of others' attraction to a store's stock of goods once and for all, because a store is not a feast: a feast's beauty is extinguished in the process of compensating its viewers for their attraction to it, but the store must remain perpetually decorated in order to stay in business, attracting others' eyes and arousing their desire on an ongoing basis.

To Orokaiva, this perpetual brightness is both the profit and the peril of owning a tradestore. It is profitable because the goods' attractiveness pulls in customers and motivates them to part with their money. But it is also perilous because either (1) people desire the goods in the store but cannot afford them, leaving them feeling 'hot,' or (2) people desire the goods and buy them, but they realize their money adds to the store's value, leading again to jealousy. Since the store continually arouses desires that cannot be satisfactorily cooled, storeowners live in fear that these hot feelings will lead to destructive actions against them. So strong is this fear that I know of many cases in which a misfortune, like the death of a child, led a store-owning family to give up its business completely and retreat to a basic subsistence lifestyle (Tok Pisin: *stap nating long bus*). Invariably the misfortune was interpreted as the result of destructive actions taken by others who were jealous of them because of their store. Because sickness, death, and misfortune are an inescapable fact of people's lives, Orokaivas' belief that stores and other businesses generate especially powerful feelings of jealousy and ill will is continually reaffirmed.[22]

In some cases, individuals decide that the risks entailed in venturing into business projects are simply not worth it. In 1993, a young Agenehambo man received a 1,300-kina (then about U.S. $1,400) grant to rehabilitate coffee trees owned by his clan, buy a coffee pulper, and build a shed in which to process the beans. This aroused intense jealousy among his clansmen and neighbors, who advanced various arguments why he should give them a share of the money he received. Some pointed out that he should use this good fortune as an opportunity to use a share of the money to acknowledge his debt to them for the nurturing and help he had received from them in the past, that made him what he was. Others argued that the member of parliament who was the source of the grant had really intended to do something for all of them in order to assure their continued political support. Still others noted that since it was their coffee trees that had been tallied in proposing the grant, they had rights to a share in it, since the money was received 'in their names.' Tensions in the hamlet ran high, and on one occasion, the man said, he was threatened by his neighbor with a grassknife. Faced with the choice between carrying out the project, which would surely fail and risk harm to his family given others' antagonism, and maintaining good relations with his neighbors and kin, he chose the latter. He distributed about half the money, giving 20, 50, or 100 kina notes to neighboring families, relatives, and a few special elderly 'grandparents' who had cared for him when he was small. The rest he consumed, buying food for his family, repaying drinking debts that his friends now called in, and traveling to Port Moresby to escape from all the hostility his grant had aroused.

The story of this grant is not an unusual one. People apply for grants because receiving them demonstrates a prestigious capacity to pull in distant wealth, but once they actually receive the money and feel the attention from others it draws, they frequently lose heart and abandon the project for which the grant was awarded. Many times projects fail because people would rather distribute the money than live with the ill will entailed by keeping it 'on their skin.' Alternatively, people may consume large portions of the money, buying nondurable items such as food, which is then shared. When money is so consumed or, as Orokaiva say, wasted in being 'eaten,' the desire aroused in others by its brightness is dissipated, just as the desire aroused by the beauty of a feast display is diffused into the various food gifts the guests take away. An especially efficient way to remove money's brightness from one's skin is to join with those who seek a share of it in shameful or secret ways of consuming it, for example by clandestinely drinking beer or consuming store-bought foods with them. In this way, the same act that compensates people for the desire that the money aroused in them draws them into complicity with the grant recipient's acts of misuse. Through such acts of shameful consumption, project-money's positive value—originally magnified by its perceived capacity to generate further future returns—is not only depleted, but the hostility it engendered is also transformed into something that is shared and thus no longer divisive (see Bercovitch 1994).

The Moral Implications of Whitemen's Wealth

White man, white man
White man with the big purse,
Since my mother born me
I've never seen such a big purse.

    —CAMEROONIAN CHILDREN'S SONG[23]

While the light color of whitemen's skin plays some role in constituting the brightness of whitemen, skin color is by no means the only factor, or even the main one. Instead, as is usual in cultural constructions of race, skin takes on meanings associated not only with a pigmentary difference but also with social and moral qualities, modes of production, activities, and social habits. Clearly, "white" skin tends to draw the eyes of Orokaiva because in the village context it is so unusual. Moreover, as we have seen in the case of adolescent girls emerging from seclusion, there are circumstances in which light skin color is aesthetically valued in traditional Orokaiva culture. But light color is not in fact essential to the Orokaiva construction of whiteness, since even dark-skinned foreigners are often categorized by Orokaiva as 'whitemen.' The more important feature that is categorically associated with whitemen and that makes them bright to Orokaiva is wealth. To Orokaiva, whitemen live in beautiful houses, drive around in fancy cars, and own rooms full of expensive household appliances, furniture, and electronic goods. The cities of whitemen are themselves bright with tall glass and steel buildings, big stores, and bustling factories. In the eyes of Orokaiva, whitemen are showy dressers, wearing shoes and socks, and shirts and neckties, items that Orokaiva say 'make the eyes move' (*tihi wasiri ai*) by attracting attention.

But whitemen are not only wealthy; they are conspicuously wealthy, and they are wealthy all the time. Unlike Orokaiva, who try to keep their wealth hidden and their outward appearances drab, whitemen seem to have no qualms about allowing their wealth to be seen by others. They walk around with expensive cameras, and regularly wear watches and jewelry. They carry wallets bulging with money bills and bank cards, and when they pay for things, instead of carefully extracting a single note from a pouch tucked deep inside a pocket or string bag, crumpling it in the hand, and passing it discreetly so that others will not notice, whitemen take the whole wallet out of their pocket or purse and hold it promiscuously open, handling their cash in the plain sight of all. Moreover, whitemen's wealth is concentrated in exactly the kinds of visible and long-lasting objects that Orokaiva find so difficult to conceal, such as good houses, cars, and businesses. Whitemen never appear to give all their wealth away, as Orokaiva systematically do at the ends of feasts and when they give up business ventures out of fear. From the perspective of Orokaiva, the conspicuous and perpetual brightness of whitemen seems to contravene all the lessons of their own experience, and is therefore enigmatic. How do whitemen manage to be so bright all the time? How is it that they attract so much attention to themselves, and yet never have their wealth and well-being undermined by others' jealousy?

This contradiction is compelling and its implications disturbing to Orokaiva, who frame this question primarily from their own perspective. Because whitemen do not acknowledge the desire their wealth creates in Orokaiva by giving them a share of it, Orokaiva are confronted with their own powerlessness. Orokaiva are continually engaged in activity directed at bringing themselves development, though it has been without success. As people often say, 'Development has not come to us. We still live like our ancestors.' Against this background of frustration, Orokaiva focus on particular relationships with individual whites who have responded to them by compensating their desires with a share of their wealth. Orokaiva often retell stories about the few whites with whom they have had exchange relationships of the sort they engage in with one another; in these cases, the desire Orokaiva have for the superior wealth of the whites was appropriately 'cooled' with expensive gifts. But it is only rarely that Orokaiva have been able to elicit wealth from whitemen through such positive relationships. Among Papua New Guineans, Orokaiva might resort to sorcery and raskolism to pull down the wealth of another who failed to respond to their desires. Yet whitemen are uncannily immune to sorcery (see below), and while individual whites have been brought to harm by raskol violence (indeed, two whites were killed in the Orokaiva region around the time of my fieldwork), Orokaiva recognize that this only leads whitemen to depart, taking their wealth away with them, and does not have the desired effect of resolving the inequality by forcing whitemen to destroy their wealth or redistribute it so that Orokaiva get a share.

An even more disturbing implication of the perpetual inequality between Orokaiva and whitemen is that whitemen do not seem to be able to see Orokaiva. According to Orokaiva assumptions about inequality, if whitemen truly saw Orokaiva, they would see that they are vastly poorer than themselves, and would thus surely be moved by pity to try to help them. The fact that they are not so moved suggests to Orokaiva not only that whitemen are ungenerous, but also, and more troublingly, that they themselves are of such little account that whitemen do not even bother to look at them.

Orokaiva understand their own villages to be 'small, backwater' places in relation to the larger, more important provincial, national, and international centers under which modern systems place them. To bring themselves to the attention of whitemen, villagers often send letters to foreign addresses they are given or find in newspapers, asking for money and gifts; they submit applications to foreign embassies requesting grants for individual and community development projects; and they visit government offices in the provincial and national capitals to try to bring their problems to the government's attention. Although a considerable number of grants and gifts are received, they do not in fact result in lasting, overall improvements in villagers' living conditions, and thus they are not really effective in making Orokaiva feel recognized by the outside world. When foreigners visit Orokaiva in their villages, Orokaiva often express their feelings of inferiority in a genre of talk they call 'sorry talk' (because it makes the hearer feel sorry for the speaker), saying things like 'we live just like pigs,' 'we are wild men who don't know how to live properly,' and 'nobody even looks at us.' The fact that even such abject talk fails to elicit responses that narrow the gap between themselves and whitemen suggests to Orokaiva that there may be some fault in themselves that makes them unworthy of others' attention.[24]

Whitemen's ability to maintain their wealth even as they are bright not only affects Orokaivas' perception of their status in relation to whitemen and the wider world but also their perception of themselves and their own communities, and it is here that the brightness of whitemen is most meaningful for Orokaiva. The problem Orokaiva are most concerned with in their own society is jealousy and the competitive emotions that arouse it, because it is jealousy that is understood to be the primary cause of the sorcery, social discord, and raskolism that undermine people's wealth, producing dearth. These negative relationships are diagrammed in figure 4.2.

The path from jealousy through sorcery and social discord to dearth and hunger is a simple inversion of the moral economy of wealth discussed earlier in this chapter. Although it may not be immediately obvious, sorcery and raskolism are classified as involving underlying social conditions because they are in most instances hidden acts that are inferred from their effects. This is especially true of sorcery, which is in fact never witnessed directly and which is believed to normally be performed under cover of night. Some kinds of raskol attacks, like highway robberies, are witnessed, but these kinds of attacks target more or less random victims and are designed to steal their money, rather than being seen as an outgrowth of jealousy harbored against particular individuals. But raskol attacks that target specific victims are a modern equivalent of traditional contracted

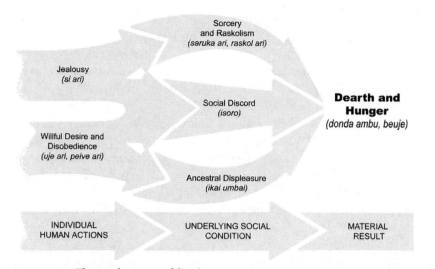

FIGURE 4.2 · The moral economy of dearth

sorcery (sorcery that the jealous person pays a third party to commit on his behalf) in that the assailants are assumed to be people the victims cannot see, know, or remember. In fact, raskols and gangs nearly always wear masks during attacks. I heard raskols describe themselves as 'wild men' who sleep by day and roam the forests at night. Again, following the pattern of traditional sorcery, raskols maintain an existence that is hidden from the rest of society, and they are feared as the instrument of the destructive forces that stem from jealousy and thwarted desire for wealth that has been seen on the skin of others (see Wardlow 2002b).

Orokaiva moral concern over jealousy and competition is also charged by a contradiction of its own, namely that between the value Orokaiva place on the assumption that all persons are autonomous and equal (at least within age-sex groupings), and the value they place on rising above one's peers in the interconnected domains of wealth, gardening, authority, and prestige. This contradiction is intensified when it comes to the forms of wealth associated with whitemen. As discussed above, whitemen's things are more various, longer lasting, and harder to hide than traditional wealth objects, creating new desires, more types of inequality, and stronger competitive impulses. Traditional Orokaiva society has specific social mechanisms for dealing with the tensions that arise from the contradiction between egalitarian and competitive values (see also Munn 1986). All of the mechanisms that Orokaiva use for managing inequality depend upon

an awareness that traditional hierarchical relationships involve reciprocity and reversal over time. In feasting, for example, at the very moment
when one man displays himself as more beautiful and wealthier than his
peers, he also compensates them for acknowledging his superior status by
giving them a share in the wealth that elevates him above them; in so doing
he begins the process of reducing himself in status, making it possible for
his peers to reverse the hierarchical relationship and one day outdo him.
But the hierarchical relationships associated with whitemen's customs are
not so flexible and episodic. Owning a manufactured-materials house;
having a university education; receiving a regular paycheck from a steady
job: these western manifestations of wealth are not so easily redistributed
or reversed, and will continue to provoke desires that cannot be satisfactorily cooled.

Orokaiva themselves see the presence of whitemen's things as exacer-
bating the problem of jealousy and competition in their society. They realize, as do Tari people in the PNG Highlands, that "there is just too much to
desire" now that people sport wristwatches, leather boots, sunglasses,
portable generators, and four-wheel-drive SUVs on their skins, and now
that in the town "people are thrown together in public spaces—church,
market, roads, stores—where they are more likely to see what other people
have" (Wardlow 1998, 5). On the whole, it seems fair to say that what
Orokaiva confront today is a widening and diversifying of inequality, and
this is a phenomenon well known to come hand in hand with capitalist
development. But to Orokaiva, this widening and diversifying of inequality
cannot be the root cause accounting for their poverty. After all, whitemen
have far more wealth than do Orokaiva, and yet that wealth apparently does
not arouse jealousy or create ill will among *them*, provoking the destruction
of their wealth by their peers. In other words, Orokaiva do not see the root
cause of jealousy as the wealth itself. Indeed, Orokaiva are quite delighted
by the possibility of owning an iron-roofed house, a motor vehicle, or
colorful store-bought goods. Instead, the fact that whitemen have what
Orokaiva themselves do not—an ability to remain bright without undermining one another's wealth—suggests that the cause of their poverty relative to whitemen must be some moral failing in Orokaiva themselves. They
therefore conclude that the flaw giving rise to their own problems is one
with which whitemen are not beset, and which differentiates them fundamentally from whitemen.

At times, people speak as if their self-undermining social problems
would be resolved if they only had bright white skin themselves. To
Orokaiva, the color of the skin is not an immutable characteristic of

individuals, but rather one that can in principle be transformed.[25] They observe that babies are born with light skin that darkens as they grow, and that when burned their black skin reveals a layer of light—almost white—skin beneath (Bashkow 2000b, 135). They also believe that the spirits of dead people sometimes return to life in white-skinned form (see chapter 2). During my fieldwork I was asked many times whether, at the time of the Second Coming, Papua New Guineans' 'bad' black skins would peel away to reveal 'good' white skins underneath, so that their bodies would become bright like whitemen and they would thus presumably live with one another in harmony, managing to avoid the problem of jealousy among themselves the way whitemen seem to be able to.

Another explanation that Orokaiva advance for why whitemen are free from the problem of jealousy hinges on the presumed unifying effects of Christianity, which, notwithstanding some vague awareness that other religions exist, is generally assumed to be the universal religion of whitemen (Bashkow 2000b). Orokaiva Christianity is intensely focused on achieving social harmony, which can only succeed if jealousy and willful desire are replaced by cooperation, good will, and obedience. Unfortunately, Orokaiva always seem to find themselves falling short of these ideals (see also Robbins 2004a). As the original bearers of the faith, however, whitemen are presumed to be better able to follow a 'Christian way of life,' and so to stamp out the negative impulses and willfulness that Orokaiva still wrestle with. As I often heard emphasized in sermons, Jesus was a whiteman, and what the missionaries brought to Orokaiva was 'light' (*usasa*). Among Orokaiva, as elsewhere, images of brightness and luminosity are emphasized in Christian discourse. Moreover, whitemen are known not to practice sorcery and are believed to be immune to sorcery's effects. People generally attribute this immunity to the superior power of Jesus, in whom whitemen believe, over sorcerers, whose evil power Orokaiva Christians—including priests—acknowledge to also be quite real (see also Barker 1990).

But the most important explanation that I heard Orokaiva offer for their poverty relative to whitemen is the entire system described above, that of sight leading to desire, jealousy, and ultimately the dismantling of wealth. When they reflect on their own society, Orokaiva perceive interrelationships and forms of coherence that they objectify—much as anthropologists do—in ideas of their own culture (*kaiva kastam, kaiva ta ari*) that are crystallized in the contrasts they draw between their own and whitemen's culture (*taupa kastam, taupa ta ari*). These crystallizations of cultural self-consciousness are various and have both positive and negative forms, reflecting the distinct sets of values that Orokaiva bring to bear in different contexts of their lives. Thus, whitemen's culture is evaluated negatively in relation to Orokaivas' ideals of open-handedness in gift exchange and hospitality, an area in which Orokaiva are justifiably proud of their own generosity. But Orokaiva are greatly troubled by the prevalence of jealousy and their inability to sustain social harmony, and these have the status of serious, destructive problems in Orokaivas' own critical discourse about the moral failings of their society. Arising as they do from the fundamental tension between Orokaivas' egalitarian and competitive values, these problems are well motivated; they express a basic contradiction inherent in Orokaiva society.

In effect, the fact that Orokaiva find themselves unable to sustain the brightness they see worn so easily by whitemen leads them to view their own cultural patterns as a moral failing or "sickness" that is the reason for their poverty. I heard this idea articulated many times in conversations with Orokaiva, and I will sum up this ethnographic discussion by stitching together the extraordinarily clear words of Peddy Orovo, a middle-aged Orokaiva friend, as he explained to me what a mare's nest of sorcery and social ills I had entered in becoming fully active in village exchange. The root cause of sorcery, Peddy explained, using the English word "unbalance," was inequality:

> Some people have more, others less. If you have big things—maybe your pigs are big, or your taro, or your store, or you have a big house—those big things of yours will be ensorcelled, and you will fall. The thought of the sorcerer will be: others will surpass us....
>
> Pigs are hard to hide; they are clearly visible under the house. But money should be kept hidden. If people see my money, I am showing off, and that invites trouble. Among you whites, people leave money right out on the table, and it's all right. But here [in the village] you cannot even leave ten kina sitting out and visible because if someone asks for it and you do not give it, you can wind up dead. So we hide our valuables and all our desirable things. That stuff may be there [hidden away], but we go about as if we have nothing (*irae-sirae*)....
>
> Sometimes it is not even necessary for a person to practice sorcery actively. Simply the fact that he carries some grievance within himself can make the object of his anger sick. Another thing that takes the place of sorcery is that wild bush men [raskols, criminals] plan an attack and then hold us up at home. These raskols are the new sorcery.
>
> Because of sorcery and raskols, instead of PNG developing, we live fear-

fully in darkness, and the land has withered. 'Withering' is something that happens to taro, but in *development*, it means that although we should by now be living in good houses and so on, just like a taro plant that withers, we cannot *change* [complete the transformation into maturity]. Or we might start to change, but then our child or our wife will die, and we will say to ourselves, it is because I made an *improvement* in myself and someone became jealous and made sorcery against me.

So people stop making improvements and just stay poor. Many *business* men do this. They leave *business* [completely] and just stay poor because of [fear of] sorcery. There is only *one way* in which we can really protect ourselves from these problems, and that is to *stop business*. By keeping ourselves very small, we *save* our *family* from harm.…

These are not mere stories. They are a real sickness (*korere*) that afflicts our *businesses* in the village. You white people stay safely up in your offices. But we go about down on the ground in a state of constant fear.

This last image of whitemen remaining safely up in offices, with Orokaiva below, brings together many of the ideas discussed here, including the idea that Orokaiva are invisible to whitemen (i.e., whitemen do not even notice Orokaiva or they would pity them and share their wealth with them). It also suggests an association between keeping hidden and the production and maintenance of whitemen's wealth. Orokaiva generally think of whitemen as people who spend most of their time indoors, unlike Orokaiva themselves, and Peddy is not the only person to have remarked to me that whitemen carry out most of their wealth-producing activities indoors where they are out of the sight and so less likely to provoke others' jealousy. That wealth magically multiplies in hidden places, quite like girls hidden away in seclusion grow fat and bright, and animals deep in the forest grow and multiply, may also be seen as contributing to the wealth whitemen achieve "up in their offices."

A more disturbing resonance of the image is its implication of segregation and arrogance. As we saw in chapter 2, segregation has long been an important part of Papua New Guineans' experience of race, as it has been for people in every other modern colonial situation throughout the world (Kennedy 1945; Balandier 1966 [1951]). But in conversations I had with many Orokaiva about this topic, I was struck by their forgiving and strongly naturalizing attitudes toward racial segregation. A common analogy people drew was between whitemen and the members of a clan: they like to stick together. Only in conversations with Orokaiva intellectuals (all but one of whom had been to university) did I hear segregation discussed not as mere clannishness but rather as a structure that systematically perpetuates inequality.[26]

Although they knew that Australian aborigines and American Indians had been dispossessed of their lands by whitemen, most Orokaiva I spoke with clearly did not see whitemen's countries like Australia and America as characterized by widespread racial segregation or economic inequality. In part, this view can be attributed to Orokaiva villagers' own historical experience of racial prejudice, which was not unmixed, and which today, in the postcolonial context, is remembered with nostalgic selectivity. Overshadowing in historical memory the routine prejudice villagers faced under colonialism are dramatic episodes of their history, like World War II and the international relief effort after the eruption of Mt. Lamington in 1951. During World War II, Orokaiva were impressed to see black soldiers in the American army, and they detected no discrimination between white and black American troops; in their eyes, the black Americans had high positions, like tending supply stores.

But the main reason why Orokaiva tend to view whitemen's home countries as places without serious problems of segregation or inequality derives from the fact that their aim in speaking of whitemen's countries is rarely to criticize or reform them but instead to hold them up as a foil for criticizing and reforming themselves. Hence, people commonly expressed the view that whitemen enjoyed a prosperity in their home places that was collective and shared—exactly like the prosperity Orokaiva wish for themselves. Rhetorically, I was often asked if my country had poor people, with the assumed answer being that, no, in my country no one was poor, and that those who could not provide for themselves were looked after by government welfare. I was also asked on many occasions whether my country had problems with raskols: this too was a rhetorical question. Such questions were not really concerned with establishing the facts about another society far away. Rather, they were intended to point up the terrible problems faced by Orokaiva themselves: that they had to work hard to grow their food (no government welfare helped them) and they suffered immeasurably from jealousy, sorcery, and raskol crime.[27] When I answered such questions by insisting that poverty and crime were in fact fixtures in my home country as well, and when I went on to describe them, people listened politely and were tolerant of my taking the conversation they had started in a new direction, but eventually they would work the discussion back to their initial point of view, which was that 'You whitemen are lucky people blessed by God. You don't have problems like we do.'

Whitemen can be soft without having to do vigorous work because they enjoy a richer cultural inheritance and more abundant ancestral favor than Orokaiva. They can be bright, attracting attention to themselves, without having their wealth undermined by others, which is the situation Orokaiva find themselves in whenever they exceed their peers in wealth and brightness. Thus, the inferiority that Orokaiva perceive when they compare themselves with whitemen reflects an interpretation of issues of physical appearance and material wealth in terms of the moral concerns that are most pressing for Orokaiva themselves.

Ultimately, both the softness and the brightness of whitemen indicate a superior ability to achieve social harmony, which Orokaiva believe to be the precondition for creating and maintaining wealth. Thus, Orokaiva consistently emphasize the creation of social harmony when engaging in those activities that are associated with development. But because the kinds of inequalities that lead to social discord are inevitably widened and exacerbated as a concomitant effect of precisely such activities, Orokaiva are not only stalled in their efforts to develop but also continually confronted with their own moral deficiency. Their persistent failure to develop confirms for Orokaiva that their inability to maintain social harmony is a destructive cultural characteristic, and the need to somehow overcome it is one of the most prevalent self-critical themes of their discourse on whitemen. In projecting onto the whiteman other those virtues Orokaiva most desire but are unable to attain, this discourse is a tragic one. In effect, it throws Orokaiva continually back onto those problems in their own society that are among the deepest lodged and most intractable. But we should recognize that there are still worse kinds of tragedy that befall indigenous cultures. In many other PNG societies, people now seek to repudiate all those parts of their traditional cultures that seem to them to stand in the way of a complete embrace of western Christianity and modernity; in so doing, they exchange their traditional notions of moral economy and the ethics of sociality for individualistic values of desire and consumption endorsed by western frameworks of economy and religion (Robbins 2004a; Knauft 2002b; Gewertz and Errington 1998; LiPuma 2000; Kulick 1992). When Orokaiva project the basic premises of their own morality onto the whiteman other, they are at least maintaining the repertoire of their own cultural values, and instead of accommodating themselves completely to a foreign sense of what is right, they in many ways reappropriate the influence of globalization according to their own noncapitalist ethos. How long can this last? How long will Orokaiva practices of seeing continue to be culturally formed so as to militate against the toleration of material inequality as a "natural" fact of life? Who could dare say? In the meantime, Orokaiva suffer from as well as enjoy their own culture's moral economy, which in making jealousy and fractiousness such intractable obstacles to the accumulation of lasting wealth, empowers them to resist the vast, enduring inequalities capitalism promotes. What doesn't destroy them keeps them poor.

5. The Foods of Whitemen

Tell me what you eat, and I will tell you who you are.

JEAN ANTHELME BRILLAT-SAVARIN, *The Physiology of Taste*

I thought that if I ate the food of the area I was visiting that I might assimilate the point of view of the people there. As if the point of view was somehow in the food.

ROBERT WILSON AND DAVID BYRNE, *"Social Studies"*[1]

In a 1990 experiment, [University of Pennsylvania psychologist Paul] Rozin tested people's implicit belief in the adage "you are what you eat" by giving several hundred American college students one of two versions of a short vignette describing the "Chandorans," an imaginary tribal society that hunts marine turtles and wild boars. Half the group read that the Chandorans ate wild boar and hunted turtles for their shells; the others read that the tribe ate turtles and hunted boars for their tusks. The students were then asked to rate members of the culture for personality traits and physical attributes that could be associated with boarness (aggressiveness and likely to have beards, for instance) and turtleness (good swimmers). Those who read that the Chandorans ate boar rated them high on the aggressive scale, while those who thought of the Chandorans as turtle-eaters rated them good swimmers. "We know 'you are what you eat' is false," explains Rozin, but despite sophisticated rational and conceptual faculties, "it nonetheless creeps into our judgment."

PETER NICHOLS, *"Arbiter of Taste"*

In the preceding chapters we have seen how the qualities Orokaiva attribute to whitemen ethnocentrically refract local historical realities and present-day experiences through the lens of Orokaivas' own cultural ideas and values. The stereotype of whitemen as light, bright, and soft is substantiated for Orokaiva in their own development activities that are identified with whitemen, and contrasted symbolically with activities such as gardening and feasting that they identify as culturally "their own." By constructing whitemen in these terms, Orokaiva project the encompassing order of their own moral economy onto the wider world of globalization and development. This is of course not to say that Orokaiva can free themselves of uncongenial outside influences by simply reshaping them in any way they please. But part of what the Orokaiva discourse about whitemen's lightness, brightness, and softness is concerned with is precisely the intractability of whitemen to the conditions that are normally placed on human action in the Orokaiva world, conditions that Orokaiva understand in profoundly moral terms. Even so, the valuation of whitemen is neither uniformly good nor bad, but is irreducibly ambivalent, with differently valued qualities foregrounded depending on people's aims in different situations.

The Orokaiva construction of whitemen also exemplifies one of the hallmarks of all cultural constructions of race, namely an enigmatic and troubling durability in the face of anomalous instances. Just as familiar western constructions of Arabs, Asians, or African Americans remain influential despite widespread recognition that these involve simplifications and distortions, the Orokaiva construction of whitemen, too, is robust, persisting even where counterevidenced by confrontation with the actual variety and complexity of whites, westerners, or other foreigners. The durability of racial stereotypes is dramatized vividly in Orokaiva ideas about whitemen's foods, which are epitomized for Orokaiva by boiled white rice and tinned meat and fish. Through the study of these foods, their associated qualities, and their uses in Orokaiva society, we will see another crucial reason why racial stereotypes can be so robust: they are not actually representations of groups of *persons*, as they are generally assumed to be (even by their critics). Rather, they symbolically identify racial categories with abstract *qualities* such as lightness, *activities* such as business, and, in the case at hand, *objects* such as foods that are detachable from persons. In the example of whitemen's foods, we see how a set of objects associated with whitemen is displayed, exchanged, consumed, and interpreted by Orokaiva themselves, substantiating the stereotype in ways that have no need for, and so cannot be disconfirmed by, the example of actual white persons.

Orokaiva Indigenous Foods Are Heavy, Hard, and Strong

Orokaiva staple foods are the starches taro, sweet potatoes, yams, and cooking bananas. These starches, which make up the bulk of what people eat, are called the 'main food' (*indari be*) or simply the 'food' (*indari*). These starches are ordinarily enlivened by a flavoring relish of meat, fish, or green vegetables called the 'greens' (*ina*), or if it includes fish or meat, the 'meat' (*o*). An ordinary meal for an adult consists of a large bowl of boiled taro or sweet potatoes topped by two or three spoonfuls of vegetable relish. Orokaiva consider their main starch to be taro (*ba*) and their main meat pork (*o*). For Orokaiva, taro and pork together are the paradigm of a proper square meal, so that the expression 'pork-taro' (*o-ba*) is used to mean 'food in general' or 'basic subsistence,' with a sense like the English idioms "bread and butter" or "meat and potatoes."

There is no prescribed number of meals in the day, though it is rare for people to eat fewer than two. Morning meals and meals cooked in the gardens during work there are usually very plain, perhaps bananas roasted on the fire or unpeeled boiled sweet potatoes, without any relish. For their evening meals, women try to obtain at minimum some young tree leaves to cook with salt as a relish. At fancier meals foods are cooked in coconut milk, and delicacies like taro flavored with ginger, and yam and coconut soup are served. At feasts, huge quantities of tubers and meat are steamed in pit ovens heated by fired stones. Over the course of the year, Orokaiva eat a great variety of plant foods, both wild and culti-vated, including breadfruits, squashes, pandanus fruits, pitpit (the heart of a fibrous stalk related to sugar cane), corn, beans, fruits, and many types of leafy greens. The animals they eat are similarly varied, including bandicoots, wallabies, tree kangaroos, birds, fruit bats, lizards, snakes, river shrimps, snails, and many kinds of insects. However, animal protein tends to be scarce and is highly prized. Most households raise pigs and chickens, but these are not slaughtered for routine consumption. Rather, people save their domesticated animals for use in honoring guests, mak-ing ritual payments, or giving away at feasts. Increasingly, Orokaiva also sell the pigs and chickens they raise to others, who will use them in turn for these same purposes.

Along with pigs, indigenous garden foods are important objects of exchange. They are transacted at feasts as well as in numerous daily con-texts where people give each other presents of raw and cooked food. In the ethnographic literature, Orokaiva are best known for their elaborate system of food exchange, which plays an important role in constituting social rela-tionships and social groupings (Schwimmer 1973; Iteanu 1983a; Newton 1985; see also Williams 1930; Crocombe and Hogbin 1963; Rimoldi 1966). One of the hardest things foreigners living in Orokaiva communities have to adjust to is the pervasive expectation that positive sentiments like affec-tion, apology, and thanks will be expressed through tangible gifts, most com-monly food. The importance Orokaiva attach to food exchange can hardly be overstated. Foods are the most important medium in which Orokaiva communicate social sentiments, build and maintain relationships, and represent their social selves to others. Food gifts are considered a medium of communication that is more valuable than talk, since talk is distrusted as potentially duplicitous, deceitful, and dissimulative; in effect, talk is cheap. Food gifts, by contrast, imply an undeniable material sacrifice on the part of the giver, and real material benefit on the part of the recipient. Gifts of both raw and cooked foods are common. A woman might bring some raw yams to her brother or sister-in-law as an affirmation of her affection; a family might send a guest on his way with a hand of bananas and several raw taros. Bowls of cooked food, like boiled taro with greens, are often delivered from one household to another in the early evening; indeed, as Eric Schwimmer observes, the exchange of cooked taro (and other cooked foods) between households is an "almost infallible index of intimacy" that symbolizes an extension of commensality (Schwimmer 1973, 112). The management of all this giving and receiving of food is an important part of Orokaiva family life.

Like people everywhere, Orokaiva have an elaborate understanding of the foods they eat, especially their main foods, taro and pork, which they regard in many ways as being like people. Taro plants are believed to have humanlike kinship relationships and friendships, to speak and understand Orokaiva, and to have a growth cycle resembling the human life cycle. Pigs, too, are held to understand human speech and are referred to using kinship terms that place them within their owners' families. Orokaiva do not eat the pigs they themselves have raised, the prospect being as abominable as eating one's own children. Men and women cry when their pig 'children' are seized and bound to be given away at feasts—in exchange for other pigs that they *can* eat because they were raised by other families. While we might say that Orokaiva ascribe humanlike qualities to taro and pigs, from the Orokaiva perspective it would be more accurate to say that the nature of taro and pigs is given, while that of humans is formed by the nature of their foods. Thus, Orokaiva see themselves as deriving particular qualities from the taro and pork they habitually eat. As we will see, the qualities of Orokaiva that derive from their taro and pork contrast markedly with those that whitemen are seen to derive from the consumption of their foods.

Producing food is the central pursuit around which the everyday lives of most Orokaiva villagers revolve, so they know their indigenous foods as living entities. They know the particular fruits that their game animals eat, their tracks through the forest, their sounds, and the places they can be found. They know the types of land on which their food plants thrive, their means of propagation, their seasons, and the insects that live upon them. The particular behavioral characteristics and patterns of growth of the animals and plants they eat are often carried over to their ideas about the resulting foods and their effects upon the bodies of those who consume them.

To Orokaiva, taro is a heavy food that is grown on heavy lands. The edible part of the taro plant is a bulbous root that when peeled and cooked resembles an extremely dense and chewy nutty-tasting potato. In cultivating taro, Orokaiva aim to produce as heavy and hard a tuber as possible. The ideal land for growing taro is dark, old-growth forest where the soil is black and heavy with moisture and rich with nutrients (*gamo*). Such land is prepared by cutting the undergrowth and trees, allowing the sun to dry the debris, and burning it. The point of the burning is not to produce fertilizing ash (though that may be one effect); indeed, in former times, "there was a tendency to sweep the ashes together to keep them out of the way" (Williams 1928, 134). Rather, the burning is primarily intended to kill weeds and to leave the land 'clean' and open to the sun. It is desirable for the topsoil's surface to be dry, so that when the taro is planted, the roots will descend, seeking the water that is retained in the heavier, darker soil below. The taro seed or rhizome (*ba bere, ba be*) is a small piece of stalk that rots away after new shoots emerge from it; in time, the plant creates a root 'body' underground by drawing solidifying substance from the ground. Eventually the plant sends up several vigorous leaf stalks, supporting very large, heart-shaped leaves. The leaves and stalks commonly grow as tall as a man stands, but after about seven months, they thin out and contract, so that only two or three short stalks and hand-sized leaves are left. The aging taro, people say, thus shrinks just like an elderly person. It condenses all of its strength into its underground body, which is thereby hardened. Hardness is the main criterion for determining the readiness of the enlarged root for harvest. Orokaiva test for this by pushing with their toes against the top of the tuber at the base of the stalk. When the taro is so strongly rooted in the ground that it cannot be moved, then it is ready to harvest and eat.

After eating taro, Orokaiva feel full, their stomachs pleasantly 'tight' and their bodies contentedly heavy with tiredness. It is said that taro's heaviness temporarily 'pushes down' the people who eat it, leaving them unable to do vigorous work and instead wanting to sleep. It is by inducing sleep that taro makes the body grow, since as we saw in the previous chapter, things grow only when hidden, and children's bodies, too, are thought to lengthen and grow only while sleeping. Food like taro that is heavy and hard is valued not only for inducing sleep (which itself, like other forms of heaviness, is necessary and positive at appropriate times), but also for 'holding' the sleeper's stomach for the duration of the night, keeping it from 'complaining' and 'biting' so that the sleeper is not constantly being awakened. It is an Orokaiva truism that sleep comes hard when the stomach is empty. (Evening or late-night meals are often spoken of as 'eating in order to sleep.') The postprandial feeling of heaviness should be dissipated by a night's sleep, but people who are weak can be so overwhelmed by taro's heaviness that they become sick (*ambure*).

Pork too is considered a heavy food, even heavier than taro, and it is thought to be full of qualities of 'motion' (*wasiri*) and 'strength' (*ivo*) that characterize a living pig. Village pigs are powerful animals that roam widely in the forest searching for wild foods and raiding people's gardens. The motion and strength of the living pig are understood to produce valued qualities of 'tightness' (*turari*) and 'hardness' (*gaiha*) in the pigs' flesh. Orokaiva often build pens for their pigs to prevent them from being speared by others whose gardens the pigs would despoil, but pigs are never kept permanently penned, since that would have the unwanted effect of causing their flesh to 'hang loosely.' In order for a pig's flesh to be tight, it must sometimes be allowed to roam freely, even if this would put the pig at risk of being speared for ruining other people's gardens.

Because Orokaiva cook chunks of pork by steaming them in earth ovens or boiling them in pots (often repeatedly, at intervals, as a form of preservation), and because the meat of animals that range freely does tend to be tough (especially in comparison to the tender meat of penned animals to which western consumers have become accustomed), the pork Orokaiva eat is indeed a very dense, hard, leathery substance. As with taro, eating pork is held to make the stomach feel tight and well satisfied, leaving the body heavy and tired. At the same time, however, eating pork is said to fill people with the living pig's quality of 'motion.' People illustrated this quality with a gesture of pumping their arms in front of them rapidly, as if they had just received an infusion of strength and vitality. Those who are 'full of motion' from having eaten pork are also considered dangerous to young taro plants, which unlike mature taro are thought to be restless and themselves all too full of motion, very much like young men, so that the living parts of young taros can all too easily be 'lured away' from gardens, killing the plants, should any additional quality of motion be communicated to them.[2]

Pork's powerful qualities of heaviness and motion are harnessed in the symbolism of feasting. Orokaiva, like other Melanesians, regard feasts as occasions for "fighting with food" (Young 1971); they sometimes liken their feast foods to ammunition and weaponry. Steven once called the foods he was gathering to distribute at a feast the "knives, guns, hand grenades, bombs, and machine guns" he would use against his opponents, who were the guests slated to receive the food. Within such a feast food arsenal, pork is the heavy artillery. When pigs are being carried to feasts, usually suspended from horizontal poles that two or more men shoulder, their heaviness is extolled in songs that liken them to the large boulders in riverbeds that only river-floods can move. I often heard it said that feast-givers use magic to increase the heaviness of their feast foods, so that each guest will be satisfied by a smaller amount of food than normal, leaving more food to feed others, and making all the guests so preternaturally heavy that they will be unable to resist sleeping for days on end. The heaviness that pork induces symbolically vanquishes those who eat it. Like taro, but more so, pork 'presses down' (*kikira ari*) feast food recipients, so that the feast-giver 'rises up' (*vihari*) over them.

Pork's quality of motion is symbolically emphasized in the way the meat is presented at feasts. Unlike other feast foods that are distributed to recipients in piles lined up on the ground, pork gifts may be thrown down vigorously from the feasting platform as recipients are called up (see plate 22), and as described in the preceding chapter, traditional dancers at feasts are sometimes literally pelted with pieces of pork that constitute payment for their dancing. Such projectiles of pork contribute to a feasting aesthetic in which the food gifts ideally 'explode out' (*pejehe*) dramatically from the feast's center, with a great momentum that will carry its 'sound' (*havi*) to distant places—and along with it, the feast-giver's name. Garden foods alone, people say, 'lack sound' and therefore the capacity to create fame. As Steven once advised me, 'taro by itself won't send up your name, but it will if you give it with pork.' The strength and motion that pork acquires by association with the living pig make it an ideal vehicle for expanding a man's 'renown' (*duru*), publicizing his name and his accomplishments in feasting, and thereby expanding his social influence (see Munn 1986). As one man explained: 'the roaming of the [living] pig spreads its owner's name, since people see it and think of him. In just this way, pork that is distributed at a feast carries a man's name to faraway places.'

By no means are all indigenous foods considered heavy and hard. But those that are not are not thought to make the body grow, and they do not make appropriate feast gifts. An example is sweet potatoes (Tok Pisin: *kaukau*; Orokaiva: *kai puteite*), which in recent decades have become the single most important calorie source in villagers' diets due to their short time to harvest and the ease with which large yields of the tubers are produced (Bashkow 1999, 124). Sweet potatoes are normally planted as a second crop in harvested taro gardens where the original heaviness of the soil has already been partially depleted, and because of this, sweet potatoes do not become a particularly heavy food. Nor are sweet potato plants personified and attributed underground travels as are young taro plants; without such motion they do not become a hard food, but rather a soft, watery food that does not hold the stomach for long. Orokaiva observe that after an evening meal of sweet potatoes people soon feel hungry again and awaken frequently to urinate. This is consistent with the sweet potato's relative softness, which makes sweet potatoes suitable for young children and others too weak to eat taro—though since the tubers do not lead to strong sleep, they are not thought to produce much growth of the body. In effect, sweet potatoes are attributed little capacity to expand a person's body or renown, and they are consequently never given as feast gifts. Instead, they are used as a day-to-day food that 'merely fills the belly.'

Other indigenous foods are likewise evaluated as more or less heavy, hard, dry, and strong, although the meaning of such qualities is different for starchy main foods than it is for flavoring relishes. Within the category of starchy main foods, it is the heavier, harder, drier foods that are valued most highly, while weaker, more watery, and less filling (i.e., less heavy) foods are disparaged as 'wet.' Thus, yams, which are esteemed as a heavy, hard growth food in the same way as taro, are proudly given as feast gifts, while the wet, soft foods sago and squashes usually are not.[3] Similarly, within the broad range of cooking bananas that Orokaiva cultivate, the varieties that have a harder, denser flesh are valued more highly than those with a softer, lighter flesh, and they are considered both better growth foods and more presentable and prestigious feast gifts.

Within the category of relish foods, however, which are expected to provide the greasiness and moistness that 'dry' starches lack, the porklike qualities of motion and strength are not felt to be contradictory with the quality of wetness, but are valued alongside it. Orokaiva do not employ complex flavor categories and are interested in few culinary subtleties, but they do appreciate the greasy 'wetness' of local delights such as tasty pork fat, creamy fat sago grubs, and coconut cream, all of which are said to 'wet the throat,' leaving it agreeably slippery. People also like relishes that are 'juicy,' with a flavorful, salty soup, like young leaves of a wild fig tree stewed in pungent traditional salt made from the ashes of burnt vines. In relishes, qualities of wetness and saltiness are valued for pleasing the palate, evoking 'interest' (hanahana) in eating, and balancing out the contrasting qualities of dryness and blandness of the starchy main foods. Main foods served without flavoring relish are overly dry and produce an unbalanced meal. As a matter of principle, it is achieving a balance in

contrasting qualities like dry/wet, hard/soft, and heavy/light that constitutes proper eating and sound nutrition in Orokaiva terms. Since the
healthy adult body is seen as mostly hard, it is a large plate of hard main
food with just a small amount of wet relish that makes for a proper, bal-
anced meal. As we will see in the next section, this balance is confounded
in what Orokaiva see as the characteristics of the foods of whitemen.

Whitemen's Foods Are Light, Wet, and Weak

Whitemen's foods are commodity foods that Orokaiva buy with money in
stores. They are not crops like corn or "Chinese taro" (a genus of taro, each
plant of which has up to ten cormels, or edible roots) that Orokaiva know as
introduced by whitemen but that they themselves cultivate. Rather, they
are foods that come to Orokaiva from the world of money, with which
whitemen are identified. The whitemen's foods most commonly seen in villages are packaged rice, packaged salt, canned fish and meat, flour, navy
hardtack crackers, ramen noodles, cheese puffs (for children), instant coffee, leaf tea, refined sugar, powdered milk, and canned evaporated milk. In
Orokaiva, these are called 'store foods' (*sitova donda*) or 'whitemen's foods'
(*taupa-ta donda*). Although Orokaiva assume that whitemen, like themselves, enjoy a great variety of foods, they also assume that whitemen have a
main staple starch and a main meat like their own taro and pork. The main
starch attributed to whitemen is white rice, which Orokaiva call *raisi* ('rice')
or *ombavuju* (lit., 'maggots'). Whitemen's main meats are canned mackerel
chunks, called *tinpis* (Tok Pisin: 'tinned fish'), *umo o gerikari* (Orokaiva:
'packaged/preserved fish'), or simply *umo o* ('fish'), and canned corned beef,
called *tinmit* (Tok Pisin: 'tinned meat') or *o miti* (Orokaiva: 'meat'). From
this point on I will follow standard usage in Papua New Guinea English and
refer to canned mackerel as "tinfish," to canned corned beef as "tinmeat."

That whitemen's foods are epitomized for Orokaiva in rice, tinfish, and
tinmeat reflects the important role these foods had in the colonial history of
the region. In Orokaiva country, as elsewhere in the colonial Territories of
Papua and New Guinea, rice, tinmeat, and later tinfish were the main foods
carried by colonial patrols. On inland journeys over rugged terrain, rice
was the favored staple because it was highly compact, did not bruise or
spoil, and was easy to cook. In addition to rice, Europeans ate canned food
and hardtack biscuits. Police constables received tinmeat with their rice,
while native carriers were fed rice almost exclusively. As the patrol officer
Ivan Champion wrote in a memoir about the provisioning of an expedition
elsewhere in Papua: "For the carriers rice is the food always chosen because

it is compact, easy to carry, and needs very little preparation for cooking; important factors with natives. The maximum load of a carrier is 40 lbs. of rice. But, of course, there are other things to carry besides the carriers' food—[tent] flys, the Europeans' food, police food, articles of trade, and various other details of camp equipment. A party comprising thirty carriers can exist . . . for a fortnight on the food that it can carry" (Champion 1978 [1932], 10). As the passage makes clear, rice, tinmeat, and tinfish were crucial in enabling whites—not only colonial patrol officers but also labor recruiters, missionaries, and other whites on the local scene—to traverse and exert their control across distances. In effect, rice and tinned protein were crucial contributors to whitemen's mobility and 'lightness.'

Histories of contact tend to emphasize guns, tools, and other durables as the primary media by which indigenous peoples came to know the nature and the mettle of whitemen. Yet from the perspective of Melanesian peoples, it was food that constituted the most salient medium of intercultural communication given indigenous notions of the person, truth, and knowledge. Like other Melanesians, Orokaiva tend to be suspicious of surface appearances, since these are known to deceive; vernacular notions of 'truth' (*be*) emphasize inner contents and immanent potentials. A thing can only be known truly by the 'effects' (*be*) or 'fruits' (also *be*) that emerge from within it, as a seed (*be*) is known by the plant it produces, and by its fruit, which contains the next seed. Similarly, a person's true nature is known by what emerges from his or her *jo* or 'inside.' As we have seen, the jo contains the person's inner thoughts and intentions, which later actions reveal, and it is also identified with the interior spaces of people's gardens and houses, where their food crops and belongings are normally stored, in effect hidden. Of all the things that a person can give, it is foods, which can be eaten by others and internalized within their own jos, that are the most convincing. Orokaiva epistemology is at once a gastronomy in that acquaintance by sight is trumped by confirmation through ingestion: seeing may be 'knowing' (*kiari*), but eating is believing. When Orokaiva saw that rice and tinmeat were the foods whites carried with them from the faraway hidden places from whence they came, hiding them in their patrol boxes and storerooms under lock and key, it only made sense for Orokaiva to identify these foods with the whitemen's innermost nature. When whites fed these foods to the carriers, policemen, and villagers who helped them, they were thereby revealing themselves to Orokaiva, showing what was inside of them, who they were.

This logic of gastronomic acquaintance is reflected in the most important Orokaiva stories about first encounters with whitemen, such as the legends of the original ancestress Sipa and the first village constable Uripa (Bashkow 1996). In such stories, the Orokaiva are initially confused and afraid of the whitemen who visit them—until the whitemen give them salt, sugar, and rice to taste, and they like it. During my fieldwork, I heard many stories about Orokaiva relationships with whitemen in different periods, and nearly all include episodes in which Orokaiva receive gifts of white-men's foods. For example, stories about Orokaiva plantation laborers in colonial times reveal little about their working conditions beyond the gen-eral fact that the conditions were hard. But the stories invariably enumer-ate the whitemen's foods—rice, salt, tinmeat, tinfish, sugar, tea, and canned milk—that the men proudly took home to distribute in their villages along with the trade goods they were paid for their work. Similarly, when vil-lagers told stories about their former village constables, they would dwell on nostalgically constructed politico-culinary events like colonial Christ-mases when the constables were reportedly entrusted with the keys to government storerooms and asked by the whitemen in charge to distribute large amounts of rice, tinfish, and tinmeat. Orokaiva World War II tales emphasize moments when foreign soldiers gave them food gifts like large (mess-hall size) cans of beef stew. Finally, stories of the 1951 Mount Lamington eruption stress the period that Orokaiva survivors spent in evacuation camps, where white aid workers are fondly remembered for the rice they doled out alongside blankets and tools (see Schwimmer 1969, 66).

Today, an average of 350 tons of rice is shipped into Oro Province each month, suggesting an annual per capita consumption of about 40 kilograms (Bashkow 1999, 129). Orokaiva villagers consume significantly less rice than that, with the per-person average for adults in Agenehambo being on the order of forty to one hundred rice meals per year. The bulk of the rice imported to Oro is consumed by town residents and workers on oil palm plantations, for whom it serves as the staple food, as it does for laborers, prisoners, and boarding students at vocational and high schools. The rice that is sold throughout Papua New Guinea is imported in bulk from Australia, where it accounts for approximately a quarter of national rice exports. It is repackaged in Lae, PNG's industrial city, by the national rice distributor, Trukai Industries, Pty. Ltd. Trukai Industries distributes rice under various brand names, of which the most common is "Trukai," a Tok Pisin coinage meaning 'real food.' Trukai is a fairly low quality, short- and broken-grain white rice packaged in distinctive, bright yellow 20, 10, and 5 kg plastic sacks, as well as in clear plastic bags of 5, 1, and 0.5 kg.[4] The smaller sizes are sold wholesale baled together in stiff plastic. Nearly all the rice consumed in Oro Province arrives by container ship to the Oro Bay wharf and is trucked to a squat yellow building, called the Trukai Industries "Rice Terminal" on Popondetta's outskirts, from which it is distributed to the five Popondetta wholesale traders and from there to local stores. Rice is the cheapest food available in stores, in terms of the numbers of people fed per kina. A kg bag of rice, which can feed five hungry adults, costs the equivalent of less than one U.S. dollar, which is about as cheap as buying sweet potatoes in the public market, and much cheaper than market taro.

Orokaiva attitudes toward eating rice are characterized by a remarkable ambivalence. On the one hand, Orokaiva consider rice a tasty and desirable luxury food. For many villagers, who have limited access to money, eating rice is a special treat, and bags of rice are among the first things villagers buy when they have money to spend. On the other hand, Orokaiva frequently disparage boiled rice as a loose, watery, light food. Unlike taro, they say, rice does not make the stomach feel full and tight, or hold it for a long time. People who have eaten rice, like those who have eaten sweet potatoes, soon feel hungry again, and at night they awaken repeatedly to urinate. This Orokaiva attitude toward rice contrasts with the attitude of many peoples elsewhere in the Pacific and Asia who esteem rice unambiguously as the prototype of satisfying, good food. The ambivalent Orokaiva attitude is not explained by the actual quality of their rice or by their cooking techniques. Orokaiva simply place rice in a covered pot with cold water and boil it until the water has been absorbed. The result is more or less soft depending on the proportion of water that was added (cooks estimate this by eye), but it is basically normal white rice, if at times a little gluey. To understand the ambivalence, we need to look at the symbolism of rice within the larger context of Orokaiva ideas about foods, themselves, and the nature of whitemen.

Ambivalence toward eating rice is most strongly marked among middle-aged men, who consider eating rice unmanly, since as a weak food it is associated with weak people—though at meals where different foods are set out side by side, men usually serve themselves rice before garden foods like taro and sweet potatoes. Women disparage rice less vociferously than men, as do very old people, whose teeth are too weak to chew taro. A few toothless old men laughed and told me straightforwardly that rice was the food they liked to eat best, sometimes adding that when they were younger they preferred taro but now it stuck in their throat. Children like rice unreservedly and adults consider this normal. Adults tell children that they should work hard in school so that they will grow up and get salaried jobs that will enable them to eat rice all the time. When very small children see others eating rice, they frequently begin to cry for it. Often, when adults are not sure why children are crying, they guess that the children are crying because they are hungry for rice.

As a food that is light, rice does not make the body feel heavy or produce the kind of heavy sleep that occasions growth of the body. Yet curiously, rice is thought to result in an even greater growth of the body than heavy indigenous foods like taro that do produce heavy sleep. When I asked people how this could be, some appealed to the word of outside authorities like schoolteachers and health workers, or ascribed the growth to a mysterious substance in rice called "vitamins," much stressed in rice advertising. Others said that although rice is weak and light for adults, it is just right for small children, given that their bodies are small and weak. Most, however, had no explanation but simply cited anecdotes which supported the assertion, naming particular children who grew up to be larger than their peers, ostensibly because they were often fed rice, or they made the general observation that children who are raised in town, where people eat rice all the time, tend to grow up to be larger than children raised on local foods in the village (which is true). The capacity of rice to cause greater physical growth than taro and other indigenous foods, even though it does not produce the kind of heavy sleep that is normally considered essential to growth, gives rice an unnatural quality of lightness which resembles the lightness Orokaiva see as characteristic of whitemen themselves.

The similarity between the lightness of rice and the lightness of whitemen can be understood in part through Orokaiva ideas about rice production. Although these are not as elaborate as their ideas about taro horticulture, people's understandings of rice follow a similar logic, according to which the manifest properties of the food when cooked, and its effects on the body when eaten, reflect the nature which the food came to have through its previous phases. During my fieldwork, I heard people discuss the production of rice in terms of the following images: mechanized farming, international shipments, milling and packaging, sale in stores, and simplicity of cooking, all of which imply qualities of lightness through culturally significant contrasts with the production of heaviness in taro. Many Orokaiva have seen photo and movie images of modern farms in the West where large tractor-combines plow huge, open fields. In such images, Orokaiva are struck by the contrast to their own small taro gardens, which are patches cut from a dark, wet jungle that hems them in on all sides, and they see in the wide openness of the machine-farmed fields that such lands are light: they have been left for a long time exposed to the drying effects of the sun. The rice plant itself also manifests lightness in fruiting on feathery stalks in the air, rather than in heavy, enlarged roots underground, like taro, yams, and sweet potatoes. Orokaiva taro is grown on specific local lands known by name to the people who eat it, and by routinely eating the taro that is harvested from these lands, people are understood to absorb and so come to embody some of those lands' essential qualities, in a process called *manata ari* or *hamo ari* ('habituation' or 'embodiment'). This process serves to bind people to their lands, reinforcing their rights of tenancy and, through these, their enduring ties to others, most notably spouses, with whom they share the land.

By contrast, Orokaiva never know specifically where the rice they eat was grown (though they sometimes asked me, just as they sometimes asked me to name the places of those farmed fields in the pictures). Rice connects a person not to the particular lands on which it was farmed, but rather to the widely distributed realm of international shipments and commodity trade, where it is associated not with the heaviness of rootedness in specific localities, but instead with the lightness implied by movement across vast distances. Rice is also associated with the lightness of money, for which it is exchanged. Although one of the vernacular terms for money is 'stone' (*karu*), modern money (which is most often called *moni*) is conceptualized as a light medium.[5] It is light to carry, often consisting of mere paper, and it is said to cause an itchy, rising feeling, a fluttering heart, in the person who has it. This itchy feeling (*kingihi*), which people say is especially acute in town and within stores, arises from a sharpening of the person's desires for the many things that money can buy, since having money brings these within (or almost within) reach. Now that one finds stores even in villages, money is the only thing a person needs in order to obtain rice, and the rice that is bought is also easily cooked—it need only be boiled in a pot with water—since all the rest of its preparation (e.g., hulling and milling) is completed elsewhere, by machine. Thus, whereas the cultivation and preparation of taro is associated at each of its stages—clearing land, collecting seed, planting, weeding, harvesting, cleaning, carrying, peeling, and cooking—with the heaviness of social obligations and the complementarities of Orokaiva work exchange, particularly within marriages, it is possible for someone to imagine living alone on just a small money income, by buying and eating rice that can be easily cooked without need of others. I once heard a man who was upset with his wife announce that he was going to divorce her and subsist on his own on rice.

Orokaiva have grown rice on their own lands sporadically since 1942. In that year an Australian Anglican missionary who was active in the coastal region organized the planting of rice as part of his attempt to establish "Christian Co-operative" rice farms and tradestores. The first rice crop he instigated was "half grown when the Japanese landed," commencing their invasion of the New Guinea mainland in World War II (Allen 1981, 114; Benson 1955). During the war the Japanese also taught Orokaiva rice cultivation as part of their cultural version of the colonial civilizing mission (Pike, Nelson, and Daws 1982; see also Ohnuki-Tierney 1995). Several years after the war, cooperative rice-growing projects were restarted under Anglican auspices (Anglican Archives). There was misunderstanding, however, between the villagers and the missionaries as to the purpose of growing rice. The missionaries assumed that it would be a good food source for villagers and would improve their nutrition, while the villagers worked on the assumption that the rice they grew would be sold to whitemen, in exchange for the money that would allow them to adopt whitemen's ways of life (Schwimmer 1969, 86; Dakeyne 1966, 60). When it turned out that their village-grown rice was not in fact to be sold, the people gave up the project, and the rice simply rotted (Anglican Archives; Dakeyne 1966, 61–62). In the decades since then, outside agencies have supported many further rice-growing projects throughout Oro Province, since the local conditions are highly favorable to dry (nonirrigated) rice cultivation and since experts have determined that the average nutritional yield of a given land area is higher when planted with rice than when planted with root crops. In a Japanese-funded project in the mid-1990s, rice seed and milling machines were imported to Orokaiva villages, and for the first time villagers planted rice that was intended solely for their own consumption. But while the rice grew well, few planted a second crop. In part this was because of the many uncertainties associated with milling: the machines sometimes broke, villagers had to compete for time slots to use the machines, and a vehicle had to be arranged to transport the harvested rice to and from the mill. But it was also because the rice grown on their own lands was not as desirable to villagers as the packaged rice they were used to. When cooked, it was a denser, harder food: less soft, less light, and less white. In short, it was perceived as inferior to the rice bought in stores.

From the Orokaiva perspective, tinfish and tinmeat are to rice what pork is to taro. They are paired with rice as its preferred accompanying relishes, scarcer and richer than the staple, and thus eaten in small amounts: a dab of one or the other is placed atop a large bowl of rice. Tinfish comes in tall, round, bright red cans containing 6 or 15 ounces of whole chunk mackerel (with bones and skin) packed in a salty broth. There are several brands, of which the better are "777" and "Sunflower," both canned in Japan. The lower quality brands, canned in Thailand and Chile, have look-alike labels bearing names like "333," "111," and "Moonflower."[6] A can of 777 costs the equivalent of about U.S. $1.80 and is much more appreciated when received as a gift than the lower quality, lower status brands that cost half as much. Orokaiva say that the fish and broth in 777 are *swit* (Tok Pisin: 'salty,' 'delicious'), while the cheaper brands are 'without flavor' (Orokaiva: *gamo ambu*). But no brand is wholly consistent, and as people open a can, usually by puncturing it with a large knife and levering around the top rim, there is a moment of expectation and wonder about the mystery of its contents, before they are poured out and assessed as tightly packed and generous, or loose and mean.

Tinmeat is canned corned beef or other canned beef and pork products. Orokaiva consume many types of tinmeat including canned stews and processed meats like Spam, but corned beef is the prototype. It is manufactured by three domestic canneries, using cattle raised around the country. The lion's share of the tinmeat market is held by Hugo canning, a subsidiary of Heinz Australia, which produces the most popular brand of corned beef, "Ox & Palm." Indeed, the name Ox & Palm has entered the Orokaiva lexicon as a general synonym for tinned beef. Ox & Palm is packaged in tapered, rectangular 12 oz. cans with bright red labels featuring an enigmatic graphic of an ox standing placidly in front of a palm tree. Some Orokaiva know the brand's catchy Tok Pisin slogan, *"katim lewa yet,"* which literally means that the product will 'cut off your inner organs [i.e., the source of desire],' an idiomatic promise to completely satisfy a desire or hunger—so much so that it will break your heart (*lewa* is Tok Pisin for the heart, liver, spleen, innards, desire, or affections).[7] The contents of a tin of Ox & Palm, like other corned beef brands, is a salty slurry of pinkish meat bits mixed with whitish pieces of membrane, fat, and gristle. While Orokaiva know that it derives from cows, they never call it 'cow meat' (*o buramakau, o kau*), nor do they use the general term for 'flesh' or 'muscle meat,' which is *visi*, but instead they treat it terminologically as a distinct animal substance, calling it *o miti* and *o tinmiti*, after the English and Tok Pisin words "meat" and "tinmeat." One quality Orokaiva seek from the tins is fatty protein; in fact "protein" has become a popular, somewhat humorous Orokaiva term for tinmeat, as well as for tinfish and indeed all foods in the vernacular categories of birds and bats (*di*) and land and sea animals (*o*).

Tinfish and tinmeat are considered soft, light, weak proteins; they are not hard and strong, like pork. In feasting, Orokaiva sometimes talk of cans (or cases) of tinfish and tinmeat as heavy objects that press down or 'pin' their recipients, but they are not thought to make a person feel heavy, tired, or weakened when eaten. They are so loose and weak that they can be eaten even by small children, whose bodies are weak, unlike pork, which often makes children sick to their stomachs, causing them to vomit, particularly after feasts when they eat it in large quantities to which they are unaccustomed. Once, when I slipped in a streambed, Steven's younger brother Alphius joked that I had slipped because I was light (*ejeba*) from having eaten tinfish for breakfast, and when I failed to get the joke, his older brother John Newman explained, only half in jest, that I was 'too light' because I ate tinfish all the time: 'you would be heavier and stronger if you ate pork.'

Yet although tinfish and tinmeat are considered light, weak foods, they are as effective as hard, heavy, strong foods like taro and pork in demonstrating the vitality and expanding the renown of a feast-giver who distributes them. As noted above, gifts of taro and pork symbolically vanquish their recipients, leaving them feeling tired and weakened, while at the same time communicating the feast-giver's vitality and motion, prefiguring the desired traveling-outward of his or her name. Tinfish and tinmeat are light; they do not weigh others down because they do not embody pork's powerful combination of heaviness and motion. The lightness of tinfish and tinmeat seems to reflect people's knowledge that they are well-traveled foods that come from faraway places. It also reflects the food's lack of rootedness in particular locales; in these respects, tinfish and tinmeat are similar to rice. Not only does the lightness of tinfish and tinmeat reify the symbolism of provenience, it also reflects the ease with which these foods can be preserved and transported, because of the hard and impervious can, which protects the soft, weak food inside. In their suitability for travel, tinfish, tinmeat, and rice in fact exceed pork and taro; they are the foods that last the longest after feasts, the foods that can be passed through the most sets of hands to reach recipients the farthest away. When guests at feasts are given tinfish or tinmeat, they are visibly pleased. The vivid red labels on the cans are attractively bright and arouse people's desire. Tinfish and tinmeat are, like other types of animal protein, considered nutritious in that they cause the body to grow, but they are also relished as especially salty, flavorful, and juicy. Thus, although tinmeat and tinfish are weak and wet, they have a vitality that does somehow lead to growth, and they have a capacity to expand their giver's renown that is in some ways even superior to pork's, primarily because of the hard, attractive cans in which they are packed.

Other types of whitemen' foods are similar to rice, tinfish, and tinmeat in being regarded as light, wet, tasty foods. Instant ramen noodles, which come with foil packets of salty soup flavoring, are a special treat that people stew with local greens, tinfish, or tinmeat to make an especially slippery, savory relish. (If nothing else is available, cooked noodles alone can serve as a relish.) Another whitemen's food that Orokaiva consider light and soft is bread. There are two bakeries in Popondetta, where villagers buy rectangular loaves of sliced white bread in plastic bags, again as a treat. In recent years, village women have been buying sacks of flour and baking yeasted bread rolls in wood-burning drum ovens, or frying unsweetened pancakes of flour and water in pans of oil on open flames. These locally produced breads, called *sikoni* (baked 'scones') or *parara* (baked or fried 'flours'), are sold by the women in early-morning produce markets and to schoolchildren at lunchtime. Although they are acknowledged to be 'heavier' and heartier than the airy loaves one finds in town, they are nevertheless eaten mainly as snacks and called by the mixed expression, "light *indari*," meaning 'light food.' Also classified as light indari are the various types of factory-baked hard crackers that are sold in small plastic packets and much desired by children. The taste preferences of people raised in the village run to greasy, salty foods rather than to sugary ones, so that village stores tend to sell children packets of biscuits with salty meat flavorings, and salty cheese- or chicken-flavored puffs, but few or no sweet cookies. (The cookies villagers like the best are greasy, sweet, and salty shortbreads, "Scotch Fingers.") At snack bars in town, people buy deep-fried batter balls, sausages in batter, fish and chips, and meat pies, all greasy and salty, and thus in vernacular terms, tasty and wet.

It is in their drinks that villagers like sugar (*jovu*). Indeed, drinking sweetened tea or coffee is often simply called 'drinking sugar.' Although Orokaiva produce coffee as a cash-crop, they do not roast and grind their own beans, but instead buy packets or jars of instant coffee ("Nescafé Niugini Blend") as a more expensive and prestigious alternative to tea, which is brewed from boxed tea leaves. When available, canned or powdered milk is added to coffee and tea to provide added richness, but sugar is considered all but a necessity, without which there would be little point in drinking coffee or tea at all. Most Orokaiva chew betel nut, which reduces the tongue's sensitivity to sweetness, and I often saw villagers add seven or eight heaping tablespoonfuls of sugar to one mug of tea. Indeed, people often joke about the proclivities of elderly people (who are often great betel nut chewers) to take up to "ten spoons." While visiting town, villagers can buy cold treats like soft drinks, ice cream, and sweet, colorful homemade ice pops that are rarely available in the village, where there is no electricity to run refrigerators and freezers.[8] At relatives' houses in town (and occasionally at feasts), people also get to drink Kool-Aid-like "cordial" (Tok Pisin: *kodil*): cold water flavored with colored sweet syrups. All such sweet drinks are recognized to have little or no nutritional value, but to provide pleasure in lubricating (wetting) the throat of one who is thirsty. To obtain this luxurious pleasure of sweetness, people I knew sometimes walked for two hours to ask for a package of sugar, or harvested foods to sell in the market to get money to buy sugar themselves; Orokaiva even have a special name for this: *jovu pure* 'work for sugar.'

To Orokaiva, whitemen's foods reverse the normal balance between dry and wet foods. I was told: 'You whitemen eat only wet foods' (*uvuvu pere ra*). Instead of eating a large amount of dry, filling main food paired with a small amount of wet relish, whitemen eat foods that are juicy, wet, and tasty, like Orokaiva relish, predominantly. Rice is the only whitemen's food that is regarded as a viable staple, and Orokaiva do refer to it as 'dry' when eaten plain, without a side dish. But, as we have seen, even rice is considered light, soft, and tasty in comparison to indigenous main foods like taro, yams, and bananas. To Orokaiva, it is as if whitemen eat only butter without the bread, or ketchup without the fries: they selfishly eat too much tasty, wet food, unbalanced by large amounts of dry staples.[9]

Whitemen, Too, Are What They Eat

Orokaiva attitudes toward whitemen's foods like rice, tinfish, and tinmeat are profoundly ambivalent. On the one hand, they are derided as light, weak, and soft, like Orokaiva baby foods. On the other hand, they are valued as nutritious (as we saw with rice) for the superior bodily growth they produce, and they are desired as tasty luxuries that, when given to others, enlarge the giver's prestige. Sharpening this contradiction, whitemen's foods produce growth (of both the body and social person) without inducing heaviness and sleep. Both the people's ambivalence toward these foods, and the unnatural lightness they embody, are strongly parallel to the construction of whitemen itself, making foods an important medium substantiating the Orokaiva construction of whitemen in people's experience. As I discuss in this section, Orokaiva conceptualize this relationship according to a vernacular logic by which people come to embody salient characteristics of the main foods that sustain them. The premise of this vernacular logic is like that expressed in the English saying, "you are what you eat." Thus, within this logic, whitemen are interpreted as having a nature like that of their foods, and vice versa, so that Orokaiva ideas about whitemen and of their foods are reinforced by one other.

The premise that people are what they eat underlies the important Orokaiva concept of *hamo ari* 'habituation.' Literally, hamo ari means 'body development,' 'body fashioning,' or 'embodiment.' But it is often used in the idiomatic sense of becoming 'habituated' or 'accustomed to' something by internalizing some portion or quality of it. In many contexts, this internalized quality is immaterial, like knowledge or a skill, and is not considered a substantive constituent of the body, but rather an influence upon its dispositions. For example, one may become hamo ari to an activity like using a chainsaw by practicing and internalizing the relevant skills that allow one to perform it well. (Trouble in performing the activity indicates that the skills were not internalized.) A first step to becoming hamo ari 'used to' a new food is simply to have tried it without becoming ill, showing that the food is potentially assimilable by the body: its qualities are sufficiently similar to the body's own to be tolerated. Alternatively, should the person dislike the new food or become sick from eating it, this would show that the nature of the food conflicts with the body. When foods are eaten habitually, that is, in large amounts and frequently, especially as a main staple, they are regarded as actually producing the body, so that the body comes to take on qualities that are thought to derive from them. In such cases, the concept of hamo ari suggests that the food makes the person: the body and its dispositions are formed and reinforced by the nature of the specific food eaten.

This logic of hamo ari, in which people's nature resembles that of their main foods, is compelling to Orokaiva because it is grounded in their own profound identification with and affection for their own main food, taro. In Orokaiva culture there is enormous elaboration of the idea that taro plants are like humans. The taro growth cycle, as we noted earlier, is likened to the human life cycle,[10] and the names for certain parts of the taro plant are the same as those used for parts of the human body; for example, the leaves of the taro plant are the 'head' (ohoru), the main stalk is the 'trunk' (uhu), and the bottom of the corm is an 'ass' (avo). Taro plants are said to have humanlike friendships and kinship relationships, and to live in humanlike communities underground, organized by clans. In the ground, taro plants talk and joke with one another, and they sometimes speak to humans in dreams. When Orokaiva go to their gardens, they enjoy seeing the healthy, growing taro plants that they have nurtured, and they feel that the plants respond to them: 'The taro plants whisper to you,' I heard from several informants. Steven once said that 'when you go to the garden, the taro plants wave their leaves to you in greeting, and you know that they are happy because you are their father coming in.' He added, emphatically, in English, that the taro plants "love at you." Orokaiva sometimes sing to the taro plants, who are thought to like the songs. Since taro are regarded as having wills of their own and the capacity to wander, gardeners worry that others who are jealous of their gardens will try to 'lure away' their taro with sweet smells and spells. To prevent this, Orokaiva often decorate their gardens with fragrant and flowering bushes so that the taro will be pleased and want to stay.

It is easy for Orokaiva to think of themselves as deriving their own nature from the taro given that they project onto it a nature so much like their own. But from the Orokaiva perspective, the nature of taro is simply a given, whereas the nature of humans is malleable and formed. This is not to say that taro are beyond human influence. To the contrary, Orokaiva have rich conceptions of the ways human actions can assist or hinder their taro's development, and they cultivate it accordingly. Taro are clearly affected by particularities of soil, water, location, and sun. But they are also believed to be highly susceptible to moral influences like human social discord; when taro plants wilt, Orokaiva see it as evidence of conflicts involving their gardeners. Indeed, taro are thought to react sensitively to many complex human conditions, according to the correspondences Orokaiva perceive between themselves and taro. For example, I was sometimes advised not to enter new taro gardens while wearing shoes, because it was thought possible that the reified quality of being encased in a thick sheathing, as my feet were in shoes, could 'jump' from me onto the bodies of the impressionable young taro plants, causing them to develop an unwelcome, thick fibrous sheathing at the base of their stalks. Orokaiva envision a kind of ideal taro nature, which they try to encourage in the taro they cultivate, and it is this ideal nature that Orokaiva say they derive from the taro they eat. It is strong and hard, and with a balance of heaviness and lightness like that found in the body of a healthy adult.

Orokaiva tend to view many aspects of their traditional culture as an adaptation to taro. Early in my fieldwork, an old man who had heard that I was there to study the "culture" offered this summary, as if to spare me the trouble of unnecessary further research: 'Our *culture* is like this,' he said. 'First we go to the garden, and we cut down trees. Then the sun dries it, and we burn the land. When it is finished, we plant taro, and then come back to the village and wait. Finally, when the taro is ready, we build a platform in the village. We pile the taro on the platform, tie up pigs, dance, and make a feast at which we distribute the pork and taro to our relations. That is our *culture.*' In such a taro-oriented culture Orokaiva derive their nature both from the way they produce and interact with their taro and from the fact that they consume it; the culture itself is understood to be organized by taro's growth and oriented toward its maximum reproduction, as a result of which humans can consume and exchange it to reproduce themselves and their families. In other words, Orokaiva conceptualize their traditional culture as a symbiosis between humans and taro in which humans are motivated to behave in particular, valued ways—for example, avoiding social conflict, doing the vigorous work of clearing the bush—specifically so as to induce the taro (and thus the people in turn) to thrive.[11]

A general principle of identification between people and their main foods is applied by Orokaiva in thinking and talking not only about themselves but about others as well. As noted in chapter 3, Orokaiva identify their ethnic neighbors, the Managalasi people, with their staple food, yams. Likewise, in talking about PNG Highlanders, who are known to Orokaiva as cultivators of sweet potatoes, the opposition between taro and sweet potatoes provides a basis for interpreting human differences. In practice, this usually means reasoning backward, making inferences about the food based on their views on the nature of the people. For example, as Schwimmer has reported (1973, 124), Orokaiva cite their history of victories in war over Managalasi as evidence for "the superiority of taro over yam." Or they cast aspersions on the lowly sweet potato by asserting negative stereotypes of Highlanders. As I once heard said, 'What do you expect [from Highlanders]? They eat only sweet potatoes!'

Just as Orokaiva apply the concept of hamo ari to themselves and other Papua New Guineans, they apply it in thinking and talking about the characteristics of whitemen that they identify with *their* foods. As we have seen, there are suggestive analogies between the qualities of whitemen and those of their foods. Most notably, we saw that the lightness of whitemen's foods resembles the lightness of whitemen themselves, whereas Orokaiva foods embody a heaviness—or more precisely, a better balance between heaviness and lightness—that is in line with Orokaiva conceptions of themselves as having to be heavy in many situations within a moral world where lightness and heaviness each have their place and are dynamically linked. We also saw that whitemen's foods are generally considered soft and weak. In this way, too, their qualities are analogous to those of whitemen themselves, inasmuch as the bodies of whitemen (as discussed in the last chapter) are regarded as unusually soft, in contrast to the bodies of Orokaiva, which like the foods that sustain them, are hard and strong. As might be expected given the logic of hamo ari, the qualities lightness and softness attributed to whitemen are especially marked in rice, since it is seen as whitemen's main staple. Thus, the logic of hamo ari constitutes a framework in which selected physical properties of foods—for example, that boiled white rice is softer and less filling than taro—authenticate and reinforce analogous qualities that are salient in the construction of whitemen.

This framework is confirmed for Orokaiva in certain facts which they interpret in terms of it. One such fact that sorely troubles Orokaiva, as I noted in chapter 3, is that most whites who visit their villages do not eat heartily when served the villagers' foods. Laughing uproariously, people tell stories of white visitors whose stomachs were filled completely after eating only the smallest chunk of taro, or they pantomime white guests picking timidly at enormous basins full of mixed local foods, taking just a little bit onto their plates 'so as not to offend us.' One woman told me, 'We Orokaiva would not hesitate to make a great heap of food on our plate. But they [whitemen] aren't used to it [hamo ari]. They are averse to these kinds of foods.' For their part, the whites I met had varying degrees of acquaintance with local foods. Some had made a point of familiarizing themselves with the local "fresh veggies" by occasionally buying them in the markets and preparing them in their own homes. However, most were frankly unable to distinguish taro from yams, or cooking bananas from sweet ones that can be eaten raw. In general, white guests to the village find local cooking anything but delicious, and they are repulsed by the Orokaiva aesthetic that attempts to impress by presenting food in large quantities. What Orokaiva find most appetizing is mixtures of tubers and bananas boiled together with forest leaves, tinfish or tinmeat, *and* ramen noodles, served up in large vessels that were intended for use as laundry basins. But white visitors often are disgusted by the sight of such mixtures, and all the more so in such vast quantities. When they have foreign guests, village women specifically make labor-intensive specialty dishes like leaf-wrapped dumplings of hand-grated taro in order to display their regard for the guests and stimulate their appetite; nevertheless, for foreigners even these fancy foods are hard to distinguish from glutinous glop. While other Papua New Guinean visitors, who are used to eating starch staples in quantity, normally put away large plates of local food to their hosts' satisfaction, white visitors who eat respectable amounts by villagers' standards are exceedingly rare.

What is emphasized in villagers' stories of whitemen's reactions to local foods is the trepidation or even fear with which they approach them, and the fact that whitemen eat absurdly little, but even so their appetites are sated. Orokaiva interpret this to mean that their local foods are too strong for the whites, too hard and too heavy. Being whitemen, the visitors are presumed to be accustomed (that is, hamo ari) to foods that are soft, wet, and light. These weak foods—rice, tinfish, tinmeat, and the other delicacies whitemen buy in stores—leave their bodies too weak to cope with the hard foods that villagers serve them. The village foods overpower them, so that they can eat only small amounts.

Orokaiva meeting me for the first time were surprised that I willingly ate local foods. The novelty of this was so great that people would sometimes hang around for hours until a meal so that they could watch me eat for the express purpose of later being able to tell others that they had seen with their own eyes this unusual whiteman who ate taro and native greens. Throughout the two years I lived with Steven and his relatives in their households, my consumption of local foods was a favorite topic of conversation that was revisited countless times, seeming to hold inexhaustible interest. It was invariably discussed whenever we shared a meal with someone for the first time, since a whiteman eating taro represented for them a kind of wondrous anomaly that countered their expectations. In my absence, Steven often enjoyed answering people's usual questions about how he provided me with the light whitemen's foods that I presumably needed. He would surprise his listeners by regaling them with stories of how 'his' whiteman ate the same things that he did, including bats and insects. I even ate the hardest of hard foods, taro roots roasted on an open fire, with deeply charred skin, something people often brought me as gifts in order to see for themselves that I really did eat them. Exaggerating, Steven would say that I built 'taro heaps' on my plate 'the size of Sumbiripa Mountain,' boasting that I ate these foods in the same huge quantities he did.

As Orokaiva see it, their indigenous foods tend to make whitemen sick. When whites who are known to have visited villagers become ill, their illness is often attributed to the effects of eating strong local foods. Such an explanation was given, for example, for the malaria that my wife suffered during a visit. As she acknowledged, she had never eaten taro before, so clearly her body was not used to eating such strong foods. Orokaiva also gave this diagnosis, a general infirmity induced by strong local foods, on several other occasions when whites who visited the village either slept late in the morning, retreated inside to rest (and to enjoy privacy) during the daytime, retired early in the evening, or left the village sooner than planned. For western visitors, staying in a New Guinea village is a physically and emotionally exhausting experience. It usually begins with a hard journey followed by a socially demanding greeting ritual, after which the guests remain the center of attention in one unfamiliar situation after the next. Visitors find it tiring to be in the spotlight, closely observed and questioned for hour upon hour by a shifting crowd of villagers. Moreover, guests find it hard to match the social stamina of their village hosts, who on such exciting occasions like to stay awake at night, talking and joking, until morning draws close. Foreign guests invariably need to withdraw inside for periods of privacy and rest. Orokaiva have no notion that people require privacy, they think it a sign of strength to go without sleep, and they rarely if ever spend daytime hours inside except to sleep or when sick. So from their perspective such behavior by whites is a clear signal of debilitation or sickness, and the most ready explanation they have for this is that it is a response to their strong village foods.

As we saw in our earlier discussion of pork and taro, Orokaiva fully expect that food gifts will debilitate their recipients, making them feel tired, heavy, weak. Indeed, it is considered gracious when Orokaiva guests express appreciation for the food they are served by telling their hosts that the food has pressed them down, destroyed them, or killed them, acknowledging their hosts' generosity, as it were, by admitting defeat. After eating, they say things like: 'Your taro and bananas have slaughtered me,' 'This food has cut my neck,' and 'The food [you have served] is like a foot pressing down on my chest, pinning me to the ground.' Thus, in attributing white visitors' sickness to the effects of foods served them, Orokaiva are construing it as an exaggerated form of the short-lived, postprandial weakness that is the expected reaction of all guests, as if whitemen were making a reasonable, or even polite, response. It is only because whitemen's bodies are weak from being accustomed to weak foods that the response is so extreme and extended.

The notion that whitemen are particularly vulnerable to local foods is also supported by white visitors themselves, who often explain their differential susceptibility to food-borne illness using the concept of "germs." Villagers are always keen to discuss food and eating with their white guests, and they sometimes draw whites out on the matter by telling stories about prior visitors' fears of sickness. As Alphius said to me in the first days of my fieldwork, speaking in English: "When we ask white people why they don't eat our food, they sometimes tell us that they are afraid it will make them sick. What does this mean?" Alphius's question suggested to me that he had heard whites speak about microbial and parasitic diseases, but as I later came to appreciate, whites' explanations of the transmission of microbes through food sound to Orokaiva remarkably like their own idea of hamo ari. At the time, even I replied to Alphius by saying that local people are "used to" certain substances in the local foods that can make white people who are "not used to" them sick. Subsequently, I heard other whites reply in similar terms to villagers' questions (as well as to villagers' hospitable coaxing to put more food on their plates). In such conversations, it was sometimes Orokaiva who introduced the term "germs," a concept known to most young and middle-aged Orokaiva like Alphius who have been to school, that represents one of the many invisible causes, like gravity, which form part of whitemen's explanatory repertoire. "Germs" is an explanation that both Orokaiva and whites can agree on, even though whites understand the term relative to a theory of immunity to microbial agents, whereas for Orokaiva it is often interpreted as a translation of the concept of hamo ari.

Another important fact that Orokaiva interpret in terms of the concept of hamo ari, confirming it in doing so, is that not only whites but also Orokaiva children raised in town often fall ill when they visit the village. Like whitemen, such urban children are nourished primarily on store-bought whitemen's foods, and because their bodies are formed by such foods, they are thought to be weak just as are whitemen. A case in point is one village girl who had excelled as a boarding student at Popondetta High School and afterward (with the support of one of her former teachers) moved to another town to take a secretarial course. When she returned home for visits, she no longer liked to eat the traditional garden foods her parents prepared. Her mother once complained to me:

> Now when you give her hard foods like taro and [cooking] bananas, her body loses its strength, it becomes weak and sick, and she sleeps night and day. Now I have to give her soft fruits like ripe bananas, pineapple, watermelon, cucumber, rambutans, and papaya. Only when she eats these [soft foods] can her body assimilate them so that she does not oversleep. As I always say, 'If you eat the bad food of people who have different ancestors, your life will be bad.' I tell her, 'You are an Orokaiva girl, but you never eat your own true food.'

The girl herself described her eating in more or less these same terms when speaking in Orokaiva, telling me that garden foods like taro were 'too heavy' and made her sick. But in English, she said "I don't like them," implying that local foods were unappetizing because they were insufficiently varied—"all the same."

As with whites who visit the village, Orokaiva who live in town interpret their sicknesses in the village in ways that confirm the logic of hamo ari, even while accepting alternative viewpoints. In town families whose children are being raised outside the village, Orokaiva parents are torn between wanting to take their children to the village on holidays so that they can get to know their lands and their relatives, and wanting to keep them away from the village since visiting often makes them sick. In addition to saying that their children come down with malaria while in the village, they also sometimes say that the children get sick from eating village foods that are too hard or strong for them.

Even the better educated parents I spoke with, who did not initially volunteer food as a cause, readily took up this line of interpretation when I suggested it, since they, too, find the hamo ari framework compelling. The two causes of sickness (foods vs. malaria parasites/"germs") are not felt to be mutually exclusive. Even where town visitors to the village are seen to regain their health by taking chloroquine, a malaria medication, their underlying susceptibility to sickness may be attributed to having eaten strong local foods, which overpowered their weak bodies.

By the principle of hamo ari, foods should be comparable in strength or weaker than the body of the person who eats them. Thus, newborn babies, who have watery, weak, insubstantial bodies, subsist only on breast milk. As they grow stronger, they are introduced to soft foods like young coconut, ripe fruits, and mashed sweet potato. In the course of development, children begin to eat ever harder and stronger foods until their diet eventually includes all the normal adult foods. At each stage, if they are only given foods that are too weak they will fail to grow and increase in strength; if they are given foods that are too strong their bodies will be overpowered and they will become sick. Ideally, the body grows by a diet that is gradually intensified in strength, constantly testing the body's limits until maturity, when one freely eats foods like taro and yams, themselves hardened, mature plants. Conversely, the town diet of whitemen's foods is seen to make people regress in strength. This food-strength scale thus implies an asymmetry: people who are hamo ari to strong foods should be able to eat weak foods with no ill effects, while people who are hamo ari only to weak foods should not be able to tolerate strong foods. That this is actually found to be so, among whitemen as well as among urban Orokaiva who are used to eating whitemen's weak commodity foods, powerfully confirms the whole hamo ari framework according to which all people—Orokaiva and whitemen alike—are what they eat.[12]

The Construction of Race and the Orokaiva Value of Rootedness in Lands

Like Orokaiva, Sursurungan people in New Ireland use food as a basic principle of racial classification. Thus, a Sursurungan girl born of a Sursurungan mother and white expatriate father, although recognized to be physically "halfway between 'white' and 'black,'" was classified as socially "black" like other villagers because she ate the same food as they did. By contrast, a politician who, just like this girl, had a village mother but a white father was classified by Sursurungans as a "whiteskin" because, as one villager said, "he buys all his food" instead of producing it (Jackson 1998, 4). As for the Sursurungans, Orokaiva assume that a person shows what he is by what he eats, so that eating habits can have an even greater racial significance than skin color or family origin. During my fieldwork, a black-skinned teacher from Ghana who taught at Popondetta High School was referred to by villagers as an 'African whiteman' because he held himself aloof from the villagers and avoided eating their food, which he told me (after visiting Rodney's village home in a party of schoolteachers) was "primitive," "dirty," and "without taste." At the same time, Orokaiva were quick to embrace certain whites as 'truly Orokaiva' and 'just like us blacks,' for example, a part-Maori New Zealander who was the Anglican Mission's diocesan engineer, and who was famous among Orokaiva for eating all local foods and chewing betel nut in large quantities. (He was eventually dismissed by the mission.) Such examples show that "the way to an Orokaiva man's heart" is as much through other people's stomachs as through his own.

We have already seen the most general reason why food is a compelling medium of racial symbolism for Orokaiva and thus an important framework used for interpreting whitemen: the logic of hamo ari, which assumes that as foods are consumed, they are incorporated into the body so as to sediment into it a kind of reduction—in effect, a digest—of the qualities those foods embody. These qualities can be quite abstract, and provide the rationale for many food aversions and prohibitions. For example, small children are advised against eating owl meat, because it can communicate to them the 'dusty' (oniho) quality that is manifest in the appearance of owl feathers, thereby making the children 'dusty' with the fungal infection grille that causes their skin to itch, flake, and peel. There seems to be no principled limit to the kinds of qualities that can be reified and transferred between elements in the natural world. Even quite esoteric qualities, like the 'dusty' skin just mentioned, excessive mucus, or a stooped posture, are believed to potentially be transferable to people from foods they eat. As in James Frazer's "homeopathic or imitative magic," the principle is similarity ("like produces like"), and a multitude of bodies and things—including food plants, medicinal plants, animals, and stones—are assumed to be capable of infecting other bodies with "their own intrinsic nature" (Frazer 1996 [1922], 39, 45).[13]

But the idea that whitemen are light, soft, and weak because of similar qualities in their foods is penumbral to a more fundamental quality that whitemen come to embody because of what they eat, namely a lack of rootedness in particular lands. Whitemen lack this rootedness, first, because it is *not* found, as a reified quality, in the foods they eat, and second, because the commodity nature of whitemen's foods allows whitemen (as a practical matter) to live without roots in lands where the food is produced. As Orokaiva see it, whitemen's foods are rooted not in lands, but rather in money. Indeed, common expressions for whitemen's foods are 'money foods' (*karu donda*) and 'store foods' (*sitova donda*), which contrast with indigenous 'garden foods' (*pure donda*), 'substantial/real foods' (*donda be*), or, as Orokaiva sometimes call them, 'land foods' (*enda ta be*), literally, 'fruits of the land.' Rootedness in land is in fact the underlying reason why indigenous garden foods are hard, heavy, and strong; and the lightness, softness, and weakness of whitemen's foods is seen to stem from a lack of this basic quality of rootedness in lands.

What I am calling "rootedness" is a meaning of hamo ari that posits an embodied relationship to particular lands. People's relationship to lands is often spoken of as having an 'embodied' (hamo ari) dimension, as if some essential quality of the land is incorporated in the people who use it. The people of Agenehambo refer to their own relationship to their lands in this way. Today Agenehambo villagers garden a broad belt of lands to the north of the village that they acknowledge formerly belonged to people of To- gaho, a community still farther to the north. These lands had been battle- grounds prior to the intrusion of colonial authority, but after pacification the grandparents and parents of today's adults began moving north, down from hamlets higher up on the volcano's footslopes, and they made new gar- dens and built new villages in areas still occupied by their descendants today. The people of Agenehambo do not assert a primordial claim to ownership of these lands, such as one based on priority of settlement or autochthonous local origin. Instead, their claim to ownership is legit- imized by historical events (notably a marriage alliance ending earlier wars that was sealed with a payment of Togaho land for the brideprice), but the claim has force primarily because of the recent history of de facto settle- ment. Since the time of their grandparents, Agenehambo people have, as they themselves say, become hamo ari to these lands. It is they who cleared the lands to make gardens; the trees they refer to as landmarks were planted by their own parents and grandparents; they have left their 'marks' (*hajire*) on the 'land's surface' (*enda ta hamo* 'the land's body or skin'). Conversely, the land has impressed itself on them in various ways. They have internal- ized a knowledge of it (e.g., its peculiarities and boundaries), and they have nourished themselves on its fruits, thus absorbing an essence of the land into their bodies. For these reasons, they are hamo ari to these lands— established on and connected to them. Such a relationship confers on them rights of tenancy and creates an effective basis for their claims of ownership.

The specific practices, like eating food grown on the land, that allow people to claim that they are hamo ari to it, are the processual here-and now counterparts of the kinds of past events—like mythic origins, migrations, and ancestral exploits—that are often also cited to justify the rootedness of people in particular lands. In principle, the claims from past events are stronger. While only past events can allow a group to claim to be the 'truly rooted' (*susu be*) of some land, the claim of ownership implied by hamo ari is shallower and weaker. But in practice, when disputes arise, hamo ari counts heavily—de facto occupancy or possession is nine-tenths of the law in customary adjudications—and it is an increasingly forceful argument the longer the relationship endures. An example of this is a large extended family whose rights to land in Agenehambo were reckoned through the matriarch, rather than through her husband. She was considered 'truly rooted' in the land because she was born into the leading village clan, and her father had been among the first men to clear gardens and settle in the area after the truce with Togaho. But her husband's 'true roots' were in another village; he was an 'immigrant' (*ombei embo*). He told me: "I came and stayed here amid my in-laws who are the landowners. I am not truly rooted [*susu be*] here. But I married their sister, a woman of the village. And I have settled here. I work the land here, and I live, eating its produce. And so eventually I have become hamo ari to this land. My children have grown up here, and their children. We are hamo ari and so we stay here."

The specifically embodied dimension of a person's connection to land might be seen as a mere figure of speech, a "conventional metaphor" (Keesing 1985) that people use in discussions of land ownership. But in Orokaiva discourse on the body—its formation, nutrition, health, dispositions, strength, and other qualities—the connection to lands is often referred to as fully physical, and it is attributed a crucial role in creating the body, giving it substance, strength, and weight. The nature of this role is illustrated by a ritual that builds the bodies of babies. Like other Orokaiva rituals, this one is simply called 'work' (*pure*): a kind of practical activity that achieves valued effects. It was performed by mothers I knew for several months to a year after a baby was born, and treated casually as part of their normal gardening routine. To understand the ritual, it is helpful to know that Orokaiva women carry babies in large net bags (Tok Pisin: *bilum*; Orokaiva: *ehi*). A folded towel or pillow is placed in the bottom of the bag, and the baby is laid down on top of it. The baby is enclosed in the bag so it cannot fall out, yet the loose mesh of the bag's sides allows fresh air to enter and lets the baby be seen. Women carry their babies in these bags on their backs, hung from the forehead at about the hairline. When a woman arrives in the garden, she removes the bag from her body and hangs it over the crook of a forked stick planted firmly in the ground, leaving her free to go about her garden work while the baby sleeps in the bag. This procedure is not only for convenience, however. It is also believed to induce the hamo (body) of the baby to form and grow by a transfer of strength from the land to the baby by way of the stick.

To Orokaiva, the human body is primarily made, not born. At birth, infants are said to consist of only *ahihi*, 'spirit.' At conception, the mother's 'blood' (*sasaga*) mixes with the father's 'milk,' 'water,' or 'sperm' (*susu, umo, bipa*), and the baby's organs and bones begin to develop in the womb in much the way that coconuts are believed to form their meat from coconut water inside the shell. However, the baby, when born, is still a wet, weak, and very soft being. Even its bones are soft, and it is toothless, unable to eat anything but liquids.[14] Although not incorporeal, it is spoken of as not yet having a hamo, the part of the body that is physically strong and relatively hard/dry. The hamo contrasts with the ahihi, which I have glossed as 'spirit' but which is not, as the western notion of spirit would imply, necessarily incorporeal. In general, the ahihi is that part of a being that has reproductive significance or the potential to influence things, but lacks solidity of substance (the hamo/ahihi relationship is discussed at length in Williams 1930, 263–66; Schwimmer 1973; and Iteanu 1983a). There are various classes of 'spirit beings' like ghosts, goblins, and forest elves that are exclusively ahihi. When a person dies, and the hamo is buried, the ahihi is released to wander, and people report seeing it at the village periphery, along paths in the forest, in gardens and forest glens, and especially near rivers, streams, pools, and other watery places. Traditionally ahihi are associated with watery elements and places, although they are increasingly today associated with the air and sky as a result of Christian influences.

When the baby is placed in the string bag that is hung from the stick in the garden, it is the stick that people call the hamo of the baby, while the actual baby in the bag is called a mere 'ahihi child' (Schwimmer 1973, 93). As André Iteanu observes, the baby-and-stick ensemble therefore "has the same structure as a taro plant" (1983a, 34). When a taro plant is mature, its ahihi is the part of the plant that is above ground, namely the water-filled petioles (stems), rising shoots, and leaves. This is the living, reproductive part of the plant and is always included with taro when it is given at feasts. By contrast, the mature taro's hamo is its edible underground root. The root enlarges and solidifies by absorbing a nutritive essence (*gamo*) from the

ground, and the baby in the baby-and-stick ensemble develops in an analogous way (see fig. 5.1). The ensemble itself resembles the short stalk or sett
(whether a rhizomic offset or the bottom piece of a stem) that people plant
in the ground when they are planting taro. The stick is like the physical
stalk, which at this stage is the new taro plant's hamo. Just as the stick does
not become the hamo of the person who grows up from the baby, the stalk
will not become the hamo of the future taro that grows from it, as it will rot
away once new shoots emerge from its center. It is thus only a temporary
pseudo-hamo that allows the ahihi of the future taro, identified with the
new watery shoots, to begin developing its own hamo by putting roots into
the ground. Similarly, the stick in the ground is a kind of temporary
pseudo-hamo for the baby. Like the taro sett that is planted, the baby does
not yet have a hamo 'body' of its own that is strong and permanent. But
when the baby is hung from the stick, it, too, is "planted" in the soil of the
garden, helping it to develop its own hamo by drawing out the ground's
essence. Eventually, of course, like the stalk, the stick becomes unnecessary
and falls away as the baby is transformed from a mere ahihi into a strong,
healthy child capable of standing on his or her own.[15]

Through the symbolism of planting, the baby-and-stick ritual illustrates
the importance of rootedness in lands. The "rooting" of the baby, which
gives it an embodied connection to garden land, is taken as the precondition
for developing a hard, strong, healthy body. When asked about the ritual,
Orokaiva offer diverse explanations, all of which reflect an underlying
assumption that the process of forming, growing, strengthening, and hardening a hamo depends upon the cultivation of its attachment to particular
lands.[16] Sometimes people speak as if the land's nutritive essence is drawn
up to the baby through the stick, and this is what forms and hardens the
body. I also heard people say that babies sleep especially soundly on garden
lands that belong to their own ancestors, and as mentioned above, it is during sleep that the body is thought to grow.

One possibility discussed at length by Schwimmer (1973, 92–94) and
Iteanu (1983a, 31–35) is that what the baby receives through the stick
is an ancestor's "soul substance" that builds its hamo.[17] According to
Schwimmer, the baby's parents initially ask the spirit of a dead ancestor to
give the baby a hamo, so that it will grow up well and look after the land in the
future. This suggests that it is the ancestor, rather than the land, that gives
"the hamo to the child . . . through the mediation of the stick" (Schwimmer
1973, 94). Note, however, that the ancestor cannot provide the hamo to the
baby directly while it sleeps in the village; the baby's hamo must in any case
be provided through a piece of garden land, to which it becomes rooted as a

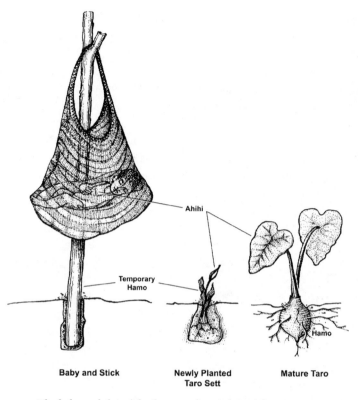

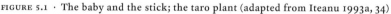

FIGURE 5.1 · The baby and the stick; the taro plant (adapted from Iteanu 1993a, 34)

consequence of the procedure. After all, it is in such a piece of garden land that the spirit of the ancestor is itself rooted. As Schwimmer writes:

> It is a fact of Orokaiva life that old people do not stop gardening as long as they have any strength left in their bodies. . . . Old people devote their reduced energies almost exclusively to their gardens, grow progressively closer to their gardens and away from the social network, until finally, after death, their spirit becomes still more closely attached to the land. . . . [Hence the spirit of a dead person is] thought to inhere in his [or her] old garden plot and in the products growing there, or more specifically perhaps in the water flowing through the garden, for it is in the water that the dead tend to live, even though in a more general sense they are everywhere in the garden. (1973, 92–94)

Since the ancestor's spirit pervades the garden with its crops, the ancestor's role in giving the baby a hamo is only a part of its larger role in developing the hamo of all of the crops in the garden. As Schwimmer observes: "The child draws soul substance through the stick all the time and as the taro and other crops fill out and become vigorous, the child will do the same" (1973, 94). Thus the baby's hamo is strengthened by virtue of the sympathetic connection that the ritual reinforces between the baby and the other crops growing in the garden where it, too, is "planted" (see also Williams 1930, 94; Iteanu 1983a, 35). This is yet another variation of the pattern according to which the child develops its body as it becomes rooted in the land; once again, it is clear that the model for human development is the development of taro. Taro, more than any of the other root vegetables that Orokaiva cultivate as their main garden crops, is exemplary in embodying the valued rootedness that is felt to form strong human bodies.

It is through food crops that people indirectly "get" their rootedness later in life as well. This happens both by eating the foods and by cultivating them. Taro themselves embody rootedness, which is expressed in taro's heaviness, hardness, and strength. As we saw earlier, Orokaiva gardeners cultivate strong, hard taro by encouraging the plants' roots to descend as deeply as possible into the soil, and by allowing mature taro to ripen until they are so strongly rooted that they cannot be moved. A person who eats taro routinely incorporates these qualities. But it is not only by eating "rootedness" that Orokaiva themselves become rooted; they also become rooted through the fact that their foods must be planted, necessarily on their own lands: they must cultivate their food gardens in order to eat. People's rootedness in their lands, in other words, is derived from practical and situational as well as mystical and sympathetic relationships. As suggested by Kingsford's joke (see chapter 3), Orokaivas' taro weigh them down with the 'heaviness of earth' because their need to grow it ties them to particular local lands. Orokaiva are tied to their taro, and their taro, in turn, are tied to the ground.

This quality of "rootedness," then, describes one way that Orokaiva talk about the qualities they derive from and share with their foods. But there is yet another way, which might in contrast be glossed as "expansiveness," a quality of mobility that we have seen associated with lightness in persons and with hardness in foods. There is a basic type of conversion from the rootedness of foods to an expansive quality in persons. For one thing, as we have seen, taro that is heavy and hard from being well rooted in the ground produces in people who eat it a deep, heavy sleep that promotes bodily growth or expansion. And when given away in feasting, it is the heaviness of such taro that 'presses down' its recipients, symbolically vanquishing them, thereby expanding its givers' name and influence. Thus, the particular qualities of heaviness and hardness that taro receive from rootedness in the ground (gardeners expend enormous effort to get their taro to root deeply) are critical to the expansion of the social person with whom the food is identified (see also Munn 1986).

The main work Orokaiva do is cultivate food that will maintain their bodies, nurture their families, and support their exchange relationships. People's garden foods are the critical resource that enables them to achieve any large aim. Hospitality and food exchanges wax when people's gardens thrive, and wane when they fail. Men plan their feasts—at which they seek renown, but also risk failure should their foods come up short—according to the state of their gardens, predicting as well as they can the time of greatest abundance, hoping they will not have to call the whole thing off because the crop fell short. Indeed, people themselves grow fat and lean with the seasons of their gardens. So people's experience continually confirms that planting crops is the necessary prerequisite for physical growth and social expansiveness: land and food are the only firm and true foundations of life. There are many sayings to the effect that a man should hold fast to his crops in order to thrive: 'You should stand on your taro, and on that basis speak' (i.e., do not over-extend yourself, do not make commitments beyond what you can back up with the taro that you have already planted); 'Your land is your true root'; 'If you stand on your land, no one can touch you.' In Orokaiva tradition, it is as basic as the fact that food is needed to fill the belly that planting and nurturing food in one's garden is the basis of legitimate wealth, influence, and prestige. The alternative to rootedness is presented as a waywardness that contracts and diminishes one's social person, as in the cautionary saying: 'If you spend too much time in the doorways of others, you will see hunger's face' (i.e., if you fail to attend to your own lands and instead merely spend your time traveling and visiting, you will invite shame, disputes, sorcery, and ultimately starvation).

This basic principle of traditional Orokaiva life, that in order to be mobile, strong, and expansive people must be rooted in lands that they cultivate, seems to be categorically defied by whitemen: whitemen and their foods are unrooted in lands, yet they nevertheless manage to be impressively expansive. The explanation Orokaiva give for this appeals to their awareness that whitemen's foods are imported commodities, rooted not in lands, but rather in money. And as whitemen's foods are not rooted in particular lands, neither are whitemen themselves; there is no essence of lands in the foods they ingest, so the foods and the whitemen who habitually ingest them are both light and weak. The commodity status of whitemen's foods allows whitemen to subsist and expand themselves without having to cultivate gardens. So rather than lands, the foundation from which whitemen grow and expand their influence is money.

Just as indigenous foods embody qualities that reflect their rootedness in lands, whitemen's foods embody qualities that reflect their rootedness in money. It is money that is understood to be the foods' final cause, what gives them their nature. This does not mean that Orokaiva are ignorant of the fact that rice, flour, sugar, and so on are derived from plants. As we saw earlier, many Orokaiva have had firsthand experience cultivating rice, and they know that refined sugar is made from plants like the sugar canes they plant in their own gardens. But simply knowing that the foods originate with plants does not in itself lead Orokaiva to think of these foods as qualitatively rooted in lands the way their own taro is. In part, this is because the images of whitemen's mechanized agriculture with which Orokaiva are familiar do not convey an impression of rootedness, since in these images the crops grow in vast, featureless fields that do not look like the lands they know (they especially do not look like heavy lands, for reasons discussed above). But more importantly, Orokaiva associate the production of whitemen's foods in any case less with cultivation than with manufacturing. When thinking about rice, flour, sugar, and so on, images of farmed fields are eclipsed by images of factories.

Whitemen's foods certainly do not *look like* foods that were grown in the earth. Unlike local garden foods that no amount of washing can divest entirely of dirt, and that normally have clods of soil, mud spatter, and insect residue on their roots and leaves, whitemen's foods have had all the traces of cultivation removed through factory processing. Whitemen's foods come packaged in manufactured wrappings, bags, containers, or cans, and the products inside are uniform, with no distinguishing marks pointing to the local conditions where the food was grown. Except for cans of tinfish, which have slight variations, the contents of individual packages are highly consistent. The uniformity is particularly striking when it comes to rice, flour, sugar, and salt, which are refined into generic bulk substances that are the same in every package.

Factory processing, commercial delivery, distribution through wholesalers, and retail sale in stores all contribute to the essential rooting of whitemen's foods in money. Orokaiva are well aware that the foods are designed to make money for those who manufacture and sell them. As Steven once said when explaining why whitemen's foods are so wet and tasty: 'The companies make them that way on purpose, in order to pull your money away.' It is to attract people's money that the foods are packaged in bright, colorful wrappings that Papua New Guineans find beautiful—so much so indeed that people sometimes use them as a form of decoration. Processed and packed in factories, whitemen's foods do not quickly spoil, so they are available at all times of the year unlike fresh garden foods, and they sit on the shelves in stores, ever ready to attract away people's money. They are made transportable by being canned, or by milling, drying, and packing them in bags or cartons. During my fieldwork, I was often asked what it was that was done to foods in factories and canneries such that they were prevented from spoiling. Individuals differed greatly in their understanding of factory processes. But everyone knew that they are places where people work making things for money wages, and that making money is their primary purpose. In short, the process of factory production is seen to be rooted in money, and thus so are the foods themselves.

When Orokaiva call whitemen 'rooted in' money, or say that they 'stand on' money, or call their foods 'money foods,' they are not actually conceding that money is equivalent to lands in being a true source of rootedness. What the notion is meant to express, rather, is simply that whitemen *require* money in order to subsist. As I was often told, 'You whitemen have to buy all your food. You have to buy everything. Without money, you starve.' To Orokaiva, the notion that a person should need money simply in order to eat is deeply immoral. Among the most common questions Orokaiva asked me was, how do people in America eat when they don't have money: what happens to them? Does the government look after them, or do they just starve? Most Orokaiva have money only sporadically; it is something that comes and goes in their lives. They might spirit away a 50-kina note in the roof thatch, or deposit a few hundred in the bank after a good harvest of cashcrops, but invariably the balance soon dwindles. It is consumed over a series of small trips to town to buy soap, salt, and kerosene; or someone might die, quickly exhausting one's savings on ritual payments and the purchase of store foods to feed mourners. Orokaiva villagers are too often penniless to be able to imagine a lifestyle in which money is an utter necessity. For them, money is just too easily stolen, wasted, or lost to be a reliable basis for survival. Thus, to Orokaiva being "rooted in money" would seem to make one highly vulnerable. Since money does not connect one to anything really solid and enduring, it is hardly considered a source of "rootedness" at all. As Steven once said of a relative who worked at a wage job and lived in company housing, 'She tries to impress us by bringing to the village large bags of rice for feasts, but we know that she is really living on [nothing more solid than] leaves' (*iki tempeto iriuja*). It was a clever pun, pointing simultaneously to leaves of money bills and the fluttering lightness of tree leaves far off the ground.

Taro Culture Is the Basis for Orokaiva Discourse about Whitemen's Foods

We have seen that Orokaiva ideas about eating and the nature of whitemen's foods form part of the construction of whitemen as a racial category in Orokaiva culture, aligning it with the qualities of weakness, softness, and lightness attributed to whitemen's foods, in contrast to the qualities of strength, hardness, and heaviness attributed to indigenous foods. These opposed qualities imply an underlying contrast between whitemen and Orokaiva in their connection to lands. From cultivating and eating their garden foods Orokaiva derive a profound rootedness in their lands, a rootedness that has many practical, mystical, social, and experiential dimensions. Whitemen, by contrast, manufacture foods in factories, and thus derive from their foods not a rootedness in lands but rather a dependence on money. The idea that whitemen are unrooted in lands has strong negative connotations, which are apparent in the negative qualities of weakness and softness ascribed to their foods. This evaluation depends upon Orokaivas' identity as people who are rooted in lands and in the culture of taro, an enduring fundamental reference point in Orokaiva cultural life.

To some extent, this notion of being rooted in lands and taro is an oppositional construct that takes on special value in light of the differences Orokaiva recognize between themselves and whitemen. If whitemen, too, were rooted in lands and needed to cultivate crops in order to eat, rootedness would not be meaningful in the same way for Orokaiva identity, because it would not be a dimension on which Orokaiva and whitemen differed. But we should not jump from this to conclude that rootedness is merely an oppositional symbol, the meanings of which are primarily constituted by the self-other relationship. And it would certainly be wrong to assume that the Orokaiva self-conception of rootedness originated as an "inversion" (Thomas 1992; cf. Friedman 1993; Sahlins 1993) of what westerners think about *themselves* (e.g., that westerners live in a materialistic society without connections to the earth). A self-other relationship with whitemen is not necessary for Orokaiva to think of themselves as people who are rooted in taro and their lands. As we have seen, their identification with taro is also motivated through contrasts they draw between themselves and neighboring peoples, such as the Managalasi, who they identify with yams. And their rootedness in lands is substantiated in many aspects of their lived experience, confirmed in the basic truth that they must plant gardens in order to eat, and elaborated through their assumptions about how the body is connected to lands in infancy through the ritual of the baby-

and-stick, and in later life through the mediation of the garden foods that a person routinely eats. It would thus be more accurate to say that it is the intense value Orokaiva place on rootedness in their vernacular culture that lends salience to the unrooted commodity nature of whitemen's foods.

The greatest changes that have been ushered in with whitemen are all in some way connected with getting or using money, most of which ends up spent on whitemen's food. Studies in the 1960s showed that, on average, Orokaiva households spent half their yearly income on store foods, with a substantial proportion of that going to rice and tinned protein (Waddell and Krinks 1968). Incomes in the 1990s were dramatically greater—as were income disparities—but the focus in spending remained on consumable items like soap, tobacco, kerosene, and a narrow selection of store foods, primarily rice, tinfish, and tinmeat, and less commonly flour, hard biscuits, oil, tea, sugar, coffee, instant noodles, and salt.

Given the importance of these foods in exchange, not to mention the long period of time that they have been familiar to people (even the great-great-great-grandparents of today's young adults knew about rice and tinfish), it is hardly surprising that they have become the subject of an elaborate vernacular discourse that is as highly conventional as are people's food purchases themselves. This modern discourse is the common stuff of mealtime talk. Although some more avid talkers and thinkers may develop quite sophisticated interpretations and others may have more information, all adult Orokaiva are conversant with the major themes described in the preceding sections, which are truisms, forming a common repertoire of stock interpretations and comments. After the first couple months of my fieldwork, I got so used to hearing certain stereotyped observations—for example, that rice is a light food and, after you eat it, your stomach does not feel pleasantly tight—that I had to make a special point of focusing my attention to record the examples. But however much Orokaiva eating and talk about foods has changed since the introduction of whitemen's foods, Orokaivas' identification with their taro and garden lands has remained compelling to them, constituting an enduring anchor of their identity.

The long historical continuity of Orokaiva identification with taro is evident in an important early response of Orokaiva peoples to colonization by whites, the prophetic "Taro Cult" movement (ca. 1912-40). Cult ritual centered on ecstatic trances (*jipari*) in which people became possessed by the spirits of taro plants. From these taro spirits, prophets received what were purported to be new varieties of taro, and they were inspired with new garden rituals that would induce new taro plantings to root deeply in the ground and thus to thrive. During a time when village men were increasingly leaving to work on plantations, cult activities sought to strengthen Orokaiva communities by reinvigorating their taro culture (Williams 1928).

A major theme developed in the taro prophets' discourse was that taro plants are like Orokaiva people. They have names, clans, communities, and kinship relationships including ones with humans. They also have human-like body parts, human language, sentiments, and will. These ideas are apparent in the statement of a former taro prophet, Edmond Donoba, from an interview done with his nephew, Orokaiva historian Willington Jojoga Opeba, in 1974:

> Taro . . . live the same way we do, sharing . . . obligations within networks of family ties. They live in communities with social institutions similar to ours—for example, all taro live in family and clan groups—and they identify their own relationships within this [family] network. . . . All taros have their own names and rather appreciate it if they are addressed according to their names and titles. There is Korove, Dabare, Goito, Biyama, Ovivi, Beanga, Kokora, Jaima, Sago [names of taro varieties] and of course many others. Biyama is addressed by other taro as an uncle, Jaima is a cousin sister and of course Sago is a brother.

The taro prophets' identification with taro was so complete that their reflections on gardening could empathetically take the taros' perspective. Donoba recalled the taro having told him,

> "We are born like you but the way you eat us and harvest us at times upsets us and disappoints us. . . . Our leaves . . . are like your hands and legs. They are an important part of us so do not harm them in any way. . . . Imagine if this had happened to you. Similarly tell our mother [referring to Donoba's wife] when she comes to harvest us and if we refuse (i.e., if she finds it hard to pull us out), 'do not attempt any further with the digging stick, because this means that we are not ready and willing.'" (Jojoga Opeba 1976, appendix 1[A], 3 [his translation here lightly edited])

Since the days of the Taro Cult, the world of Orokaiva people has changed profoundly. But what has remained virtually constant is Orokaivas' intense positive identification with taro. Taro cultivation is an area of impressive Orokaiva historical continuity, an area where the ways of the ancestors and people's present-day lives converge. In the mid-1920s, F. E. Williams wrote that the digging stick was "still" the main Orokaiva gardening tool (Williams 1928, 160), and today, eight decades later, it remains "still" so. While people are keen to use hoes, spades, forks, rakes, and even tractors in planting sweet potatoes, the digging stick is still in their eyes the best-adapted tool for planting taro, in part because of the peculiar requirements of the plant's propagation and rooting, and in part because the plants themselves are ascribed—today, as in the time of the Taro Cult—a traditional sensibility and conservative preferences. Taro *like* things done the way the ancestors did them, and after all, they are said to have thrived in the ancestors' time.

It is in their taro gardens, surrounded by their forest lands, where changes associated with whitemen are the least visible, that people feel closest to the traditional past of their ancestors. Virtually the only store-bought objects in gardens are the few that people have on their persons, like the clothes they are wearing (and in the garden these are always their oldest and most ragged), their work tools (a machete, an ax), perhaps a knife and a pot for cooking, and the nylon string that has replaced bark fibers in the knotted string bags used for carrying crops.[18] In their gardens, people are surrounded by the plants, trees, vines, and birds that their forebears also knew. They are surrounded by streams and pools where their ancestors bathed, by individual trees their ancestors planted, and by features of the land that form part of the knowledge their ancestors left them. In this setting people are most acutely aware that they are merely the current occupants of lands their ancestors gardened before them, and people often feel that their deceased forebears are actually with them in the gardens, protecting the taro.[19]

Thus, Orokaiva taro culture is a remarkably stable anchor of their identity. It is continually renewed in an area of people's lived experience that has remained both central for Orokaiva and very largely outside whitemen's influence. In saying that taro cultivation is an area where cultural continuity is concentrated, I am not claiming that the culture as a whole has remained constant, as if taro culture truly were Orokaiva culture writ small. Rather, I am identifying a privileged domain within the culture that continually grounds and resubstantiates in people's experience the terms in which both indigenous and imported elements are understood and evaluated (see also Mosko 1999). The historical continuity of Orokaiva identification with taro, and the many ways in which the basis for this identification is mirrored in their interpretations of whitemen and rice, suggest that whitemen's foods, in being the object of a century's worth of talk and action, have been conceptually well "worked over" through a process of cultural interpretation. No doubt this is part of why the discourse about whitemen's foods has become so highly standardized and culturally coherent.

The historical continuity of taro culture is not the only reason why it serves as a crucial ideological reference point in people's discourse about whitemen's foods. Another is its role in establishing a self-identity for Orokaiva that is positive. One of the most striking things about people's talk and action involving whitemen's foods is the disjuncture between people's well-developed critique of the foods (they are too light, weak, soft, unsatisfying, etc.) and the enormous expenditures people lavish on them, the gusto with which they eat them, and the desires they acknowledge the foods to arouse. So powerful are these desires that I was often warned to keep any tinfish or bags of rice I owned well hidden, since if they were visible others might ask for or steal them, or else try to 'pull' them from me using any number of stratagems. I became quickly acculturated to keeping these food items better hidden than almost any of my other belongings, some of which were of much greater objective value (such as my microphones and tape recorder), since people's attention would otherwise inevitably come to rest on them. While these foods have positive social uses and are indeed highly valued as gifts, such sentiments are not normally reflected in the ways people talk about them. When asked, people can say they enjoy such items as rice, tinfish, and sugar because they are tasty, greasy, or 'wet,' and the fact that they please others for the same reasons makes them valuable in exchange. But people are very comfortable criticizing whitemen's foods, a perspective which often leads to lengthy and animated elaborations of the positive qualities of their own foods, one of the best developed topics in the Orokaiva conversational repertoire. By the pervasive logic of hamo ari, which identifies people with their main foods, such talk is a way of expressing Orokaivas' sense of their own value in contrast to whitemen. Indeed, it is generally through talk about foods that people articulate views of whitemen that are the least ambiguous and most highly critical.

So in the construction of whitemen's foods we see a discourse that is anchored in the positive value of indigenous Orokaiva food production, just as were the discourses of earlier times. Although it is possible for people of every culture to think and talk critically about a given topic, some cultures offer much greater ideological resources for doing so than do others, and Orokaiva culture offers people substantial ideological resources for thinking and talking about food. This is especially true for the production and exchange of indigenous foods like taro and pork that are closely bound up with Orokaivas' most positive self-conceptions and core cultural values.[20] As we have seen, Orokaiva people's identification with taro is charged with the intensely positive value of garden work; it is tied to their sense of the past because of its unusually strong historical continuity; and it carries all the significance of a highly elaborated complex of reproductive rituals, food and body symbolism, and subsistence and social exchange functions, all of which serve to reaffirm Orokaiva people's rootedness in their land. With so much in the balance, it is easy to understand why Orokaiva might speak critically of whitemen's money foods. They evaluate whitemen's money foods from a standpoint of their rootedness in taro culture, to which they see whitemen's foods as opposed.

Clearly this is not a neutral discourse, but rather a deeply ethnocentric one, and its ethnocentrism is precisely what reveals the nature of the culture in which it is produced. In this discourse, indigenous foods are represented correctly as the foundation of vernacular cultural life, the form of life that Orokaiva identify as 'their own.' In reality, of course, this does not encompass the complex lives Orokaiva now lead in their entirety; those lives have come to include things imported from whitemen and from other cultures as well. But the vernacular form of life, in which Orokaiva cultivate taro and other crops on their lands, still frames the perspective from which they construct the whitemen's world as an inferior, ungrounded world. This kind of asymmetry has also been noted in the discourse of Samoans, who similarly contrast modernity with tradition as the 'customs of whites' versus the 'customs of Samoans.' Because people identify tradition with the customs of their own particular society, whereas modernity is experienced only "in its international dimension [as] money, the market, individualism, etc.," that is, in disembodied cultural features that seem to be untethered from any particular community, the terms in which such contrasts are cast "on balance favor tradition" (Tcherkézoff 1997, 334–35).

But if anything, it is this same solidity of Orokaiva rootedness in taro culture that makes possible the exuberance with which Orokaiva engage and incorporate the foreign. On the one hand, Orokaiva have an ethos of cultural importation and experimentation; there is a constant scanning of the horizon for new forms of value. On the other hand, they retain a kind of security in their traditional culture through the ongoing renewal of taro cultivation. And in fact, the cultivation of taro on their ancestral lands is a viable alternative to which people can retreat when they experience disappointment and problems in business, town life, or schooling. Orokaiva are able to eat their imported cake, and have their taro, too.

How Whitemen's Foods Are Used

Not only do Orokaiva talk about whitemen's foods, they also use them to represent themselves as whitemanlike in certain valued ways. Whitemen's foods are today becoming increasingly prominent in Orokaiva feasting, hospitality, family consumption, and gift exchange. When hosting important guests in their homes, as when feeding helpers and guests at a feast, people enliven indigenous garden foods with boiled rice, canned protein, and tea with milk and sugar. Quantities of whitemen's foods, raw in their packages, are used to decorate feasting platforms before being distributed to guests on top of piles of taro. Parents like to buy hardtack biscuits, frozen chickens, instant noodles, and cheese puffs to please their children and to promote good nutrition and growth. Visiting townspeople bring whitemen's foods to their relatives in the villages as gifts, and the foods are also increasingly important exchange objects within the village, where they are given as gifts to express social sentiments, acknowledge debts, and strengthen social relationships.

Given the overwhelmingly negative evaluation of whitemen's foods in people's talk about them, the positive value they are accorded in hospitality, feasting, nurture, and gift exchange might seem surprising. But the contradiction is only apparent. In talk, whitemen's foods are identified with whitemen simply and generically, and their deficiencies as light, soft, and weak are emphasized by the framing of the foods in terms of a discourse of self-other contrasts with regard to bodies, relations to lands, exchange customs, and so on. The evaluative framework is different, however, when whitemen's foods are used not as a basis for drawing cultural contrasts, but instead to achieve particular social aims through people's own actions. Under such circumstances, the general identification of whitemen's foods with whitemen is subsumed by the identifications between particular items, like a package of rice, and the specific individuals who own, display, and transact them. When rice is given as a gift, it is not only 'whitemen's food' generically identified with the whiteman other; it is also a particular gift item identified with the people who appropriate its value by giving and receiving it.[21]

Unlike in talk where whitemen's foods are figuratively situated within a contrasting separate and parallel whitemen's world, the foods as they are used in exchange are fully integrated into people's lived cultural world, where, as we shall see, they are most commonly transacted *alongside* indigenous foods: not in contrast to them, but supplementing them. This supplementary use of whitemen's foods reflects the kind of relationship with whitemen that Orokaiva would ideally like to have: a relationship in which they retain the rootedness in lands that allows them to reproduce their own forms of value, while simultaneously appropriating the special powers of whitemen they value, in particular whitemen's special capacity to expand their prestige and influence.

Feasting provides the most dramatic example of how Orokaiva appropriate whitemen's foods to their own ends. Indeed, the conversion of commodity foods into feast gifts has become an essential part of contemporary Orokaiva feasting. Although people assert that it would still be possible to hold a feast with 'only pork-taro,' that is, with only indigenous foods, most Orokaiva feast-givers today would in fact be embarrassed to do so, and in the year leading up to a feast they go to great lengths to obtain and save money specifically in order to buy the necessary whitemen's foods. Indeed, it is in anticipation of feasting that many village business projects are started. Some village men prepare for feasts long in advance by rehabilitating long-neglected coffee and cocoa gardens; others take short-term jobs; many taboo their betel nut trees so that the nuts will later be plentiful and can be sold in bulk at the markets. Women spend long days in the town market selling garden vegetables, forest products, coconuts, and bread rolls ('scones'). To convert the incremental income from such ventures into the large lump sum needed for feasting, villagers form rotating savings associations to which each individual contributes a fixed amount every fortnight; someone planning a feast can then look forward to a turn receiving the full pot of pooled contributions at a future date preceding the feast. (For more on these rotating savings associations see Ardener and Burman 1995.) Feast planners also contact relatives in town for help with contributions of store foods. During my fieldwork, I was asked to contribute to dozens of feasts, and I continue to receive letters asking for money gifts when feasts are being planned.

But while whitemen's foods have become all but essential to successful feasting, without pork and garden foods like taro they are not sufficient. As one man put it: 'Today we use your whitemen's foods to beautify the feast and please the guests. But whenever you make a feast, your taro and pork is what you must stand on.' By themselves, light foods such as rice and tinfish would be inadequate to truly satisfy and 'press down' feast recipients. They are unsuitable to effect the transfer of heaviness that we have seen is central to the symbolism of feasting, in which feast-givers make themselves light and raise up their own names by pushing down others under the weight of the heavy foods they are given as gifts. When whitemen's foods are given raw and in great quantities this is less of a problem, and people do sometimes say that such gifts as sacks of raw rice and wholesale cases of canned fish and meat 'pin down' or 'push down' their recipients. But the main reason feast-givers are able to exploit the valued qualities of whitemen's foods in feasting even though these foods are light and weak is that they use them as a supplement to, rather than as a substitute for, indigenous taro and pork.

This principle of supplementation is revealed in the way food piles at feasts are constructed. These piles are covered with an eye-catching top layer of betel nut, pork, rice, tinfish, tinmeat, and other whitemen's foods. But they are invariably built around a base pile of taro, surrounded by the other heavy garden staples bananas and yams. This is diagrammed in figure 5.2 (also see plate 3). Whitemen's foods are positioned with betel nut and pork at the top or outer edge of the pile where they are most visible, like the garnish on a western plate. Their colorful packaging is eye-catching and attractively bright. The beauty of the foods is exploited not only by feast-givers but also by feast-recipients, who bring to the feast reciprocal payments (*tihanga*) of food (see plate 5). The loose-mesh string bags in which tihanga payments are delivered can be huge, up to five feet wide and containing 150 lbs. of produce, and they are meant to draw the eyes of spectators when carried into the feasting area on a woman's back. Since earth-colored taro roots can be hard to see through the mesh, women sometimes incise designs into their peels that show up as pale white, and they artfully arrange the taro so that the other foods like bananas set them off. It is where the bag bulges out most visibly that they place the bright whitemen's foods: red cans of tinfish and tinmeat, white bags of sugar and rice, and bright yellow packets of noodles, cheese pops, and crackers. A variant form of tihanga consists of elaborate displays of foods on open, stretcherlike platforms carried in by young men. Here again, the foundation is taro and bananas under a dazzling spread of betel nut and eye-catching whitemen's foods. Orokaiva appropriate not only whitemen's foods but also the attention-getting qualities of their packaging, using these according to an indigenous aesthetic to create attention-getting images that enhance their own reputations. In several feasts I saw, shiny packages of cheese puffs and crackers fluttered high above the tihanga platforms and feast displays, hung on thin sticks like pennants.

All feasts present spectators with representations of the social selves of the feast-givers. Whatever the ritual purpose of a feast—whether for payment of a brideprice, the debut of a girl in puberty seclusion, the 'finishing' of the memory of a deceased, or the opening of a church—in its larger symbolism it serves as a representation of who the feast-givers are and what they are capable of. (This explains the intense material commitment that feast-givers put into it.) It renders visible their relationships to others who help them, and it externalizes their power to mobilize normally hidden resources. Large feasts in particular incorporate symbols of all the most valued elements of people's moral world: vitality, prosperity, fecundity, beauty, strength, social harmony, ancestral favor, rootedness, and so on. And one especially important value that people strive to represent in feasting is their capacity to extend their influence over people over distance. For

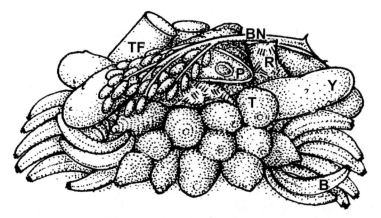

FIGURE 5.2 · Structure of the feast pile. The base of taro (T) is surrounded by yams (Y) and bananas (B), then topped with the most attractive and eye-catching items such as betel nut (BN), pork (P), and brightly packaged whitemen's foods like rice (R) and tinfish (TF).

example, at one brideprice payment feast, a man went to great lengths to bring in a group of foreign friends from the swamp country far to the north. He hired a truck to fetch them, paid them with a whole pig, and seated them conspicuously in a special shelter at the front of the feasting ground where they could easily be seen by everyone, sitting and drumming until the feast's end. In rendering visible his private exchange relationships with these distant people who were strangers to most of his fellow villagers (and potentially dangerous strangers at that, as the region they hailed from is assumed to be a bastion of sorcery), the feast displayed his influence with them as an aspect of his public persona.

In the present day, then, Orokaiva feast-givers simultaneously project two images of themselves that are created from elements of different symbolic repertoires. One image asserts their powers in the indigenous realm, through the medium of taro, yams, bananas, and pigs. They invite their Orokaiva exchange partners, perform traditional dance-songs, and display traditional ornaments like a feathered ceremonial staff and headdresses of plumes. The other image feast-givers project represents their power in the whitemen's world, and this they do through the medium of commodity foods like rice and tinfish. They hire trucks using money, and they display whitemen's ornaments like wristwatches, neckties, and cameras and film (see plate 17).

That Orokaiva recognize these images as distinct is apparent in many comments people make at feasts that evaluate traditional and whitemen's foods separately, as if the single feast pile were an amalgamation of two separate accounts. At one feast I attended I heard the feast-givers depre-cated by some of their relatives for not having assembled more store foods, although it was conceded that the amount of taro and pigs distributed was truly impressive. At another feast the host villagers were shamed when their guests arrived with a truckload of mostly whitemen's foods as their tihanga. In a blitz of activity the visitors unloaded the truck and created a gigantic feast pile more than ten feet in diameter covered in rice and flour bags. While the host villagers had prepared an impressive display of tradi-tional garden foods to give away, they had still been outdone. As one man from the host village put it, 'we are okay in taro, but our rice is like the tooth of a fruit bat compared to theirs, which is like the tusk of a pig.'

Ultimately, what feast-givers say about themselves with the whitemen's foods they give away at their feasts is not that they are entirely like white-men, but that they have whitemanlike powers that they can put into the service of their own ends. The food demonstrates these powers both in the way it comes into the feast and in the way it goes out. In coming into the feast, it shows the feast-givers' buying power, their power to obtain whitemen's wealth. Note that this is not a case like ordinary western consumerism, where symbolic value is attached to product choices that express individuals' personal identities. Here the choices are standardized: rice, tinfish, tinmeat, and such. When Orokaiva give away caseloads of these foods in feasting, rather than consuming them themselves, they man-ifest resistance to the powerful desires these foods are acknowledged to elicit.[22] In so doing, they demonstrate their ability to detach whitemen's wealth from the realm of commodities identified with factories and stores, and redirect it within the traditional system of reciprocity (*minekara*) where it expresses the indigenous virtue of generosity.

In the way whitemen's foods leave a feast, they create for the feast-givers a whitemanlike power to project their influence across distance. As we have seen, whitemen's foods embody an especially potent quality of light-ness associated with mobility and expansion, since in contrast to indige-nous foods, rice, tinfish, and tinmeat can be kept almost indefinitely without spoiling. The foods feast guests take away will be divided when they reach home among other people, who will in turn further subdivide them and carry them farther away still, at each step handing over the story of the feast along with the foods. In this way, the food serves as a vehicle for the feast-givers' names, publicizing their accomplishment in feasting and increasing their fame as it travels. In the tropical climate of lowland New Guinea, the travels of indigenous foods are sharply limited by time.

Without refrigeration pork spoils in hours, and whereas taro can in principle be kept for upward of ten days, feast taro is always harvested several days before the feast takes place, leaving little time for it to circulate before it rots. Of all the foods distributed at a feast, rice and canned foods preserve the longest, so people use them for sending shares to their relatives who live farthest away. Whitemen's foods are thus the foods that actually carry feast-givers' names to the most distant places.

Another arena where Orokaiva exploit the valued qualities of whitemen's foods while compensating for their limitations by balancing them with indigenous foods is hospitality. Hospitality is an important medium of Orokaiva social relationships. It enables people to travel to places where they are not self-reliant, and it serves as a means for hosts to build prestige and create debts that will invite later reciprocation. Although hospitality takes diverse forms, a major focus of attention is the host's provision of betel nut and foods. Hosts rarely allow guests who have seated themselves in their homes to leave without having consumed something, and if the visit was planned in advance, the guests are important, or they have come from afar, the meal that is served will be elaborate, with additional gifts of raw foods given to the guests to carry with them when they depart. The hope is that guests will leave with lasting positive memories of their hosts' generosity that will lead them to one day reciprocate.

As the recipient of much hospitality, I was often amazed and somewhat embarrassed to be offered expensive delicacies like margarine sandwiches on white bread bought in town by very poor villagers. But lavishing such expense on whitemen's foods was not done uniquely for me as a visiting white. On many occasions I saw families who were poor even by local standards buy goods on credit at a village tradestore in order to serve boiled white rice, or at the very least sugared tea, to a visiting relative from another part of the country, to a visiting church or government official, or to visiting members of a Christian "outreach" group who had been invited from another village. As one woman told me, guests will see 'from the way we live that these are not foods we eat all the time, but that we bought them just for them so that they will know what kind of people we are. They will know that we are people who take care of guests well, and that we are happy they came.' Indeed, it is in part an effect of poverty that whitemen's foods are so meaningful in hospitality, since the knowledge that they are a real sacrifice heightens the impression of generosity. The relative scarcity of whitemen's foods in the village also increases their desirability, thus confirming their status as luxury foods that can be used to build prestige.

However, hosts prefer not to serve whitemen's foods alone. Most commonly guests are served 'mixed food' (*mikis indari*): large trays or basins of garden staples in thin coconut milk mixed with local greens, store-bought instant noodles, and chicken, tinfish, or tinmeat. Alongside such mixed food, which Orokaiva credit to the historical influence of Polynesian and Filipino missionaries, meals served to guests also generally include a large bowl of white rice and bowls of plain boiled tubers, as well as small dishes of salty cooked greens to be eaten as relish. People set out large quantities of indigenous garden foods not only because they always have them on hand, nor only because people's own garden produce is such a source of pride. Orokaiva simply consider whitemen's foods insufficient to fully satisfy their guests, since such foods are too light. I found that even in town, where many Orokaiva eat rice on a daily basis as their major starch staple, women would go to the market and buy heavy, hard root crops and cooking bananas for serving at fancy meals (as on Christmas) and to special guests (like me). A well-educated Orokaiva friend in Port Moresby habitually calls such village-style garden food "real food," his English gloss for the vernacular expression, *indari be*, 'true food' or 'substantial food.' Like villagers, he contrasts this "real food" with whitemen's "light food, which is not enough to make us feel really full."

In the villages, where whitemen's food is often called "light *indari*" ('light food'), an increasingly popular format for elaborate hospitality is to offer a separate first course of light indari appetizers—wet, cooling, soft foods like white bread spread with margarine, ripe bananas and papaya slices, hardtack biscuits, and sweet drinks—before the main course of rice and filling garden foods.[23] This format, with its concentrated display of whitemen's foods, allows hosts to demonstrate their strength in the domain of taupa kastom without sacrificing clarity in the show of strength in heavy indigenous foods. There is a feeling that something is missing from any meal that does not include heavy foods, so that whenever hosts serve foods like rice and tinfish alone, they apologize that 'it is only light.'

The one village context in which light whitemen's foods are served alone without apology is in the new form of feasting called rice or tea "competitions." At these raucous events, a group of men, like a soccer team, youth group, or subclan or hamlet group, prepares an uncommonly huge amount of boiled white rice or milky sugared tea for another group that they challenge to come consume it. The competition pits the hosts against the guests. The guests win if they manage to consume everything, while the hosts win if they succeed in setting out so much that the guests cannot possibly finish it; in that case the rice or tea is said to have 'killed' the guests in much the way that guests at a feast are said to be 'killed' by the pork-taro they are given. I saw only two of these and heard of four others, including two at which the hosts proved unable to amass enough food to make the challenge worthwhile, so that the competition reverted to a normal hospitality meal. At both the competitions I saw, the hosts were reciprocating earlier challenges, and in one they were soliciting potential dancers in advance of a large feast; here the cauldrons of rice the guests were served with tinfish were also understood as their inducement and payment for the dancing. (In classic Orokaiva fashion, the outcome was ambiguous, both sides claiming victory.)

In answering my questions about why they hold these sorts of events, people emphasized the contrast between their exaggeratedly heavy eating at the competitions, which they said is typical of 'us crazy Kaiva,' and the light eating habits of whitemen, who eat only small amounts and yet somehow feel full. The competitions generate enormous anticipation and interest, with rumors of the hosts' preparations circulating widely in advance. The excitement is charged by the promise of a kind of impossibility: that the normal scarcity of whitemen's foods might be overturned in an awesome display of abundance, and that the foods' unsatisfactory quality of lightness might be overcome by their sheer quantity. The quantity would be transformed into quality such that the huge amounts of the light food would give it the same qualities as a heavy food. For once there would be too much of the rice that there is never enough of; for once people would feel their stomachs to be full and tight, indeed, almost bursting, from having eaten so much of this otherwise insufficiently filling food. Instead of the reliable heaviness of pork and garden foods, rice and tea competitions are premised on the hope that the lightness of rice and sugar will be transformed into a heaviness that, like taro, will weigh the guests down as it lifts the hosts up, expanding their fame as they give it away.

Anomalous Categories in the Racial Symbolism of Foods

There are some introduced and commodity foods that are not strongly identified with whitemen and are not classified as 'whitemen's foods.' When we compare these foods to those Orokaiva *do* regularly classify as whitemen's foods, we find that they do not fit the pattern; they do not authenticate the opposition Orokaiva draw between themselves and whitemen. It is those foods that do—like taro and pork versus rice and tinned protein—that Orokaiva commonly focus on in their talk. These are the foods that have the clearest position and most highly developed symbolism in Orokaiva culture, and it is these I have focused on in illustrating the basic premise of hamo ari, that people come to embody the qualities of the foods that they eat. But other foods are more ambiguous or anomalous, since they lack the neat alignment of oppositions such as heavy/light, hard/soft, and rooted/unrooted that I have described, and these other foods are not so closely identified with categories of people, Orokaiva or anyone else. In Orokaiva people's ordinary talk about themselves and whitemen, their respective foods and the ways they differ, these anomalous foods are rarely mentioned; they are simply swept under the ideological rug. By examining these anomalous instances, we can better understand how the Orokaiva system of foods forms the basis for a cultural construction of race, in which the foods are primary objects supporting stereotyped racial categories. Table 5.1 presents my analysis of the full system of Orokaiva foods, which I discuss in the following pages.[24]

Most of the information condensed under categories I and V is already familiar; categories II, III, and IV are new. There are three crucial dimensions of symbolism that motivate the classification. The first of these dimensions, which we have not needed to discuss until now, is the food's cultural origin. It is needed to distinguish category III, which consists of foods that are not considered whitemen's foods even though whitemen are known to have introduced them, because Orokaiva now grow these foods themselves. This shows that cultural origin matters less in determining whether foods are whitemen's than does their place of cultivation or production. It is where the food is produced—that is, whether it is grown on local lands or manufactured in a distant factory—that establishes its basic value as either rooted in local lands or rooted in money, the second main dimension of symbolism. The third dimension, iconicity, is a composite of the properties of foods like hard/soft, heavy/light, and strong/weak that are understood to be transferred between people and their foods according to the logic of hamo ari.

For foods in categories I and V these three dimensions of symbolism are closely aligned, which is why these foods are so strongly identified with categories of people and so focal in people's talk about the social meaning of foods. Category I foods are 'whitemen's foods'; category V foods are the contrasting Orokaiva foods. Although I have not represented it in the table, each of these categories is centered on a core of main foods (taro and pork, rice and tinned protein). These core main foods are used emblematically for the corresponding identity category and form the subject of the elaborate discourse that has been presented at length in this chapter; it is in these foods that the symbolic system of self-other contrasts is best supported by

TABLE 5.1 The System of Foods

	Category				
	I	II	III	IV	V
Description	'Whitemen's foods'	Other foods sold in stores	Locally grown, western-introduced foods	Other locally grown indigenous foods	'Orokaiva foods'
Examples	White rice, tinfish, tinmeat; white bread, instant noodles, flour, sugar, milk powder, salt, hot and cold sweetened drinks, crackers, cookies, other packaged snacks; frozen chickens	European-type fresh vegetables sold in stores (e.g., broccoli, carrots, English cabbage, onions, Irish potatoes); fresh or frozen red meat (esp. cases of frozen lambflaps)	Chinese taro, corn, local rice, pumpkin-squashes, green onions, peanuts, green peppers, tomatoes, cucumbers, mangos, papayas, watermelon, pineapples; cows, ducks	Sweet potatoes, soft bananas, greens, local fruits, nuts, breadfruit; most wild game (wallabies, bandicoots, fruitbats, snails, insects, tree squirrels, possums, etc.)	Taro, yams, hard bananas; pork, village fowl. Also soft, light, cool foods that provide balance (e.g., coconuts, betel nut, sugar cane, pitpit, sago, pandanus)
Cultural origin	Whitemen	Whitemen	Whitemen	Indigenous (incl. other New Guinea)	Indigenous
Rootedness in local lands	Manifestly factory processed and packaged (rooted in money)	Sold as a commodity, but may *look like* foods grown on local lands	Locally grown: rooted in local lands	Locally grown: rooted in local lands	Locally grown: rooted in local lands
Iconicity	Markedly whitemenlike qualities: soft, light, and weak; not well-balanced	Anomalously Orokaiva-like, ambiguous, or muddled qualities	Ambiguous or muddled qualities	Ambiguous or muddled qualities	Markedly Orokaiva-like qualities: hard, heavy, and strong; well-balanced
Identification with whitemen or Orokaiva	Strongly identified with whitemen; significant conceptual elaboration of hamo ari ideas ('whitemen are what they eat')	Weakly identified with whitemen; hamo ari ideas are elaborated only where they fit with the foods' iconicity (see explanation in text)	Weakly identified either with whitemen or Orokaiva, depending on iconicity; generally very little elaboration of hamo ari ideas	Weakly identified with Orokaiva; eclectic elaboration of hamo ari ideas	Strongly identified with Orokaiva; enormous conceptual and ritual elaboration of hamo ari ideas; some foods personified
Given as feast gifts (raw)	Yes	No, except for cartons of frozen lamb that are substituted for pork	No, except for locally raised cows that are substituted for pork	No	Yes

Orokaivas' selective perceptions about the foods. While peripheral foods in these categories (e.g., instant noodles and flour in category I; coconuts and sago in category V) are associated unambiguously with Orokaiva or white-men, people's discourse about them is less highly conventionalized, they are less often talked about, and they are not used on their own as emblems of identity. While these foods do not contravene the symbolic system of self-other contrasts overtly, they also do not substantiate it as compellingly and completely as do the core foods; even though they are rooted in local lands they do not fully realize the ideal values of heaviness, hardness, and strength. In short, foods of categories I and V are the ones that best lend themselves to a rich and densely integrated oppositional symbolism, which is why they play such a prominent role in Orokaiva discourse on race, why they are ideologically limelighted. As discussed in the previous section, these two categories also contain nearly all the foods that may be given raw as feast gifts.[25]

For category IV foods, which have been a part of Orokaiva diets for a very long time, hamo ari ideas are similarly well developed. But they are also highly eclectic, both in the range of properties that can be transferred (recall the 'dustiness' of owls' meat) and in the differential ways that men, women, and children are thought to be susceptible to them (hence they form the basis for a highly complex system of food prohibitions).

Hamo ari ideas are least developed—and certainly least conventional-ized—for category II and III foods where the dimensions of symbolism are not clearly aligned. In racial terms, these foods are ambiguous or anom-alous. Category II contains foods that are identified with whitemen because they are sold in the foreign-owned supermarkets in Popondetta, but Orokaiva do not see marked similarities between their properties and those of whitemen themselves. The main members of this category are European-type vegetables such as brown onions, carrots, potatoes, broc-coli, cauliflower, and cabbage, and fresh or frozen red meats. The vegeta-bles are ambiguous because they are whitemen's in cultural origin and shipped in from afar, but they look more like products of the soil than like products of factories.

The ambiguity of European-type vegetables is reflected in people's talk about them, including in the fact that they do so only rarely. When people do mention them, they ignore their appearance of rootedness that is anom-alous in the vernacular scheme, instead stressing the vegetables' inferior size and limpness when compared to the large, fresh, healthy, vigorous veg-etables grown by Orokaiva in their own gardens. In point of fact, the veg-etables sold in the Popondetta stores generally do look meager, sickly, and limp. Stocks are small since both the supply and the demand are highly irregular. Even in the fanciest of the town stores, the refrigerator cases hardly overflow in the kind of bounteous produce display familiar from American supermarkets. If there is any fresh produce in stock at all, it is likely to consist of but a few tiny cauliflowers, a few stalks of rubbery broccoli, and one or two bunches of drooping carrots. It is therefore understandable that Orokaiva do not consider European-type vegetables to be suffused with strength and vitality. I was sometimes told that these vegetables had 'lost their strength' by 'sitting in the cold' of the refrigerator, since extreme cold is regarded as antithetical to power, vigor, and health. I once heard Steven call them, in his idiosyncratic English, "unproductive veggies." They "do not produce blood," he said, unlike "our garden veggies" which "produce a lot of blood." By blood he seemed to mean hot blood, the kind Orokaiva associate with masculine vigor, strength, and productivity. Because they regularly eat these kinds of vegetables, Steven suggested, Australian visitors to the village are too weak to assimilate the Orokaiva garden foods they are fed without getting sick.

The only European-type vegetable that villagers commonly purchase is brown onions. People like the flavor that onions add to foods stewed in coconut milk, and they regard the use of onions as part of the modern urban and whitemen's style of cooking that is especially favored for dishes contributed to village church gatherings and other high prestige functions. Yet I never heard people actually refer to onions as a 'whitemen's food.' People did not speak of them to me as my own food, nor did they ever mention them when discussing what whitemen's foods were like in general. What people did mention was that the onions they bought were grown in the PNG Highlands. To Orokaiva it makes sense to attribute these hard root vegetables to the lands where they are actually cultivated rather than to their original cultural source, whitemen, who are associated not with gardening but with money.

A similar ambiguity characterizes potatoes, which Orokaiva call "English potatoes" (*inglis potete*). The potatoes for sale in PNG stores are displayed without having been scrubbed clean, so that they still have dirt clods clinging to their skins. Of all the foods available in stores, these tubers bear the closest resemblance to indigenous staples like taro or sweet potatoes. As with onions, potatoes are identified simultaneously with stores and with the lands where they are grown, again, in the PNG Highlands. I never heard Orokaiva volunteer potatoes as a general example of 'whitemen's foods.' And when I mentioned that potatoes were a staple starch I ate at home in America, people sometimes said this meant that I was really 'the

same' as them in culture and nature. Ever quick to extrapolate from qualities of a food to broad social generalizations, my Orokaiva interlocutors
took it to show that *Americans* are really an anomalous sort of whitemen
who eat good, hard, strong food as do Orokaiva. This in turn they took to
explain why American individuals are physically large and why the United
States is such a big and strong country. It moreover explains why
Australians needed American help during World War II; the Australians, as
"normal" whitemen, ate only light, weak foods, and so were too weak by
themselves to prevail against the Japanese. Thus notwithstanding that they
are called "English" potatoes, that they are sold in stores, and that whitemen eat them, potatoes are even more racially ambiguous than are onions.

The other ambiguous store foods that make up category II are fresh and
frozen meats. In recent years, the use of store-bought meat in the village
has increased dramatically. Village tradestores do not sell meat, since there
is no electricity for their refrigeration. But the larger stores in town sell beef
and lamb in various cuts, of which the most popular among villagers is the
most inexpensive, frozen lambflaps—fatty sheep trimmings that are
lumped together with pieces of bone, frozen, and then cut crosswise into
sheets. Like other fresh and frozen red meat, lambflaps are similar to
Orokaiva fresh pork. When cooked, they are tough, chewy, and greasy.
Lambflaps are categorized as *o visi* 'animal flesh,' or *o sipsip* 'sheep/lamb
meat,' in contrast to the beef found in tinmeat, which, as mentioned earlier,
is treated as its own type of animal substance in vernacular speech; it is not
generally referred to by the normal vernacular term for 'meat' or 'flesh,' *visi*,
which has connotations of strength and hardness. (The fresh or frozen beef
sold in stores is similarly called visi and *o bulamakau*, 'the animal cow.')
Lambflaps are considered so similar to pork that they can be used as a substitute for it. It is increasingly common for lambflaps to be distributed in
place of pork at small feasts, where whole or half cases of frozen lambflaps
(also called *sip katen*, 'sheep/lamb [in a] carton') are presented as the equivalent of segments of a pig.[26] Although pork and lambflaps may both be
used in a feast, I never saw both presented concurrently in a single feast gift.
In contrast, pork, tinfish, and tinmeat are often presented together, suggesting that they are treated as different *kinds* of meat, while lambflaps and pork
are treated as alternative varieties of a single kind.

As with store vegetables, lambflaps are a racially ambiguous food. On
the one hand, they are sold in stores and are understood to be a commodity
imported from the whitemen's country of New Zealand ("Product of New
Zealand" is usually printed in large letters on the wholesale cartons). On
the other hand, in their properties lambflaps closely resemble pork in being

hard, heavy, and strong, and, unlike tinmeat, they have not been factory processed to the point where their animal origin is no longer easily recognizable. Like the other ambiguous category II foods, lambflaps and other red meat bought in stores are not strongly identified as 'whitemen's food.' People did not tell me that lambflaps were 'my food,' and when I replied to questions about the foods I ate at home by saying that we actually ate not tinmeat but rather fresh meats more like these, it always struck people as a novel and unexpected idea.

The other ambiguous category is category III. These are foods that whites have introduced, but that Orokaiva themselves cultivate on their own lands. Since they have therefore become rooted in local lands, they are treated very much like the indigenous foods of category IV. With few exceptions they are not called 'whitemen's foods,' and they are attributed to whitemen only historically. A clear example is Chinese or Singapore taro (*Xanthosoma sagittifolium*), which thrives in Orokaiva gardens (people plant it especially on steep valley slopes) and which in recent years has become a major source of calories in the Orokaiva diet. The aboveground portion of the plant looks like a much larger version of true taro (*Colocasia esculenta*), but its growth cycle is different, and whereas true taro has only one corm, or edible root, the mature Chinese taro plant has up to ten edible cormels that grow out from an inedible main 'mother' corm (often fed to pigs). Chinese taro cormels range in size from about three to fifteen inches and, when roasted or boiled are similar to true taro, only somewhat less gluey. It is freely cited as the same kind of hard, heavy food that makes villagers strong. At the same time, however, its introduction among Orokaiva is widely credited to an early white Anglican missionary, Henry Holland. People seem not to notice that the plant's vernacular name, *ba barija*, 'Wariya taro,' hints at an origin among the culturally and linguistically similar people of the Wariya River area to the north.[27] The story of Father Holland's importation of Chinese taro is continually republicized by Orokaiva supporters of the Anglican Mission who use it as evidence that the church has materially improved people's lives, so it enjoys wide currency throughout the region. But even so, there is no implication that Chinese taro is therefore a 'whitemen's food.'

Similarly, certain other foods that Orokaiva cultivate, including peanuts, green onions, and several varieties of bananas, although generally considered to have been introduced by whitemen, are neither called 'whitemen's foods' nor strongly identified with whitemen. Things are somewhat more complicated in the case of corn, pumpkin-squashes, watermelon, pineapple, and papaya, foods which were in fact introduced by whites into New

Guinea but which diffused into some Orokaiva areas via intermediary peoples in advance of whites.[28] Among Orokaiva today, it is ambiguous whether these foods are introduced or indigenous. While a few very old people I asked affirmed that corn and pumpkins were introduced by whites, most others thought them indigenous. Many people consider papayas indigenous, but there is no consensus on pineapples or watermelons. But even those who maintain that the foods did come from whitemen historically do not therefore call them 'whitemen's foods.'

As to whether people believe that these are foods that whitemen eat, it appears to depend not on the foods' imputed origin, but rather on their iconic similarity to whitemen according to the logic of hamo ari. So whitemen are said to eat ripe fruits, which are light, wet, and sweet; whitemen are *not* thought to eat corn and pumpkin-squashes, which, albeit not very heavy and filling, are enough so that they can be used as the main food in a meal. When I mentioned that corn and squashes were indeed widely grown and eaten in America, people were surprised, and would again cite the overlap with their own foods to support the idea that this meant I as an American was more like them than like typical whitemen. In short, what this overview of categories II and III foods shows is that where it is possible to distinguish degrees of identification with whitemen, such as with broccoli and papaya versus brown onions and corn, the identification with whitemen is stronger where the food more closely resembles whitemen iconically. And we consistently find that foods that are cultivated locally are not strongly identified with whitemen because they are rooted in local lands.

There are only two exceptions to the generalization that locally raised foods are not classified as 'whitemen's foods': certain market vegetables and what are called 'whitemen's chickens' (*taupa di*). Tomatoes, green peppers (capsicums), and English cabbages are all locally grown 'whitemen's foods,' but they are all cultivated by villagers primarily as cash-crops to sell at market. English cabbages (called *bol kabis* 'ball cabbages') in particular are highly marked as whitemen's because they are the only garden crop grown in the village that can be sold to stores.[29] Moreover, growing cabbages successfully in the region requires very expensive hybrid seeds that must be bought in the capital; villagers cannot reproduce the plants by taking seeds from their own flowering plants. Cabbage seedlings require nurserying, and even the transplants must be given elaborate care and watering until they are harvested. The expense and effort of raising cabbages is offset by the high price they fetch and the prestige of transparently producing for the local commodity market represented by town stores. Although people specifically value the heaviness and hardness of cabbages (qualities that differentiate them from local greens), they do not dwell on the discrepancy between these qualities and whitemen's lightness and softness. Instead, cabbages are attributed to whitemen because they participate in a wider set of relationships among money, markets, and stores. They are cultivated explicitly as a business, like other cash-crops.

The second exception, and final food I will discuss, is village-raised 'whitemen's chickens.' Like English cabbages, these chickens are raised as a form of business, and again as with cabbages, part of their reproduction cycle is purchased as a commodity. Day-old chicks must be ordered from a government agency, air-freighted in, and picked up in town. Once they are brought back to the village, they are installed in a coop. Unlike 'village chickens' (*da di*), which wander freely around the village and are cooped only at night, if at all, the whitemen's chickens stay in their large coop permanently and always separately from the local birds. Unlike the village birds, they do not subsist on insects, worms, and villagers' food scraps, but rather on factory-processed store-bought chicken feed. These chickens thus live and eat like whitemen: they always stay indoors, they do not roam in the forest, and they eat store-bought food. The unmistakable whiteman-like nature of these chickens is cast into sharp relief by indigenous fowl. Whereas the free-ranging village birds are lean and muscular, and their meat when cooked is tough and leathery, the permanently secluded white-men's chickens are plump and weak, and their meat when cooked is tender. People sometimes laughingly call it 'light meat,' *visi ejeha*, a vernacular oxy-moron, implying that it differs from the heavy, strong meat of village chick-ens and pigs and of all wild game. The racial symbolism is underscored by the contrast between their bright white plumage and the plumage of the vil-lage birds, which is mottled brown. That the chickens are white like their eponymous whitemen makes for a great deal of joking in which the birds are called by the same humorous hyperbolic nicknames (like 'flaring torch-skin men,' 'flaring Coleman lantern men,' and 'white cockatoo men') as are whitemen themselves. Indeed, in their close identification with whitemen, these chickens resemble category I foods, and like these other foods they are acceptable for use in feasting.

Because foods in categories II, III, and IV are ambiguous in their racial symbolism, they tend to be overlooked or attenuated in people's talk about race. Instead, attention is focused on foods like taro and rice where the various dimensions of racial symbolism are clearly aligned and which thus form opposite poles of identification. The meanings of these ideologically polarized foods are highly elaborated in conventionalized discourse so that their racial symbolism is continually reinforced in everyday speech. In contrast, there are no vernacular labels corresponding to the intermediate categories; indeed, there is virtually no talk at all about any food's ambiguity with respect to race. In constructing whitemen's foods as soft, Orokaiva overlook the hardness of lambflaps; in constructing them as light, they overlook the manifest heaviness of English cabbages and packaged salt. As always, typification depends on throwing out the deviations (Canguilhem 1978 [1943]; Foucault 1979). The net effect is that the continuous nature of the overall system is ideologically hidden from view.

The Construction of Race not in Persons, but in Objects

As we have seen, Orokaiva individuals inherit from their culture an elaborate system of ideas about whitemen's foods that are conventionalized in vernacular moral discourse, materialized in activities where the foods are used, and grounded in the particularities of Orokaiva lived experience, such as how whitemen's foods in their packages draw people's eyes, and how the foods, when eaten, affect people's bodies. The conventionalized meanings and institutionalized uses of whitemen's foods within Orokaiva experience substantiate crucial aspects of the Orokaiva construction of whitemen. Most obviously, the fact that whitemen's foods must be bought with money continually reaffirms for Orokaiva the basic notion that whitemen subsist on things that are bought, rather than on things that they themselves produce. They do not eat from the land, but instead purchase what they need in stores. Unlike Orokaiva, who often emphasized to me that they could live entirely outside of the cash economy, whitemen are understood to inhabit a world in which even the most basic necessities of food and shelter must be bought. To Orokaiva, this confirms the assumption that whitemen are wealthy: how else could they afford to buy all the expensive foods that they require for basic subsistence? The lightness of their foods is consistent with whitemen's light eating habits and weak and soft bodies, while whitemen's mobility—their impressive capacity for traveling and extending control across distance—is clearly facilitated by their foods' preservability, ease of transport, and ubiquity in stores wherever one travels. Moreover, because whitemen's foods are not rooted in lands, the whitemen who subsist on them are likewise unnaturally light, unbalanced by what Orokaiva see as normal and necessary moral and interpersonal attachments.

What is so interesting about this system of foods is what it teaches us about the cultural construction of race. All too often in discussing race, we assume that it must be defined in terms of heredity, class, or ethnicity, effectively reducing race to some stable quality of persons that we take as more real (Omi and Winant 1994; Smedley 1999). And we are confounded in these well-worn approaches by applying them always to our own society, where the familiar theories are so widely taken for granted that they form part of the problem itself, and where issues of race are so morally and politically charged that our ability to think creatively about them has come in some respects to a standstill, hung up as it is on the divergence between the simplicity of our racial categories and the incontrovertible complexity of populations of persons. One reason why the discourse of otherness is often treated as "suspect" (Carrier 1995a, 1) is that the construction of cultural others is generally taken to be primarily a representation of people, when in fact it is primarily a construction of objects, images, practices, places, and institutions. As we well know, an entire movement of modern art, primitivism, was able to develop with virtually no recourse to actual "primitive" people in the flesh, relying instead almost entirely on a category of artifacts: African masks. And how different, after all, are U.S. whites' stereotypes of African Americans, which are so largely constructed in terms of elements like body gestures and ways of moving, styles of clothing and genres of music (blues, hip-hop, gangsta rap), types of cooking, models of cars, and images of rural poverty and urban street culture (housing projects, drug-peddling gangs), symbols that are independent of actual African American persons?

The analysis of whitemen's foods developed in this chapter shows that a cultural construction of race is more than just a set of ideas, bad or otherwise. It is rather a complex integration of ideas, objects, and practices that substantiate and reinforce one another. In Orokaiva foods we see clearly how the popular understanding of a racial other is built upon a socially relevant set of categories that need not correspond to any well-defined population of real persons. The fact that the categories are not reducible to essential qualities shared by actual persons means that (western scientific theories of race notwithstanding) *race is not an inherent quality of persons at all*. Where the construction of whitemen is substantiated for Orokaiva is in objects such as foods, activities such as business, and places such as town, all of which are themselves imbued with racial characteristics. These qualities exist independently of white persons and are experienced by Orokaiva people as a part of their own lives, within their own cultural and moral world. As we have seen, Orokaiva constructions of race *do* correspond to reality—just not to the realities of actual persons and groups.

The Orokaiva system of foods has the characteristic structure we expect of a system of racial categories; it is anchored by neatly opposed prototypes which are ideologically foregrounded and which fail to adequately comprehend the continuum of intermediate instances that have ambiguous, anomalous, or hybrid characteristics. Category I and V foods, prototypical whitemen's and native foods, correspond of course to Orokaiva typifications of whitemen and themselves. The foods in categories II, III, and IV correspond to what people know about real individuals that exceeds the typifications, involves variation, and introduces complexities as with English potatoes that have clods of dirt still clinging to them and so have the appearance of being rooted, or with pineapples that Orokaiva grow in their own gardens but which are a sweet, wet, and weak food associated with whitemen. These intermediate cases involve mismatches among their features, just as white women, Orokaiva children, nonwhite foreigners, and Orokaiva migrants to town all defy the neat primary (gendered) racial opposition between blackmen and whitemen. Such realities make it impossible to analyze the Orokaiva construction of whitemen versus Orokaiva blacks as a racial classification of actual persons. But because foods are an ideologically focal domain of racial symbolism for Orokaiva that is central to their own identity, it *is* possible to analyze racial categories as they are manifest in the Orokaiva system of foods.

With this analysis of the symbolism of race, it becomes clear that raced objects (including places, activities, institutions, images, etc.) are sufficient to substantiate racial stereotypes, so that direct experience with actual persons is rendered unnecessary. Because people know raced objects as part of their own lived experience within their own cultural world, the racial ideas they embody are substantiated in particularly compelling ways; people experience them as really true. Orokaiva know that whitemen are soft and light from their own bodily sensation of hunger soon after eating rice, just as they know that they themselves are hard from the tight feeling in their belly just after a meal of taro. Such viscerally acquired knowledge cannot be readily unseated by mere evidence that a racial category applies imperfectly to any actual person.

This experiential immediacy of raced objects helps explain why my informants' views of whitemen were so remarkably durable in the face of the obvious counterexample I presented as an actual white man. From my own perspective rice and tinfish were emphatically not "my" people's main foods, though I was often asked (and often told) by Orokaiva to confirm that they were. The question of what foods I ate at home was one I was asked very often, and at first I tried to evade the question for fear of distorting my findings. But once I had gotten past my naïve preconception that people's views would be fragile and liable to shift, I tried out various answers that were truer from my own perspective, and found that none of them really stuck. I began to speak freely of eating English potatoes, pasta, bread, and fresh meats and vegetables—sometimes adding, when mentioning bread, that in my home country I did not eat the kind of white, airy, light loaves that were found in Popondetta, but rather another type of bread that was dark-colored, dense, and heavy, a bread that really made one feel full. On occasion, I even explained that in my country we ate different kinds of food in the morning, afternoon, and evening; indeed, we ate different foods from one day to the next, so that we did not really have 'main foods' the way Orokaiva do. But the one answer I never gave was the one people expected, namely that at home I ate boiled white rice with tinfish as my main food, and at times I even went so far as to contradict this notion outright: 'We in America do not eat much rice. That is the main food of people in China, Japan, and Indonesia. Nor do we eat tinmeat or tinfish. People here consider these good foods, but at home we consider them rubbish.' When I said such things, people did not openly disagree, and they did not question my authority as a white person to discuss my own foods. But neither did they accept what I said; except insofar as they suggested that I (or Americans, etc.) was thereby atypical, they did not pursue my iconoclastic contentions in conversation, and they did not repeat them. Moreover, when they would subsequently serve me rice in their homes, they would still call it 'you whitemen's food,' ignoring my disavowal. In short, the truth about whitemen that I might have been thought to represent as a white person was shown to be very largely irrelevant in the local context of the village, where rice and tinfish truly are whitemen's foods in the things people say and do in their everyday lives.[30]

Just as the racial symbolism of foods is substantiated by their embeddedness in Orokaiva people's lived world, so too is their moral ambiguity. People evaluate whitemen's foods either positively or negatively, depending on their particular aims in the context of speaking. The rice and tinfish that are disparaged in one context as merely light, soft, and weak may be valued by the same person in another context for being tasty, wet, and handy to transport. Rice is disparaged, as we have seen, in the common genre of talk that opposes it to taro, since Orokaiva identify taro so fully with the best in themselves; but where rice is used as an adornment on feast piles, it becomes associated with the positively valued powers of whitemen that Orokaiva want to appropriate for themselves, such as the power to extend one's influence over distance and in the world of money. Because objects like rice exist outside of persons, they are appropriable by individuals who can represent the objects' symbolic connection to the foreign other in morally selective ways depending on whether the aim is self-critique or self-aggrandizement.

While the racial classification of foods is clearly a symbolic cultural construction, it is by no means entirely arbitrary; it is motivated by the nature of the foods and supported by years of reinforcement within Orokaiva culture. We should recall that the prototypical whitemen's foods, rice and tinned protein, were among the first commodity foods that were introduced historically, and their initial selection by the European colonists was guided by criteria of transportability and preservability that are still relevant today. Moreover, people's understanding of the foods is reinforced by modern marketing, not to mention the process of commodification itself. Whitemen's foods *are* rooted in a world that turns on money; they *are* carefully refined in flavor and texture and packaged deliberately brightly in order to appeal specifically to Papua New Guinea villagers as a target group of consumers. The system is thus one that selects from the possibilities presented in the reality of Orokaiva lived experience, even if it is one that has been polarized and refined in its racial symbolism as, over time, people—in cooking, eating, working, shopping, talking, thinking, acting, and interacting—have progressively sharpened the contrasts and caused the inconsistencies to recede.

6. Conclusion: Whitemen Beyond

In the preceding chapters we have explored the meaning of whitemen in the Orokaiva cultural world. We have seen that Orokaiva attribute to whitemen morally charged qualities, of which the most salient are lightness, softness, and brightness. The lightness of whitemen connotes an uncanny mobility and lack of encumbrance by the obligations of debt to others that Orokaiva experience as an unavoidable part of human existence. Whitemen's lightness is also identified with a lack of rootedness in the land. Unlike Orokaiva, who are tied to their lands by the need to cultivate food gardens, whitemen are rooted in the cash economy, relying for their subsistence on light commodity foods that are produced in factories and purchased in stores. The softness of whitemen's bodies, epitomized by their uncallused hands and feet, confirms that whitemen do not do the kinds of heavy outdoors work that Orokaiva themselves must do in order to subsist, yet whitemen nevertheless enjoy far greater material wealth than do Orokaiva, living lives of extraordinary ease and comfort. The light color of whitemen's skin is identified with the attractive brightness and conspicuousness of whitemen's extravagant wealth. Whitemen seem not to be subject to the normal moral economy of interpersonal relations, in which the sight of wealth arouses desire in others, setting in motion processes that diminish that wealth either by requiring that persons who see it receive a portion of it in compensation, or else by arousing negative feelings of frustrated desire and jealousy that lead people to reciprocate destructively with crime or sorcery.

As we have seen, whitemen are morally ambiguous: Orokaiva ascribe to them qualities that are good as well as bad. The Orokaiva construction of whitemen does not mark only Orokaiva superiority over whitemen, or vice versa, but rather provides Orokaiva with a rich moral symbolism encompassing diverse evaluative possibilities that are invoked depending on people's particular interests and aims in the context of speaking. At times Orokaiva use whitemen as a foil for highlighting their own virtues, like solidarity and strong emotions in kinship, proper grieving for the deceased, and generosity in feasting, hospitality, and gift exchange. At other times they use whitemen as a foil for criticizing problems in their society, such as competition, disunity, unbridled jealousy, sorcery, and gang violence (raskolism), from which whitemen are held to be immune. Whitemen are often seen as uncanny beings who escape the basic moral principles that govern the lives of Oro-kaiva, for example by managing to sustain conditions of extreme inequality that Orokaiva cannot tolerate among themselves. In this sense, whitemen are exceptions to the human condition as Orokaiva understand it. Yet even when constructed as uncanny, exceptional beings, whitemen properly belong to the Orokaiva moral and cultural world. Their position within that world is one of a cultural outsider, a moral other which is accorded a prominent role in ver-nacular moral discourse.

The Construction of Whitemen in a Heterogeneous Society

As with any group of people, Orokaiva individuals differ from one another in knowledge, experience, personal temperament, and myriad other ways. Their society is, in its own way, a plural one, incorporating individuals who have married in from many other regions. One can subdivide Orokaiva soci-ety along the lines of age, gender, and status (and increasingly class), as well as in terms of people's knowledge and degree of experience in the white-men's world. There is growing division between Orokaiva villagers and Orokaiva living in towns, plantation compounds, and other quasi-urban environments. Even within the village, Orokaiva individuals differ widely from one another in their formal education, competence in Tok Pisin and English, and literacy skills; in their familiarity with town life and wage work; and in their ability to operate effectively within western-style institu-tions like business, church, schools, and government. Orokaiva also differ in their degrees of travel experience, their direct acquaintance with whites and other foreigners, and their knowledge about different nations and the differ-ent foreign nationalities represented in PNG.

Given such differences, it might be expected that the construction of whitemen would differ across individuals and sociological groups, and in fact there are some discernible differences in emphasis along sociologi-cal lines. Young people, for example, are particularly attracted by the light-ness of whitemen insofar as it presents for them an appealing model of individualistic freedom, an escape from the heavy traditional social obli-gations that the looming world of adulthood promises soon to enmesh them in (this is most notable for young men and high-school educated young women). Similarly, it is men who are most fascinated by white-men's abilities to extend their influence across distance, and it is mainly men who actively seek out leadership roles in the prestigious domain of development, for example by applying for government grants, starting vil-lage businesses, attending bible study courses and development training workshops, and organizing clan- and community-wide church and devel-opment projects. But in their talk about whitemen, I found that Orokaiva individuals do not differ greatly in the kinds of subjects they raise or the basic moral stances they take; nor do they differ in the salient qualities they predicate of whitemen or in their basic views on what these qualities mean. Just as there are not separate moral models for women and for men in Mt. Hagen despite the differences in their interests that guide how they apply them (Strathern 1981), there is no Orokaiva women's construction of whitemen that is qualitatively distinct from Orokaiva men's, and there do not exist distinct constructions of whitemen for other sociological cate-gories either. To the contrary, in the basic moral categories and assump-tions people applied to whitemen, I found only broad commonality.[1]

In its high degree of conventionality, the Orokaiva construction of whitemen contrasts with other areas of vernacular culture that do differ significantly along lines of gender, age, clan affiliation, status, or simply idiosyncratically by individual. Sorcery, healing, feast politics, political rhetoric, ornament-making, and so on all have their experts, usually men, within Orokaiva communities. Among women, there are acknowl-edged specialists at preparing particular medicines, using certain tech-niques for making textiles, and incising designs into feast taro. Spe-cialization is especially notable in the domain of traditional knowledge such as origin stories, since authority over these is tied to particular clans that own the lands where events recounted took place (Bashkow 2000b). There is also clear specialization and differentiation in people's practical knowledge of whitemen's culture, such as how to run a business, work for a company, participate in bible study sessions, chair a meeting, and give evi-dence in court; in this regard Orokaiva individuals may have quite different degrees and areas of competence in frameworks of western expectations.

But for all their differences in knowledge, habits, predisposition, and skills, Orokaiva individuals *do* share common cultural categories and sen-sibilities in the realm of morality. In an important way, what it means to be part of an Orokaiva community is to share in a set of culturally elaborated moral assumptions: the inherent virtue of generous hospitality; the impor-tance of positive reciprocity in creating and maintaining relationships; the efficacy of compensation payments for effacing wrongs; the supreme importance of social harmony in producing material abundance and community well-being; the fear of jealousy and ill will as primary causes (via sorcery and criminal acts) of want, sickness, and death; the recognition of ongoing debt to one's ancestors for livelihood and prosperity; and the value of feasting as one of the highest manifestations of social good.

The Orokaiva construction of whitemen is a moral phenomenon of precisely this order. Indeed, as we have seen throughout this book, whitemen are constructed in dialectic with these very values. Over the course of more than a century the construction of whitemen has been worked over within Orokaiva culture, bringing it into coherence with indigenous moral assumptions and integrating it with people's ideas about right and wrong, cause and effect, the visible and the hidden, spatial and social relationships, and food, work, growth, and productivity. Because the construction of whitemen is woven so tightly into the fabric of Orokaiva morality, it now has the same sociological generality.[2]

European ideas of "the primitive" and "Oriental" others are analogously deeply motivated within western morality and widely assumed across sociological lines, so much so that it is only recently that a superelite critical discourse in cultural studies and anthropology has begun to question them. As with such widely shared others in western societies, the whiteman-other of Orokaiva culture allows a collectivity to create and "intensify its own sense of itself by dramatizing the distance and difference between what is closer to it and what is far away" (Said 1978, 55; see also Deloria 1998; Carrier 1995c; Mason 1990). It is as if the foregrounding of whitemen's otherness allows individual differences among Orokaiva to be eclipsed by the shared opposition. In this way, the construction of whitemen serves as a discourse affirming Orokaivas' own shared identity.

Like other Pacific peoples Orokaiva place a premium on unity and agreement as a discursive norm (see, e.g., Brenneis and Myers 1984). In ordinary conversation, people go to great lengths to avoid saying anything that might be divisive or that might offend anyone present, lest they create ill will, engendering destructive consequences in the future. To the same end they also devote a large share of their discourse to diplomatically rehearsing truisms that are sure to meet with common approval and create positive feeling and alignment among interlocutors. Whitemen are an ideal topic for the creation of unity and avoidance of discord. Because the discourse about whitemen posits such clear moral contrasts between Orokaiva and a well-established, culturally salient category of others, and because this discourse is so well-worn, employing tropes that are widely recognized and intelligible throughout the community, individuals enjoy in this repertoire of talk a powerful experience of cultural self-assuredness, shared morality, and unity. So well-suited is it for creating common feeling, establishing agreement, and affirming Orokaiva identity, that it is often used as a safe idiom in which to broach matters that speakers know will be divisive. For example, at one Agenehambo village meeting, the topic turned to young men's frustration at their elders' unwillingness to pass on leadership positions to the next generation. Rather than risk antagonizing the old men by expressing this directly, the young men cast their grievance indirectly through extended speeches about whitemen's lack of sorcery. The implicit meaning of these speeches was that the current village leadership was incapable of bringing prosperity through development because it was held by a generation that busied itself with such condemnable aspects of tradition as sorcery, something younger leaders presumably would not do—indeed could not do—since sorcery is held to be the special province of old men. By thus cloaking their criticism of the old men's leadership in statements about whitemen that were beyond reproach, the young Orokaiva speech-makers sought to protect themselves from the old men's resentment and the possible charge of divisiveness by exploiting the moral community Orokaiva share through their discourse about whitemen.

The fact that the construction of whitemen is so widely shared allows it to be used to overcome even differences in the degrees and kinds of experience Orokaiva individuals have with taupa kastom. There is little doubt that these differences of expertise in whitemen's culture are among the most economically and sociologically consequential for Orokaiva today. Not only do they affect an individual's prospects of gaining desirable forms of wage employment such as public service jobs, but they also influence such matters as choice of marriage partner, access to development aid, and prestige in the community. Precisely because of the material significance of these differences, speakers are keen to downplay them to avoid arousing jealousy, and so even those individuals with the greatest expertise in taupa kastom tend to emphasize in their talk about whitemen familiar interests and moral assumptions they share with their Orokaiva interlocutors, rather than alienating them by speaking of things beyond their comprehension. For example, when two young Agenehambo men successfully elicited Anglican mission and Rotary Club sponsorship to spend three months in Australia learning carpentry, masonry, and other building trades, their reports upon their return were cast remarkably mundanely in terms of villagers' expected concerns with exchange relations and hospitality, whitemen's mobility, and food and eating. Apart from making a few incisive cultural observations ('guests who arrive at mealtime do not receive a share of the food they see being eaten; they only get offered tea or coffee,' 'the people grow large from eating so much ice cream'), the men dwelled upon details like who greeted them, who paid for their meals, and the gifts they received; the types and sizes of the vehicles in which they traveled and how far they went; and the types and amounts of main foods and relishes served at different meals.[3] In contrast, they hardly spoke at all about the useful skills they gained that now set them above other villagers, except when the topic was forced by people's questions about the photographs that were taken by their Australian hosts, which showed them dressed like white tradesmen, operating machinery and working with tools.

In its effectiveness as a vehicle for achieving valued forms of social agreement and unity, the Orokaiva construction of whitemen resembles the many discourses about whitemen that have been historically noted by studies of cargo movements throughout Melanesia. In such movements, whitemen, often alongside the ancestors, serve as a shared moral other that allows people of otherwise disparate identities to unify, in some cases across vast distances and for the very first time (Worsley 1968 [1957]). Unity is a central theme in all cargo movements, where it is expressed not only in discourse but also in a strong ritual emphasis on synchronized activity, sharing, goodwill, and equality (Bashkow in preparation; Leavitt 2001; Errington 1974; LaBarre 1971; Worsley 1968 [1957]).

Thus, the highly conventional nature of the Orokaiva construction of whitemen is not a function of the sharedness of Orokaiva culture in general, but rather derives from its integration in a framework of categories and moral assumptions which *are* widely shared, and its very conventionality contributes to its pragmatic value and vitality in the culture.

Whitemen and the Urban Experience

As I have been at pains to show, the Orokaiva construction of whitemen is culturally particular and can only be understood from the point of view of Orokaiva people's experience within their own cultural world. It is centered in Orokaiva morality and cast in terms of vernacular ideas like the concept of hamo ari, the growth and life cycle of taro, the inexhaustible heaviness of obligations to progenitors, the association of visible wealth with the skin, and so on. But the larger phenomenon it represents is nevertheless not limited to a few Orokaiva village communities; it is one that extends throughout the nation of Papua New Guinea as a whole—and even beyond. When Orokaiva migrate to town, their experiences there are easily (if imperfectly) assimilable to their cultural preconceptions, and so serve to confirm the construction of whitemen they brought with them from the village. And the foreign discourses they encounter about whitemen and the West, while likewise culturally distinctive, are readily intertranslatable with their own, because the binary contrasts they all posit are structurally homologous. There is thus no contradiction between the cultural distinctiveness of ideological constructs and the open-ended nature of people's cultural experience. Cultural particularity does not depend on insularity.

For Orokaiva who leave the village community to take up jobs or live in squatter settlements in town, the wider world they enter into is one they understand and participate in through their construction of whitemen. Although town is no longer a place where many whites actually live, it is closely associated with whitemen historically, symbolically, and practically. A settlement pattern that is clearly not derived from local forms, towns were originally built to serve as white colonial administrative centers. Town structures are predominantly built of manufactured materials, and they are laid out largely in a rectilinear grid. Virtually everything one does in town— subsistence, transportation, wage labor, market peddling, recreation—costs money or is done to obtain it. While we might expect that the town experience would disabuse Orokaiva of their village ideas, replacing their culturally idiosyncratic construction of whitemen with a more cosmopolitan and realistic one, to the contrary, the experiences Orokaiva have in town and beyond tend to *confirm* their basic construction of whitemen and reinforce their conventional ideas about the essential ways in which whitemen differ from themselves.

For example, the Orokaiva idea that whitemen's foods are epitomized in rice, tinfish, and so on might seem like an obvious falsehood that would be dispelled for those individuals who leave the village and migrate to town. But to the contrary, because this belief shapes what people want from the world of commodities, in turn influencing the choices that are made available to them, it actually forms part of a mediating complex that connects Orokaiva village culture with the wider world of town and even other countries. Village notions about whitemen's foods are confirmed by people's experience with modern institutions like schools, hospitals, and prisons, where the meals served consist ordinarily of plates of rice and tinned protein. What villagers consider to be whitemen's foods are also the mainstays of the diets of Papua New Guineans who live in town. Accordingly, these are the foods most actively advertised on the radio, in newspapers, and on television (see Foster 2002).

Moreover, since rice and tinfish do in fact make up the bulk of the commodity foods that people want and consume throughout Papua New

Guinea, Orokaiva find confirmation of their village assumptions about whitemen's foods in small locally run tradestores all over the country and even in the large foreign-run supermarkets in PNG's towns and cities. The local tradestores virtually always carry the same basic stock of food items: rice, tinfish, tinmeat, flour, salt, oil, hardtack biscuits, instant noodles, powdered milk, sugar, coffee, and tea. Indeed, in the larger, more professionally run town supermarkets, huge amounts of shelf space are devoted to these popular categories, which along with soaps account for around four-fifths of the value of nonalcohol, nontobacco PNG grocery sales. They are displayed in vast quantities, with entire aisles taken up by row upon row of nearly identical packages of rice, tinned protein, and crackers, and with the same items often placed near the entrance to greet shoppers with impressive displays of red-labeled cans stacked by the case or pallets loaded with baled bags of rice. In effect, the stores people encounter throughout PNG affirm the reality and centrality of these foods in the whitemen's commercial realm.

The Papua New Guinean version of whitemen's foods affects not only native people like Orokaiva villagers, but it even shapes the behavior of the expatriates they encounter, who thereby also substantiate and confirm it (see also Bateson 1958 [1936], 184–85). Many whites in Papua New Guinea keep rice, tinfish, and tinmeat on hand at home in their cupboards, since it quickly becomes apparent to them that foods like rice and tinfish are the most appropriate, cost-efficient, and appreciated foods to feed "grassroots" Papua New Guineans when hosting them or compensating them for work, and to give uncooked to them as gifts. From the whites' perspective, buying and providing such foods is merely a response to the people's own expectations and intense desire for them. But from the perspective of the Papua New Guineans, it is only natural that whites should give them whitemen's foods, given their superior access to money, and when they do so, it only confirms that they are indeed whitemen's foods; they are the foods whites have on hand to give them.

Another aspect of villagers' construction of whitemen that is confirmed rather than contradicted by town life is whitemen's lightness. Many Orokaiva find in the lightness of whitemen an alluring model of freedom from the burden of social obligations placed on them by their culture. But when they leave the village to live out the fantasy of a 'light' life in the town, they are virtually always disappointed. Wages in PNG are low, often equivalent to only U.S. $20 to $40 per week for unskilled work, and so with consumer prices still high, a dependence on cash subsistence comes with its own form of economic and social heaviness and anxiety. Rather than realizing the ideal condition of unencumbered wealth and mobility, Orokaiva migrants to town find themselves struggling just to get by. They find their wages grossly inadequate to feed, house, and transport themselves, let alone pay school fees and raise a family. In town, money is also needed to support a whole additional set of social relations with friends, co-workers, neighbors, and fellow church congregants who require reciprocal gifts of betel nut, cigarettes, food, and for men, often beer. As James Ferguson (1999, 111) observes of urban life in Zambia, the "apparent anonymity... is deceptive," since "there is a steady stream of family members coming to visit, to seek jobs, to demand lodging, and so on." Because town is the place of money, migrants' village kin are quick to assume that they must have some to share. So migrants are not only unable to meet their own basic needs, but they also feel the anxiety of often having to disappoint the expectations of their extended kin, to whom they must plead that "the town has impoverished [them], and [they] can give only little" (M. Strathern 1975, 314; see also Sykes 1999). Visits from villagers often exacerbate people's indebtedness to their town friends, to whom they must turn for the money they need to at least give their visiting kin a proper meal to get them to leave and to help mitigate their resentment at having had their requests denied.

Townspeople are acutely conscious of the need to maintain the goodwill of their village kin. As in the colonial African economy described by Claude Meillassoux (1981), the PNG urban sphere supports workers only during their peak wage-earning years, and does not attempt to compensate participants in the cash economy for the cost of living over the full life cycle. Nor does the PNG government step in to fill this gap with any kind of social benefits program analogous to unemployment insurance, welfare, or social security in the United States. Only the higher-tier civil service and company jobs come with formal pensions, but even these are unreliable because employers such as government agencies do not always pay in the required contributions, the pension funds may be mismanaged, and the payments some people do eventually receive are severely devalued by inflation. Urban workers are thus acutely aware that they may well need to return to their village lands when they are forced by sickness or age to retire. Given the fluidity of the system of customary land tenure back in the village, the claims townspeople have to village lands must be continually reasserted lest they be decisively superseded by others' de facto occupation. Since this would mean losing the only basis most town dwellers have for true security, they must maintain good relationships with village kinsfolk, contribute to important feasts, and return periodically to the village on social visits. All these things are expensive. Trips home are particularly costly, since not only are town visitors expected to bring along lavish quantities of commodity foods, but all key village relationships must also be reaffirmed with tangible gifts.[4]

Orokaiva migrants to town find their ideas about whitemen's lightness further corroborated by their experience of class hierarchy. The traditional egalitarian ethos of Melanesian communities has not prevented the emergence of class differences over the last forty years as a national black urban elite has rapidly arisen in the place of the old colonial white elite. With few exceptions, middle- and upper-class Papua New Guineans feel pressed to disentangle themselves from their impoverished kin if they are to preserve those few comforts and privileges their fragile class advantage allows them. For this very reason, villagers and less fortunate townspeople tend to look to their more elite kin with resentment as *skin masta*, 'superficial whitemen' who are trying to appropriate for themselves an unjust lightness that does not rightly belong to them. And for elite blacks themselves, this sense of illegitimacy that is so difficult to shake off in turn reinforces the notion they share with their village brethren that lightness is essentially a quality of whitemen. Indeed, the importune interference of their kin forces even the most elite Papua New Guineans to feel the heaviness of their Melanesian black skin, no matter how successful they are and no matter how hard they may try to escape it. This, then, is the classic bind of the urban classes in PNG (Gewertz and Errington 1999).

The general predicament of townspeople, caught between their superior access to money and their obligations to extended kin, is very well recognized throughout PNG. It has become an important theme elaborated in literature, cartoons, and popular songs. One of its most compact and humorous dramatizations may be found in the lyrics of a song by the PNG pop band Tarbar, "There Goes My Pay." First recorded in 1980, the song remained perennially popular throughout the 1980s and 1990s, invigorated by the release of a new jazzed-up recording in 1992. It takes the point of view of a young urban government worker who finds himself besieged by the importunate requests of his extended kin (his *wantoks*) every payday. As "There Goes My Pay" shows, the possibility of an existence free of heavy obligations to extended kin is highly elusive for most urban Papua New Guineans. Far from enabling them to achieve a whitemanlike lightness, participation in town life squeezes them between the difficulty of surviving in the cash economy and the anxious burden of their social obligations. And their social obligations are only increased as their wage-earning status brings the most diverse requirements of needy relatives to their door:

I've got a little house out in Gerehu [a Port Moresby neighborhood]
I've got a wife and a little baby too.
I've got the job, I work in Waigani [government office district]
The government, it pays my salary.

I think that I am contributing to the nation,
But after tax and superannuation
There goes my pay. Oh oh oh oh . . .
(Oh, no woman no cry.)

At ten past four [quitting time], I catch the PMV [public bus].
I find them in my house all watching EM TV [PNG TV station],
Kids, cousins, uncles, sitting round the floor,
And some of them I've never seen before!

I think that I am contributing to the nation
Cause all my money goes to my relations.
There goes my pay. Oh oh oh oh . . .
(This wantok system [of extended kinship] is driving me crazy!)

My wife complains that I don't earn enough.
She likes Big Rooster [a PNG fast food chain] and all that kind of stuff.
But we buy rice and [tin]fish at the local store,
Two loose B&H [fine western-style cigarettes], if I'm lucky three or four.

I think that I am contributing to the nation,
Cause all my money goes to my relations.
There goes my pay. Oh oh oh oh . . .
(I'll have to go back to Mutrus [cheap, rough, locally manufactured cigarettes]
    soon.)

And every fortnight [i.e., payday] they gather at the door.
Somebody's school fees have to be paid for.
[School] uniforms and bus fares, they never seem to end.
And I never get back all the cash I lend.

I think I'm helping to educate the nation,
But I'm fed up with making big donations.
There goes my pay. Oh oh oh oh . . .
(Hey! I'm not the bank!)

And all the time my in-laws pressure me.
They say I ought to buy a big utility [pickup truck]
To pick them up and drive them round Mosbi [Port Moresby].
But it will end up as their personal taxi!

I think that I am contributing to the nation,
Cause I'm responsible for wantoks' [extended relations] transportation.
There goes my pay. Oh oh oh oh ...
(Where [do] you want to go? Sogeri [suburb on the outskirts]?! You've got to
  be joking!)

And now my wife is getting bigger every day.
Somehow we got another baby on the way.
Another pile of bills, another mouth to feed.
As CPI [the Consumer Price Index] increases, that's what I really need!

I think that I am contributing to the nation,
I accidentally increased the population!
There goes my pay. Oh oh oh oh ...

[Chorus calls:] Here it comes! Here it comes! Here comes our pay!
[Narrator responds:] There goes, there goes, there goes my pay.

[Loose translation of Tok Pisin coda:]
"Wantok, you got a few bucks for me?"
"Aw, just this morning some of my other relatives came over and cleaned me
  out. All I have left is small change."
"Just small change, huh? Just a few coins? Oh, alright, I'll take 'em."[5]

The Construction of Whitemen as a National Phenomenon

Outside the village, Orokaiva find the basic outlines of their construction of
whitemen confirmed not only in their experience of the realities of urban
life but also in what they hear others say. Other Papua New Guineans, too,
have their cultural constructions of whitemen, and these are similarly cast
in terms of basic assumptions that are broadly common in Melanesian cultures: for example, that human life alternates between states of heavy social
encumbrance and periods of relative mobility and social freedom, or that
persons comprise an unknowable, agentive, hidden will and a visible skin
embodying one's history of nurturing social relations. People throughout
Melanesia display a similar ambivalence toward individual autonomy,

which, while necessary for personal influence and success, is inherently undermining of the ideal of egalitarian unity and the social harmony necessary for collective wealth and well-being; and they share a dependence on land as a symbolic anchor for people's identity, as well as the only truly reliable source of wealth and security. All Papua New Guineans comfortably contrast themselves with whitemen from the viewpoint of such premises. They depict themselves as burdened by social obligations from which whitemen are free, as afflicted by sorcery to which whitemen are indifferent, as divided and debilitated by people's competitive impulses while whitemen's wealth grows ever larger in countries marked by virtuous social harmony, and as dependent on hard, physical labor for subsistence while whitemen inexplicably build fortunes without appearing to do any hard work (see, e.g., Robbins 1997b, 2004a; Englund and Leach 2000; Knauft 2002b; Smith 1994, 1995; Kulick 1992; Brison 1991; Lederman 1986, 373; Strathern 1990, 31; Lattas 1998; Foster 1992; Worsley 1968 [1957], 97).

While other Papua New Guineans' discourses about whitemen are not identical to Orokaivas', the similarities are sufficient to make them easily intertranslatable and mutually intelligible. In some cases the similarities are strikingly close, as with the Melanesian islanders who speak of whitemen as "floaters, like driftwood, stringy and flabby because they have no enduring relations to the earth but are compelled to move about in search of money" (Strathern 1988, 80; see also Reed 2003; Gewertz and Errington 1995, 176; LiPuma 2000, 120; Wardlow 2002a). In other cases the similarities are less obvious. For example, there is a historical tendency, noted especially in the literature on PNG Highlanders' early contacts with white exploratory patrols and gold prospectors, for whitemen to be identified with spirit entities and specific categories of sorcerers. But here too people were interpreting whites as powerful outsiders who seemed not to be bound by ordinary social relations and who were exceptions to what they understood to be the human condition (Clark 2000, 45–47; Schieffelin and Crittenden 1991; Connolly and Anderson 1987; see also Stasch 2001). And even when this discourse eventually gave way to a general "perception that whites were, after all, human" (Clark 2000, 39), they remained a different sort of human who, for example, was less given to sorcery. At bottom, the discourses about whitemen that Orokaiva encounter in talking with Papua New Guineans from elsewhere in the country are all basically commensurable, confirming many aspects of their own culturally particular discourse, reinforcing their fundamental inclination to approach the issue of whitemen in moral terms, and providing them with additional avenues for elaborating whitemen's relationship to themselves.[6]

One important domain in which culturally distinct discourses that are diverse in their particulars are nevertheless broadly commensurate is the representation of whitemen in origin stories. The Orokaiva story of the original ancestress Sipa depicts whitemen as the Orokaiva people's original forefathers. Having come from afar, three whitemen find the native woman Sipa sitting alone in the forest. They win her over with salt and sugar, clothe her, and marry her, but after the twelve children she bears them all turn out to have skin that is black like her own (and not theirs), they depart, taking the blessings of their inheritance away with them. The sons later prepare a feast in order to supplicate their mother and gain the blessing from her side, since without ancestral favor one cannot prosper. But in the process of preparing the feast, the brothers quarrel, completing their alienation from the favor of their ancestors and presaging the jealousy and conflict that inexorably besets the modern-day Orokaiva, their black-skinned descendants. In its details the Sipa story is distinctive to Orokaiva culture; indeed, even within the Orokaiva region the story exists in numerous village and clan variants.[7] But whitemen figure prominently in the origin stories told by many other PNG peoples today, reflecting the importance of whitemen in all their cultural and moral worlds. For example, people in many Sepik societies tell stories about two brothers who quarrel and separate, with one leaving, possibly to become the progenitor of modern-day whitemen who are now unknowingly returning to their place of origin (Burridge 1960, 1969; Lawrence 1964; Kulick 1992; Tuzin 1997; Leavitt 2000; Bashkow 2000b; see also Lattas 1998).[8] In their narrative content, all these stories symbolize whitemen's mobility, material wealth, and white skin, while seeking to account for people's tragic disinheritance from whitemen's material prosperity. The close original kinship to whitemen they posit, while negative, is nonetheless appealing because it offers a precedent for the kind of relationship with whitemen Papua New Guineans would wish to have, namely one involving paternal or fraternal closeness, solicitude, and exchange (see Leavitt 1995, 2000). Papua New Guineans from different areas like to exchange the outlines of their origin stories with one another, noting, highlighting, and indeed often exaggerating the similarities between the relationships narrated.

One reason why Orokaiva find so much corroboration for their construction of whitemen in other Papua New Guineans' discourses is the high value noted earlier that they place on establishing commonality and agreement in conversation. The imperative to do so is felt all the more strongly in interethnic interactions, where the bases for relationships may be relatively thin, leading people to diplomatically try to accentuate their commonalities and minimize their differences. In this they are supported by "the friendly ambiguities of language" (Sapir 1949 [1932], 516), which allow what is said by people of different communities to be interpreted in ways that maximize meaningfulness, necessarily in terms of the listener's own cultural categories, interests, values, and so on. The ease with which Papua New Guineans translate between different languages and discourses is also facilitated by the frequent use of a third language, the PNG lingua franca Tok Pisin, as the medium of the translation, smoothing over many of the culturally particular connotations and nuances that inhere in vernacular utterances. The result is a mutual intelligibility that may be only partial, though to conversational participants it feels quite complete. It is something like the game of telephone, played out on a cultural scale. Thus, just as Orokaiva find common ground with one another in their village communities through their discourse on whitemen, talk about whitemen serves to establish community with the people they encounter from elsewhere in PNG.

Another reason why the Orokaiva construction of whitemen can be supported by the discourse of other Papua New Guineans notwithstanding some differences has to do with the fact that the material objects through which whitemen are symbolized lend themselves, as all objects do, to multiple interpretations. Orokaiva are hardly the only Papua New Guineans who emblematically associate objects like foods and building materials with racial identities. All over the country, rice and tinfish are eaten as urban staples and village luxury and feast foods, and virtually everywhere they have meaning as whitemen's foods, contrasting with the local garden foods emblematically associated with native people and their livelihood (Clark 2000, 164; Lederman 1981, 23). While the specific qualities attributed to whitemen's foods may differ from place to place depending on the nature of the foods and the specific way local ideas about eating are elaborated, the ideological correspondences need not be worked out in full detail. Virtually everywhere in PNG the local foods are stick-to-the-ribs garden foods that evoke memories of home, which is one reason why village foods are so often sent as gifts to town relatives; villagers know that such foods will remind them of their village identity. So it is enough for Orokaiva just to see rice and tinfish used by others as whitemen's foods to call up and confirm their own ideological scheme in its entirety.

But perhaps the most important source of the confirmation people find in others' discourses about whitemen is the homologous structure these discourses share. All Papua New Guineans' discourses are alike in being structured in terms of a binary contrast between black self and white other. The very simplicity of this stark dichotomy makes the basic terms of others' discourses readily intelligible and easily intertranslatable, with whitemen universally aligned with certain key symbols like money and business. Inherent in any such simple opposed self/other structure is the possibility for ambivalence that we have seen emphasized in the Orokaiva discourse about whitemen, the same use of the other as a foil, inverting the virtues and vices people feel in themselves. Thus, Orokaiva are never in the position of having their own unambiguous evaluations of whitemen challenged by others' critiques or expressions of admiration. Since Papua New Guineans from elsewhere are also rhetorically adept at evaluating whitemen both negatively and positively depending on their aims in the context of speaking, for example, depending on whether they are trying to cast their own virtuous generosity into relief or to bemoan their own fractiousness, Orokaiva are well accustomed to hearing their friends from Kainantu in the PNG Highlands (for example) speak ambivalently of whitemen just as they do.

In addition to finding confirmation for their distinctive cultural construction of whitemen in the local discourses of other PNG cultures, Orokaiva find resonant themes in the well-established national discourse on whitemen in Tok Pisin and English that has become a prominent feature of PNG urban life. Stemming from the "creole culture" (Hannerz 1987) that emerged during colonial times in places like police barracks, prisons, plantations, and boarding schools, this national discourse circulates widely today in many of the "modern" settings such as workplaces, schools, churches, and sports, youth, and women's groups, where people of different ethnic and regional backgrounds come together, and it is presupposed and elaborated by PNG newspapers, radio, TV, and popular music (Knauft 2002b; Zimmer-Tamakoshi 1996, 1998; Foster 2002; Levine and Levine 1979; Rew 1974). The national discourse contrasts whitemen broadly with Papua New Guinean nationals (*nesenel*), Papua New Guinean blacks (*blaks*, *blaksikin*), or black Melanesians in general.[9] The various terms used for whitemen include 'whitemen' (*ol waitman*), "Europeans," 'masters' (*ol masta*), and people from the "overseas countries" (or *ol kantri*, i.e., the predominantly white developed West). As most of these terms suggest, the discourse represents national belonging as an aspect of race and vice versa, so that notwithstanding the citizenship of naturalized whites and Chinese, *Papua Niugini* is represented as a nation that is essentially black (see also Robbins 2004a, 172). It is not only black Papua New Guineans who command the use of this discourse; most expatriates and others of foreign origin quickly become acculturated to it as well. As a result, Orokaiva find that their racial ideas are congruous with the views they hear expressed in newspapers, on TV news, and even by the whites they encounter.

Like the homologous discourses of villagers from elsewhere in Papua New Guinea, the national discourse on whitemen is structured as a simple binary opposition between black and white, self and other, as an all-encompassing framework for dividing a complex reality into two moral spheres. People in PNG speak assuredly of two dissimilar worlds, European and Melanesian, as though the reality laid out before them continually forced upon them a choice between two contrasting domains of action: the modern urban, cosmopolitan world of money, personal freedom, and technology, and the traditional village "grassroots" world of subsistence gardening, kinship, and ritual. This ubiquitous discourse resembles the "pervasive and familiar dualism" James Ferguson found among Africans in Zambia, where even the least educated people seemed to be fluent in the "clichéd dualistic stereotypes of modernization theory," giving him the "unsettling sense" that he was "listening to an out-of-date sociology textbook" (Ferguson 1999, 84; see also Rebhun 1999, 2; Strathern 1990, 31). As scholars have argued, this kind of dichotomous framework is intrinsic to the discourse of modernity, which characteristically represents tradition as a delimited quality of the past to be broken free from and exceeded (see Knauft 2002a, 2002b; Mitchell 2000). Nevertheless, it is *within* such a dualistic framework that the people themselves conceptualize modernity, and invariably they assimilate it to the whitemen's side of the dichotomy, so that modernity itself becomes raced.

The binarism common to Papua New Guineans' discourses about race has the effect of obscuring the real diversities and "finer gradations of the racial spectrum" (Schumaker 2001, 137). This is reflected in a "generification" of traditional life, in which cultural particularities are conceived of as representing "equally valid variations on common themes" (e.g., initiation, brideprice, feasting, dance, kinship, etc.) associated with a generalized, regional culture (Errington and Gewertz 2001; 2004, 93; see also Pigg 1992; Wilk 1995b). Such generification is politically useful for fostering agreement and solidarity across ethnic lines and for supporting a sense of pan-Melanesian black identity among otherwise culturally disparate peoples. Paralleling this, there is also a generification of foreigners and the modernity they are held to instantiate. As discussed in chapter 4, Orokaiva do have knowledge of many distinctions among foreign ethnic/racial/national groups such as Chinese, Malaysian, American, Australian, German, Japanese, and such. But these are opposed to one another not as different races that contrast differently with the self, but rather as subspecies of a larger category of privileged foreigners or, in other words, whitemen. While

there is some basis for arguing that the prototypical subcategory of whitemen is white Australians, it is not Australians specifically, but a generic construction of whitemen (albeit based largely on Australians historically) that
stands as the most relevant outsider Papua New Guineans use to dialectically
construct their own identity. People can certainly distinguish among sub-
categories of whitemen when it is contextually appropriate, and it is even a
sign of worldliness to be able to do so. But it is not by contrast to any particular subcategory of whitemen that they express their own moral worth
through conventionalized discourses opposing the ambiguities of the self to
an other. So long as no actual foreigners are specifically at issue in the context of speaking, it is immaterial to people precisely which kinds of whitemen their talk is about. It really does not matter whether they are Americans
or New Zealanders, Caucasians or Orientals, because these are our categories
of importance, not Papua New Guineans', and it is *their* distinctions that are
of direct moral significance to them. After all, from their perspective whitemen of all kinds are wealthy, making them naturally assimilable to a single
moral category in the discourse.

The PNG national racial discourse has three main themes that amplify
those central in the Orokaiva vernacular discourse about whitemen. The
first of these is the "wantok system," which expands people's traditional
obligations to engage in material reciprocities with their kin into a generalized system of gift exchange and reciprocal favors, creating extended networks of kinlike exchange friends. A concept drawn upon heavily in urban
settings where people from different home regions intermingle, *wantok* has
the core meaning of someone from one's own cultural and linguistic region
with whom a connection of kinship, however remote, can always be established, making them a natural town ally.[10] But the label is often extended to
anyone with whom one has exchanged any material favors, even if only a
betel nut or cigarette, on the presumption that such gift exchange implies a
kinshiplike relationship (see Levine and Levine 1979, 71). In address
between Papua New Guineans, the term is often used to express friendship
and camaraderie, as in "Hello, wantok!" or "I'm going off to visit my wantoks." The hybrid term "wantok system" is known to every Papua New
Guinean, from illiterate rural people to university professors; it is known to
all expatriate residents, all who visit PNG on business or development con-
sultancies, and even most foreign tourists. It is widely discussed in newspaper articles and letters, travel guidebooks, and development bank reports,
where it is used to evoke a distinctly Melanesian sphere of exchange that
contrasts with the presumably normative sphere of western capitalism
(much as in the analysis presented by Gregory 1982).

The wantok system is often hailed by both Papua New Guineans and foreigners as "a valuable safety net in times of sickness and distress," "an effective form of social insurance and shared responsibility . . . in an environment where it is difficult to save and store wealth" (AIDAB 1994, 51–53). Bernard Narokobi, an influential Papua New Guinean public intellectual and political leader who has forcefully advocated for a positive Melanesian morality and identity, often appeals to the wantok system as a vernacular model of communal responsibility and mutual aid through which Papua New Guineans can avoid the alienation and impoverishment of individualistic capitalism (Narokobi 1983; Otto 1997; Temane 1998). This view is not just idle talk. It makes great sense to Papua New Guinean town-dwellers and squatters, for whom the informal exchange of favors is generally the main means of finding housing, jobs, food, leisure, company, protection from harm, and a sense of belonging and self-respect. At the same time, however, the wantok system is widely recognized to be an impediment to economic development, because people find the "intense pressures to share income" a "strong disincentive" to steady "work in paid employment" (AIDAB 1994, 52–53; recall, too, the Tarbar lyrics transcribed above). The wantok system is also often spoken of as synonymous with corruption. In countless newspaper letters and editorials, everyday conversations, and even political speeches, Papua New Guineans lament that jobs, government contracts, and investments in public infrastructure are monopolized by the wantok networks of those who owe others for their power and wealth, through a vast system of nepotism, cronyism, and political favoritism—in a word, "wantokism."

In sum, the PNG discourse about the wantok system betrays a moral ambivalence that is closely paralleled by Orokaiva villagers' discourse on whitemen's lightness. Whitemen have their counterpart in talk about the wantok system, and it, too, is morally ambivalent. The discourse extolling the wantok system's communalism draws on an implicit contrast to a darkly tinted whitemen's world marked by inhospitality, ungenerousness, indifference, and alienation. In that world of unchecked individualism, people are believed to be moved to act only out of greedy self-interest, so that everything good depends on having money. Critiques of the wantok system similarly draw on an implicit contrast with whitemen, but this version of the whitemen's world is a rose-tinted one. In this idealized vision of western capitalism, commerce is assumed to be impartial and the apportionment of jobs, social benefits, and infrastructural investments in roads, schools, clinics, and so on, based on merit and fair (see also Reed 2003, 165–66). One profound consequence of the

PNG discourse on corrupt wantokism is that black Papua New Guineans cannot escape the limitations of their race. No matter how much elite Papua New Guineas may be regarded as whitemanlike in other respects, when it comes to partiality to their wantoks they are always suspected of being "not quite/not white" (Bhabha 1994, 92). By contrast, for all that whites in PNG are criticized as arrogant, ungenerous, and inhospitable, they are rarely, if ever, criticized for nepotism and corruption. The partiality to wantoks may be the most essential racial characteristic black Papua New Guineans attribute to themselves, though it is not obviously symbolically connected to skin color. Rather, it seems to derive from an awareness that all Papua New Guinean blacks are necessarily born into a world of wantoks, gaining whatever power they do have by means of their wantoks, and so they are constitutionally embroiled in a network of obligations.

The second theme in Papua New Guineans' national discourse on race is the continual reassertion of Melanesian peoples' close ties to the land. Notwithstanding the steady growth of PNG's cities since the 1960s (King 1998, 188; Koczberski, Curry, and Connell 2001), 85 percent of the population remains rural (NSO 1994b), and with few exceptions (such as formally employed teachers, clinic workers, and priests) the people of this rural majority maintain themselves by working ancestral lands.[11] The PNG situation regarding land tenure differs from that of most other postcolonies throughout the world. Whereas indigenous peoples elsewhere were extensively dispossessed of their lands by colonial decree and economic transactions conducted according to western norms, the expropriation of land in colonial Papua and New Guinea was minimal, and native land rights have been little disturbed over 97 percent of the country's land area (James 1985).[12] In contrast to familiar western private land ownership, which involves state registration of survey data and land transactions, customarily held land in PNG is undocumented by the state; with very few exceptions the government holds no records whatsoever demarcating land parcels, authenticating ownership, or documenting transaction history. Instead, PNG customarily held lands are tied to social collectivities, both those of the present and those of the past—including spirits of ancestors who continue to inhabit and control the land. As Margaret Mead commented of the New Guinea Arapesh: people "do not conceive of themselves as owning [their] ancestral lands, but rather as belonging to the lands" (1935, 16). Hence the focus of discourse on customarily held lands is on rights of use: trusteeship rather than ownership. While a group of people may have the right to use certain lands held under customary tenure arrangements in PNG, they are not thereby empowered to "receive income from the property independent of use" (i.e., act as landlords) or to alienate land on their own initiative by selling, leasing, or giving it away (Harding 1973, 107). On principle, then, lands are never permanently and completely alienable from people who have rights to them. This inalienability of land is protected in practice because latent rights are always distributed fairly widely among a multiplicity of groups, and because all land claims (and land boundaries) are disputable given the essentially memory-based system of reckoning.

Melanesian people's attachment to their lands is validated by virtually every element of their traditions, and it is the one theme in the national discourse in which they construct themselves in terms that are primarily positive. Villagers throughout PNG value their lands not only for the material subsistence and social security they provide, but also for the connections they establish to the ancestors and the continuity of locally distinctive traditions. The importance of people's attachment to particular lands is even validated by the legal system, which awards land-owning groups huge settlement payments in successful compensation claims for lands that are exploited by businesses such as mines or occupied by government infrastructure such as airstrips, roads, schools, clinics, and so on; these are the "compo claims" that are continually being publicized in the PNG media. Among townspeople, who like to point out that through their families they own vast tracts in their home areas, there is a strong mythology of the village as the place of enduring connections, true belonging, stability, and self-sufficiency. People romantically celebrate the honest toil of village gardening, and oppose it to the kinds of work town-dwellers do for pay, where the tasks are not self-determined and the fruits are not one's own to enjoy (see Wardlow 2002b, 158; Rapport and Dawson 1998). PNG town life does have a "city lights" attraction for the opportunities it can offer to make and spend money, and to satisfy one's urges through drinking, drugs, and prostitution. But towns are also pervasively derided as places that are bad: dirty, dangerous, immoral, alienating, and enervating. Where everything must be paid for, one can never be completely comfortable or satisfied, and the very fact that with money, so many needs can be met—and desires aroused—ensures that there will never be enough of it. The value placed on people's attachment to lands in the national discourse is a readily recognizable variant of the Orokaiva village discourse on rootedness that was discussed in chapter 5. As in the village discourse, the theme derives its significance through an implicit contrast with whitemen, who represent dependence not on lands, but on money. Unlike lands, which ground an enduring, authentic, morally valued way of life, the world of money is unreliable, decentering of one's identity, and morally ambiguous. To many Papua New Guineans, there is something terribly immoral—even incomprehensible—about whitemen's treatment of land as a mere commodity that can be bought and sold.

The intensity of Papua New Guineans' feelings about their ties to lands is shown dramatically by the widespread protest that took place in 1995, when it was feared that a government land reform proposal would open the way for banks and the government to expropriate people's customarily held land. The government proposal, which was part of a Land Mobilization Program associated with the World Bank's Structural Adjustment Program for PNG, was widely understood as a condition for the national government to receive $330 million worth of emergency "rescue" loans it was then seeking from the World Bank, the International Monetary Fund (IMF), and other international aid agencies (Tannos 1995a).[13] When the proposal was announced, the PNG Trade Union Congress (PNG TUC) expressed vehement opposition, and as news of the proposal spread, the PNG newspapers began being flooded with letters and editorials denouncing it; in one of them the PNG TUC criticized the plan as "legalised piracy," a "sinister and devious plot . . . targeted at freeing chunks of customary owned land towards capital development" (*Post-Courier*, July 7, 1995, 14; see also Abare 1995; Lakau 1995a, 1995b, 1995c; Millett 1995). At the University of Papua New Guinea (UPNG) in Port Moresby, students voted to strike and then marched in protest, rioting and burning several government vehicles (Waibauru 1995; Iorere and Setepano 1995). Following several days of protests and public meetings with high government officials, where they were joined by thousands of angry citizens and PNG Defense Force soldiers, the students extended their strike indefinitely in order to allow student representatives to return to their home provinces to mobilize villagers to defend themselves against what they saw as "the beginning of alienation . . . of the land from its true caring inhabitants" (Kombako 1995; Pamba 1995; Temane 1995). In the provinces, the agitation over land registration was fueled by powerful currents of resentment and mistrust of the government, whose officials, people said, were liable to misuse the new international loan money as they had misused government funds in the past: to reward their own wantoks and to support their expensive whitemanlike lifestyles (consuming luxuries like wine and beer, sporting fancy clothes, cruising around in expensive SUVs, etc.). Having thus wasted the money, the corrupt politicians would be unable to repay the huge international loans when they came due, and so to settle the debts created by all the government consumption and waste, the lenders would repossess the country's only remaining possession of value—

the villagers' lands, which government registration would have rendered visible and thus appropriable. Facing explosive protests in many cities and towns, and amid fears of a rumored military insurrection, the government backed down and the land registration proposal was "axed" (Bashir 1995; Kepson 1995; *Post-Courier*, July 19, 1995, 1).[14]

The third theme in the PNG national racial discourse laments the moral failings that prevent Papua New Guineans from achieving the kind of secure and prosperous society they believe whitemen to have and that they would like to have for themselves. In contrast to the first theme, the wantok system, which is morally ambivalent, and the second theme, attachment to lands, which casts Papua New Guineans in an essentially positive light, this third theme of moral deficiency is strikingly negative: it is a discourse of abjection explaining the tenacious problems of poverty and crime in the Papua New Guinean nation in terms of pervasive negative characteristics of Papua New Guinean selves. In this vernacular jeremiad, Papua New Guineans represent themselves as given to quarrelling and clashing, lying, stealing, adultery, and wastefulness. As villagers in Gapun said of themselves, all we do is "get angry, fight, swear, steal, lie, and talk behind people's backs" (Kulick 1992, 60). Married couples argue too much, and men beat their wives; people of opposite sex cannot be left alone together, since they are prone to losing control and committing infidelity. This pungent discourse of hyperbolic self-critique borrows heavily from the colonial motif of undisciplined savagery and the Christian discourse of sin (Brison 1996, Robbins 2004a). Nevertheless, the critique emphasizes two moral concerns which are ubiquitous in Melanesia and undoubtedly indigenous. One of these is the problem of what is sometimes called "unlawfulness," the inability to control selfish impulses that leads people to engage in destructive behaviors, such as improper sex, improper consumption (e.g., getting drunk), theft, and violence. The other is "bigheadedness," an insistence on autonomous action that undermines communal undertakings and that derives in part from the feeling that one is wronged whenever others receive credit for an undertaking to which one has contributed (see also Robbins 2004a; Knauft 2002b; Leavitt 2001; Kulick 1992; Brison 1991). Bigheadedness is often spoken about in terms of the problem of "having too many bosses," a dissolution into political fractiousness that results from people refusing to accept others' authority for the sake of the common good. The bigheadedness problem often becomes troublingly apparent to people when they attempt to carry out communal activities such as village work days or development projects, where multiple individuals must coordinate with one another to synchronize their efforts. Because individuals cannot be relied upon to do their part (at best they continually need special coaxing; often, they just slink away when events requiring their participation are taking place), people continually experience their society as a weak one that cannot be made stronger because of the essential intractability of its members.

The most commonly bemoaned manifestations of Papua New Guineans' reprehensible lack of self-control and bigheadedness are sorcery and its modern counterpart, raskol crime. In present-day Papua New Guinea, there is a generalized discourse about sorcery that is abstracted from the numerous sorcery discourses of particular PNG societies. Everyone in PNG today can speak with conviction about the existence and nature of several basic patterns of sorcery by which a person may be sickened or killed through fearsome magical means: the victim may come into contact (more or less directly) with a magically active substance, often placed on a road and then walked or driven over; some bit of substance associated with the victim's body, such as a hair or piece of half-eaten food, may be acted upon by a sorcerer without one's knowledge; or a victim may be stunned and assaulted, have his or her innards invisibly tampered with, and then be released as a zombie to soon fall sick or die. Sorcerers often perform these evil deeds under contract by a third party with a grievance against the victim. But one way or another, such acts epitomize the moral problem of improper behavior toward others resulting from unchecked destructive impulses. It is axiomatic for Papua New Guineans that this problem (together with the wantok system) is to blame for their lack of prosperity and failure to develop. Indeed, many of the transitory institutions people create to try to bring on development, including cargo cults and Christian revivals, are explicitly focused on stopping sorcery (see, e.g., Knauft 2002b; Lattas 1998; Tuzin 1997; Wesch 2006).

The other great racial failing on which Papua New Guinea's lack of development is blamed is the violence and crime called "raskolism" that people fear when circulating outside the safety of the village, especially when traveling along the roads and in town. Armed robberies of public buses and of stores and houses in town are today "regular occurrences" (Wardlow 2002b, 145) that cast a pall over everyday life. Reminders of the raskol problem are ubiquitous in PNG. They are seen in the barbed wire fences that surround urban private houses, and the uniformed security guards and ferocious dogs posted outside stores. The threat of raskolism constitutes a real disincentive to investment in public facilities and business development. No doubt, raskolism is in some sense stimulated by the enormous commodity wealth that modern life makes available, in light of the economically hopeless reality of unemployment and low wages faced especially by young men (Wardlow 2002b; Roscoe 1999;

Goddard 2005). But for most Papua New Guineans, what is salient about raskols is the fear they spread through their shameless unlawfulness and big-headed lack of restraint, and these degenerate moral qualities are often empha-sized in the stories told about them. In fact, these qualities are ones that raskols themselves co-opt and take to an extreme. Not only are raskol incidents often violent, but also in many cases the violence is excessive, extremely transgres-sive, and shocking: rooms in robbed houses are smeared with feces, murder victims are dismembered, pregnant women are raped (Sykes 1999). People's sense that the raskol problem is insidious and endemic in PNG society is only magnified by rumors that raskols have well-established connections to the highest echelons of the national government (see Dinnen 1999).

Papua New Guineans often speak of these moral failings as an essential characteristic in themselves that contrasts with the superior self-control, obedience, and ability to unify they attribute to whitemen. Not that this attribution is absolute and unambivalent; in certain contexts Papua New Guineans readily portray whites as given to unrestrained arrogance and expressions of anger such as cursing. But in this racial discourse of self-critique, where morally charged qualities are mapped onto the contrast between black and white skin, they read onto their own black skin the stigma of moral failing (Lattas 1992a, 1998; Kulick 1992; Robbins 2004a; Jebens 2004). In taking their skin as evidence for the moral deficiencies that prevent them from enjoying a whitemanlike prosperity and develop-ment, Papua New Guineans are adopting a discursive framework that is thoroughly homologous with colonial racism and the western hierarchy of peoples and nations. This recapitulation of the terms of western hegemony has been criticized by Papua New Guinean intellectuals like Narokobi, who warns Papua New Guineans against "constantly measuring them[selves] against outsiders," since it leads them to devalue their own moral strengths, producing an unfortunate and unwarranted "inferiority complex" (Narokobi 1983, 57). This critique of the "colonial hangover" has continued to have resonance; in 1998, for example, the prominent journalist Frank Senge Kolma excoriated Papua New Guineans in the pages of the PNG daily *The National* for continuing their "unconscious elevation" of whitemen for reasons as spurious as "the colour of their skin," an "irrational syndrome" he dubs the "masta [colonial white master] complex" (Kolma 1998). But such admonitions notwithstanding, there is today an undeniable perva-sive current of self-condemnation and self-denigration in Papua New Guineans' talk about themselves, their blackness, and their nation. Recent PNG ethnographies document well how people closely associate a sense of themselves as incorrigibly willful, undisciplined, and divided with Papua

New Guinea's position at the bottom of the international hierarchy of more and less developed countries (Foster 2002, 136; Lattas 1998; Zimmer-Tamakoshi 1996, 168; Kulick 1992). As Joel Robbins has put it in describing how Urapmin "see their national identity as a source of much that they dislike and wish to reject in themselves," Papua New Guineans' nationalism is often a negative one (Robbins 2004a, 171; 1998). Or as Jeffrey Clark was surprised to hear his Papua New Guinean collaborator vehemently insist, "I hate PNG" (Clark 1997, 74).

Like the other two themes, the wantok system and villagers' strong attachment to their lands, this third self-denigrating theme of abject moral failing organizes people's concerns in a way that is similar to the Orokaiva village discourse of race discussed in previous chapters. As in the Orokaiva vernacular construction of whitemen, there is a basic premise that abundance and prosperity derive from an antecedent condition of social harmony and lawful obedience, leading people to infer from whitemen's obvious wealth a corresponding virtue that makes their own experience of dearth all the more morally charged and troubling, as it stands as a constant reminder of their own moral deficiency.[15] So we see once again that the ready intertranslatability afforded by the homologous racial discourses of the village and nation means that the cultural particularity of the Orokaiva construction of whitemen in no way requires an isolation of Orokaiva people from the wider world of the nation (and indeed, as we will see below, from the international realm as well).

Implications for Orokaiva People, Anthropology, Race Studies, and the Place of the West in the World

The Continued Vitality of Orokaiva Culture

As the foregoing pages make clear, the western modernity Orokaiva identify with whitemen is an integral part of the moral world of Orokaiva people today. Like other Papua New Guineans, Orokaiva villagers are experiencing cultural change as a formidable force in their lives. Although they are poor, villagers are increasingly targeted as a market for soft drinks, cigarettes, detergent, and a range of other products, which has the effect of increasing the role of capitalist desire in organizing village life (Foster 2002; Wardlow 1998). This in turn legitimizes individualistic patterns of consumption and notions of selfhood that are devalued in the indigenous order. Individual notions of selfhood are also encouraged by Christianity, particularly in its charismatic and Pentecostal variants which have become major competitors of the old-line Anglican church (Robbins 2004a, 2004c; Bashkow 2000b). Moreover, the distinctiveness of villagers' cultural identity is being reshaped by the external forces of the state and modern institutions that encompass them, framing them as but one parochial ethnicity among so many structurally equivalent others (LiPuma 2000). This "cultural generification" reduces Orokaiva to a mere position within "structures of common difference," so that what is distinctively Orokaiva becomes just another regional variant of a generic Melanesian cultural identity distinguished by a particular form of body decoration, dance, feasting, brideprice custom, and so on (Errington and Gewertz 2001; Wilk 1995a; Hannerz 1996).

At the same time, however, we should not underestimate the robustness and resilience of Orokaiva vernacular culture. For all the changes it has undergone in response to colonial rule and its aftermath, an impressive degree of cultural continuity is evident among Orokaiva peoples over the past century. Unlike some other New Guinea peoples that have been studied particularly in parts of the far western Highlands and Sepik, Orokaiva seem to be culturally predisposed to construct for themselves an identity that is very largely centered in and generated out of their own traditions and locally experienced world, which protects them from some of the most culturally erosive effects of globalization. It is thus quite possible that Orokaiva people will enjoy continued cultural vitality into the future, even with the pressures of globalization in force, so long as they remain grounded in the local experiential world that their culture invests with meaning and relevance, reinforcing the culture in turn.[16]

It is also for this reason that the Orokaiva construction of whitemen, which might seem by virtue of its very content to draw Orokaiva away from their own culture, actually leads them back into it. On the face of it, of course, Orokaiva people's admiration of whitemen's wealth as indicating a moral position superior to their own would appear to be writing on the wall for their distinctive cultural worldview; since Orokaiva so highly value what they see whitemen to have, it might seem like only a matter of time before they give up their own culture in order to get it. Indeed, there is an undeniably tragic aspect to the Orokaiva construction of whitemen. With so many of the virtues of indigenous Orokaiva morality being projected onto the whiteman other, these become alienated from Orokaiva selves, to the point where people's own ideals (like extension of influence across distance, social harmony, and abundant wealth and prosperity) become all but unattainable. But we should remember that Orokaiva also construct whitemen as in many ways *inferior* to themselves (e.g., in hospitality, hard work, and capacity for true feelings), so one must recognize that they see foreign others as better than themselves only *in certain respects*. Moreover, Orokaiva portrayals of whitemen as superior often serve rhetorical ends (such as the critique of sorcery) that are culturally valued and consistent with traditional morality, so that even when people represent themselves as inferior to whitemen and express the desire to be like them, they may be doing so in a medium that actually perpetuates distinctively Orokaiva moral premises, categories, and concerns. While it is true that Orokaiva long to enjoy a whitemanlike prosperity that would give them access to abundant rice and tinfish, roofing iron, transportation, kerosene for their lanterns, and so on, they have not (yet) internalized the western point of view that such wealth exacts a necessary social toll in the form of material inequality. They do not accept, as we all too easily do, that disparity between rich and poor is natural, and that it is unproblematic for those with wealth to hold it for themselves even when directly confronted with others' dearth.[17] In projecting onto whitemen an achievement of their own ideal of social harmony, it is apparent that the prosperity they associate with whitemen is in many ways a collective and communally shared prosperity of just the sort they would wish for themselves.[18] Thus, their admiring representations of whitemen do not impel them necessarily toward the individualistic ethos of western capitalism, and their use of whitemen as a foil for cultural self-critique does not actually hinder them in maintaining robust traditions in their everyday lives.

Because Orokaiva culture is so dependent on the particular world of experience in which it is embedded, the most critical factor for its continued vitality is the continued availability of ancestral garden lands that yield the food that Orokaiva not only subsist on but also use to create their social selves through feasting and exchange with others. The threat to this world of experience rooted in lands is in fact a real one, and it comes from the potential for further expansion of the World Bank–funded Higaturu Oil Palm Project, which has become the region's anchor in the cash economy. In 1976, one year after Papua New Guinea's independence, the World Bank, together with the Commonwealth Development Corporation (now called CDC), a commercial arm of Great Britain that operates in former British colonies, initiated a multi-million-dollar project to develop an oil palm industry in Oro Province. In addition to creating several large, foreign-managed plantations or "nucleus estates" on land that had been appropriated for the state early in the period of Australian colonial rule, the project created 1,500 miniplantations to be tended by Papua New Guinean "smallholders," about one-fifth of whom were settlers from other provinces, and the rest Orokaiva. Of these miniplantations, six hundred were planted near Orokaiva villages on lands formerly used for food gardening. So much of the region's land has been devoted to growing oil palm that evenly spaced rows of the bushy palm trees have come to dominate the landscape one sees when flying into Popondetta and while traveling along area roads. Indeed, many of the roads were built with project funds, as was the only major industrial facility in the region, the huge, smoke-belching mill where fruit from the palms is processed into a low-grade palm oil (see plate 24). With its company housing compounds (replete with clinics and schools) and its elaborate system for transporting the palm fruit from each of the miniplantations to the mill every fortnight, the project represents in some respects a model of expertly planned "big development." And the cash it introduces into the local economy has undoubtedly contributed to the viability of Orokaiva village existence in modern times. Because of the project Orokaiva are less compelled to leave their villages to gain access to money, as are many other PNG villagers.[19]

Although the project's economic performance has typically "fallen short of original expectations" (World Bank 1999, 23), its success relative to other big development schemes that have been tried in the region (e.g., coffee, cocoa, and cattle ranching) led to an expansion of the project in the mid-1990s that has more than doubled the land area devoted to oil palm, to more than 80 square miles (Koczberski, Curry, and Gibson 2001, 6–8). The land used to plant new nucleus estates was taken over from prior failed development schemes, but virtually all of the new land planted by smallholders was customary land, much of it garden land, in the close environs of villages. The project expansion also extended the road network, bringing oil palm plantings to many new parts of Orokaiva country, including new areas around Agenehambo. Oil palm has now come to occupy a considerable proportion of Agenehambo villagers' lands, including virtually all land suitable for gardening that is close to the roads. Oil palm plantings have a harvestable lifespan of about fifteen years, after which the massive, fast-growing palms must be poisoned, cut down, and replanted. The expansion of the project in the 1990s piggybacked on the necessary reinvestment occasioned by this life-cycle transition, so there is reason to expect further expansion at the end of the current planting cycle. Based on the dates of the original plantings, a new replanting cycle will inevitably be discussed and funded by 2008 in order to support replanting over the following few years, with a peak around 2010.[20]

The threat of the expanding oil palm industry intensifies land pressures already being felt due to the growth of the local population and the use of land to grow other, less agriculturally disruptive and less externally regi-mented cash-crops such as coffee and cocoa. The permanent withdrawal of large tracts of land from the swidden gardening system has meant a shortening of the periods during which rotational garden lands are left fal-low. While these changes have not significantly degraded people's garden yields or patterns of gardening activity as of yet, Orokaiva land resources have now been extended to the point where further pressure is likely to stress indigenous gardening in consequential ways. As nearby lands get diverted to oil palm, food gardens must be established ever farther away, burdening families and especially women, who bear the brunt of repetitive garden tasks and who are the ones who normally carry harvested foods back to the village. Moreover, unlike coffee and cocoa, which create inten-sive work only in occasional short bursts of activity, participation in the oil palm project requires a regular, heavy time commitment for tending, har-vesting, and transporting the bunches of palm fruit to the road every fort-night. This regular time commitment necessarily detracts from gardening and community activities, including feasting (see also Schwimmer 1973, 27; Waddell and Krinks 1968). Since feast foods are ideally grown in gardens cut from dark, wet forest lands that have not been planted in many, many years, the reduced length of fallow periods resulting from oil palm land pressure will soon leave people squeezed between the needs of feasting and the preservation of their surrounding rainforest landscape, the old-growth forests that serve as hunting grounds, reservoirs of fecundity, and an impor-tant reference point in their culture.

When presented with an opportunity to participate in the oil palm proj-ect, Orokaiva individuals can hardly afford *not* to accept the huge sums the project pays participants upfront in loans for tools, seedlings, and so on, and they find the promise of a regular cash income an overpowering incentive (see also Newton 1982).[21] But in the long view, development does poor peo-ple little justice if it binds them to a life at the lowest rungs of western modernity that exchanges the wealth of their own cultural forms for only the lowest-grade trappings of western civilization: broken-grain rice and canned mackerel. The oil palm expansion reinforces other trends of globalization that undermine the traditional culture by legitimating indi-vidualistic patterns of consumption, livelihood, and selfhood. In making people dependent on market commodity prices and relations of produc-tion, it furthers their transformation from free people centered in a world that belongs to them, where their livelihood and place is secure, to vulnera-ble peasants in a world economy to which they are marginal and easily replaceable.

The threat to Orokaiva lands and the way of life they support is thus the most serious issue for the continued vitality of Orokaiva culture. Further large-scale diversion of garden lands for oil palm farming would have grave material and cultural consequences for Orokaiva people's lives, and given the ineffectiveness and aid-dependence of the PNG government, it is up to no one but the West to prevent this from happening.

Recuperating Otherness: Toward an Anthropology of the Foreign

Over the last three decades, there has arisen an interdisciplinary discourse on culture and identity that is dominated by a critique of the dichotomous contrast between self and other. This discourse pursues the issues raised by Edward Said's thesis that western "orientalist" discourse, which is structured in terms of a self/other dichotomy, functions in the interest of imperialism and racial domination and is inherently hostile to and depreciatory of those portrayed as other. According to Said's influential critique, western scholars and British colonial officials self-servingly constructed Europeans as rational, restrained, and responsible—and hence fit to rule—by contrasting them with "Oriental" others, such as Egyptians or Indians, who were depicted as irrational, indolent, mystical, cunning, and "inclined toward despotism"—and hence fit to be ruled (Said 1978, 1989, 1993; Kabbani 1986; McAlister 2001, 9). Since Said, scholars have applied analogous critiques to virtually every western genre in which others find representation: colonial reports, travel memoirs, literature, philosophy, history, ethnography, photography, film, and so on. According to these critiques, construing others as culturally distinct is pernicious when it perpetuates their exclusion from the superior category identified with the West and legitimates colonial and neocolonial domination (Abu-Lughod 1991; Young 1995). For this reason, it is unacceptable to portray cultural others as inhabiting a time or place distinct from our own, since this denies others "coevalness" with the self (Fabian 1983). Even depicting others in positive terms, for example as more authentically spiritual than us, improperly exoticizes them, covertly devaluing them as "primitive" by implicit contrast with our own self-satisfied western modernity (Torgovnick 1990; Di Leonardo 1998; see also Rosenblatt 1997). Indeed, so thoroughly have critics repudiated cross-cultural understandings cast in terms of binary self/other oppositions, "difference," and "alterity," that the traditional subject of ethnographic study would seem to be all but "dead and buried" (Kurasawa 2002, 2).

The Orokaiva construction of whitemen studied here points to a fundamental problem with this critical framework. Based as this framework is

240 · CHAPTER SIX

on the multiplication of a set of examples virtually all of which were produced by westerners and which are often specifically chosen for their association with imperial expansion and racial domination, the critique reflexively generalizes what is actually a historically and culturally particular moral valence and political function to all self/other dichotomies, as if any form of othering is ipso facto bad (see also Dirlik 1997). But it is a mistake to universalize the moral valence of this form of understanding without bothering to look carefully at the discourses of otherness that are produced within other cultures. And we are too often poised to dismiss those foreign discourses of otherness that we consider as mere internalizations of hegemonic western ideology cultivated through the experience of colonialism. But the connection between self/other dichotomizing and imperial expansionism and racial domination is not in fact a necessary one. In studying literary and ethnographic sources that reveal diverse peoples' constructions of others and otherness for an undergraduate anthropology course I regularly teach, How Others See Us, I have amassed enormous support for the conclusion that self/other dichotomizing is hardly distinctively European: people everywhere create representations of others opposed to themselves. Indeed, it appears that the impulse to do so is intrinsic to culture itself and always has indigenous motivations, even when it simultaneously reflects external influences such as colonial ideologies. We could say it is only human, then, for people to construct others in dialectical relation to themselves—as more virtuous or more vice-ridden, more primitive or refined, more natural or ethereal, and so on—always taking the self as the implicit point of reference (Lévi-Strauss 1969; Brightman 1990; Lovejoy and Boas 1997 [1935]; Boas 1997 [1948]; Bartra 1994).

These pan-human discourses of otherness serve an important moral function in providing an evaluative metacommentary on aspects of the self that the other casts into relief: a ready framework for exploring alternatives to one's own culture's conventional morality. Given this function, discourses of otherness must always be understood to be part of the culture in which they are *produced*, rather than the culture they appear to be *about*. When Orokaiva construct whitemen as inverting the virtues and vices they see in themselves, they are engaging in a form of moral reasoning that is cognitively natural and culturally universal, albeit one unacknowledged in the model of morality taken for granted in western folk ideology, religion, and philosophy. In this model, morality is identified with a system of rules or principles that people apply to particular situations. But as Mark Johnson (1993) has argued, moral reasoning may be better understood as an imaginative act involving metaphorical extension from conventionalized core cases that serve as moral prototypes. Although Johnson does not deal directly with moral reasoning involving cultural others, they clearly serve as just such moral prototypes, "mak[ing] criticism possible" by giving us "alternative viewpoints and concepts from which to evaluate the merits of a particular moral position" (Johnson 1993, 3). If this is indeed a fundamental mode of human thinking, as Johnson suggests, for scholars to repudiate morally charged self/other comparison as such is to seriously misplace our critical focus.

In other words, to oppose the self to an other is a human phenomenon, not a European or colonial one (Carrier 1995c). Nor is it morally reprehensible in and of itself. It is not a flaw inherent to culture, an original sin that besets our perceptions of difference and distances us from the longed-for Eden of true human community. As we have seen in the case of Orokaiva, who in many contexts construct whitemen as epitomizing virtues that they themselves find difficult to achieve, ideas of "the foreign" and the "own"/"other" distinction are not invariably depreciatory or dehumanizing of the other, but may be characterized by admiration and regard (see also Sax 1998). Far from being a mere internalization of hegemonically imposed views of the western self, such positive evaluations of the other are powerfully motivated from within the culture itself, where they serve an important creative function in providing people with terms in which to articulate moral criticism of themselves and their society. Ideas of own versus other are uniquely suited to the exploration of problems that trouble people in their own society, problems which appear absent in the alternative world of the other. It is the very fact of an other's difference from the self that opens the possibility of "questioning that which appears normal or natural," to denaturalize, relativize, estrange, and interrogate the self (Kurasawa 2002, 3–4; 2004; see also Wagner 1975, 15–16; Marcus and Fischer 1986; Mason 1998; Ellingson 2001; Bashkow 2000a, 322–24).

All people need some way to interpret and assimilate the foreign, even though in doing so they necessarily reinterpret and resituate it within the terms of their culture. Orokaiva perceive whitemen as foreign beings whose nature could not have been formed within their own cultural bounds. Nevertheless, as we have stressed repeatedly, the way Orokaiva construct whitemen *is* an integral part of their contemporary vernacular culture: it is cast in terms of Orokaiva categories, values, assumptions, and interests; it is made integral to distinctively Orokaiva activities; and it is perpetuated by Orokaiva themselves within their communities even in the absence of white people. As such the Orokaiva construction of whitemen exemplifies what I have elsewhere termed the "zone of the foreign"—an intrinsically flexible and accommodating area of culture that is concerned with the things in people's lives that they categorize as foreign, not culturally their own (Bashkow 2004). It is the zone of the foreign that allows people to make sense of all manner of extraordinary intercultural experiences, albeit using preconceived notions of others that are constructed dialectically with their ideas of themselves. In Orokaiva culture this zone of the foreign includes not only the many various things that are identified with whitemen and taupa kastom but also things identified with other foreign sources, such as the yam house Kingsford designed in the style of the Managalasi people to the north (see chapter 3). In being recognizably foreign, the yam house was not thereby removed from Orokaiva cultural experience but was rather assimilated to it on that very basis.

People's marking of foreignness productively complicates our conventional understanding of culture change. Ordinarily, we think about "foreign influence" as a force that impels change by presenting people with cultural alternatives they may adopt. A given item of influence can be more or less consequential depending on the specifics of how it articulates with preexisting conditions, so that in New Guinea societies the introduction of axes, for example, occasioned relatively little social structural change, whereas single family housing has tended to be quite disruptive. We know that people are selective about which foreign influences they adopt, and that they tend to transform those they do adopt by interpreting them from their own cultural standpoint. But what we have learned from our example of the Orokaiva construction of whitemen is that people, as they interpret things, distinguish between "own" and "other," and that this allows them to regard imported alternatives as part of a foreign complex and not "their own" culturally. Imports may be exoticized, their very alienness serving to support native powers and traditional purposes (as when Orokaiva use whitemen's foods in feasting, or when a U.S. cable television channel achieves audience share by showing films about "tribal" peoples). Alternatively, imports may be relativized, culturally compartmentalized to specific identities or contexts of use (like the Orokaiva practice of whitemen's business, or Chinese food in the United States). Particularly where people associate a category of the foreign with superior status, such compartmentalization can accelerate the loss of standing of traditional ways. But it can also be part of a dynamic through which foreign influence and cross-cultural interaction themselves contribute to the preservation of cultural distinctiveness, through the ongoing marking of valued differences from objects, activities, styles, and so on that remain framed as foreign.

As we have seen, the distinctiveness of Orokaiva culture does not depend on its insularity: Orokaiva people no more "lose" their culture when they distribute whitemen's rice and tinfish at feasts than Americans lose *theirs* when they hang New Guinea spirit masks on their living room walls. Indeed, the example of western New Age spirituality, with its rapacious consumption of the culturally exotic, illustrates well how the pursuit of the foreign can itself become a means through which people reproduce the basic structures of their own culture (westerners pursuing an "exotic" New Age lifestyle end up reproducing their western individualism, consumerism, and evangelism). An example farther afield is the value traditionally placed on importation in New Guinea Mountain Arapesh culture, where the most highly valued rituals and dance complexes were ones imported from other peoples, creating an ever-changing round of fashionable practices central to traditional culture itself (Mead 1938; Dobrin and Bashkow forthcoming 2006). In some circumstances it is an object's very foreignness that lends power to the actions people take that symbolically appropriate it and turn it to their own indigenous ends, as we have seen Orokaiva do with whitemen's foods in gift exchange and feasting. By demonstrating their ability to exert control over the foreign and the distant in this way, people claim a particularly dramatic form of power in terms that are convincing in their own local cultural world (see also Rutherford 2003; Sahlins 2000; Helms 1988; Munn 1986).

The foreign is part of everyone's world. Even if its role may be to epitomize cultural difference and otherness, anthropology needs to recognize the foreign for the significant cultural force that it is. If we do so, we take an important step toward a more realistic conception of culture that is open and "outward-looking" (Massey 1994, 147), offering us a way out of the old (and false) conundrum in which the reality of cultural particularity seems to contradict our understanding that human cultures are not discrete entities. In an anthropology of the foreign, the boundaries distinguishing cultures would not be confused with barriers that block or hinder people, ideas, or objects from passing across them, but rather would be conceptualized as thresholds or frontiers that allow and indeed even create motivation for things to be pulled in from outside (Bashkow 2004). The boundaries people draw as they distinguish their own culture from all others may appear to them to surround or enclose them, but such boundaries are in fact what allow them to extend their culture and its categories, values, assumptions, and so on across the symbolic thresholds the boundaries mark. While this extension of culture through notions of the foreign may oftentimes be imperialistic and condemnable, this should not prevent us from appreciating that it may also serve cultural functions that are positive and creative. In many cases, the zone of the foreign constitutes a field in which cultural alternatives are explored and from which cultural self-critiques may be launched, a field in which the novel and the experimental are incubated and where particular intercultural experiences and relationships among people find meaning. The field of anthropology may itself be understood as just such a zone of the foreign. Unfortunately, the intense problematization of cultural othering has tended to promote "a withdrawal of the western human sciences to their own cultural horizons" (Kurasawa 2002, 15). But the truest calling of the discipline remains to expand these horizons by providing a productive framework for engaging other cultural worlds that, while undeniably part of western culture, is nevertheless deeply interested in and profoundly open to the lives and voices of others, as well as morally constructive for ourselves.

Race Is Culturally Constructed, but How? And Where Does That Leave Us?

In this book I have argued that race is constructed not only in persons and groups but also in objects, institutions, activities, and places which are interpreted as having racial characteristics. Raced objects provide an illusion of clarity that the actual complexity of racial categories of persons does not support, and so we find that it is primarily through objects that racial categories find confirmation within people's lives. After three decades of postcolonial white flight, Orokaiva stereotypes of whitemen are only minimally grounded in the experience of actual interaction with whites, which is now rare, and are instead substantiated primarily in symbolic elements that exist independently of whites as persons. These elements include whitemen's material culture such as motor vehicles, roofing iron, guns, baby powder, paper and books, shoes and socks, wristwatches, radio-cassette players, machines of all kinds, pots and pans, canned corned beef, and rice—in effect, everything one can buy with money in a store, and the money and the store itself. They embrace institutions like wage work, markets, churches, schools, banks, clinics, courts, the government, and development agencies. They include whitemen's habits like freely intermingling the sexes, celebrating birthdays, cursing and barking commands, timing work by the clock, sitting in chairs, sleeping on mattresses, serving guests cake, and writing things down. They include whitemen's languages, especially Tok Pisin and English, and foreign media like video movies, amplified music, television, radio, faxes, phones, and computers.

It might be thought that the disjuncture between the salience of white-men as culturally constructed and the paucity of direct experience with white persons reflects the social dynamics of an anomalous racial situation. But extremely limited or circumscribed interaction between cultur-ally opposed racial groups is by no means uncommon. For example, as Philip Deloria makes clear in his illuminating history of European American ways of "playing Indian," from the Mohawk disguises assumed by Boston Tea Party participants to the modern vision quests of contem-porary New Agers, the meanings of Indianness constructed by European Americans have been "largely disconnected from Indian people," with the forms of "Indianness" that have most interested European Americans generally being those promoted by non-Indians, including some who indeed take up fictive native identities in order to "lay claim to the cul-tural power of Indianness in the white imagination" (Deloria 1998, 159, 168). Last week, my four-year-old son Elie surprised my wife and me by excitedly reporting that he wanted to dress up as a "Native American" for Halloween. When we questioned him about this, he could not tell us anything about Native Americans apart from their (to him very attractive) association with bows and arrows and hunting. This is not an association he has gotten from direct experience with Native American people. Nor did it come from media portrayals, as we have drastically limited his exposure to electronic media and media-savvy peers and environments. Instead, the idea (and along with it the conscientious term "Native American"!) came from his playmate Ezra, who also has plans to dress up as a Native American this year. This example shows how racial stereotypes may come to us at some remove from the persons so stereotyped, that they are trans-mitted through culture-internal relationships, and that they associate racial categories with categories of objects and activities.

Or it might be objected that the Orokaiva emphasis on objects reflects a peculiarity of their culture. After all, many have observed that in societies throughout Melanesia the person is constructed as a composite of social relationships, which are constituted in turn by the history of objects exchanged between people; in this way the person is imbued with the char-acteristics of objects, and vice versa (Strathern 1988). If Orokaiva and other Melanesian cultures construct persons in an artifactual medium *in general*, then the association of whitemen with objects would simply be an extension of the cultural construction of persons, and not necessarily about race at all.[22] This could undermine my suggestion that the racialization of objects is a general and important medium of race symbolism in culture. The response to this objection is that first, it is not only material objects but also institutions, places, and styles of activity that acquire racial connotations, and second, the objectification of persons (and personification of objects) is by no means uniquely Melanesian, even if the particular ways in which it is accomplished in Melanesia are distinctive and thus easy for us to see (Carrier 1995b; LiPuma 2000). In modern western societies, too, there is no denying that objects are pervasively used to construct the person, for example through shopping, consuming, and the giving of presents. The personification of objects is diligently cultivated by marketers eager to differentiate their products and position their brands in a crowded marketplace. And there is no shortage of western institutional contexts in which persons are objectified: in electoral politics and government services as demographics; in schooling as test scores or "problem children"; in wage work as surplus value; and in pornography as sex objects. Indeed, racism itself is a prominent mode in which persons are objectified.

One major strength of the race-in-objects view elaborated here is that it begins to explain why popular racial stereotypes are persistent even in the face of persons who are racially ambiguous or who counterexemplify them. The Orokaiva stereotype that whitemen have soft skin because they do not do hard physical work is not abandoned when villagers encounter whites who do work with their hands and have thick calluses to show for it; instead, such whites are simply considered unusual individuals. Similarly, the basic construction of whitemen as frustratingly light and arrogantly aloof from exchange relations with villagers is in no way overturned by whites who do generously reciprocate villagers' help and hospitality; instead, such persons are appreciated as happy exceptions. So robust is the stereotype, indeed, that whites who are generous often provoke Orokaiva to speculate that they may not be true whitemen at all but rather reincarnations of Orokaiva people, returning in disguise (see chapter 2). Of course, the robustness of racial stereotypes is hardly unique to Orokaiva society. All over the world, well-entrenched racial stereotypes have proven enormously difficult to dislodge, and racial stereotypes continue to affect people's lives even where ambiguous or anomalous individuals would clearly seem to disprove them (see Rockquemore and Brunsma 2002; Derricotte 1997).

So robust indeed are the racial stereotypes in our own society that they have persisted in the face of a century of sustained critique by social scientists. The enormously important critique of race pioneered by Franz Boas in the early twentieth century debunked the pervasive assumption that races are distinct "human types" in which anatomical features correlate with mental aptitudes and levels of moral worth. Not only were scientists wrong in thinking that acquired cultural characteristics were inherited "with the blood," biologically, but actual human populations were in fact anatomically and mentally quite heterogeneous, and even anatomical characteristics such as head form could be dramatically affected by differences of environment (Boas 1965 [1938]; Stocking 1968, 1974, 1992; Barkan 1992; Gould 1996; Smedley 1999; Pierpont 2004). As expressed in successive Statements on Race published by the United Nations Educational, Scientific, and Cultural Organization (UNESCO) since 1950, race is an ideology of human difference that is culturally fabricated, not biologically real. And the field of anthropology has repeatedly argued that the popular conception of races as culturally significant human groupings rooted in biological difference is simply illusory; it is pure ideology that does not reflect reality—it "does not exist" (Gilroy 2001; Montagu 1972; AAA 1998; IUAES 1995; see also Proctor 2003). This critique of the biological ("biologistic") basis for popularly held racial categories has provided an important response to the most overt and egregious forms of racism like segregation, eugenics, and genocide. But even after a century of elaboration, the critique has eliminated neither racial stereotyping nor the covert, insidious racism that motivates discrimination in housing, employment, education, and so on in our society.

One reason for this lack of impact is surely the tactical error of denying the reality of race simply because its categories are underdetermined by the explanatory parameters we take as given by the natural sciences. Indeed, calling race an illusion, critics have made their own voices largely irrelevant to political debates about the problem of racism (Baker 1998; Haney López 1996; Appiah and Guttmann 1996). And as scholars have noted, the "no-race posture" implied by the critique of biologistic theories of race gives unintended support to the "color blind racism" of white racial conservatives (Harrison 1995, 47; Bonilla-Silva 2003; Winant 2001b). Appropriating Martin Luther King's dream of a color-blind society, whites can now profess that all people are only individuals and "the same" whether "black, brown, yellow, or green" (Frankenberg 1993, 149) and thereby argue against affirmative action as a correction for institutionalized racism. Taking the invalidation of biological race to mean that we can only legitimately speak about individuals and diversity in the abstract, we effectively deny the reality of social and cultural structures that perpetuate discrimination. It is no solution to racism for us all to "forget" culturally constructed racial categories. Pervasive race avoidance by the white majority only supports white privilege and dominance, even as race continues to occupy an important place in people's experience and everyday lives (Winant 2001a; Frankenberg 1993; Conley 1999, 2000; Hartigan

1999; Prashad 2000; Dyer 1997; Bonilla-Silva 2003; Royster 2003; Bush 2004; Dijk 1984, 1987).

But another reason for the slight impact of the critique of biological racial classifications is its narrow concentration on the human body. This concentration reflects the ideological centrality of the body in the western folk theory of race which was "elevated to the ranks of scholarly discourse when scientists began developing rationalizations and justifications for . . . unequal power relationships" in terms of the concept of racial inheritance symbolized by "blood" (Smedley 1999, 321; see also Drake 1987–1990; Schneider 1984). But this folk theory of race is inadequate to characterize how race is actually symbolically constructed in culture.[23] The body is in fact only one of many kinds of objects in which race is signified in people's everyday lives. As Boas showed us so long ago, people's ideas about race cannot be explained by biology. Nor, I now argue, need their symbolic content necessarily be anchored in the body in any way. In tacitly accepting the "scientific" definition of racial constructs as ideas (albeit false ones) about the cultural correlates of biological difference, the scholarly critique of race unconstructively perpetuates the false premise that racial categories are, at bottom, classifications of persons and groups of persons.[24] This premise has been an obstacle to our understanding of the cultural process by which racial categories are constructed in culture because it keeps drawing our attention to the same set of problems with biologically based racial classification, leading us again and again to frame the same kinds of critiques, which show that racial stereotypes are unreliable as depictions of groups of persons. The western folk theory of race thus distracts us from considering how objects other than the body serve to reproduce racial constructs, as if it is not about race if it does not relate to the body or a classification of persons.

The alternative view developed in this book is that the cultural construction of race that matters in people's everyday lives can be grounded in objects. The meanings popularly associated with racial constructs like whiteness and blackness are substantiated not in properties of the skin, but rather in the characteristics of race-signifying objects, institutions, places, and styles of activity that exist independently of actual persons. In this view, it is not so important whether the classification of persons we normally think of as "race" is constructed on the basis of ancestry, skin color, other visible phenotypic characteristics, or invisible genetic ones (Táíwò 2003); its cultural content derives from a parallel classification of objects which are meaningful as racial symbols. Once it is understood that race is constructed in this way, it becomes clear why counterexemplifying persons could never really disprove or displace racial stereotypes. In fact, racial stereotypes do not find their primary confirmation in persons at all; their robustness derives from their very *independence* from persons. As we have seen throughout the book, Orokaiva find confirmation for their cultural construction of whitemen in objects like rice, activities like business, institutions like church, and places like town, all of which exist independently of white persons, thus allowing the qualities of whitemen that they embody, like lightness, to be experienced directly, making the stereotypes that are based on them seem real and compelling.

Because race-signifying objects, activities, institutions, and places are independent of persons, the features that ground stereotypes are manipulable and materially appropriable. We have seen how Orokaiva use foods like rice and taro as conventionalized objectifications of racial categories, so that eating them is to eat in a raced way. Because an object like food can be incorporated within a wide range of contexts, the appropriation of food as a racial symbol supports varying kinds and gradations of racial identification and contrast. Eating tinfish and rice can be a mere indulgence in a culinary pleasure associated with racial others, but it can also represent one's own identification with whitemen as part of a fashioned "crossover" racial identity (see also Pilcher 1998, 143–44; Seneviratne 1992, 196; Sutton 2001; Weismantel 1988). We see another example of this in John Hartigan's ethnography of race in Detroit, where working-class whites and blacks draw upon a shared vocabulary of raced foods to understand each other and manipulate racial categorizations. Because white hillbillies "were known to love pinto beans while blacks ate chitlins," a white man who ate chitlins could be called "kin" by a black man in a gesture of solidarity (Hartigan 1999, 114–15; see also Witt 2004). Where multiple raced elements are appropriated all at once, individuals can identify with racial others more dramatically, experiencing their stereotypes mimetically from within. The most widely discussed example of this kind of racial crossover in the United States is when white youths imitate African American styles of music, language, dress, and body attitudes, creating what is sometimes derided (and at other times celebrated) as "wigger" identities (Roediger 2002, 221ff; Wimsatt 1994; Wagner 1996). This phenomenon of racial crossover is also recognizable in numerous postcolonial settings, including in PNG, where the elites take on a lifestyle—and often even the racial category—associated with the particular version of whiteness that is salient locally (Segal 1993; Gewertz and Errington 1999; Al Ahmad 1984 [1962]; Memmi 1965 [1957]; Fanon 1967 [1952]; Sheriff 2001; Winant 2001b).

The point to draw from this is not that individuals, by manipulating raced objects, can fully control how others perceive and classify them, since once again, the construction of the categories of race, with their symbolic meanings, connotations, values, and so on, is a cultural process at a different level from the racial classification of individual persons. Obviously, there is a difference between voluntarily adopted racial crossover identities such as "wigger" and involuntarily ascribed ones like "nigger." But persons everywhere may be attributed "honorary" or "pseudo" racial identities that contradict their clearly marked phenotypic ones. Even someone who "looks black" unambiguously can be associated with whiteness by acting or speaking "white," and people with ambiguous looks often move between different racial identities by the way they act in different contexts. The fact that the racial categorization of individuals is so often uncertain, complicated, shifting, and multifaceted makes it clear that groupings of persons are not the source of the clarity and stability of popular racial stereotypes.

By focusing on the way racial stereotypes are grounded instead in objects that are independent of persons and hence appropriable and manipulable, we are led to understand how race can be *performative*: race is not only a category people ascribe to others; it is something that people *do* (Willie 2003; Jackson 2001). A performative view of race is consistent with recent research on how race and racism is learned by children. Children learn racial stereotypes not by observing the people so stereotyped, but rather by observing and imitating acts of stereotyping, often using objects as props for this purpose, and by acting out the stereotypes themselves. As Debra Van Ausdale and Joe Feagin argue in their book *The First R*, "children learn . . . not just by parroting the views [i.e., words] of adults"; instead "they act, practice, and do race" in "the physical and social worlds around them." One important way children *do* race is by incorporating it into their interactive play. For example, the authors cite the story of a black child who sat down, put his feet up on a table, and crossed his arms majestically over his chest, explaining, "I've been playing white man." It is this kind of role-playing that "embeds these things strongly in [the children's] minds." These researchers, too, recognize that too much focus on the racial identifications of persons leads us to underestimate "the material, interactional, and action-oriented aspects of racial and ethnic realities" (Van Ausdale and Feagin 2001, 23, 34, 35; see also Chin 2001).

The role of objects in the performative construction of race has been intuitively understood by people throughout Melanesia who have responded to the experience of European power (particularly after World War II) by participating in "cargo cults," popular movements that seek to magically elicit an abundance of whitemen-style wealth items or cargo. In many such movements, the arrival of cargo was expected to usher in a new era in which the New Guineans would miraculously come to enjoy white-manlike lifestyles, powers, and even light-colored skin: the hoped-for cargo was understood as a means for transforming them into a new kind of people on a par with whitemen.[25] Cargo cults have traditionally been treated by anthropologists as some combination of politics, religion, and confabulated notions about how wealth is achieved. But to the extent that the movements' aim was nothing less than a total transformation of racial status, the traditional term "cargo cult" is something of a misnomer: the term should really be "race cult."

Because the cultural construction of race is invariably hierarchical, and serves as the basis for inequality and prejudice, we have repeatedly tried to explain the persistence of racial categories as a reflection of the power interests they serve. But such explanations do not adequately account for racial categories' hegemony; again and again we see them perpetuated even by the people they are held to subordinate. Explanations of racial stereotypes in terms of power relations also share a problem characteristic of all functional explanations for cultural phenomena: they cannot account for the specific constellations of features that ground the construction of race; all they can account for is the hierarchical order itself. This problem is only obscured when we accept that racial categorizations refer (even if falsely) to bodily characteristics, since then the grounding of race in certain characteristics like skin color and hair "that we are very good at recognizing" (Appiah and Guttmann 1996, 68) distracts us from these features' own arbitrariness and thus explanatory insufficiency. In fact, power interests could be served just as well by categories or stereotypes that differ profoundly in their details. They could be served just as well by the Orokaiva notion that whites are people who are light, soft, and bright with wealth as by the western notion that whites are people who have light-colored skin.[26] And they are certainly well served by the grounding of race in objects that are themselves symbolically meaningful in hierarchical terms. From this perspective we can see how the hegemony of race is extended and deepened through people's consumption of material items that have symbolic meaning in racial terms. For example, Mary Pattillo-McCoy has described how African Americans use prestigious goods like designer clothing, imported scotch, and fancy vehicles to challenge and equalize the power differentials from whites that they experience, so that poor black men have historically been more likely than poor white men to buy expensive, luxury cars like Cadillacs. In buying such goods, she observes, the consumer "signifies first to him- or herself, then to friends, and finally to 'the whiteman' that he or she has made it"; yet this "symbolic affront" to white power does not actually liberate the buyer from the hegemony of racial categories, but indeed it merely reproduces this hegemony with its hierarchical order intact (Pattillo-McCoy 1999, 147-48).

By recognizing that race is symbolically constructed in objects, places, institutions, and activities that are independent of persons and hence materially appropriable, we are able to see much more clearly how specific constellations of symbols are organized into highly redundant systems of homologous dichotomous contrasts. These constellations harness the power of a very simple structure, which makes them readily graspable as well as resistant to disproof, and they are therefore particularly well suited for ideological manipulation. As we have seen in the example of Orokaiva foods, many symbolic dimensions are aligned and contrasted in a simple structure of "bipolar conceptualizations" (Drake 1987-1990, 1:64), so that they are all easily mapped onto one another. While no one dimension is strictly the signifier and none directly signified, the parallel structuring of the dimensions serves to reinforce each one. So it is *not* the case that rice and taro are equivalent here to two kinds of bodies that carry the "meanings" of white and black race. Rather, they are themselves raced in being constructed through the same series of analogous contrasts—between light and heavy, soft and hard, weak and strong, rootedness in local lands as opposed to money, and so forth—which are used to construct and contrast whitemen and Orokaiva. Like other raced objects, rice is thus both the meaning of a racial category and the symbolic vehicle through which it is expressed. In this view, the hierarchical values associated with such objects (which are more masculine or more feminine, more refined or more earthy, more or less nutritious, and so on) ground the hierarchical ordering of the racial categories with which they are identified, providing the basis for such evaluative rules of thumb as "the clothes make the man" and "you are what you eat" (see Bourdieu 1984; Sahlins 1976, 176).

It is because of the highly redundant, simple dichotomous structures in which racial categories are constructed that ambiguous and complexifying information comes to so little account. This too was made clear in chapter 5, where we saw how anomalous foods like onions and lambflaps that find no comfortable home at one or the other racial pole of the system fall into the ideological background. This kind of ideological manipulation, in which assimilable patterns are given more weight than anomalous ones, is a natural part of category organization, and to focus our antiracist energies on eradicating this structural feature of stereotyping constitutes yet another instance of misdirected activism.

This view of racial meaning as constructed in various kinds of objects, of which the body is but one—and not necessarily the key one—gives us a new, and I hope more productive, understanding of what in the United States has come to be known as "racial coding." People (especially whites) are said to speak in *code* about race, using terms like "work ethic, crime, standards, merit, welfare, and urban areas [to] conjure up definitely racialized images ... without the stigma of racism" (Bush 2004, 224; see also Royster 2003; Dijk 1984). Racial coding is politically insidious when it serves as a "cryptic vernacular" to camouflage race-baiting and covertly racist policies such as defunding public education and health care (Steinberg 1995, 214; Edsall and Edsall 1991). Racial coding also allows whites to deny their racial privilege in everyday talk: for example, "What we should be rewarding people for is merit" (Bonilla-Silva 2003; Bush 2004; Frankenberg 1993). But from the point of view developed here, racial coding is not "code" at all; talk about raced objects *is* talk about race. Talk about raced objects is often portrayed as a new form of euphemism that responds to a liberal trend of policing discourse for its "political correctness." But the only thing that may perhaps be new is the perception that such talk is euphemistic at all. To regard talk of raced objects as a phenomenon that responds to the multicultural sensitivities of our times is to forget just how much importance it was given by whites in earlier periods. In the segregationist South, for example, racial contrasts were communicated through discourses about the differences between civilization and savagery, fine dress and tatters, symphony and spiritual, big house and cabin, free worker and slave, and so on (Heneghan 2003; Roediger 1999). Indeed, as Grace Hale (1998) argues, much of the impetus for the creation of rigidly segregated "racialized spaces" such as black and white railway compartments was the prospect of having to cope with racial ambiguities that began arising when conflicting symbols of race were encountered simultaneously in an increasingly anonymous public sphere (for example, when meeting a finely dressed dark-skinned man on a train).

The important point to take away from this discussion is that the premise underlying the whole notion of "coding" is false: that "real" talk about race will be about persons or groups or categories of persons. It is not talk of race through objects that is bad, but only the mistaken notion that such talk is not really talk about race. We only legitimize this notion if we continue to reject racism while repudiating the validity of biological race, all without offering an alternative understanding of the cultural mechanisms by which race is actually constructed (Cowlishaw 2000, 111). Once race is recognized to be grounded not just in persons but in objects, activities, institutions, and places such as "vanilla suburbs and chocolate cities" (Barlow 2003, 93; see also Knowles 2003; Kochman 1981; White 1998), it becomes clear that there is no one symbolic component of racial stereotypes that can be dislodged to demolish them; there is no one symbolic "key" to solving racial problems. What is truly troubling about race is not that humans differ from one another in small particulars such as skin color, hair type, or susceptibility to certain diseases. What is troubling is the experience of discrimination and poverty to which racially marked groups of people are so often subject. The interpretation of salient human differences is an ineluctable fact of culture, and to single out for reform people's attitude toward any one objectification of race can lead at best to only superficial change, since racial categories' highly redundant dichotomous structure makes human difference invariably reframable in other terms. What we *really* need to work to change are the structures of inequality which oppress all but the most privileged categories of people, in the West and throughout the rest of the world. Not only would it be more valuable intrinsically to end discriminatory practices and inequality than to end racial talk; if indeed it is impossible to eliminate stereotypes as such, we can still change the material structures within which raced objects have meaning, and look forward to a time when new realities made the old stereotypes' hierarchies seem anachronistic and false.[27]

The Place of the West in the World

In Africa, there is—and it is hard to admit this—a reverence for whiteness. Africans have been brainwashed into believing that anything white is better, anything American is better. Even their black people are better.

ALEXIS SINDUHIJE, *"Welcome to America"*

Q: Who's winning in life, you or the *mzungu's* [whitemen's] dog?
A: The dog.
Q: Then what are you waiting for? Just die.

Swahili street repartee formula frequently rehearsed (and found hilarious) by teens in Tanzania[28]

A final set of implications to be drawn from this study of the Orokaiva construction of whitemen concerns its meaning for the role of the West in the world. Throughout much of the world today we encounter comparable figures of the white European or American foreigner as a stock character that personifies and represents an evaluation of western modernity, wealth, and racial privilege. That these stereotypical whitemen differ somewhat from place to place reflects the diversity of the cultural worlds in which the figures are produced. But all constitute symbols of the legacy of colonialism and the force of globalization. The global phenomenon of the cultural construction of whitemen challenges the conventional relativist view that all cultures are equivalent and are to be understood in their own terms, as if they represent so many simple alternatives, each of which can be chosen independently of the others. This kind of relativism is insufficient to the world we actually live in, a world in which cultures not only continually interact, but do so on the basis of such marked inequalities that some cultures' indigenous ideals and "visions of the future" have been "cannibalized" and replaced by foreign ones. As Ashis Nandy points out, it is thus a form of denial to speak of leaving "cultures to their own devices." The real challenge we face is learning to "live with an alien culture's estimation of [ourselves]" (Nandy 1987, 16–17).

What we have seen in this book is just one such alien construction of ourselves. How we appear to Orokaiva differs markedly from how we appear to ourselves, since the version of us they see is constructed from *their* cultural standpoint and rendered meaningful in *their* cultural terms. In other words, the Orokaiva construction of whitemen is ethnocentric. But the term "ethnocentric" should not be taken to necessarily imply "false." Knowledge is always culturally constructed, and the cultural knowledge others have of us may nonetheless reflect powerful truths. Orokaiva people's collective working ethnography of whitemen and the West is neither all wrong, nor wholly unfamiliar to western anthropology. While many Orokaiva ideas about whitemen are obviously specific to their own morality and culture, many of their ideas parallel notions familiar from western social theory, such as the contrast between collectively owned land and exchange-based sociality on the one hand, and private property and individualistic personhood on the other. Upon encountering the Orokaiva notion of lightness, with its implications of a lack of binding social ties, we may be tempted to identify it with the notion of individual alienation that we often note is the cost of modern technological progress and the dissolution of traditional ways of life. And just as we may observe such similarities between their ideas and ours, Orokaiva are struck by the way *our* ideas reflect *theirs* when they encounter them in social science courses at secondary schools and universities, and when traveling (as some do) overseas. In other words, even though the Orokaiva construction of whitemen might at first seem esoteric and strange to us, when we look at it closely it is not entirely unmotivated, even from our own point of view.

One powerful truth that it rarely occurs to us to think about without the kind of prompting the Orokaiva perspective provides is that attracting and holding onto wealth is so acceptable within our society, so highly facilitated by our law (individual property ownership rights have unchallenged primacy over personal relationships) and economy (geared as it is toward cultivating individual desire and the acquisition of wealth), and in general so unproblematically natural to us, that we have virtually no social or cultural mechanisms in place to check inequality (see also Rouse 1995). From the Orokaiva point of view, there is nothing natural about the way in which western society encourages us to indulge our acquisitive impulses and accumulate wealth, so that owning any fewer possessions than would fill a small truck is interpretable as "living humbly" (see Applbaum 2004; Schor 1998). After all, in Orokaiva experience, the inequality that owning even one article of new clothing creates in turn tends to generate intense social pressure to give it away. A skin bright with wealth draws the attention of those to whom an Orokaiva individual is obligated. Since there are so many people to whom one is indebted, and since such moral primacy is accorded to social obligations (recall that Orokaiva are inexhaustibly indebted to their kin for their own bodies), others' claims become all but inescapable, and people do not assume that the possessions they acquire will, or should, remain only their own. In effect, Orokaiva culture imposes strong checks on the production of inequality. With its social and moral incentives for redistributing wealth, and its obstacles to accumulating and retaining it, Orokaiva culture casts into stark relief the remarkable wealth-complex of our own society, in which accumulating possessions is unproblematic, and in which even dramatic inequalities are accepted as a natural fact of social life.

This unchecked inequality affects not only our own society. Through the globalization of western capitalism, it has also been spread to the rest of the world. For centuries now, an increasingly dominant West has taken the entire world as a field of economic opportunity, impoverishing by comparison the others at its margins, if not outright dispossessing them. Under colonialism, the cultural worlds of other peoples were remade as markets for western commodities and sources of raw materials and labor. Continuing and even accelerating this process has been the subsequent regime of "free trade" imposed on poor nations by the World Bank and IMF as a condition for receiving international aid, leading to the collapse of local industries in the face of cheap foreign imports, and reducing poor nations' populations to "labor pools" that must compete against one another to offer multinational companies the lowest wages and benefits in a "race to the bottom" of the scale (Rodrik 1997). In order to fill western malls and "big box" stores with electronics, clothing, and housewares at the cheapest possible prices, vast numbers of people, predominantly women, work under tight supervision in "export processing zones" in Mexico, China, Tunisia, Sri Lanka, Malaysia, the Philippines, the Dominican Republic, Bangladesh, Mauritius, and other "low income" countries for salaries as low as $15 per week, minus taxes and company deductions, with no security or benefits (Perman et al. 2004). For corporate titans scanning the world for opportunities to profit, no place is too small to consider if a resource might be cheaply extracted. Nonetheless, this process of globalization has reduced entire nations and geographic regions to the status of economic "basket cases" (Dirlik 1999, 51), valueless as sites for international investment, and so integrated into the world economy only as potential markets for foreign-produced goods, with the vast majority of their people thus left to watch from afar as the world's rich grow ever richer.

The many figures of whitemen we find throughout the world today are a response to this kind of global inequality. But why are these whitemen figures, like the Orokaiva construction of whitemen, to a large extent positive, rather than expressing unmitigated resentment at the West for the poverty it has created? The answer has to do with the fact that discourses of otherness are intrinsically self-anchored. We in the West would do well to recognize this, since it is an important part of what has sheltered us from the effects of our exploitative actions in the rest of the world. We tend not to see ourselves as being incorporated through globalization into others' moral worlds; we tend to focus primarily on our role in their economies, pop culture, organized religion, and development. But as we have seen with Orokaiva, the figure of whitemen is a salient moral other with qualities that invert the virtues and vices Orokaiva see in themselves. Like marginalized people the world over, Orokaiva associate whitemen's power and material wealth with moral virtue. Interpreting this wealth primarily from the point of view of the relative poverty of their own society, Orokaiva are continually led to contemplate their shortcomings and problems. For Orokaiva, these problems include jealousy, disunity, and sorcery, all moral failings endemic to and well recognized within their indigenous culture. By projecting onto whitemen inversions of these moral failings, whitemen's wealth becomes emblematic of a higher morality; hence, the attribution to whitemen of virtues that might seem to us surprising, such as social unity, ancestral favor, and self-control. Through this same projective process, Orokaiva also come to see their failings as accounting for their relative poverty.[29] Such projection helps sustain people's desire for western-style development despite the pervasive failure of local development interventions, and even though the widening inequalities development brings actually aggravate the very problems of jealousy and discord that Orokaiva blame for their backwardness and poverty. It is this tragic conversion, transforming people's material lack into their own moral humiliation through a discourse about whitemen others, that has shielded us from the resentment that the world's many subordinated people could by all rights be directing against our power and wealth.

Of course, Orokaiva are not alone in projectively constructing a salient cultural other as a foil for exploring and expressing their moral concerns. Nor, as we have learned from numerous studies of western Orientalist and primitivist discourses, is such a process found only in Papua New Guinea or the nonwestern world. But in order for these discourses to function self-critically, it helps for there to be some separation from the actual others the discourse portrays, so that their influence on local life is unobvious, and they can serve as foil rather than foe. This kind of separation is now common in many postcolonial contexts, where actual whites are few and where their activities seem sufficiently distant from the immediate sources of people's ills that a higher moral nature can be projected onto them without dissonance. But not all discourses of otherness are anchored in the self and self-critique. When people are led to interpret the other as the true cause of their misfortunes, so that the other is symbolically constructed not as a foil to the self but as the cause of the most significant problems afflicting the self, othering can take a destructive turn. Such blame-casting discourses of otherness are ubiquitous in anticolonial rebellions, xenophobic hate groups, genocidal nationalism, war-mobilizing propaganda, and guerilla and terrorist movements.

That the one kind of othering can give way to the other is an unhappy lesson of recent world events. Just forty years ago Arab societies throughout the Middle East looked to the United States as a model of development, political organization, and culture, embracing, as one Egyptian intellectual put it, "the America of fiction and jazz": "At home in the Sixties one seemed to have no need to be aware or beware of political America. . . . But then you didn't really meet Americans around Cairo" (Soueif 2002, 79–80). But a long series of self-serving American interventions—coups d'état, the fomenting of insurgencies, "the prolongation and intensification of regional conflicts," and the propping-up of unpopular kleptocratic regimes—has transformed this earlier goodwill into a rising tide of anti-American rage (Mitchell 2004, 100; Makdisi 2002; Boot 2002; Prados 2002; Kinzer 2003; Coll 2004). It is these interventions, about which Americans remain profoundly unaware, that make the argument of groups like al-Qaeda so compelling to people throughout the region: that the United States is the source of Middle Eastern societies' ills (Voll 2001; Bulliet and Gerges 2001). The flames of resentment are only fanned when the West invades and occupies Middle Eastern lands (Criss 2002; Beeman 1983, 2003). This kind of destructive othering is the bitter consequence of all expansionism that seeks to project America's will onto foreign others through the evangelism of "freedom" and other "American values" that have proven so effective in mobilizing Americans at home politically (McPherson 2003; Ross and Ross 2004).

What, then, are we to do? Clearly, the intensification of coercive force is the wrong response to the sense of threat now felt by many Americans. Because the threat stems from others' perception that the United States is causing them harm, coercion and violence abroad cannot bring lasting security; it can only increase and spread anti-Americanism. But the search for more productive responses will undoubtedly require us to be more willing to see the world, and our own role in it, as others do. For scholars this means moving beyond our current obsession with self-critique, and opening ourselves to the manifold ways our undeniable power and wealth are actually understood and felt by others. For those of us active in public life it means avoiding constructing others solely in terms of whether they "love us or hate us," when in reality others' ideological constructions of us are undoubtedly more complex, including elements of both love and hate, admiration and resentment, attraction and repulsion, all at the same time.[30] What is really called for, then, is learning "to squeeze ourselves into other bodies, to see with the eyes of others, even and especially our enemies'—not to become inert in relativism, but to be enlarged and informed for action" (Weisbuch 2004, 2). America could come a long way toward achieving a less anxious place for itself in the world if it acted with less arrogance, more openness, and more compassion.

Notes

1   As I will explain, "black" and "white" are common terms used to designate racial categories in Papua New Guinea English, and they correspond to a range of other expressions in English, PNG's lingua franca Tok Pisin, and local vernaculars.

2   In their interesting study of Cameroonians' ideas about the *whiteman kontri* (whitemen's countries), the sociologist Francis Nyamnjoh and the geographer Ben Page note that the young people they interviewed spoke "less frequently in terms of the place, *whiteman's kontri*," than in terms of "white people": "Whilst this could have been a consequence of the questions put to the focus groups, it was more often the case that questions about places quickly slipped back into answers about people" (Nyamnjoh and Page 2002, 629).

3   For more on current nostalgic views of colonialism in Papua New Guinea, see chapter 2 as well as Thomas 1997; Gewertz and Errington 1999; Reed 2003, 166–67; Burce 1991; and Robbins 2004a, 45–47.

4   Since Orokaiva perceive their own power to be an extension of the potency of their ancestors, portraying one's ancestors as having been limited in their agency disempowers oneself.

5   Oro Province (formerly called Northern Province) has an area of 8,120 square miles, about the size of the state of Massachusetts. The total land alienated to the Crown during the colonial era was 77,000 acres, which is about 120 square miles, or 1.5 percent of the total (PAR 1921, 16). An additional 25,000 acres (0.5 percent) was converted from customary to individual (indigenous) tenure under a 1960s scheme. For Papua New Guinea as a whole, the usual figure given is that customary lands account for 97 percent of the country's land area.

6   Not that this was entirely fanciful; see Waiko 1989 and Maclean 1998.

7   See, e.g., Lewis 2003; Stoler 2002, 1995; Cooper and Stoler 1997; McClintock 1995; Comaroff and Comaroff 1997, 1991; Stocking 1991.

8   In the vernacular, Orokaiva specially mark the gender of white women, saying *taupa evohu* ('whiteman woman'), whereas white men may be called simply *taupa* ('whiteman'), the masculine being unmarked.

9   Writers on race have worried much about their own perpetuation of the opposition between white and black (or whiteness and blackness, etc.) through a scholarly literature that aims to challenge the basic notion of

"race" as a principle of human classification (see, e.g., Rasmussen et al. 2001; Haney López 1996, 175; Frankenberg 1997; Razack 1998, 11). But if we seriously want to challenge the folk dichotomy between black and white, we must begin by establishing what it is, by finding out empathetically how it "helps individuals to formulate their thoughts [by giving] them unreal categories into which to cast their observations" (Shanklin 1999, 676). As Vron Ware points out, we must make things *comprehensible* before we can explain them well critically (Ware and Back 2002, 30–31). The challenge is analogous to that faced in the study of other objectionable human phenomena like sex discrimination, terrorism, cannibalism, genital mutilation, terrorism, and infanticide. In such cases, we are most likely to succeed in what Richard Handler has called "destructive analysis" if we first have insight into the way the phenomenon is seen by those who engage in it (Handler 1985).

10   The social evolutionist anthropology of Lewis Henry Morgan, E. B. Tylor, and other late nineteenth-century thinkers can be viewed as an attempt to break down the specifically racial (biological) boundary and shift it to a softer boundary of culture epochs or stages of civilization. Nevertheless, their frameworks were still anchored in the image of "the dark-skinned savage" (Stocking 1968, 1987).

11   See, e.g., Rabinow 1989; Hall 1991; Mitchell 1991, 2000; Stoler 1995. Useful reviews of the vast critical literature on modernity may be found in Knauft 2002a; Fischer 1999; Miller 1994; and Giddens 1991.

12   See Barlow 1997; Watson 1997; Rofel 1999; and Tavakoli-Targhi 2001. Another interesting critique of the association between modernity and European whiteness inverts the assumption that Europeans have a natural hold on the rationality that is considered a central prerequisite for modernity. See, e.g., Fabian 2000, which documents the mad antics and irrational excesses of Europeans in central Africa. A powerful countercritique, reasserting the centrality of race in modernity, is Winant 2001a.

13   Englund and Leach 2000 make a similar point. One may contrast this negative view of power in fieldwork by American anthropologists with the French anthropologist Marcel Griaule's disturbingly frank adoption of colonial and other forms of coercive power in a fieldwork style that almost seems designed to provoke ethnographic truth into being, rather than observing it passively (Clifford 1988, 75–79).

14   I have in mind here the self-aggrandizing "Kurtzian" dimension of Malinowski's fieldwork archetype, following the notorious example of Joseph Conrad's character Mistah Kurtz (Conrad 1999 [1902]; Clifford 1988; Stocking 1992).

15   To Spanish *gringo*, Chinese *laowai*, and Akan *obroni*, we can add further illustrations such as *blanco* in Spanish, *gaijin* in Japanese, *pakeha* in Maori, *sahib* in Hindi, *indaa* in Western Apache, *balanda* in Australia, *papalagi* in Samoan, *dimdim* in eastern New Guinea, *farangi* in Persian, and *farang* or *falang* in several of the languages of Southeast Asia. This list could be made much longer.

16   A resource for accessing newspapers from around the world is the "Today's Front Pages" Web site, which is updated daily by the Newseum (interactive

museum of news) at http://www.newseum.org/todaysfrontpages/(accessed July 23, 2005).

17 A similar point is made by Clifford (1988, 256); hooks (1992, 166); Roediger (1998); Taussig (1993, xv); and Nyamnjoh and Page (2002, 609).

18 This is precisely the problem with the genre of "anthologies of others' perspectives" on the West or on America, such as Lips 1966 [1937]; Burland 1969; Blackburn 1979; DeVita and Armstrong 2002; and Rinder 2003 (along with the book's associated exhibition). Because they cannot assume their western readers will be acquainted with the particular histories and cultures of those represented, the editors of such volumes have no alternative but to select readings and images whose meanings are readily assimilable to categories that make sense to us in our own terms, such as "problems faced by native peoples" (dispossession of lands, destruction of environment, loss of ancestral language, etc.). Thus, no matter whose stories we read, their common framing in opposition to the West reduces their particularity to a generic voice of the oppressed native. Except for the introductory passages that valiantly attempt to provide some cultural and historical context (for some excellent examples see Rosenstiel 1983 and Arkush and Lee 1989), the low ratio of explicated context to native voices unfortunately means that the voices can rarely do more than confirm what western readers already believe.

19 As Doris Lessing remarks in an essay written in the wake of September 11, 2001, "Americans ... at last learned that they are like everyone else, vulnerable to the snakes of Envy and Revenge.... They say themselves that they have been expelled from their Eden. How strange they should ever have thought they had a right to one" (Jack 2002, 54).

20 "O wad some Power the giftie gie us/To see oursels as ithers see us!/It wad frae monie a blunder free us...." (Burns 1989, 37).

Chapter Two

1 I derived this estimate by culling census figures for village populations in the Hujara, Aeka, Sohe, Saiho, North Coast (southern one-third), and Oro Bay census divisions. I then added 75 percent of gross population figures for Popondetta town and the smallholder settler blocks and company villages of Higaturu Oil Palms and associated development projects. This proportion, on the one hand, may slightly overestimate the numbers of Orokaiva living in town and project areas. On the other hand, I have excluded the substantial number of Orokaiva who are temporary outmigrants to other provinces. Since the PNG census is more likely to under- than overcount, the present estimate is, if anything, a low one (NSO 1993; 1994a, 77; 1994b, 7, 96–97; on outmigration see Baxter 1973, 116, 126, 128).

2 Linguists conventionally divide the Binandere language family into fourteen languages, all of which are spoken in Oro Province or along the coast north of it. Wurm's estimate of a total of 59,000 speakers of Binandere family languages is based on 1970s figures and should be revised upward significantly to reflect subsequent population growth (Wurm 1982, 157–59; see also Wilson 1969; Foley 1986, 235).

3   Scholarly documentation of the Orokaiva language is not extensive. Apart from Healey et al.'s 1969 "Preliminary Notes on Orokaiva Grammar," which is extremely concise, the main sources are several unpublished papers and a pedagogical grammar by the missionary linguist couple Robert (Bud) and Marlys Larsen (1985), who translated the New Testament into Orokaiva in two dialectal editions, Ehija and Etija (Larsen 1988), during their lengthy stay in the province as part of the Summer Institute of Linguistics (SIL) and Wycliffe Bible Translators. There has also been work on other Binandere family languages by SIL missionaries, particularly on Korafe, by Cynthia and James Farr (Farr 1999), and Binandere (with Suena), by Darryl Wilson (1969, 1974).

4   This is true everywhere except in the vernacular language preschools being created now throughout PNG, where lessons are to be conducted in Tok Pisin or the children's local vernacular.

5   When asked what "Orokaiva" means, people invariably explained it to me as a cry used in greeting, having connotations of welcoming, hospitality, happiness, joyous motion, conviviality, and so on. No informants tried to construct a denotational meaning; it might be said not to have one. The most that can be said is that *oro* is used alone to mean 'house'—any type of house, not only 'men's house' as reported by Williams (1930, 4)—and *kaiva* is the name, as William notes, of one of the principal varieties of taro. Around Agenehambo, people often say "Kaiva" as a short form of "Orokaiva" the identity category, but never as a short form of the greeting. The greeting is instead shortened to "Oro! Oro!"

6   I am indebted to Septimus Evovo of Handarituru for sharing with me his authoritative knowledge of this story.

7   True for Orokaiva is Mervyn Meggitt's formulation of the "contingent, optative nature of the relationship between leader and follower in Melanesia, such that both parties must recognize and constantly exploit factors of friendship and greed, persuasion and bullying, in their attempts to achieve their own ends" (1967, 20).

8   The literature on Melanesian regions and regional cultural complexes is reviewed in Douglas 1996. On the construction of regional worlds through particular types of experience and transaction, see Munn 1990.

9   The notion of alternating states is important in many areas of Orokaiva life. As Eric Schwimmer writes, it applies even to enemies and allies: "According to Orokaiva ideas, associations [i.e., relationships] go through alternating periods of positive reciprocity (friendship) and negative reciprocity (war). Whereas in western thought permanence is considered normal and quarrels a deviation from the norm, the Orokaiva do not envisage either friendship or enmity as permanent states but rather as alternating temporary states" (Schwimmer 1977, 320).

10   Language is another arena in which contradictory claims of centrality are routinely sustained. Throughout the Orokaiva region (and indeed, throughout Papua New Guinea), people are convinced that the dialect they speak is superior and normative; it is 'straight' and correct, unlike all other related dialects, which are said to be 'crooked' and incorrect. But when traveling among others whose speech is intelligible but sounds different, 'crooked,' or strange to their ears, Orokaiva diplomatically defer to the evaluatory point of

view of their hosts, or else they draw the focus of conversation to the linguistic features they *share* with their hosts in contrast to some third speech variety that all can agree is inferior.

11 The PNG currency is the kina, which in the mid-1990s was worth roughly the equivalent of one U.S. dollar.

12 In the vernacular, people called themselves *ugorota* 'central [Kaiva]' or simply "Kaiva" (without a modifier); this was glossed for me as "Kaiva stret" (Tok Pisin: 'straight Kaiva') and "pure Kaiva."

13 My first trip to the area was a one-month visit in 1991. The main research was conducted over about two years in 1993-95, and I made a subsequent visit to Agenehambo for two weeks in 1998.

14 In Sivepe village in the 1960s Schwimmer found that over 50 percent of a clan's land parcels had been transferred to them in this way (1973, 100). See also the discussion of land transfers in Crocombe and Hogbin 1963 and Rimoldi 1966, as well as Williams 1930; Waddell and Krinks 1968; and Iteanu 1983b.

15 As Schwimmer perceptively describes, "individuals derive their land, and therefore their sustenance, from a cluster of corporate groups [i.e., clans or subclans] in only one of which they are a corporate member, although they maintain permanent exchange relationships with the others. These other corporations do not make them permanent gifts but leave them conditional upon the successful continuation of the relationship. The fact that a man holds land on such terms *forces* him to continue the relationship" (Schwimmer 1973, 108; original emphasis).

16 The administration's ambiguous policy is illustrated by an instance of land alienation that has been consequential in shaping the present-day Oro Province economy. In the 1920s, the Crown "purchased" fourteen large lowland tracts from Orokaiva under an ordinance for "compulsory labor in the natives' own interest" (PAR 1920-21, 16). These lands were not initially made into a normal plantation, but were instead planted with commodity trees by villagers, who received half the proceeds. The other half, which was kept by the colonial administration, paid the salary of Government Anthropologist F. E. Williams (Crocombe 1964, 8-15; see also Harris 1981, 133-34; Murray 1920, 22). The existence of this large tract of previously alienated land allowed for the creation of a number of subsequent development projects. Today this land forms the nucleus of the huge World Bank–funded Higaturu Oil Palm development project, which is majority-owned by the CDC (formerly known as the Commonwealth Development Corporation), a multinational company owned by the government of Great Britain through its subsidiary Pacific Rim Palm Oil Ltd. (see chapter 6).

17 This movement toward secularizing their schools was initially resisted by the missions, but because of increasing government subsidies they were ultimately forced to accept it. The Anglican mission which served the Orokaiva region succumbed to "the dragon, secularization" in 1970, when its schools were placed within the national education system (Dickson 1971, 270, 274).

18 Around 1963, the New Guinea Research Unit of the Australian National University established a research center at Popondetta, upon receiving a

grant from the Rural Credits Development Fund of the Reserve Bank of Australia to conduct a series of studies "on the relation of subsistence agriculture to cashcropping and the influence of indigenous social organization on agricultural productivity" in Orokaiva communities (Bettison 1963). New Guinea Research Unit studies on Orokaiva include Crocombe and Hogbin 1963; Crocombe 1964, 1967; Howlett 1965; Rimoldi 1966; Dakeyne 1966, 1977; Morawetz 1967; and Waddell and Krinks 1968. Other researchers whose writings were based primarily on fieldwork through 1981 are Eric Schwimmer (1969, 1973, 1987); Michael Baxter (1973, 1977); Janice Newton (1982, 1985, 1989); and André Iteanu (1983a, 1983b, 1990). Additional sources can be found in the Oro Province bibliography by Barker and McKellin (1993).

19 These figures count persons born in the countries mentioned, not country citizens. In the two territory-wide censuses conducted prior to independence, there was of course no PNG citizenship as distinct from Australian citizenship, so country of birth was the basis for tabulating the "nonindigenous" population, along with an added category for "nonindigenous" persons born in the territory that covered PNG Chinese and PNG Australians who were born to Chinese and Australian parents working in the colony (NSO 1994a). Postindependence census figures give breakdowns by country of birth as well as by citizenship, the population category I use in most contexts; wherever I compare pre- and postindependence figures, I use the postindependence country of birth figures to be consistent. Basically, the group that is hardest to identify given the census categories is PNG Chinese. The major PNG Chinese families have been in the country for several generations, but individuals vary in citizenship and in country of birth. My impression is that most of the resident Chinese in Popondetta appear in the census as Australian citizens. The PNG Chinese community is the subject of an anthropology dissertation by Margaret Willson (1989). There has also been a dissertation on Filipinos in PNG (Munro 1992).

20 It is impossible to obtain figures on expatriate visitors to the country broken down by province, but for Papua New Guinea as a whole, foreign arrivals were only 17,000 in 1998. According to immigration statistics, 28.3 percent were tourists, 6.5 percent came to visit friends and relatives, 63.6 percent came for business purposes, and 1.6 percent came for other reasons, including research (*The National* [PNG], May 5, 1998). Only a tiny fraction of foreign visitors to PNG enter Oro Province, and so the number of foreigners visiting the province, like the number of resident foreigners, is quite small.

21 The criminals themselves are called *raskols*. Recent studies of rascalism include Roscoe 1999; Sykes 1999; Dinnen 2001; and Goddard 2005. The significance of rascalism in the Orokaiva symbolic economy of race relations is discussed in chapter 4.

22 According to a 1998 study commissioned by the Asian Development Bank, about 17,000 expatriates hold jobs in PNG, predominantly in the mining industry, forestry, and retail trade (*The National* [PNG], January 7, 1998). Some hint of how this number might be broken down by country of citizenship is found in 1990 census figures, which report a total expatriate popula-

tion of 25,600 including 7,300 from Indonesia, nearly all of them indigenous refugees from Irian Jaya. The remainder include 6,700 Australians (including many PNG Chinese); 1,800 Americans (USA); 1,600 Filipinos; 1,300 New Zealanders; 700 each from the UK, Republic of Ireland, and Malaysia; 600 from the USSR; and fewer than 450 each from India, Sri Lanka, Africa, the Solomon Islands, Korea, Canada, Fiji, and other countries (NSO 1994b, 108-9).

23 Also, it should not be supposed that the racial attitudes of nonwhite expatriates are more enlightened than those of whites. Indeed, some are reminiscent of Nigel Barley's observation that elite postcolonial Africans tend to be quite similar to the white imperialists of the former colonial era in their faith in the ideal of progress and their "certainty that natives were characterized by stubbornness and ignorance and had to be forced into the present for their own good" (Barley 1983, 150).

24 An illustration is the white manager of the Popondetta branch of the Oil Palm Industry Corporation (OPIC), which is the statutory body that provides agricultural extension services to village and smallholder oil palm growers. In 1991, when I first visited the province, the manager was a young Englishman who committed himself to making a daily excursion in his Land Cruiser to areas served by the project. Eventually, during one of these site visits, he was assaulted (by a man later elected member of parliament!), prompting him to leave the country. His replacement leaves routine site inspection and extension work to local employees.

25 This assessment is echoed in a recent published statement by the senior public servant in East Sepik Province in 1999, Peter Maginde. In a full page newspaper advertisement taken out by Maginde to rebut charges of wrongdoing, he states at one point, by way of explaining the "lack of competency" of provincial officers under his direction, that "it is common knowledge, that the entire national public service is incompetent" (Maginde 1999, 7).

26 Although Schwimmer (1987, 107) concluded that "globally . . . it is definitely the negative image of the white man that has prevailed in Oro," this evaluation results from excluding from the category of whitemen all those white individuals Schwimmer discusses who could be recognized in a positive light due to their participation in exchange.

27 I also heard stories that retrospectively attributed an Orokaiva identity to the kind Australian doctor who had supervised Saiho health center in the 1960s. Schwimmer writes that this doctor, together with his wife, took part in traditional dances at a Christmas feast in Orokaiva attire and that he was "the only white man in the district (omitting the anthropologists)" who attended village feasts and ate the local foods along with the people (1969, 62-63).

28 A similar argument made by Stephen Leavitt is that when Melanesians construe specific whites as departed ancestors returning in disguise, they "see us not as 'gods' but as 'relatives'" (2000, 305). Leavitt's perceptive analysis recalls Kenelm Burridge's characterization of the "moral European" sought by Tangu people in New Guinea in the 1950s: "An imaginative or ideal rather than a pragmatic category, potentially inhering in every European though unlikely to be realized in any particular one, the moral European represents

the kind of European Tangu themselves would like to encounter because he would engage in reciprocal relations with them" (Burridge 1969, 35). For more on views of whites as ancestors, see Lawrence 1964; Leavitt 1995; Kulick 1992, ix, 271–72; Lattas 1992a; Stephen 1995, 77; Robbins 1997b; and Tuzin 1997.

    At the opposite extreme from whitemen-as-one's-own-relatives are images of whitemen as bogeymen who are so radically disconnected from the self that they are capable of any abomination. I saw this view of whitemen expressed frequently to children, who were admonished in my presence to behave, or else "the white man will eat you" (see also Wormsley 1993; Rumsey 1999, 111–12; Stephen 1995; Lederman 1986). Such threats to children did not appeal uniquely to whitemen, but also to other strangers on the periphery of the social universe, including Managalasi, Highlanders, and with small children, even animals.

29 As Karen Brison has written of Kwanga in East Sepik Province, Orokaiva desire "to cultivate a relationship with a benevolent higher power who will rescue villagers from their present poverty" (quoted in Leavitt 1995, 180).

30 The notorious White Women's Protection Ordinance of 1926 forbidding unchaperoned contact between native men and white women was repealed in 1958 (Inglis 1975, 144). Most other racist legislation followed suit soon afterward, such as the blue laws banning the consumption of alcohol by natives, which were lifted four year later (Marshall 1980, 1982).

31 Nicholas Thomas (1997, 211) observes that anthropologists and historians have mostly regarded such nostalgia as "simply too embarrassing to discuss." For a careful consideration of the topic in an African context, see Bissell 2005. It should be noted that this nostalgia for colonialism felt by those who were formerly colonized is different from the "colonial nostalgia" felt by former colonizers, of which Renato Rosaldo (1989) writes.

Chapter Three

1 Schwimmer (1973, 68–72) analyzes an interesting speech by an Orokaiva village official in which the culture hero responsible for the introduction of money and wage labor was Jesus.

2 When I first visited Agenehambo shortly after the Gulf War, some villagers reported having seen war news broadcasts (on a television at the Anglican high school) that included images transmitted from video cameras mounted in the heads of American missiles as they approached their targets. What they found most impressive in this was the projection of force over space combined with instantaneous feedback about the results. Watching it led one man to fantasize about recording the view from the head of a war club as it smashed an opponent's skull.

3 Orokaiva often spoke as if the main purpose of my fieldwork was to produce the feast that would acknowledge and compensate the people who helped me do it. In this diplomatic way of portraying it, my fieldwork was focused on the unimpeachably virtuous matter of cultivating reciprocity and my own exchange relationships with the people.

4 'Heaviness of earth' can also refer to the fact that Orokaiva are bound to their lands in ways that are explained in chapter 5.

5 To my knowledge, osaga and 'heaviness' (*boka*) are the Orokaiva terms that most closely approximate the English notion of "debt," but as my account indicates, they do not square well with the objectivist, circumstance-independent "bookkeeping" implied by the English. A broader treatment of the subject would have to consider Orokaiva ideas of 'remembering' (*hotembari*) and 'forgetting' (*jenaupa ari*), as well as the cultural construction of the 'body' (*hamo*) as a sort of corporeal memory of all significant things that a person has been given by others and consumed—and in this sense as the reality corresponding to the "latent debts" which derive from the past but imply relations in the future (see Iteanu 1990, 40; Strathern 1988; Munn 1986, 1990). Ruth Benedict's famous discussion of indebtedness and reciprocity in Japan presents a variation on these issues outside Melanesia (Benedict 1974 [1946]).

6 In precolonial times too, young men would live apart from the rest of the community for lengthy periods, especially while preparing for initiation, when they were secluded in special men's houses, or off in some secret forest location (Williams 1930; Iteanu 1983a, 1990).

7 When I began to appreciate the importance of this topic during my fieldwork, I was initially skeptical about Orokaiva views of whitemen that did not accord with my expectation that they would be overwhelmingly critical. Such an expectation was fueled by my reading of works such as Keith Basso's *Portraits of "the Whiteman"* and Said's *Orientalism*, as well as studies of western discourses of primitivism, all of which are emphatically critical of white western power. It was only when I overcame my characteristically anthropological wariness of anything smacking of western superiority that I was able to stop listening selectively for criticism and begin taking seriously the full evaluative range of what people were expressing. In my subsequent surveys of other societies' discourses about the West, I have found cases of black-and-white evaluative stances toward others, like the Nazi construction of Jews, to be the exception, rather than the rule. It is much more common to find others constructed in ways that can have both positive as well as negative interpretations, depending on context (see page 258, as well as Ellingson 2001; Deloria 1998; Creighton 1995; Chen 1992).

Chapter Four

1 Quoted in Kulick 1992, 55. The published quotation, a translation from Tok Pisin, has been edited and condensed.

2 As Iteanu writes, "a 'big-man' (*embo okose*) or a 'big woman' (*evohu okose*) is someone who has a 'big' social person, that is, who has many social relations. . . . One should really say that a big-man 'is' a big social person in the sense that he 'is' numerous social relations, an expression whose very oddness in English reflects accurately the difference between the Orokaivas' point of view and ours. . . . When we say that men 'have' social relations, we imply that men as such exist apart from their relations and that their 'possession' of

these relations is in some sense secondary. Precisely the opposite is true in Orokaiva logic" (Iteanu 1990, 40).

3   This identification of a truck with its owner makes it simultaneously a source of pride and, for reasons we will discuss, a potential cause of misfortune. If ill should befall the owner or his family, a likely reason he will consider is others' jealousy of the truck.

4   This is not to say that they *could not* be of greater concern, or that they have not been under other circumstances, only that they are not so today. Historically, ideas that whitemen drink more responsibly than Papua New Guineans became matters of concern and criticism in many parts of the country when the colonial blue laws forbidding the consumption of alcohol by "natives" were lifted in 1962 (Marshall 1980, 1982; Schwimmer 1982). Looking toward the future, it is not hard to imagine a growing interest among Orokaiva—especially well-educated women—in contrasts between Orokaiva men and whitemen in matters of sexual expectations, sexual jealousy, and sex relations. For one exceptionally worldly Orokaiva woman, an internationally known artist married to a white Australian, it was hard to say whether women had greater "respect" in the whiteman's world or in the village, but there was no question that in the whiteman's world they enjoyed more freedom from constraints associated with promiscuity and sexual pollution. However, for most villagers today, sexual liberation is a less significant part of the vision of development than is western-style prosperity; and "modern" Orokaiva women in PNG towns often face greater problems than their village sisters in terms of domestic violence, lack of a support network, and restrictions on their movements (see Newton 1989). One particularly important context in which a discourse about lack of sexual self-control is cultivated is charismatic and Pentecostal Christianity (Robbins 2004a; Brison 1996), which is currently growing in influence among Orokaiva.

5   Consistent with this, Schwimmer found in the 1960s that, "No great value was usually attached to conversion [of work and money] to western commodities, except where these became valued prestations. Thus, when transistor radios became valued prestations, they began to appear in large quantities in the villages ... mostly paid for by absentee workers" (1979, 303).

6   The white patrol officers, missionaries, and traders that Orokaiva encountered in early colonial times were surely superior in their bush skills to the whites who visit Orokaiva country today. Before the widespread availability of motorized transport, the whites who worked in the region were generally accustomed to walking long distances on native forest trails. By contrast, in Papua New Guinea today, as we saw in chapter 2, most jobs requiring rural travel are filled by Papua New Guineans, while whites tend to occupy managerial office positions. The whites of an earlier era may appear to have been very rugged "hard men" when compared in retrospect to their successors or perhaps to ourselves, but we would not be justified in assuming that they were so regarded by Orokaiva at the time. Colonial-era Orokaiva compared the whites they encountered to themselves, no doubt evaluating their bush skills less positively than we would. After all, the whites needed native helpers to widen trails for them, build shelters, and so on.

7   Another exceptional class of hard-skinned whitemen includes superheroes like Rambo, Tarzan, and the Phantom, all of whom have exciting adventures in dangerous jungle environments. These superheroes were popular icons for young village men during my fieldwork, when Rambo videos set in the rainforests of Southeast Asia were favorites at the village video "theater" set up underneath the house of a retired public servant who had invested part of his pension in a TV set, VCR, and portable diesel generator. (He showed video movies there twice a week—when there was fuel for the generator and nothing was broken—charging a small admission fee.) I also saw Rambo decals on the cabs of trucks and magazine photos of Rambo on the walls of bachelors' houses. I was asked several times whether Rambo stories were true and whether Rambo himself was a real person. When I asked about distinctive cries each young Orokaiva man would use to let others know his whereabouts in the forest, I was told they were not traditional, but rather imitations of Tarzan's call in the videos. Another popular superhero is the comic strip character the Phantom, an Australian version of the masked white Superman, who fights evil plots designed to overturn the natural order of life in the jungles of Africa, where he lives in a cave and enjoys (and returns) the help of wild animals and primitive tribesmen with bones in their noses (Friese 1999). Orokaiva find these jungle-based heroes much more captivating than their more urban and futuristic counterparts like Rocky and the Terminator. It has been argued that the Phantom represents for Papua New Guineans a nostalgically desired colonial paternalism readapted to the postcolonial context (Burce 1991). The Phantom, like Tarzan, is appealing to villagers because he straddles the color line and enjoys authority and infallible competence in the natural realm of birds and animals, the traditional realm of "tribes" and their elders, and the modern realm of development identified with whitemen—all simultaneously (see also Metcalf 2001 on Hulk Hogan in Sarawak).

8   There is remarkably little in the Orokaiva literature on the seclusion and debut rituals for girls. This makes it hard to confirm that the current popularity of this ritual is completely continuous with the past, as my informants maintained. Formerly, collective initiation rituals that involved seclusion of groups of both girls and boys were organized periodically within a village (Williams 1930; see also Chinnery and Beaver 1915b on initiation rites of the "Koko"). In most areas, these collective rites fell into desuetude in the years surrounding World War II. A notable exception is the Aeka village Jajau studied by Iteanu (1983a, 1990). Indeed, when I visited there with Iteanu in 1994, the villagers were in the midst of preparing a collective seclusion for both boys and girls in a house that had been constructed especially for the ritual. In Agenehambo, the traditional initiation ceremony was revived once within living memory, in 1984, when Kingsford obtained a grant of 2,500 kinas (about U.S. $2,800), and called together the oldest men in the village to teach the esoterica of the defunct *embahe* spirit cult to a few initiates, including himself. The money was donated specifically for this purpose by the nearby Anglican high school, which invited visitors from its Australian sister school to witness the ceremony's climax at which pairs of sacred flutes and the bullroarer were sounded.

Certainly, the current popularity of girls' seclusions makes a striking contrast to the discontinuation (except in Jajau) of the boys' seclusions in traditional initiations. Many factors could be adduced to explain this contrast, including the expectation that girls will be more obedient than boys in submitting to seclusion, and the fact that girls' families, unlike boys', can anticipate receiving brideprice payments in the future that they can use to pay back the debts they will incur in the initiation feast. Note too that the absence of a 'softening' seclusion ritual for boys is consistent with the value placed on 'hard' male bodies.

9 I finally supplied a pig myself so that the girl's life could return to normal.

10 Such joking also points to the gender contradiction in the softness of whitemen, since the softness that is idealized in the girls is not proper in men. But for Orokaiva, the key contradiction in whitemen's softness does not turn on gender, but rather, as I have tried to emphasize, on the production of wealth, which happens to require work that has gendered dimensions.

Notwithstanding the Orokaiva presumption that women are generally softer than men, softness is not an ideal associated with femininity as such. Rather, it is an ideal specific to the situation of debutante girls, where it is associated with a complex of things (only some of which are discussed here) including youthful beauty, fecundity, hiding and revelation, the display of wealth, and the visible rendering of the investment of nurture that parents and kin have made in the girl's body. In grown women, who must be adequate to the constant heavy work they are expected to perform, it is hardness that Orokaiva value in a woman's body.

11 My conversations with villagers about tractor farming would often wind up on the topic of chemical fertilizer. At the time of my fieldwork, the World Bank–funded Higaturu oil palm project in the region was encouraging villagers to buy chemical fertilizer for their oil palms to maximize yields, but villagers were not quick to do so. Even those, like Kingsford, who had good results fertilizing their oil palms worried that fertilizing food crops would ruin them.

12 Indeed, this is the true meaning of what has come to be known as "Yali's question" in the literature on New Guinea cargo movements, now popularized by Jared Diamond (1997), who extends it to the larger phenomenon of third-world poverty vs. first-world wealth (see also National Geographic Television and Film 2005). For an excellent discussion of the problems with so globalizing Yali's question, see Errington and Gewertz 2004.

13 The other cause of disinheritance in the story is black skin. It is the sight of the children's black skin that leads their white fathers to leave them. There are three reasons for this that are consistent with the story: first, that the fathers were racist; second, that the children looked different from them, resembling only their mother; and third, that black skin itself betokened fractiousness, lack of self control, and the inability to live harmoniously. I hope to elaborate further on this important story in a future publication.

14 This kind of moral community of humans with plants, animals, and the land is sometimes romanticized in western images of the "ecological savage" at one

with nature (Krech 1999; Brightman 1993). It should be emphasized, however, that there is nothing necessarily ecological about reading human moral causes into natural outcomes, and given that social discord is unavoidable, it is really quite burdensome to fear that it will have repercussions in the failure of one's food supply through the loss of livestock and crops.

15 The masculine gender in this discussion accurately reflects the unmarked masculinity of Orokaiva notions of inheritance and ancestral intervention in human affairs. Orokaiva women often do inherit lands from their fathers, and in such cases they are thought to enjoy and be dependent upon their male ancestors' favor, but inheritance in the unmarked case goes from fathers to sons (Iteanu 1983b; Schwimmer 1973). While Orokaiva do not deny the importance of female ancestors and try to remember them in their genealogies, in contrast to males their names tend to be forgotten after one or two generations, and it is the spirits of forefathers who are thought of as more active and influential.

16 The main exception is the Chinese storekeepers. Known almost exclusively from the perspective of their consumers and employees, they are often spoken of as ungenerous, either using the English word "greedy" or the derogatory vernacular expression 'money face.' But for the most part they are assimilated, like other foreigners, to the more general class of whitemen. Like whitemen generally, Chinese were perceived as aloof from positive exchange relationships with Papua New Guinean nationals, and those who engaged in them were considered exceptional. For more on PNG Chinese, see Willson 1989; Wu 1982; Wood 1995; Jackson 1998.

17 Such cases also illustrate the importance of traversing great distance, arriving from afar, and having a whitemanlike mobility (or lightness) in contributing to people's impression that one is, indeed, white.

18 The association between hiddenness and growth is also confirmed for Orokaiva in the great fertility of gardens cut from dark, old-growth forests. In general, Orokaiva assume that there is an inverse correlation between the growth potential of forested land and the amount of light the forest cover admits, i.e., the degree of visibility into it. By this principle, the very greatest growth potential should be found in those forests that admit virtually no light at all; in effect, in areas that are invisible. These are the places that 'only the pig knows,' where it finds the tender shoots and other pig delicacies that, when eaten, will make it grow best. These unknown places are also where wild forest animals hide, to multiply and increase until they reappear in the known places they occupy in their seasons of plenty. When I would ask about the locations of these places, people usually pointed to the high, unpopulated slopes of the Mt. Lamington volcano, or else told me that they were deep in lowland areas that are hard to reach because of the surrounding swamps. Calling them 'true forest,' *ariri be,* Orokaiva describe these lands as the darkest, coolest, stillest parts of the rainforest. It is here that the widest variety of wildlife can be found: unusual plants and fruit trees that nourish every kind of bird, including cockatoos, hornbills, and birds of paradise. There is plentiful game like wild pigs, cassowaries, wallabies, tree kangaroos, lizards, bandicoots, and echidnas. Fish spawn in the streams and "in some

cases there are ... flying fox caves, where thousands of flying foxes and bats of many different sorts are found" (Waiko 1983, 5). Although all these forms of wildlife are real, the remote lands they inhabit are semilegendary in that they are necessarily invisible.

19 It is also created, albeit unintentionally, by PNG prisons when they incarcerate inmates. In his fascinating ethnography of a PNG prison, Adam Reed notes that inmates observe that in prison "their bodies grow fat and strong." They attribute their growth in part to the effects of three daily meals, the enforced rest, and the separation from women, but do not regard such factors as sufficient to explain it. Also crucial is the incarceration itself, which "renders them unseen." Indeed, some inmates likened imprisonment to traditional village rituals in which young men were secluded in "dark, windowless" ceremonial houses as an integral part of their preparation for initiation (Reed 1999, 47).

20 The two common terms for menstruation are *hariga* 'moon' (see chapter 3) and *ambure*, which literally means 'lacking in strength or vitality'; idiomatically, it means 'sickness.'

21 The tendency toward competitive emotions aroused by the sight of beautiful dancers may explain the surprising reaction my informants gave to an old photograph of an Orokaiva dancer that they saw in my photocopy of F. E. Williams's *Orokaiva Society* (1930). The picture, which is the monograph's frontispiece, shows the dancer standing at stiff attention, dressed in the magnificent traditional regalia of an earlier age. When we discussed his antique ornaments, pointing them out one by one, my informants seemed impressed and spoke of their superiority to those they themselves wear. But when they regarded the image as a whole, my informants mostly responded to the photograph with whoops of laughter, and they jokingly disparaged this proud character from an earlier time, nicknaming him derisively the "Typical Orokaiva Youth." The nickname lampooned and deflated the extraordinary photo as a representation of cultural typicality, but what I think made it so funny for people was the way the phrase "Orokaiva youth" (which was part of the original printed caption) resonated to the current national discourse about youth crime problems, a discourse in which "Orokaiva youths" are notorious as gangsters and criminals—as if the long ago dancer in the photograph would today be at risk of becoming a gang member and thief. My informants were not sufficiently distant from the culture of the boy's era to suppress their competitive impulse, and I imagine this is why they could only speak in ways that diminished his beauty (though they were able to acknowledge the impressiveness of his ornaments) and placed him in the shadow of contemporary social ills.

22 Another type of business that is especially risky is the operation of a truck or bus transport service. In this case, the heightened risk comes because the vehicle is constantly moving about, thus multiplying the number of people whose eyes are attracted to it. To be sure, when a truck or bus is brand new, its owners are proud of it and like to show it around, but this pleasure is soon tempered by anxiety lest it bring on misfortune. To forestall this feared possibility, truck and bus owners and crews passively allow the vehicle to sustain considerable

cosmetic damage which is never repaired, so that it becomes less bright; they sometimes offer free rides especially to old men (who are potential sorcerers) and young men (who are potential criminals); they publicly donate the services of their truck or bus for church purposes, thus offering reciprocation at a community level; they talk up their own generosity in giving free rides to widows, the indigent, the seriously sick or injured, and other unfortunates; they widely disseminate the amounts of their loan payments and imply that the vehicle is still largely owned by the bank; they assiduously cultivate good exchange relations with known gang leaders and members; and they often maintain large crews of young male hangers-on for protection.

23 Quoted in Nyamnjoh and Page 2002, 607.

24 This inability of whitemen to truly see Orokaiva is also a manifestation of their lightness: they appear not to be bound by the normally inescapable consequences of social relationships, instead maintaining themselves aloof from them—a posture of arrogance. However, the notion that whitemen are arrogant does not do away with the implication of Orokaiva inferiority, which is clearly the more disturbing possibility from an Orokaiva perspective. The same possibility is reflected in the paucity of Orokaiva-white marriages. Orokaiva, like other people throughout the Pacific, view marriage as an alliance that can advance the political status and economic well-being of one's family, and whitemen, as wealthy and powerful outsiders, are in this respect ideal marriage partners (see also Nyamnjoh and Page 2002). However, whites' lack of interest in Orokaiva liaisons or the exchange obligations which flow from them implies a rejection of Orokaiva as unworthy alliance partners. Although I did not hear this point explicitly discussed, Orokaiva did appear to find it troubling. For example, people were fascinated by those few cases where whites and Orokaiva *did* marry, and such cases seemed to be known to everyone in the region. Or in my own fieldwork, I was impressed by the way my politically astute hosts would regale all important new visitors to our compound with an elaborately embroidered account of my girlfriend at home, who they would portray as all but my wife in that she was said to routinely perform such canonical wifely duties as cooking meals for my guests, tending to my dependents (a pet) in my absence, and helping to care for my parents, her eventual in-laws. In telling this fanciful story, my hosts were surely seeking to bolster my reputation against what to Orokaiva was the questionable aberration of being unmarried and childless at my age. But in part, too, it was their own face they were saving: the elevation of my relationship with the absent girlfriend was a way of forestalling the obvious question of why I had not taken up with any of the available village women, even though I was living there for the better part of three years as a single man on his own (i.e., I couldn't because I was to all intents and purposes already married). Although it is not within the scope of the present work to pursue the methodological implications of this issue, suffice it to say that it problematizes the common presumption that sexual abstention in the field is a fieldwork practice that is ethically neutral.

25 Lest the Orokaiva belief in the possibility of such transformation seem far-fetched and exotic, we might recall that many westerners, too, have

speculated that skin color (and race) might actually be changeable. A promi-nent historical example is Samuel Stanhope Smith, who as president of the College of New Jersey (later Princeton) in the late nineteenth century wrote a treatise on the "change of complexion" to which "nations are susceptible as well as individuals" when they are brought to a new climate, becoming in time physically "so *assimilated* [to the new climate] that we cannot say with certainty whose ancestor was the native of the clime, and whose the intrud-ing foreigner" (Smith 1787, 8–10). On this basis Smith suggested that blacks in America were beginning to turn white and would continue to do so—the more so to the extent they were allowed to enjoy not only the cool, northern clime but also whitelike conditions (57–58; Gould 1996, 71). Similarly, the public was fascinated by the case of a Philadelphia man named Henry Moss whose skin seemed to have turned from "entirely black" to "white and fair" in 1796, while his "wool" became replaced by "straight hair similar to that of a white person" (Yokota 2004). As Kariann Yokota has noted, whites gener-ally paid less attention to the converse possibility that they themselves might turn black, even though such an unwelcome transformation of social and legal status was by no means unheard of in many parts of the United States where the infamous "one drop of blood" rule could be applied to make those of mixed ancestry "black" (see also Malcomson 2000; Haney López 1996).

26   This idea was expressed most forcefully by David Ivahupa of Popondetta, who cited the securely gated compound called The Ridge that housed the highest-level, mostly expatriate managers of the World Bank–funded oil palm project as "a kind of apartheid" on the South African model (which at the time of his speaking in 1991 had not yet been overthrown) that was being implemented in Oro Province right under people's noses.

27   The gravity with which Orokaiva perceived raskol crime as a pressing prob-lem was heightened in the years surrounding my fieldwork. In 1991, during my first month-long visit to the region, I was aware of several holdups and killings, and I myself was nearly held up on two occasions when armed raskols staked out locations that the truck I was riding in was expected to pass, in order to ambush it. By December 1992, when I arrived to begin my main fieldwork, lawlessness in the province had become a flashpoint of eth-nic tensions as well as a focus of national attention that was underscored by frequent articles and front-page headlines in PNG's newspapers. Escalating the crisis, an Orokaiva politician, Sylvenus Siembo, declared the situation intolerable, and blaming it on an "invasion" of Papua New Guinean migrants from other provinces, he set up a vigilante-style "home force" that intimi-dated oil palm settlers, workers, squatters, and businessmen, ostensibly to curb lawlessness (see also Koczberski and Curry 2004, 363–64). While pro-ponents of this "Oro for Oro" campaign blamed local crime problems on non-Orokaiva, the outsiders themselves—and even most Orokaiva villagers I interviewed—apportioned blame for crime differently, and it is possible that much of the worst violence in those months was instigated or justified by the campaign itself, including many rapes, several murders, and more than fifty cases of armed holdups, shootings, and robberies (Livinai 1992; Kakas 1993; Yalu 1993). Eventually, reports of a mass exodus of settlers from other

provinces sparked a national outcry (see, e.g., "10,000 Set to Flee [Oro] Province," *Post-Courier*, January 25, 1993, 1), leading the national government to send in a team of paramilitary police—the notorious "Mobile Squad." As Siembo issued a formal retraction of his "Oro for Oro" statements (*Post-Courier*, February 19, 1993, 2; February 22, 1993, 32), and was placed under arrest, the Mobile Squad was regularly seen at the provincial hospital trucking in beaten suspects, and its unofficially sanctioned brutality, in tandem with a gentler "community relations" campaign conducted by a team of visiting specialists, surprisingly proved effective in stopping the crime wave almost completely and generally calming things down.

In the years since those fearful months, I have seen the local incidence of violent crime fluctuate through better and worse periods, but all the while there is a sense of fragility about the maintenance of public safety. Many of the province's stores, banks, and public facilities that closed in 1992-93 have never reopened, and Popondetta has retained its nickname of "cowboy town," connoting lawlessness; Oro Province is called "cowboy country." In short, Orokaiva are all aware that in the national context their region is associated closely with raskolism, and thus the problem of raskolism has remained among the preeminent moral concerns of their society.

Chapter Five

1 From *Music for The Knee Plays*, ECM Records, 1985.
2 Young taro are said to roam about at night, like human adolescents, and to be quite frisky, so that during the early phases of taro gardening people focus on inducing the plants to 'sit down' and 'stay' (see also Williams 1928). The imagined movements of taro plants are consistent with the notion that taro is a hard food, since qualities of hardness are associated with the effect of motion more generally, as discussed in chapter 4.
3 In some Orokaiva areas sago *is* used in feasting, but then it is always parceled in large leaf-wrapped bundles of hard-packed dry starch that manifest the qualities of hardness and heaviness that make its use as a feast gift appropriate.
4 The other brands distributed by Trukai Industries include "Roots Rice" and "Power Rice," which are similar to Trukai (though sold in bags with different graphics), as well as "Sun-Long," which is a higher quality, long grain variety packaged in Australia for the PNG market and sold for a few pennies more. A brown rice, also marketed by Trukai, is almost never bought by villagers.
5 'Stone' refers to money in general and to coin money in particular. A second term, 'leaves' (*iki*) is used to specify money bills. Historically, coin money circulated earlier and more widely in this region than money bills, a circumstance that perhaps explains why it is 'stones,' and not 'leaves,' that mean 'money in general.'
6 The account here refers to the time of my main fieldwork in 1993-95. Since then, there have been changes in the brands and kinds of tinfish available,

occasioned by the opening of the first domestic mackerel cannery in Lae. Government incentives to attract the cannery, which is owned by International Food Corporation (IFC), a subsidiary of the Malaysian trading and processed foods conglomerate, Kumpulan Fima Berhad, included granting it a five-year monopoly on the sale of canned mackerel products in Papua New Guinea, effectively discontinuing the importation of foreign brands such as 777. (In subsequent years, there was a schedule of tariffs, decreasing in steps from 70 percent in 1999–2001 to 15 percent in 2006 and beyond [Tai 2004].) Following the successful marketing model of Trukai rice, IFC packages a main brand, "Besta," and a number of subsidiary brands, including "Supreme" (the lowest quality grade) and a domestic version of "Sunflower." Unfortunately, the cannery, which it was hoped would lead to the creation of a domestic commercial fishing industry, has instead made liberal use of a loophole in its deal with the PNG government that allows it to import bulk cooked-and-frozen mackerel from overseas suppliers until such time as a local mackerel fishing fleet provides an assured supply (an unlikely eventuality in the near term). Notwithstanding criticism in the news media, and allegations that the firm had bribed government officials to secure its lucrative deal, the cannery has continued to import bulk frozen mackerel which must be thawed and recooked, resulting in tinfish products that are widely recognized as appalling in quality (see, e.g., *Post-Courier*, May 13, 1998, 10; February 4, 1999, 5). Since 1997, IFC products have faced competition from a new domestic tuna cannery which has quickly gained an estimated two-thirds share of the PNG tinfish market (Hernandez 2003). Owned by the Philippines-based RD Corporation, RD Tuna Canners Ltd. in the coastal city Madang successfully exports high quality canned tuna to Europe under numerous labels, and for the domestic market it packages large (14 oz.) tinfishlike tins of low quality, reddish brown tuna flakes and scrapings under the brand name "Diana." As of early 2005, two additional tuna canneries are being planned for the towns of Wewak and Kokopo, primarily to supply foreign exchange earnings by the duty free export of PNG tuna to the European Union, but also to satisfy PNG domestic and Pacific regional tinfish demand.

7   My thanks to Dan Jorgensen for help with this gloss.

8   In the last several years, however, Coca Cola–Amatil, which bottles and distributes Coke in PNG, has been attempting to increase rural sales by providing free soft drink refrigerators to village tradestore owners who own portable generators with sufficient capacity to run them (see also Foster 2002; Errington and Gewertz 2004).

9   As R. K. Dentan was told by Semai rice-eaters on the Malay Peninsula: "What do you think we are, cats [that we only eat meat]?" (quoted in Manderson 1986, 6).

10 People draw analogies between newly sprouted taro plants and human babies (both are weak, watery creatures), between taro and human adolescents (both are frisky and roam around at night), and between taro plants and humans of ripe age (both shrink in height). Alternatively, people point out that taro roots ripen in nine months, the same as human gestation.

11 The identification of humans with taro is further supported by myths that represent human-taro metamorphoses (see Schwimmer 1973, 114–18; Iteanu 1983a; Iteanu and Schwimmer 1996).

12 A slightly different reaction was given to whitemen's food by young men from Kaliai, West New Britain, who visited Port Moresby in the late 1980s. The men complained that western foods like breakfast cereal were too "soft" for them and made them sick when they ate them regularly: "Their solution was to demand to be taken to the [produce] markets in Port Moresby where they bought 'Papua New Guinea food.' The young men contrasted soft debilitating western food with the 'strong' food they normally ate" (Lattas 1998, 322n13).

13 It should be noted that, just as reified qualities are transferred from foods to humans by eating, so are they transferred from humans to growing plants in the context of gardening. Many gardening practices and prohibitions are designed to control such transfers. An example mentioned earlier is the prohibition against wearing shoes in a new taro garden, lest the taro develop an overly thick fibrous casing (*goru*: casing, pouch, womb) like the shoes on one's feet (shoes are called *utu goru*, 'foot casings'). Many prohibitions attempt to prevent unwanted or harmful qualities from 'jumping' from humans to crops; others aim to induce beneficial qualities by the same means. So for instance, when Orokaiva are planting yam seed, they generally make a point of sitting down on the ground or crouching low beside each yam mound, instead of standing and bending over, so as to communicate to the seed a quality of 'sitting down in the ground' which will help the yams root.

A further manifestation of Orokaiva concerns over the transfer of qualities between plants and humans is exemplified by prohibitions that are designed to prevent some harmful quality associated with one plant from being communicated to another via the gardener. For example, gardeners who have recently eaten sago should refrain from entering new taro gardens. The prohibition is an attempt to prevent the young taro from growing soft inside and rotting, which could happen were they to indirectly contract, through the mediation of the person, the quality of 'inside softness' (*jo suruha*) that is found in the sago palm, which has a soft inner pith. This softness is too weak to affect the strong, fully-formed body of a person (the gardener), or of taro that is mature. But it can nonetheless be invisibly carried by such a body, as when a person has just eaten sago, and it can then be relayed from his or her body to another more susceptible body like that of an infant or a fledgling taro plant that it might then harm. For further examples, see Williams 1928, 1930; Schwimmer 1973; Iteanu 1983a.

14 For Orokaiva, hard teeth (*ti*) are an essential symbol of the body's strength and vitality. The expression *ti gasa* 'mature/hard teeth' likens the teeth to nuts or seeds that have ripened fully and are therefore hard. This expression is often used as a synecdoche for a person's maturity and the ability to chew betel nut. When elderly people lose their first tooth, they often hold a feast-meal for associates in their age-set, in order to publicly admit that their bodily strength has begun to diminish and thereby (it is hoped) to prevent some of the embarrassment that their weakness might cause them.

15 Among Orokaiva, parallels between their taro plants and their children are commonly acknowledged, for their ideas of the growth and maturation of

taro plants and of humans are modeled closely on one another. People use taro seed as a metaphor for babies, and babies as a metaphor for taro seed. They also use taro names as endearments for their little ones, calling them gently, 'taro seed' and 'rhizome.'

16 Iteanu's apt term for the sympathetic connection that is cultivated between a child and a particular piece of land is "localization" (1983a, 35).

17 Although the ancestor is an ahihi or 'spirit being,' it does not, as the "soul substance" account might imply, impart its ahihi 'spirit' to the baby. Schwimmer speculates that the act of naming a baby for a dead person effects a transfer of ahihi (1973, 93), but Orokaiva name children not only after dead people but also after the living, creating 'namesake' (*saso, dombo*) relationships that are an important part of Orokaiva kinship. Namesake relationships are focused not on matters of the ahihi but rather on those of the hamo. Namesakes are expected to 'look after' (*simba*) each other's hamo, the elder looking after the younger namesake's hamo until the younger is fully grown, and the younger looking after the elder's when the elder becomes old and weak. It is thought that a sympathetic connection comes to exist between namesakes' hamos; this is indicated in the use of *dombo* 'likeness' as a common term of mutual address and reference for namesakes. For more on namesakes, see Iteanu 1983b.

18 It might be thought that bushknives (machetes) and axes would be an exception, since like all steel tools, these are known to be imported from overseas and to come from whitemen originally. Nevertheless, they are not ordinarily marked as *taupa kastom* 'whitemen's things.' Like certain ambiguous store foods that I examine in the next section, machetes are more strongly identified with indigenous than with whitemen's culture, probably because the work for which they are used in the forest and gardens is itself strongly marked as indigenous, not a kind of work that whitemen do.

19 In using gender-neutral language here I am acknowledging that both men and women experience strong ancestral identification with their lands. Even though it is men who are normally said to inherit lands bequeathed by their fathers, as Schwimmer observes, "the transfer of land to sisters and daughters is [also] very common," and I knew of several families who gardened lands associated with ancestors of the wife or mother (Schwimmer 1973, 102; see also Crocombe and Hogbin 1963; Rimoldi 1966). Orokaiva also acknowledge their in-law ancestors as much as they do their lineal forebears, and in long-married couples both wives and husbands remember how their deceased in-laws, when alive, used to work in the gardens. I heard report of such ancestors protecting taro against pig and human intruders, invisibly slapping dogs who had stepped on new shoots (explaining why the dogs had begun to cry out suddenly for no apparent reason), and generally 'looking after' (*simba ari*) the taro to ensure that it thrived.

20 Indeed, to discourse on these topics is considered a rhetorical virtue. Mackenton Seambo once criticized a church sermon on the divisive subject of Christian denominationalism by contrasting it with topics exemplary of the 'true and constructive speech of our ancestors,' chief among which was food and how people 'wipe away one another's tears' (help each other through hard spots) by exchanging food in times of scarcity.

21 Also relevant here is the difference between giving an item away and consuming it oneself. People who give away whitemen's foods show their own transcendence of the desires these foods arouse, which is not the case when they consume rice and so on themselves. Indeed, when people spoke disparagingly of whitemen's foods while they were eating them, I sometimes had the impression that they were in some measure compensating for giving in to these desires they were not proud of.

22 The emphasis on giving whitemen's foods away as gifts is consistent with the general devaluation in Orokaiva morality of consuming food oneself. While the body is recognized to need sustenance, it is also felt that the consumption of excess food produces 'only sleep' and wastes resources that could be better put to use developing positive relations with others (see Munn 1986).

23 This cooling first course is an enlargement upon the traditional custom of offering betel nut and young drinking coconuts to newly arrived guests in order to refresh them after their long, hot journey.

24 The model for my thinking in this section is Stanley Tambiah's classic essay (1985 [1969]) analyzing Thai villagers' classification of the edibility of animals. Tambiah shows how classes of animals correlate with spatial and symbolic categories centered on the Thai house as well as with the animals' behaviors as seen from the point of view of human marriage and sex rules. Other influential works on food classification and eating include Lévi-Strauss 1966; Douglas 1966, 1997; Sahlins 1976; Feeley-Harnik 1994; Kahn 1986; Mintz 1985; Meigs 1984; Jolly 1991; and Weismantel 1988.

25 Virtually any foods may be served at feasts cooked. Note that neither sweet potatoes, in category IV, nor Chinese taro, in category III, are ever given raw as part of a feast gift, even though both have become true staple foods for Orokaiva, providing at least as many calories in the diet as true indigenous taro.

26 Lambflaps are particularly useful for accomplishing small rituals like ending mourning for a baby that nonetheless require meat to be distributed. As a friend explained to me: 'Lambflaps are good when you don't have money to buy a whole pig, but a chicken would be too little.' Lambflaps are also used at feasts when meat gifts are given to Seventh Day Adventists, since pork is forbidden to them. This is increasing in significance as the number (and ritual adherence) of Orokaiva Seventh Day Adventists grows.

27 That Chinese taro came to Orokaiva from this area is also suggested by the English name Orokaiva use for Chinese taro: "German taro." The Wariya area was formerly part of German New Guinea; i.e., it is across the border that formerly separated the Australian Territory of Papua from German New Guinea. Of course, it is quite possible that Holland himself became acquainted with "German taro" from somewhere else still, such as another mission station, and that he imported it along with the names it was referred to by there.

28 There is a good deal on the importation of these foods in Williams (1928, 117, 120–21) and in early patrol reports, especially BNG 1894, xvii, and NDPR: Buna patrol report October 1915.

29 English cabbage also keeps for a much longer time than do other greens under local conditions (no refrigeration). In this way it might well be considered the vegetable counterpart to rice and tinned protein.

30 Papua New Guineans who have traveled overseas do become aware that the foods villagers think of as whitemen's foods are but an insignificant part of most whites' actual diets. For example, an Agenehambo village man, Neville Deiko, spent three months in Australia on an internship where he stayed in the homes of white Australians, eating the same foods as they did. He returned to describe breakfasts of cereal and milk, lunches of sandwiches, and dinners consisting of no main food at all or sometimes just a small amount of rice or potatoes, but large amounts of several different relishes, usually a meat, some vegetables, or spaghetti. Nevertheless, before long I heard him revert to referring to rice and tinfish as 'whitemen's foods.' When I asked him about it, he thought for a moment, then said with a laugh, 'well, these are whitemen's foods over here.'

Chapter Six

1 The one exception I found was a handful of Orokaiva men who had been to university in the decades surrounding independence, where they learned the anticolonialist discourse of the mostly foreign left-leaning academics who taught in PNG at the time. But while these individuals would readily assign blame to whitemen as the primary factor in Orokaiva poverty using the discourse of dependency theory, they shared with other villagers the same moral problematic of whitemen's lightness (how are they so socially unencumbered), softness (how do they get their wealth without doing hard work), and brightness (how can they have such wealth yet escape the negative consequences of inequality). Indeed, it was only by assimilating their exogenous critique to the terms of this problematic that the critique could be made compelling in the village context.

2 The trend in recent anthropological work has been to devalue the culturally shared and conventional in contrast to the diversity and individuality of specific persons and contexts. This trend may be appropriate as a response to an earlier tendency to equate culture with what is shared, but we should not overlook the importance of conventional categories in enabling meaningful communication and individual creativity (see Rosenblatt 2004). As Fritz Kramer observes in his brilliant study of images of Europeans in African spirit possession and art, Africans portrayed these others to gain a measure of control over them, which depended precisely on conventionalizing them, "raising them to the status of types and making them part of [people's] own tradition[s]" (Kramer 1993, 240).

3 See also chapter 5, note 30, on one of these men's reflections on the foods.

4 In a perceptive discussion of the difficulties town migrants face in reactivating their claims to village lands, George Curry and Gina Koczberski note that, while "the maintenance of exchange relationships with home is a precondition for the resumption of resource rights for migrants returning home after a long absence," it is not always enough, particularly where the migrant's exchange with villagers has targeted too few or the wrong individuals, or where the villagers themselves face rising pressure on land resources (Curry and Koczberski 1999, 141). Because of such pressure, those who migrate to town are increas-

ingly at risk of losing access to village land permanently, impelling a breakdown of the "established patterns of short-term circular migration" (in which town migrants someday return home) and a growing trend toward migration to town that is long-term or permanent (143).

5 The version of the song transcribed here was recorded by the band Tarbar (Louie Warupi, Paul Warupi, Albert Hoada, John Aisi, and Charlie Auwa) in 1992 at Pacific Gold Studios in Port Moresby, updating the earlier solo version recorded by Louie Warupi in 1980 (see also Foster 2002, 180). The actual text of the Tok Pisin coda is as follows: "Wantok, yu gat sampela kina i kam long mi o nogat." "Ei, long moning ol sampela ol wantok i kam kisim planti moni long mi i go pinis. Nau mi gat ol lus toea tasol i stap, ya." "Lus toea tasol, ei? Tu toea tasol? O orait."

6 On the association of whitemen with social harmony in other Melanesian societies, see, e.g., Leavitt 2001; Smith 1994; Kulick 1992; Errington 1974.

7 The Sipa story presented here in its basic outlines was popularized during the period of accelerated development interest and activity surrounding national independence in 1975 (see also Schwimmer 1987; Iteanu and Schwimmer 1996). I am indebted to Gideon and MacNeill Pueka for an authoritative telling of the story, which I recorded. I also heard many other versions of the story in villages throughout the region.

8 An interesting parallel to these New Guinea tales are the many African myths about Noah's sons, which are similarly focused on skin color and which explain the dispossession of blacks from the prosperity that whites enjoy by the primordial curse that Noah put on his son Ham (Kramer 1993, 21ff.).

9 The vernacular terms in this paragraph are Tok Pisin.

10 *Wantok* is commonly glossed hyperliterally as 'one-talk,' evoking a solidarity based on the sharing of a vernacular language. While this gloss may be correct etymologically, it gives the misleading impression that linguistic commonalities are a primary traditional basis for cultural unity and social alliances, when in fact, throughout New Guinea, cultures and social networks regularly cross linguistic lines (see also Bashkow 2004). A more revealing gloss might be 'someone with whom one can talk,' where what is shared is not a language, but rather the possibility of speaking together and positive interactions.

11 Even the proprietors of tradestores and other rural businesses ordinarily run their businesses as a supplement to, and not in place of, subsistence horticulture.

12 The 3 percent of land that *was* alienated to the Crown now comprises virtually all of the country's most highly developed urban, commercial, industrial, and plantation areas, so the impact of colonial interventions in the land system is not to be minimized. But particularly in comparison to other colonial situations throughout the world, it is important to positively acknowledge the paternalistic policies instituted in the early twentieth century by Papua's longtime colonial administrator J. H. P. Murray—over objections by Australian settler, commercial, and plantation interests—which resulted in so much of the land remaining under the indigenous peoples' uncompromised control (Murray 1920, 24; West 1968; Lewis 1996).

13   Those defending the World Bank in this case have pointed out that the Land
     Mobilization Program was not technically "part of the structural adjustment
     program nor ... a condition of the structural adjustment loan" (Smith 1996).
     Nevertheless, in policy recommendations going back as early as the first
     World Bank mission to the colonial territories of Papua and New Guinea in
     1962, the World Bank, together with other international aid agencies, often
     called for measures to overcome "the grave limitations to agricultural devel-
     opment imposed by existing land-tenure systems" and to "remove the tenure
     obstacles to more efficient land use" and "cash production" (World Bank
     1965, 173, 175; see also AIDAB 1992, 48; World Bank 1988, vol. I, 19–20;
     AIDAB 1994, 50–52; Fingleton 2005a, 2005b, 2005c). Consistent with such
     recommendations, one of the goals of the PNG Land Mobilization Program
     begun in 1989 was to develop a framework to allow "the use of customary
     land for modern commerce, including usage for security as credit" (Gov-
     ernment of Papua New Guinea, *Economic and Development Policies, 1994*,
     quoted in AIDAB 1994, 52). According to draft Structural Adjustment
     Program (SAP) policy documents circulating in the government at the time of
     the land controversy, legislation that would create this framework was
     indeed one of the prerequisites of the SAP loan (Yadi 1995)—even if the
     World Bank did remove it in subsequent drafts of the requirements list
     (Smith 1996; see also AusAID 1997, 66, 105).

14   The popular protest against land reform appeared to many foreigners to be
     an overreaction by ill-informed villagers based on unfounded fears inflamed
     by the students. And in the proposals' defense, government officials and
     reform proponents observed that the proposed legislation involved "no com-
     pulsion on the customary landowners to register their land" in the first
     instance, and that registration would not make customary lands permanently
     alienable by outright sale or make them subject to repossession by banks
     (Tannos 1995b; Kone 1995; Smith 1996). But while these claims may have
     been strictly true, they were not wholly truthful. In order to fulfill the moti-
     vating objective of the reform, which was to make customary lands accept-
     able to banks as loan collateral, the proposed legislation would in fact have
     allowed registered lands to be *leased*, so that banks could "lend money on the
     security of a lease of land, and if the loan is [not] repaid, the bank will be able
     to take over the lease until debts are settled" (Iorere 1995; Waram 1995;
     Tannos 1995a, 2). This would have enabled customary landowners not only
     to accept loans using a lease on their land as collateral but also to *rent out* their
     lands to foreign developers for long periods—thus "effectively utili[zing]
     their land for their own economic benefit," as the PNG Lands Minister put it,
     "by just becoming landlords" (Tannos 1995b). But from the viewpoint of
     villagers' livelihood and security, the extended loss of land use rights could be
     nearly as damaging as the loss of titular ownership; moreover, one can well
     imagine villagers being effectively prevented from regaining use of their
     leased-out lands because of contractual loopholes (e.g., having to compensate
     leaseholders for the value of improvements such as tree plantings and build-
     ings). So in my opinion, the widespread alarm and suspicion was by no
     means unjustified. Indeed, even if the proposal was only for voluntary land

registration as such (i.e., without rights to lease), it would still not be innocu-
ous, since over the long term it would create a necessarily simplified, official
register of land demarcations and ownership that, by rendering customary
land "legible" to the state, would significantly alter the balance of power
between the state and customary landowners, thus making it possible for the
state to enact policies that would more radically transform customary tenure
in the future (see Scott 1998; Tararia 2005).

15 In other words, this devaluation of their society and sense of its impotence
reflects people's tendency to reckon the virtue of their society in terms of levels of wealth. By doing so, however, they wind up counting *against* their society those aspects of manifest strength and cohesiveness that they recognize in
other contexts through their experience of the inescapability of social obligations and heaviness.

16 Accounts of cultural change may be exaggerated when we fail to distinguish
long-term cultural transformations from ordinary, culturally appropriate
life-cycle transitions. So even when young men's desires and comportment
express an individualism that seems to depart from community norms, this
is not necessarily a sign of fundamental cultural transformation, since an
individualistic phase is not culturally unexpected for young people, especially men, before they begin families and enter into the network of obligations that comes with full adulthood. Especially given that the version of
modern western individualism available to people is so economically unre-
warding and offers so little in the way of long-term security, it is normal for
the young progressivists of one period to become pillars of tradition twenty
years hence.

17 Interestingly, it is often young men who are particularly averse to accepting
such disparities. Although in so many other ways, young men are clearly the
advance guard of cultural change toward individualistic desire and consumption, they are also often the quickest to offer and respond to Robin
Hood–like appeals for action (usually illegal) to reverse inequalities.

18 This connects to the emphasis on communal elicitation and reward noted in
studies of cargo movements. Were the desired cargo to actually materialize,
it would immediately raise the problem of how to distribute it equitably
and nondivisively. Hence Kenelm Burridge's important observation that
"nowhere in the available literature is there any indication of how the cargo
would be distributed were it [actually] to arrive" (1960, 42).

19 Sources on the Higaturu Oil Palm Project include Newton 1982, 1985; IASER
1989; FAO 1987; Tyrie and Bleeker 1990; Koczberski, Curry, and Gibson
2001; and Koczberski and Curry 2004.

20 I am indebted to Donald Munro, Oro Province Project Manager for the PNG
Oil Palm Industry Corporation, for information on the project expansion.
An expansion of the oil palm processing factory is already underway (*Rural
Industry Weekly* 2005). Concerning prior development schemes tried in the
region, see Crocombe 1964; Schwimmer 1973; Newton 1985.

21 Notwithstanding this, there has been significant, if sporadic, local opposition
to various facets of the oil palm project, including a series of complaints spear-
headed in the 1990s by a local Orokaiva politician, Sylvenus Siembo, who was

subsequently elected a member of parliament and the province's governor. Those complaints focused on the environmental and health consequences of wastewater runoff from the oil palm factory and the fertilizer used on oil plantations, a large percentage of which unavoidably winds up in the rivers. There have also been protests against the expansion of the project and its "invasion of our customary land and usurpation of our resources," in opposition to which landowners in the province held a Forum on Land Rights and Community Based Natural Resource Management in March 2004, with organizational assistance from the Forest People's Programme, a European-based NGO, and the PNG Center for Environmental Law and Community Rights (CELCOR 2004). The cause of halting the rapid expansion of palm oil plantation projects on rainforest lands is one that Orokaiva share with indigenous people in other parts of Papua New Guinea as well as in Malaysia, Indonesia, and elsewhere, and it has recently been taken up in its global environmental and health-related dimensions by western advocacy groups such as the Center for Science in the Public Interest (2005) and Friends of the Earth (2004a, 2004b, 2005), and by members of the United Kingdom Parliament (2004).

22　This is analogous to the position taken by Mary Weismantel in her evocative study of race in the Andes: "In the Andes, race is indeed corporeal, but the definition of the physical self is extended beyond flesh and hair and teeth to include the clothing and objects that extend, shield, and adorn the body" (Weismantel 2001, 184). The clothing and objects that define whiteness there thus include leather jackets, good shoes, expensive cars and jeeps, wristwatches and CD players, cash, and noisy gadgets like a battery-powered razor (185–93). In discussing portrayals of Indians on picture postcards, Weismantel recognizes that such objects are manipulated by the postcard photographers to "confer a race upon the people photographed. Manufactured goods . . . bestow whiteness upon the people around them; their absence performs the operation in reverse. Without wristwatches, radios, and blenders (objects that are, in fact, commonplace in indigenous homes) the people in the photographs are immediately recognizable as nonwhites" (180). For other work in the same spirit, see Bridget Heneghan's superb historical archaeology and literary study of the material culture of race in the American South (2003), and Anne McClintock's discussion of "commodity racism" (1995, 207–31).

23　Another way of putting this is that discourses about bodily characteristics, however important they may be in some contexts of racial discrimination and genocide, account for only a portion of the symbolic building blocks composing popularly held racial stereotypes. And indeed, given the way scientific criteria for race, like head shape and size, have changed over time, it would seem they are constructed to fit the content of the stereotypes rather than the other way around (Smedley 1999; Gould 1996).

24　This is precisely the kind of effect that George Lakoff writes about in his book on political discourse, *Don't Think of an Elephant!* (2004). In just the same way that it is well nigh impossible, when confronted with this phrase, not to think of an elephant, the critique of race itself evokes the very notion it attempts to negate, that is, the whole premise that differences constituted in the human body offer a key for understanding social problems about which nothing can be done except turning a blind eye. We will keep on giving discursive prominence to this idea until we are able to develop a frame for discussing it that is different.

25 Thus Errington and Gewertz point out that the attraction of cargo to Papua New Guineans is "not its inherent and instantly recognizable value," but its perceived potential to "transform the relations of inequality between whites and blacks that were pervasive in colonialism" (Errington and Gewertz 2004, 26).

26 The fact that it often makes no difference whether categories are grounded in bodily characteristics or not explains why there is so little analytic value in distinguishing rigorously between race and ethnicity.

27 While stereotypes *per se* may not be eradicable, they clearly change over time and are subject to trends. John Earl Joseph has described how the prestige of persons is transferred to associated features like language, a process which explains why some ways of speaking come to be seen as prestigious while others are stigmatized, a phenomenon that finds no explanation in terms of dialects' "intrinsic worth" (Joseph 1987, 31). The implication of my argument for antiracism, then, is that the best strategy may well be the old-fashioned one of working to improve the livelihoods and status of disadvantaged people, since this might in turn raise the relative status of the objects and stereotypes with which they are associated.

28 Recorded during thesis research by my undergraduate student Leslie Anne White (personal communication; White 2005, 58–61).

29 As Kramer points out (1993, 29), this tendency of the underprivileged "to blame themselves for their unfortunate situation" can also be understood as a way in which they "avoid despairing at the injustice of a world which is outside their effective grasp." A similar observation is made by Leavitt (2000, 306) who notes that "casting modernization issues in the context of local relations" offers at least "some promise of control over one's destiny in a world that otherwise defies understanding."

30 Since 2001, there has been a great deal of interest in the United States in the phenomenon of "anti-Americanism" in different parts of the world. However, when others' views are collected together solely on the basis of a shared negative evaluation, we are led all too easily to focus our attention on whether the ideas seem justified: Are they well founded in realistic assessments of the U.S. impact on their lives, and thus worth taking seriously? or do they merely reflect people's local traditions of cultural insecurity, protest, nationalism, or whatever, in which case they can be dismissed? What this way of framing the issue fails to confront is the simple reality that these expressions—whatever we think about them—are real: they have a cultural life wholly apart from our evaluation of them, and thus *need to be understood in the context of others' own lives* if we are to know how to respond to them productively. It is of course true that local traditions of anti-American criticism are in many places longstanding (Roger 2005; Hollander 2004; Rubin and Rubin 2004; Shiraev and Zubok 2000; Granatstein 1996; Rubinstein and Smith 1985). But the American tradition of denying the significance of others' criticism is hardly less timeworn. Indeed, the dismissive message of

several recent works is remarkably similar to that expressed as long ago as 1828 by James Fenimore Cooper, who wrote from Switzerland that he was "disgusted" by those Americans who were eager "to know what other nations think of us," since jaundiced European opinions about America were the "utterly *worthless*" product of unjustifiable snobbery and ultimately of "jealousy and dislike" of "our growing power" (Cooper 1908, 47–49; see also Gibson 2004; D'Souza 2002; Hollander 1992; for notable exceptions, see Stephan 2005; Balis and Serfaty 2004; Ross and Ross 2004; McPherson 2003; Boroujerdi 1996).

References

The following abbreviations are used in the references.

AAA   American Anthropological Association
AIDAB   Australian International Development Assistance Bureau
AusAID   Australian Agency for International Development
BNG   Commonwealth of Australia, British New Guinea
CELCOR   Center for Environmental Law and Community Rights, PNG
FAO   United Nations Food and Agriculture Organization
IASER   Papua New Guinea Institute of Applied Social and Economic Research
IUAES   International Union for Anthropological and Ethnological Sciences
NDPR   Northern District Patrol Reports
NSO   Papua New Guinea National Statistical Office
PAR   Commonwealth of Australia, Papua

Archive Sources

Anglican Archives held in the New Guinea Collection, University of Papua New Guinea Michael Somare Library. Port Moresby.

Anglican Board of Missions Records held in the Mitchell Library, Sydney. Anglican Missionaries' letters and newsletters are Box ML MSS 4503/21.

Australian Archives, ACT. Canberra, Australia.

Bishop Philip Strong Papers, National Library of Australia, MS 3921. Canberra.

Francis Edgar Williams Papers, Papua New Guinea National Archives. Port Moresby. A microfilm copy is available in the Mitchell Library, Sydney.

Northern District Patrol Reports (NDPR), 1909–74. Originals held in Papua New Guinea National Archives, Port Moresby. Pre-WWII reports for Kokoda and Buna are also available on Microfilm produced by Commonwealth Archives Office (G91 Series). Postwar reports for Kokoda and Higaturu, until 1948, and for Popondetta, from 1951, are available on microfiche produced by University of California at Santa Diego Library Melanesian Archive. See http://sshl.ucsd.edu/melanesia/patrols.htm.

Published Sources

AAA (American Anthropological Association). 1998. American Anthropological Association Statement on "Race." Available online at http://www.aaanet.org/stmts/racepp.htm, accessed September 16, 2005.

Abare, Grego. 1995. How the World Bank and IMF Are Taking Over (Letter to the Editor). PNG *Post-Courier*, July 7, 10.

Abu-Lughod, Lila. 1991. Writing against Culture. In *Recapturing Anthropology: Working in the Present*, ed. Richard Fox, 137–62. Santa Fe, NM: School of American Research Press.

Achebe, Chinua. 2000. *Home and Exile*. Oxford: Oxford University Press.

Adas, Michael. 1981. From Avoidance to Confrontation: Peasant Protest in Precolonial and Colonial Southeast Asia. *Comparative Studies in Society and History* 23:217–47.

AIDAB (Australian International Development Assistance Bureau). 1992. The Papua New Guinea Economy: Prospects for Recovery, Reform and Sustained Growth. International Development Issues, no. 27. Canberra: AIDAB.

———. 1994. Papua New Guinea: The Role of Government in Economic Development. International Development Issues, no. 33. Canberra: AIDAB.

Akin, David, and Joel Robbins, eds. 1999. *Money and Modernity: State and Local Currencies in Melanesia*. Pittsburgh: University of Pittsburgh Press.

Al Ahmad, Jalal. 1984 [1962]. *Occidentosis: A Plague from the West*. Trans. R. Campbell. Berkeley: Mizan Press.

Allen, Bryant. 1981. The North Coast Region. In Denoon and Snowden 1981, 105–27.

Appiah, K. Anthony, and Amy Guttmann. 1996. *Color Conscious: The Political Morality of Race*. Princeton, NJ: Princeton University Press.

Applbaum, Kalman. 2004. *The Marketing Era: From Professional Practice to Global Provisioning*. New York: Routledge.

Ardener, Shirley, and Sandra Burman, eds. 1995. *Money-Go-Rounds: The Importance of Rotating Savings and Credit Associations for Women*. Washington, DC: Berg.

Arkush, David, and Leo Lee, eds. 1989. *Land without Ghosts: Chinese Impressions of America from the Mid-Nineteenth Century to the Present*. Berkeley: University of California Press.

Asad, Talal. 1973. *Anthropology and the Colonial Encounter*. Atlantic Highlands, NJ: Humanities Press.

AusAID (Australian Agency for International Development). 1996. The Economy of Papua New Guinea: 1996 Report. International Development Issues, no. 46. Canberra: Australian Agency for International Development.

———. 1997. Economic Survey of Papua New Guinea. Canberra: Australian Agency for International Development.

———. 1998. Papua New Guinea: Coping with Shocks and Achieving Broad-Based Economic Development. International Development Issues, no. 52. Canberra: Australian Agency for International Development.

Baker, Lee. 1998. *From Savage to Negro: Anthropology and the Construction of Race, 1896–1954*. Berkeley: University of California Press.

Balandier, Georges. 1966 [1951]. The Colonial Situation: A Theoretical Approach. In *Social Change: The Colonial Situation*, ed. Immanuel Wallerstein, 34–61. New York: Wiley.

Balis, Christina, and Simon Serfaty. 2004. *Visions of America and Europe: September 11, Iraq, and Transatlantic Relations*. Washington, DC: Center for Strategic and International Studies.

Barkan, Elazar. 1992. *The Retreat of Scientific Racism: Changing Concepts of Race in Britain and the United States between the World Wars*. Cambridge: Cambridge University Press.

Barker, John. 1990. Encounters with Evil: Christianity and the Response to Sorcery among the Maisin of Papua New Guinea. *Oceania* 61:139-55.

———. 1996. Village Inventions: Historical Variations upon a Regional Theme in Uiaku, Papua New Guinea. *Oceania* 66:211-29.

Barker, John, and William McKellin. 1993. A Bibliography of Oro Province. *Research in Melanesia* 17:123-81.

Barley, Nigel. 1983. *The Innocent Anthropologist: Notes from a Mud Hut*. London: British Museum.

Barlow, Andrew. 2003. *Between Fear and Hope: Globalization and Race in the United States*. Lanham, MD: Rowman and Littlefield.

Barlow, Tani, ed. 1997. *Formations of Colonial Modernity in East Asia*. Durham, NC: Duke University Press.

Bartra, Roger. 1994. *Wild Men in the Looking Glass: The Mythic Origins of European Otherness*. Ann Arbor: University of Michigan Press.

Bashir, Mohammad. 1995. Land Plan Axed. *The National* (PNG), July 19, 1.

Bashkow, Ira. 1991. The Dynamics of Rapport in a Colonial Situation: David Schneider's Fieldwork on the Islands of Yap. In Stocking 1991, 170-242.

———. 1996. The Symbolism of Space and the Power of Whitemen in Historical Narratives in Papua New Guinea. Paper presented at the American Anthropological Association Annual Meeting, San Francisco, November 20.

———. 1999. "Whitemen" in the Moral World of Orokaiva of Papua New Guinea. PhD diss., Anthropology, University of Chicago.

———. 2000a. "Whitemen" Are Good to Think With: How Orokaiva Morality Is Reflected on Whitemen's Skin. Theme issue, "Whiteness in the Field," *Identities: Global Studies in Culture and Power* 7 (3): 281-332.

———. 2000b. Confusion, Native Skepticism, and Recurring Questions about the Year 2000: "Soft" Beliefs and Preparations for the Millennium in the Arapesh Region, Papua New Guinea. Theme issue, "Millennial Countdown in New Guinea," *Ethnohistory* 47 (1): 133-69.

———. 2004. A Neo-Boasian Conception of Cultural Boundaries. *American Anthropologist* 106 (3): 443-58.

———. In preparation. The Globalization of Time: "Whitemen's Time" in Papua New Guinea. (Article.)

Basso, Keith. 1979. *Portraits of "the Whiteman": Linguistic Play and Cultural Symbols among the Western Apache*. Cambridge: Cambridge University Press.

Bateson, Gregory. 1958 [1936]. *Naven*. Stanford, CA: Stanford University Press.

Baxter, Michael. 1973. *Migration and the Orokaiva*. Port Moresby: University of Papua New Guinea Department of Geography, Occasional Paper No. 3.

———. 1977. Orokaiva Rural-Urban Contacts and Attitudes. In *Change and Movement: Readings on Internal Migration in Papua New Guinea*, ed. R. J. May, 162-72. Canberra: Australian National University Press.

Beaver, W. N. 1919. Notes on Homicidal Emblems among the Orokaiva, of the Mambare and Kumusi Divisions. In PAR 1918-19, 96-99.

Beeman, William. 1983. Images of the Great Satan: Symbolic Conceptions of the United States in the Iranian Revolution. In *Religion and Politics in Iran: Sh'ism from Quietism to Revolution*, ed. Nikkie Keddie, 191–217. New Haven, CT: Yale University Press

———. 2003. Iran and the United States: Postmodern Culture Conflict in Action. *Anthropological Quarterly* 76 (4): 671–91.

Belshaw, Cyril. 1951. Social Consequences of the Mount Lamington Eruption. *Oceania* 21:241–52.

Benedict, Ruth. 1974 [1946]. *The Chrysanthemum and the Sword: Patterns of Japanese Culture*. New York: New American Library.

Benson, James. 1955. Christian Co-operatives. *The Anglican* (Sydney), December 30, 9.

Bercovitch, Eytan. 1994. The Agent in the Gift: Hidden Exchange in Inner New Guinea. *Cultural Anthropology* 9:498–536.

Bettison, D. G. 1963. Introduction to the Series. In The Erap Mechanical Farming Project. Port Moresby: Australian National University New Guinea Research Bulletin No. 1.

Bhabha, Homi. 1994. *The Location of Culture*. London: Routledge.

Biersack, Aletta. 1987. Moonlight: Negative Images of Transcendence in Paiela Pollution. *Oceania* 57 (3): 178–94.

Bissell, William. 2005. Engaging Colonial Nostalgia. *Cultural Anthropology* 20 (2): 215–48.

Blackburn, Julia. 1979. *The White Men: The First Response of Aboriginal Peoples to the White Man*. Foreword by Edmund Carpenter. New York: New York Times Books.

Boas, Franz. 1965 [1938]. *The Mind of Primitive Man*. New York: Free Press.

Boas, George. 1997 [1948]. *Primitivism and Related Ideas in the Middle Ages*. Baltimore: Johns Hopkins University Press.

Bonilla-Silva, Eduardo. 2003. *Racism without Racists: Color-Blind Racism and the Persistence of Racial Inequality in the United States*. Lanham, MD: Rowman and Littlefield.

Boot, Max. 2002. *The Savage Wars of Peace: Small Wars and the Rise of American Power*. New York: Basic Books.

Boroujerdi, Mehrzad. 1996. *Iranian Intellectuals and the West: The Tormented Triumph of Nativism*. Syracuse, NY: Syracuse University Press.

Bourdieu, Pierre. 1984. *Distinction: A Social Critique of the Judgement of Taste*. Trans. Richard Nice. Cambridge, MA: Harvard University Press.

Brenneis, Donald, and Fred Myers, eds. 1984. *Dangerous Words: Language and Politics in the Pacific*. Prospect Heights, IL: Waveland Press.

Brightman, Robert. 1990. Primitivism in Missinippi Cree Historical Consciousness. *Man* 25 (1): 108–28.

———. 1993. *Grateful Prey: Rock Cree Human-Animal Relationships*. Berkeley: University of California Press.

Brillat-Savarin, Jean Anthelme. 1975 [1826]. *Physiologie du goût*. Paris: Hermann.

Brison, Karen. 1991. Community and Prosperity: Social Movements among the Kwanga of Papua New Guinea. *The Contemporary Pacific* 3:325–55.

———. 1996. Becoming Savage: Western Representations and Cultural Identity in a Sepik Society. *Anthropology and Humanism* 21 (1): 5–18.

Buckley, Thomas. 1987. Dialogue and Shared Authority: Informants as Critics. *Central Issues in Anthropology* 7:13-24.

Bulliet, Richard, and Fawaz Gerges, eds. 2001. *CIAO Responds to the Terrorist Attacks against the United States: A Recruiting Tape of Osama bin Laden*. Available at Columbia International Affairs Online (CIAO) http://www.ciaonet.org/cbr/cbr00/video/cbr_v/cbr_v.html, accessed August 3, 2005.

Burce, Amy. 1991. Tarzan and Colonial Nostalgia in Representations of the Papua New Guinean Nation. Paper presented at the American Anthropological Association Annual Meeting, Chicago, November 22.

Burland, Cottie. 1969. *The Exotic White Man*. Photographs by Werner Forman. London: Weidenfeld and Nicolson.

Burns, Robert. 1989. *The Essential Burns*. Selected and with an Introduction by Robert Creeley. New York: Ecco Press.

Burridge, Kenelm. 1960. *Mambu: A Study of Melanesian Cargo Movements and Their Ideological Background*. New York: Harper and Row.

———. 1969. *Tangu Traditions: A Study of the Way of Life, Mythology, and Developing Experience of a New Guinea People*. Oxford: Oxford University Press.

Bush, Melanie. 2004. *Breaking the Code of Good Intentions: Everyday Forms of Whiteness*. Lanham, MD: Rowman and Littlefield.

Byrnes, G. M. 1989. *Green Shadows: A War History of the Papuan Infantry Battalion*. Newmarket, Australia: published by the author. (Held in Australian War Memorial Library, Canberra.)

Canguilhem, Georges. 1978 [1943]. *On the Normal and the Pathological*. Trans. Carolyn Fawcett. Dordrecht, Holland: Reidel.

Carrier, James. 1995a. Introduction. In Carrier 1995c, 1-32.

———. 1995b. Maussian Occidentalism: Gift and Commodity Systems. In Carrier 1995c, 85-109.

———, ed. 1995c. *Occidentalism: Images of the West*. Oxford: Clarendon Press.

CELCOR (Center for Environmental Law and Community Rights, PNG). 2004. Oro Landowners' Declaration on Large-Scale Commercial Extraction of Natural Resources and the Expansion of Oil Palm Nucleus Estates. Available online at http://www.forestpeoples.org/Briefings/SocialDev/png_landowners_decl_mar04_eng.htm, accessed May 26, 2005. See also http://www.celcor.org.pg/.

Center for Science in the Public Interest. 2005. Cruel Oil: How Palm Oil Harms Health, Rainforest, and Wildlife. Washington, DC: Center for Science in the Public Interest. Available online at http://www.cspinet.org/palmoilreport, accessed September 17, 2005.

Chalk, Andrew. 1986. The King's Reward: The Australian Army's Execution of Papuan and New Guinean "Natives," 1942-1945. BA honours thesis, University of New South Wales, Sydney.

Champion, Ivan. 1978 [1932]. *Across New Guinea from the Fly to the Sepik*. New York: AMS Press.

Chen, Xiaomei. 1992. Occidentalism as Counterdiscourse: "He Shang" in Post-Mao China. *Critical Inquiry* 18:686-712.

Chin, Elizabeth. 2001. *Purchasing Power: Black Kids and American Consumer Culture*. Minneapolis: University of Minnesota Press.

Chinnery, E. W. P., and W. N. Beaver. 1915a. The Movements of the Tribes of the Mambare Division of Northern Papua. In PAR 1914-15, 158-70.

———. 1915b. Notes on the Initiation Ceremonies of the Koko, Papua. *Journal of the Royal Anthropological Institute* 45:69-78.

Chittleborough, Anne. 1976. *A Short History of the Anglican Church in Papua New Guinea*. Stanmore: Australian Board of Missions.

Clark, Jeffrey. 1997. Imagining the State, or Tribalism and the Arts of Memory in the Highlands of Papua New Guinea. In *Narratives of Nation in the South Pacific*, ed. Ton Otto and Nicholas Thomas, 65-90. Amsterdam: Harwood Academic Publishers.

———. 2000. *Steel to Stone: A Chronicle of Colonialism in the Southern Highlands of Papua New Guinea*. Ed. Chris Ballard and Michael Nihill. Oxford: Oxford University Press.

Clifford, James. 1988. *The Predicament of Culture: Twentieth-Century Ethnography, Literature, and Art*. Cambridge, MA: Harvard University Press.

Cohn, Bernard. 1996. *Colonialism and Its Forms of Knowledge: The British in India*. Princeton, NJ: Princeton University Press.

Coll, Steve. 2004. *Ghost Wars: The Secret History of the CIA, Afghanistan, and Bin Laden, from the Soviet Invasion to September 10, 2001*. New York: Penguin.

Comaroff, Jean, and John Comaroff. 1991. *Of Revelation and Revolution, Vol. 1: Christianity, Colonialism, and Consciousness in South Africa*. Chicago: University of Chicago Press.

Comaroff, John, and Jean Comaroff. 1997. *Of Revelation and Revolution, Vol. 2: The Dialectics of Modernity on a South African Frontier*. Chicago: University of Chicago Press.

Commonwealth of Australia. British New Guinea (BNG). 1894-1906. Annual Report(s) with Appendices. (Cited by the years the report covers, rather than the year in which it was published.)

Commonwealth of Australia. Papua (PAR). 1906-22. Annual Report(s). (Cited by the years the report covers, rather than the year in which it was published.)

Conley, Dalton. 1999. *Being Black, Living in the Red: Race, Wealth, and Social Policy in America*. Berkeley: University of California Press.

———. 2000. *Honky*. Berkeley: University of California Press.

Connolly, Bob, and Robin Anderson. 1987. *First Contact: New Guinea's Highlanders Encounter the Outside World*. New York: Viking.

Conrad, Joseph. 1999 [1902]. *Heart of Darkness*. Peterborough, ON: Broadview Press.

Cooper, Frederick, and Ann Laura Stoler, eds. 1997. *Tensions of Empire: Colonial Cultures in a Bourgeois World*. Berkeley: University of California Press.

Cooper, James Fenimore. 1908. Letter: As Others See Us. In *Seventh Year Book*, 45-53. Boston: The Bibliophile Society.

Cowlishaw, Gillian. 2000. Censoring Race in "Post-Colonial" Anthropology. *Critique of Anthropology* 20 (2): 101-23.

Creighton, Millie. 1995. Imaging the Other in Japanese Advertising Campaigns. In Carrier 1995c, 135-60.

Criss, Nur Bilge. 2002. A Short History of Anti-Americanism and Terrorism: The Turkish Case. *Journal of American History* 89 (2): 472-84.

Crocombe, Ron. 1964. Communal Cash-Cropping among the Orokaiva. Port Moresby: New Guinea Research Unit Bulletin No. 4.

———. 1967. Four Orokaiva Cash Croppers. In Papuan Entrepreneurs, 3–22. Port Moresby: New Guinea Research Unit Bulletin No. 16.

Crocombe, Ron, and G. R. Hogbin. 1963. Land, Work and Productivity at Inonda. Port Moresby: New Guinea Research Unit Bulletin No. 2.

Curry, George, and Gina Koczberski. 1999. The Risks and Uncertainties of Migration: An Analysis of Recent Trends amongst the Wosera Abelam of Papua New Guinea. *Oceania* 70 (2): 130–45.

Dakeyne, R. B. 1966. Cooperatives at Yega. In Orokaiva Papers: Miscellaneous Papers on the Orokaiva of North East Papua, 53–68. Port Moresby: New Guinea Research Unit Bulletin No. 13.

———. 1969. The Small Market at Popondetta, Northern Papua. In *Pacific Market-Places*, ed. H. C. Brookfield, 25–34. Canberra: Australian National University Press.

———. 1977. Labour Migration in Papua New Guinea: A Case Study from Northern Papua. In *Change and Movement: Readings on Internal Migration in Papua New Guinea*, ed. R. J. May, 155–61. Canberra: Australian National University Press.

de L'Estoile, Benoît. 1997. The "Natural Preserve of Anthropologists": Social Anthropology, Scientific Planning, and Development. *Social Science Information* 36 (2): 343–76.

Deloria, Philip. 1998. *Playing Indian*. New Haven, CT: Yale University Press.

Denoon, Donald, and Catherine Snowden, eds. 1981. *A Time to Plant and a Time to Uproot: A History of Agriculture in Papua New Guinea*. Port Moresby: Institute of Papua New Guinea Studies.

Derricotte, Toi. 1997. *The Black Notebooks: An Interior Journey*. New York: Norton.

Devereux, George. 1967. *From Anxiety to Method in the Behavioral Sciences*. The Hague: Mouton.

DeVita, Philip, and James Armstrong. 2002. *Distant Mirrors: America as a Foreign Culture*. 3rd ed. Belmont, CA: Wadsworth.

Diamond, Jared. 1997. *Guns, Germs, and Steel: The Fates of Human Societies*. New York: Norton.

Dick, Gordon, and Bob McKillop. 1976. A Brief History of Agricultural Extension and Education in Papua New Guinea. Port Moresby: Department of Primary Industry Extension Bulletin No. 10.

Dickson, Donald. 1971. Government and Missions in Education in Papua and New Guinea with Special Reference to the New Guinea Anglican Mission, 1891 to 1970. Master's thesis, University of Papua and New Guinea Department of History. Port Moresby.

Diderot, Denis. 1964 [1772]. Supplement to Bougainville's "Voyage." In *Rameau's Nephew, and Other Works*, 179–228. Trans. Jaques Barzun and Ralph Bowen. Indianapolis: Bobbs-Merrill.

Dijk, Teun A. van. 1984. *Prejudice in Discourse: An Analysis of Ethnic Prejudice in Cognition and Conversation*. Amsterdam: John Benjamins.

———. 1987. *Communicating Racism: Ethnic Prejudice in Thought and Talk*. Newbury Park, CA: Sage.

Di Leonardo, Micaela. 1998. *Exotics at Home: Anthropologies, Others, American Modernity*. Chicago: University of Chicago Press.

Dinnen, Sinclair. 1999. Militaristic Solutions in a Weak State: Internal Security, Private Contractors, and Political Leadership in Papua New Guinea. *The Contemporary Pacific* 11 (2): 279–303.

———. 2001. *Law and Order in a Weak State: Crime and Politics in Papua New Guinea*. Honolulu: Center for Pacific Islands Studies, School of Hawaiian, Asian, and Pacific Studies, University of Hawai'i Press.

Dirlik, Arif. 1997. *The Postcolonial Aura: Third World Criticism in the Age of Global Capitalism*. Boulder, CO: Westview Press.

———. 1999. Globalism and the Politics of Place. In *Globalisation and the Asia-Pacific: Contested Territories*, ed. Kris Olds, Peter Dicken, Philip Kelly, Lily Kong, and Henry Wai-chung Yeung, 39–56. London: Routledge.

Dobrin, Lise, and Ira Bashkow. 2006. "Pigs for Dance Songs": Reo Fortune's Empathetic Ethnography of the Arapesh Roads. In *Histories of Anthropology Annual*, vol. 2, ed. Regna Darnell and Frederic Gleach. Lincoln: University of Nebraska Press, forthcoming.

Douglas, Bronwen. 1996. Introduction: Fracturing Boundaries of Time and Place in Melanesian Anthropology. *Oceania* 66 (3): 177–88.

Douglas, Mary. 1966. *Purity and Danger*. London: Routledge.

———. 1982. *In the Active Voice*. London: Routledge.

———. 1997 [1971]. Deciphering a Meal. In *Food and Culture: A Reader*, ed. Carole Counihan and Penny Van Esterik, 36–54. New York: Routledge.

Drake, St. Clair. 1987–1990. *Black Folk Here and There: An Essay in History and Anthropology*. 2 vols. Los Angeles: University of California, Los Angeles, Center for Afro-American Studies.

D'Souza, Dinesh. 2002. *What's So Great about America*. Washington, DC: Regnery.

Durkheim, Émile. 1933 [1893]. *The Division of Labor in Society*. Trans. George Simpson. New York: Free Press.

Dyer, Richard. 1997. *White*. New York: Routledge.

Edsall, Thomas, and Mary Edsall. 1991. When the Official Subject Is Presidential Politics, Taxes, Welfare, Crime, Rights, or Values . . . The Real Subject Is Race. *Atlantic Monthly* 267 (May): 53–74.

Ellingson, Ter. 2001. *The Myth of the Noble Savage*. Berkeley: University of California Press.

Ellison, Ralph. 1952. *Invisible Man*. New York: Random House.

Englund, Harri, and James Leach. 2000. Ethnography and the Meta-Narratives of Modernity. *Current Anthropology* 41 (2): 225–39.

Errington, Frederick. 1974. Indigenous Ideas of Order, Time, and Transition in a New Guinea Cargo Movement. *American Ethnologist* 1:255–67.

Errington, Frederick, and Deborah Gewertz. 2001. On the Generification of Culture: From Blow Fish to Melanesian. *Journal of the Royal Anthropological Institute* 7:509–25.

———. 2004. *Yali's Question: Sugar, Culture, and History*. Chicago: University of Chicago Press.

Fabian, Johannes. 1983. *Time and the Other*. New York: Columbia University Press.

———. 2000. *Out of Our Minds: Reason and Madness in the Exploration of Central Africa*. Berkeley: University of California Press.

Fanon, Frantz. 1967 [1952]. *Black Skin, White Masks*. Trans. Charles Markmann. New York: Grove Press.

Farr, Cynthia. 1999. The Interface between Syntax and Discourse in Korafe, a Papuan Language of Papua New Guinea. Canberra: Australian National University, Research School of Pacific and Asian Studies, Pacific Linguistics Series C, no. 148.

Feeley-Harnik, Gillian. 1994. *The Lord's Table: The Meaning of Food in Early Judaism and Christianity*. Washington, DC: Smithsonian Institution Press.

Ferguson, James. 1999. *Expectations of Modernity: Myths and Meanings of Urban Life on the Zambian Copperbelt*. Berkeley: University of California Press.

Fingleton, Jim. 2005a. What Is Land Titles Registration? PNG *Post-Courier*, March 15, 11.

———. 2005b. PNG Has History of Registration. PNG *Post-Courier*, March 22, 11.

———. 2005c. Land Matters for PNG to Decide. PNG *Post-Courier*, March 29, 11.

Fischer, Michael. 1999. Emergent Forms of Life: Anthropologies of Late or Postmodernities. *Annual Review of Anthropology* 28:455-78.

Flint, L. 1924. Report on a Patrol from Buna to Kokoda by A. R. M. Flint. Patrol no. 3 of 1924-25, Kokoda Station, dated October 29, 1924. In NDPR (G91, Item 403).

Foley, William. 1986. *The Papuan Languages of New Guinea*. Cambridge: Cambridge University Press.

Foster, Robert. 1992. Commoditization and the Emergence of Kastam as a Cultural Category: A New Ireland Case in Comparative Perspective. *Oceania* 62:284-94.

———. 1995. *Social Reproduction and History in Melanesia*. Cambridge: Cambridge University Press.

———. 2002. *Materializing the Nation: Commodities, Consumption, and Media in Papua New Guinea*. Bloomington: Indiana University Press.

Foucault, Michel. 1979. *Discipline and Punish: The Birth of the Prison*. Trans. Alan Sheridan. New York: Vintage.

Frankenberg, Ruth. 1993. *White Women, Race Matters: The Social Construction of Whiteness*. Minneapolis: University of Minnesota Press.

———, ed. 1997. *Displacing Whiteness: Essays in Social and Cultural Criticism*. Durham, NC: Duke University Press.

Frazer, James. 1996 [1922]. *The Golden Bough*. Abridged ed. Introduction by George Stocking. New York: Penguin Books.

Friedman, Jonathan. 1993. Will the Real Hawaiian Please Stand: Anthropologists and Natives in the Global Struggle for Identity. *Bijdragen Tot de Taal-, Land-en Volkenkunde* 149:737-67.

Friends of the Earth. 2004a. Greasy Palms—Palm Oil, the Environment, and Big Business. London: Friends of the Earth. Available online at http://www.foe.co.uk/resource/reports/greasy_palms_summary.pdf, accessed September 17, 2005.

———. 2004b. Press Release: UK Government Faces Legal Threat over Palm Oil Investments. August 16. Available online at http://www.foe.co.uk/resource/press_releases/uk_government_faces_legal_16082004.html, accessed September 17, 2005.

———. 2005. Greasy Palms—The Social and Ecological Impacts of Large-Scale Oil Palm Plantation Development in Southeast Asia. London: Friends of the Earth.

Available online at http://www.foe.co.uk/resource/reports/greasy_palms_ impacts.pdf, accessed September 17, 2005.

Friese, Kai. 1999. White Skin, Black Mask. *Transition*, no. 80: 4–17.

Geertz, Clifford. 1973. *The Interpretation of Cultures*. New York: Basic Books.

Gewertz, Deborah, and Frederick Errington. 1991. *Twisted Histories, Altered Contexts: Representing the Chambri in a World System*. Cambridge: Cambridge University Press.

———. 1995. Duelling Currencies in East New Britain: The Construction of Shell Money as National Cultural Property. In Carrier 1995c, 161–91.

———. 1996. On Pepsico and Piety in a Papua New Guinea "Modernity." *American Ethnologist* 23 (3): 476–93.

———. 1998. Sleights of Hand and the Construction of Desire in a Papua New Guinea Modernity. *The Contemporary Pacific* 10:345–68.

———. 1999. *Emerging Class in Papua New Guinea: The Telling of Difference*. Cambridge: Cambridge University Press.

Gibson, John. 2004. *Hating America: The New World Sport*. New York: Regan Books.

Giddens, Anthony. 1991. *Modernity and Self-Identity*. Cambridge: Polity Press.

Gilroy, Paul. 1993. *The Black Atlantic: Modernity and Double Consciousness*. Cambridge, MA: Harvard University Press.

———. 2001. *Against Race: Imagining Political Color beyond the Color Line*. Cambridge, MA: Harvard University Press.

Goddard, Michael. 2005. *The Unseen City: Anthropological Perspectives on Port Moresby, Papua New Guinea*. Canberra: Pandanus Books.

Gould, Stephen Jay. 1996. *The Mismeasure of Man*. Rev. ed. New York: W. W. Norton.

Granatstein, J. L. 1996. *Yankee Go Home? Canadians and Anti-Americanism*. Toronto: HarperCollins.

Gregory, Chris. 1982. *Gifts and Commodities*. London: Academic Press.

Hale, Grace. 1998. *Making Whiteness: The Culture of Segregation in the South, 1890–1940*. New York: Pantheon.

Hall, Gwendolyn Midlo, ed. 1995. *Love, War, and the 96th Engineers (Colored): The World War II New Guinea Diaries of Captain Hyman Samuelson*. Urbana: University of Illinois Press.

Hall, Stuart. 1991. The West and the Rest: Discourse and Power. In *Formations of Modernity*, ed. Stuart Hall and Bram Gieben, 275–320. Cambridge: Polity Press.

Handler, Richard. 1985. On Dialogue and Destructive Analysis: Problems in Narrating Nationalism and Ethnicity. *Journal of Anthropological Research* 41 (2): 171–82.

Haney López, Ian. 1996. *White by Law: The Legal Construction of Race*. New York: New York University Press.

Hannerz, Ulf. 1987. The World in Creolization. *Africa* 57:546–59.

———. 1996. *Transnational Connections: Culture, People, Places*. London: Routledge.

Harding, Thomas. 1973. Land Tenure. In *Anthropology in Papua New Guinea: Readings from the Encyclopaedia of Papua and New Guinea*, ed. Ian Hogbin, 106–21. Carlton: Melbourne University Press.

Harris, G. T. 1981. Papuan Village Agriculture, 1884-1960. In Denoon and Snowden 1981, 129-41.

Harrison, Faye. 1995. The Persistent Power of "Race" in the Cultural and Political Economy of Racism. *Annual Review of Anthropology* 24:47-74.

Hartigan, John. 1999. *Racial Situations: Class Predicaments of Whiteness in Detroit*. Princeton, NJ: Princeton University Press.

Hasluck, Paul. 1976. *A Time for Building: Australian Administration in Papua and New Guinea, 1951-1963*. Carlton, Australia: Melbourne University Press.

Healey, Alan, Ambrose Isoroembo, and Martin Chittleborough. 1969. Preliminary Notes on Orokaiva Grammar. In Papers in New Guinea Linguistics, no. 9, 33-55. Canberra: Australian National University Pacific Linguistics Series A (Occasional Papers), no. 18.

Hegel, G. W. F. 1977 [1807]. *Phenomenology of Spirit*. Trans. A. V. Miller. Oxford: Oxford University Press.

Helms, Mary. 1988. *Ulysses' Sail: An Ethnographic Odyssey of Power, Knowledge, and Geographical Distance*. Princeton, NJ: Princeton University Press.

Heneghan, Bridget. 2003. *Whitewashing America: Material Culture and Race in the Antebellum Imagination*. Jackson: University Press of Mississippi.

Hernandez, Alfredo. 2003. RD Tuna Export Hits US$23.42 Million. *The National* (PNG), September 22.

Hill, Jonathan, ed. 1996. *History, Power, and Identity: Ethnogenesis in the Americas, 1492-1992*. Iowa City: University of Iowa Press.

Hollander, Paul. 1992. *Anti-Americanism: Critiques at Home and Abroad, 1965-1990*. New York: Oxford University Press.

———, ed. 2004. *Understanding Anti-Americanism: Its Origins and Impact at Home and Abroad*. Chicago: Ivan R. Dee.

hooks, bell. 1992. Representing Whiteness in the Black Imagination. In *Black Looks: Race and Representation*, 165-78. Boston: South End Press.

Howlett, Diana. 1965. The European Land Settlement Scheme at Popondetta. Port Moresby: New Guinea Research Unit Bulletin No. 6.

Hudson, W. J., and Jill Daven. 1971. Papua and New Guinea since 1945. In *Australia and Papua New Guinea*, ed. W. J. Hudson, 151-77. Sydney: Sydney University Press.

Hymes, Dell, ed. 1972. *Reinventing Anthropology*. New York: Vintage Books.

Inglis, Amirah. 1975. *The White Women's Protection Ordinance: Sexual Anxiety and Politics in Papua*. New York: St. Martin's Press.

International Bank for Reconstruction and Finance (the World Bank). 1965. *The Economic Development of the Territory of Papua and New Guinea*. Baltimore: International Bank for Reconstruction and Finance.

Iorere, Denys. 1995. Customary Land Is Safe: Henao. PNG *Post-Courier*, July 17, 2.

Iorere, Denys, and Nellie Setepano. 1995. Students Smash, Burn over Land. PNG *Post-Courier*, July 17, 12.

Iteanu, André. 1983a. *La ronde des échanges; De la circulation aux valeurs chez les Orokaiva*. Cambridge: Cambridge University Press.

———. 1983b. Idéologie patrilinéaire ou idéologie de l'anthropologue? *L'Homme* 23:37-55.

———. 1990. The Concept of the Person and the Ritual System: An Orokaiva View. *Man* 25 (1): 25-53.

————. 1991. Person, Society and the Ritual System among the Orokaiva (a reply to critics). *Man* 26 (2): 345–48.

————. 2004. Partial Discontinuity: The Mark of Ritual. *Social Analysis* 48 (2): 98–115.

Iteanu, André, and Eric Schwimmer. 1996. *Parle et je t'écouterai: Récits et traditions des Orokaïva de Papouasie-Nouvelle-Guinée*. Paris: Gallimard.

IUAES (International Union for Anthropological and Ethnological Sciences). 1995. Proposed Replacement Statement for the UNESCO Documents on Biological Aspects of Race. Available online at http://www.leidenuniv.nl/fsw/iuaes/08-race.htm, accessed August 3, 2005.

Jack, Ian. 2002. What We Think of America: Episodes and Opinions from Twenty-Four Writers. *Granta* 77:9–81.

Jackson, John L. 2001. *Harlemworld: Doing Race and Class in Contemporary Black America*. Chicago: University of Chicago Press.

Jackson, Stephen. 1998. Real Men Eat Like Us: "Racial" Categories in New Ireland. *Anthropology Newsletter* 39 (2): 1, 4.

James, Rudi. 1985. *Land Law and Policy in Papua New Guinea*. Port Moresby: Law Reform Commission of Papua New Guinea, Monograph, no. 5.

Jebens, Holger, ed. 2004. *Cargo, Cult, and Culture Critique*. Honolulu: University of Hawai'i Press.

Johnson, L. W. 1983. Colonial Sunset: *Australia and Papua New Guinea 1970–74*. St. Lucia, Australia: University of Queensland Press.

Johnson, Mark. 1993. *Moral Imagination: Implications of Cognitive Science for Ethics*. Chicago: University of Chicago Press.

Jojoga Opeba, Willington. 1976. Taro or Cargo: A Study of the Taro Cult among the Orokaiva of the Northern Province. BA honors thesis, University of Papua and New Guinea Department of History, Port Moresby.

————. 1982. The Migration Traditions of the Sebaga Andere, Binadere and Jaua Tribes of the Orokaiva: The Need for Attention to Religion and Ideology. In *Oral Tradition in Melanesia*, ed. Donald Denoon and Roderic Lacey, 57–68. Port Moresby: University of Papua New Guinea.

————. 1993. The Papuan Fighters Republican Army: What Was It? In *Islands and Enclaves: Nationalisms and Separatist Pressures in Island and Littoral Contexts*, ed. Garry Trompf, 263–88. New Delhi: Sterling Publishers.

Jolly, Margaret. 1991. Gifts, Commodities and Corporeality: Food and Gender in South Pentecost, Vanuatu. *Canberra Anthropology* 14 (1): 45–66.

Jolly, Margaret, and Nicholas Thomas, eds. 1992. The Politics of Tradition in the Pacific. *Oceania* 62 (4): 241–354.

Joseph, John Earl. 1987. *Eloquence and Power: The Rise of Language Standards and Standard Languages*. London: Frances Pinter.

Kabbani, Rana. 1986. *Europe's Myths of Orient: Devise and Rule*. Houndmills, Basingstoke, Hampshire: MacMillan.

Kahn, Miriam. 1986. *Always Hungry, Never Greedy: Food and the Expression of Gender in a Melanesian Society*. Cambridge: Cambridge University Press.

Kakas, Dominic. 1993. Oro Business Houses Threatened: "Send All Foreigners Away." *Times of PNG* (weekly newspaper), February 11, 2.

Keesing, Felix. 1952. The Papuan Orokaiva vs. Mount Lamington: Cultural Shock and Its Aftermath. *Human Organization* 11 (1): 16–22.

Keesing, Roger. 1985. Conventional Metaphors and Anthropological Metaphysics: The Problematic of Cultural Translation. *Journal of Anthropological Research* 41 (2): 201–17.

Kennedy, Raymond. 1945. The Colonial Crisis and the Future. In *The Science of Man in the World Crisis*, ed. Ralph Linton, 306–46. New York: Columbia University Press.

Kepson, Philip. 1995. Soldiers' Move Sparks Panic. *The National* (PNG), July 19, 2.

King, David. 1998. Elites, Suburban Commuters, and Squatters: The Emerging Urban Morphology of Papua New Guinea. In Zimmer-Tamakoshi 1998, 183–94.

Kinzer, Stephen. 2003. *All the Shah's Men: An American Coup and the Roots of Middle East Terror*. Hoboken, NJ: John Wiley.

Kituai, August Ibrum. 1998. *My Gun, My Brother: The World of the Papua New Guinea Colonial Police, 1920–1960*. Honolulu: University of Hawai'i Press.

Knauft, Bruce. 1996. *Genealogies for the Present in Cultural Anthropology*. New York: Routledge.

———, ed. 2002a. *Critically Modern: Alternatives, Alterities, Anthropologies*. Bloomington: Indiana University Press.

———. 2002b. *Exchanging the Past: A Rainforest World of Before and After*. Chicago: University of Chicago Press.

Knowles, Caroline. 2003. *Race and Social Analysis*. London: Sage.

Kochman, Thomas. 1981. *Black and White Styles in Conflict*. Chicago: University of Chicago Press.

Koczberski, Gina, and George Curry. 2004. Divided Communities and Contested Landscapes: Mobility, Development and Shifting Identities in Migrant Destination Sites in Papua New Guinea. *Asia Pacific Viewpoint* 45 (3): 357–71.

Koczberski, Gina, George Curry, and John Connell. 2001. Full Circle or Spiralling Out of Control? State Violence and the Control of Urbanisation in Papua New Guinea. *Urban Studies* 38 (11): 2017–36.

Koczberski, Gina, George Curry, and Katherine Gibson. 2001. Improving Productivity of the Smallholder Oil Palm Sector in Papua New Guinea: A Socioeconomic Study of the Hoskins and Popondetta Schemes. Canberra: Australian National University Research School of Pacific and Asian Studies Department of Human Geography.

Kojève, Alexandre. 1969. *Introduction to the Reading of Hegel: Lectures on the Phenomenology of Spirit*. Trans. James Nichols Jr. New York: Basic Books.

Kolma, Frank Senge. 1998. Colonial Hangover: On the "Masta Complex" That Lives on in Us All. *The National* (PNG), August 21, 4.

Kombako, David. 1995. Land Registration: Think of the Negative Effects (Letter to the Editor). PNG *Post-Courier*, July 17, 10.

Kone, Eric. 1995. Students Misleading People: Lawyer. *The National* (PNG), July 19, 2.

Kramer, Fritz. 1993. *The Red Fez: Art and Spirit Possession in Africa*. Trans. Malcolm Green. London: Verso.

Krech, Shephard. 1999. *The Ecological Indian: Myth and History*. New York: Norton.

Kulick, Don. 1992. *Language Shift and Cultural Reproduction: Socialization, Self, and Syncretism in a Papua New Guinean Village*. Cambridge: Cambridge University Press.

Kurasawa, Fuyuki. 2002. A Requiem for the "Primitive." *History of the Human Sciences* 15 (3): 1–24.

———. 2004. *The Ethnological Imagination: A Cross-Cultural Critique of Modernity*. Minneapolis: University of Minnesota Press.

LaBarre, Weston. 1971. Materials for a History of the Study of Crisis Cults: A Bibliographic Essay. *Current Anthropology* 12 (1): 3–44

Lakau, Andrew. 1995a. Customary Land Reform Needs Careful Handling (Letter to the Editor). PNG *Post-Courier*, July 6, 10.

———. 1995b. An Expert Looks at the Pros and Cons of Customary Ownership of Land (Part I). PNG *Post-Courier*, July 11, 11.

———. 1995c. An Expert Looks at the Pros and Cons of Land (Part II). PNG *Post-Courier*, July 12, 11.

Lakoff, George. 2004. *Don't Think of an Elephant! Know Your Values and Frame the Debate*. White River Junction, VT: Chelsea Green Publishing.

Langmore, Diane. 1989. *Missionary Lives: Papua, 1874–1914*. Honolulu: University of Hawai'i Press.

Larsen, Robert, trans. 1988. *God Ta Duru Jawotoho: The New Testament in the Ehija Dialect of the Orokaiva Language and Today's English Version*. South Holland, IL: World Home Bible League.

Larsen, Robert, and Marlys Larsen. 1985. Orokaiva Language Lessons and Grammar Notes. Ukarumpa, Papua New Guinea: Summer Institute of Linguistics Workpapers in Papua New Guinea Languages, vol. 30.

Lattas, Andrew. 1991. Sexuality and Cargo Cults: The Politics of Gender and Procreation in West New Britain. *Cultural Anthropology* 6 (2): 230–56.

———. 1992a. Skin, Personhood and Redemption: The Double Self in West New Britain Cargo Cults. *Oceania* 63 (1): 27–54.

———. 1992b. Introduction: Hysteria, Anthropological Disclosure and the Concept of the Unconscious—Cargo Cults and the Scientisation of Race and Colonial Power. *Oceania* 63 (1): 1–14.

———. 1998. *Cultures of Secrecy: Reinventing Race in Bush Kaliai Cargo Cults*. Madison: University of Wisconsin Press.

Latukefu, Sione. 1985. The Modern Elite in Papua New Guinea. In *Education and Social Stratification in Papua New Guinea*, ed. Mark Bray and Peter Smith, 31–48. Brisbane: Longman Cheshire.

Lawrence, Peter. 1964. *Road Belong Cargo: A Study of the Cargo Movement in the Southern Madang District, New Guinea*. Manchester: Manchester University Press.

Leavitt, Stephen. 1995. Political Domination and the Absent Oppressor: Images of Europeans in Bumbita Arapesh Narratives. *Ethnology* 34 (3): 177–89.

———. 2000. The Apotheosis of White Men? A Reexamination of Beliefs about Europeans as Ancestral Spirits. *Oceania* 70 (4): 304–16.

———. 2001. The Psychology of Consensus in a Papua New Guinea Christian Revival Movement. In *The Psychology of Cultural Experience*, ed. Carmella Moore and Holly Matthews, 151–72. Cambridge: Cambridge University Press.

Leclerc, Gérard. 1972. *Anthropologie et colonialisme, essai sur l'histoire de l'africanisme (Anthropology and Colonialism: An Essay on the History of Africanist Anthropology)*. Paris: Fayard.

Lederman, Rena. 1981. Sorcery and Social Change in Mendi. *Social Analysis* 8:15–27.

—————. 1986. The Return of Redwoman: Field Work in Highlands New Guinea. In *Women in the Field*, ed. Peggy Golde, 359-88. Berkeley: University of California Press.

Legge, J. D. 1971. The Murray Period: Papua 1906-40. In *Australia and Papua New Guinea*, ed. W. J. Hudson, 32-56. Sydney: Sydney University Press.

Levine, Hal, and Marlene Wolfzahn Levine. 1979. *Urbanization in Papua New Guinea: A Study of Ambivalent Townsmen*. Cambridge: Cambridge University Press.

Lévi-Strauss, Claude. 1966. *The Savage Mind*. Chicago: University of Chicago Press.

—————. 1969. *The Raw and the Cooked*. New York: Harper.

—————. 1974. *Tristes tropiques*. Trans. John and Doreen Weightman. New York: Atheneum.

Lewis, D. C. 1996. *The Plantation Dream: Developing British New Guinea and Papua, 1884-1942*. Canberra: The Journal of Pacific History.

Lewis, Laura. 2003. *Hall of Mirrors: Power, Witchcraft, and Caste in Colonial Mexico*. Durham, NC: Duke University Press.

Liep, John. 1990. Gift Exchange and the Construction of Identity. In *Culture and History in the Pacific*, ed. Jukka Siikala, 164-83. Helsinki: Finnish Anthropological Society Transactions, no. 27.

Lips, Julius. 1966 [1937]. *The Savage Hits Back*. New Hyde Park, NY: University Books.

LiPuma, Edward. 2000. *Encompassing Others: The Magic of Modernity in Melanesia*. Ann Arbor: University of Michigan Press.

Liston Blyth, A. 1922. Patrol Report Number One of 1922-23, Kokoda Station, dated July 7, 1922. In NDPR (G91, Item 401).

Livinai, Judith. 1992. National Community Relations Crisis: Mass Move to Quit Oro (Province) by Milne Bay Settlers. The *Eastern Star* (weekly newspaper of Alotau, Milne Bay Province, PNG), November 23, 1-2, 6.

Lovejoy, Arthur, and George Boas. 1997 [1935]. *Primitivism and Related Ideas in Antiquity*. Baltimore: Johns Hopkins University Press.

Lutton, Nancy. 1978. C. A. W. Monckton: Reprobate Magistrate. In *Papua New Guinea Portraits: The Expatriate Experience*, ed. James Griffin. Canberra: Australian National University Press.

MacGregor, William. 1894. Despatch Reporting Visit of Inspection to the North-East Coast. In BNG 1894, 30-37.

Maclean, Neil. 1998. Mimesis and Pacification: The Colonial Legacy in Papua New Guinea. *History and Anthropology* 11 (1): 75-118.

Maginde, Peter. 1999. Response to Allegations of "Sepik Mess" in East Sepik Province (paid advertisement). The *Toktok* (independent newspaper published in Wewak, East Sepik Province, Papua New Guinea), issue 3, April 30, 6-7.

Mair, Lucy. 1970 [1948]. *Australians in New Guinea*. Rev. ed. Carlton, Australia: Melbourne University Press.

Makdisi, Ussama. 2002. "Anti-Americanism" in the Arab World: An Interpretation of a Brief History. *Journal of American History* 89 (2): 538-57.

Malcomson, Scott. 2000. *One Drop of Blood: The American Misadventure of Race*. New York: Farrar Straus Giroux.

Malinowski, Bronislaw. 1984 [1922]. *Argonauts of the Western Pacific*. Prospect Heights, IL: Waveland Press.

Manderson, Lenore. 1986. Introduction: The Anthropology of Food in Oceania and Southeast Asia. In *Shared Wealth and Symbol: Food, Culture, and Society in Oceania and Southeast Asia*, ed. Lenore Manderson, 1–25. Cambridge: Cambridge University Press.

Marcus, George, and Michael Fischer. 1986. *Anthropology as Cultural Critique.* Chicago: University of Chicago Press.

Marshall, Mac. 1980. A History of Prohibition and Liquor Legislation in Papua New Guinea, 1884–1963. Port Moresby: Institute of Applied Social and Economic Research Discussion Paper, 33.

———, ed. 1982. Through a Glass Darkly: Beer and Modernization in Papua New Guinea. Boroko, Port Moresby: Institute of Applied Social and Economic Research Monograph, 18.

Mason, Peter. 1990. *Deconstructing America: Representations of the Other.* New York: Routledge.

———. 1998. *Infelicites: Representations of the Exotic.* Baltimore: Johns Hopkins University Press.

Massey, Doreen. 1994. *Space, Place, and Gender.* Minneapolis: University of Minnesota Press.

McAlister, Melani. 2001. *Epic Encounters: Culture, Media, and U.S. Interests in the Middle East, 1945–2000.* Berkeley: University of California Press.

McAulay, Lex. 1991. *Blood and Iron: The Battle for Kokoda 1942.* Sydney: Hutchinson Australia.

McCarthy, Dudley. 1959. *South-West Pacific Area—First Year: Kokoda to Wau.* Canberra: Australian War Memorial.

McClintock, Anne. 1995. *Imperial Leather: Race, Gender, and Sexuality in the Colonial Contest.* New York: Routledge.

McPherson, Alan. 2003. *Yankee No! Anti-Americanism in U.S.-Latin American Relations.* Cambridge, MA: Harvard University Press.

Mead, Margaret. 1935. *Sex and Temperament in Three Primitive Societies.* New York: William Morrow.

———. 1938. *The Mountain Arapesh*, vol. 1, *An Importing Culture.* New York: Anthropological Papers of the American Museum of Natural History, vol. 36, pt. 3.

Meggitt, Mervyn. 1967. The Pattern of Leadership among the Mae-Enga of New Guinea. *Anthropological Forum* 2:20–35.

Meigs, Anna. 1984. *Food, Sex, and Pollution: A New Guinea Religion.* New Brunswick, NJ: Rutgers University Press.

Meillassoux, Claude. 1981. *Maidens, Meal, and Money: Capitalism and the Domestic Community.* Cambridge: Cambridge University Press.

Memmi, Albert. 1965 [1957]. *The Colonizer and the Colonized.* Trans. Howard Greenfeld. New York: Orion Press.

Metcalf, Peter. 2001. Global "Disjuncture" and the "Sites" of Anthropology. *Cultural Anthropology* 16 (2): 165–82.

Miller, Daniel. 1994. *Modernity: An Ethnographic Approach.* Oxford: Berg.

Millett, John. 1995. Clearing the Air on Land Registration. PNG *Post-Courier*, July 7, 11.

Mintz, Sidney. 1985. *Sweetness and Power: The Place of Sugar in Modern History.* New York: Penguin Books.

Mitchell, Timothy. 1991. *Colonising Egypt*. Berkeley: University of California Press.

———, ed. 2000. *Questions of Modernity*. Minneapolis: University of Minnesota Press.

———. 2004. American Power and Anti-Americanism in the Middle East. In Ross and Ross 2004, 87–105.

Monckton, C. A. W. 1922a. *Taming New Guinea*. New York: Dodd Mead.

———. 1922b. *Last Days in New Guinea*. New York: Dodd Mead.

Montagu, Ashley. 1972. *Statement on Race: An Annotated Elaboration and Exposition of the Four Statements on Race Issued by the United Nations Educational, Scientific, and Cultural Organization*. New York: Oxford University Press.

Morawetz, D. 1967. Land Tenure Conversion in the Northern District of Papua. Port Moresby: New Guinea Research Unit Bulletin No. 17.

Morgan, Thomas. 1967. *Among the Anti-Americans*. New York: Holt, Rinehart and Winston.

Mosko, Mark. 1999. Magical Money: Commoditization and the Linkage of *Maketsi* ("Market") and *Kangakanga* ("Custom") in Contemporary North Mekeo. In Akin and Robbins 1999, 41–61.

Munn, Nancy. 1986. *The Fame of Gawa: A Symbolic Study of Value Transformation in a Massim (Papua New Guinea) Society*. Durham, NC: Duke University Press.

———. 1990. Constructing Regional Worlds in Experience: Kula Exchange, Witchcraft and Gawan Local Events. *Man* 25:1–17.

Munro, Nancy. 1992. Expatriates in Papua New Guinea with Special Reference to the Filipinos. PhD diss., Sociology, University of New South Wales, Australia.

Murray, J. H. P. 1912a. General Review of the Year 1911–1912. In PAR 1911–12, 5–9.

———. 1912b. *Papua, or British New Guinea*. New York: Charles Scribner's Sons.

———. 1920. *Review of the Australian Administration in Papua from 1907 to 1920*. Port Moresby: Government of Papua. (Included in microfilm of Papua Annual Reports by the Pacific Manuscripts Bureau, PMB 313 Reel 2.)

Nandy, Ashis. 1983. *The Intimate Enemy: Loss and Recovery of Self under Colonialism*. Delhi: Oxford University Press.

———. 1987. *Traditions, Tyranny and Utopias: Essays in the Politics of Awareness*. Delhi: Oxford University Press.

Narokobi, Bernard. 1983. *The Melanesian Way*. Suva, Fiji: University of the South Pacific.

National Geographic Television and Film. 2005. *Guns, Germs, and Steel* (videodisc release of PBS television program based on Diamond 1997). Produced and directed by Tim Lambert and Cassian Harrison. Burbank, CA: Warner Home Video.

Nelson, Hank. 1974. *Papua New Guinea: Black Unity or Black Chaos?* Rev. ed. Ringwood: Penguin Books Australia.

———. 1976. *Black, White, and Gold: Goldmining in Papua New Guinea, 1878–1930*. Canberra: Australian National University Press.

———. 1982. *Taim Bilong Masta: The Australian Involvement with Papua New Guinea*. Sydney: Australian Broadcasting Commission.

Neumann, Klaus. 1994. "In Order to Win Their Friendship": Renegotiating First Contact. *The Contemporary Pacific* 6:111–45.

Newton, Janice. 1982. Feasting for Oil Palm. *Social Analysis* 10:63–78.

———. 1985. Orokaiva Production and Change. Canberra: Australian National University Development Studies Centre Pacific Research Monograph, no. 11.

———. 1989. Women and Modern Marriage among the Orokaivans. *Canberra Anthropology* 12 (1 and 2): 28–47.

Nichols, Peter. 1999. Arbiter of Taste. *University of Chicago Magazine*, April, 20–23.

Norwood, Hugh. 1984. *Port Moresby: Urban Villages and Squatter Areas*. Port Moresby: University of Papua New Guinea Press.

Nyamnjoh, Francis. 1995. *The Disillusioned African*. Limbe, Cameroon: Nooremac Press.

Nyamnjoh, Francis, and Ben Page. 2002. *Whiteman Kontri* and the Enduring Allure of Modernity among Cameroonian Youth. *African Affairs* 101 (405): 607–34.

Ohnuki-Tierney, Emiko. 1995. Structure, Event and Historical Metaphor: Rice and Identities in Japanese History. *Journal of the Royal Anthropological Institute* 1:227–53.

Omi, Michael, and Howard Winant. 1994. *Racial Formation in the United States from the 1960s to the 1990s*. 2nd ed. New York: Routledge.

Opeba, Willington Jojoga. See Jojoga Opeba, Willington.

Oram, N. D. 1976. *Colonial Town to Melanesian City: Port Moresby 1884–1974*. Canberra: Australian National University Press.

Oro Province. [ca. 1978]. Oro Province Development: Past, Present and Future. Pamphlet held in the library of the PNG National Research Institute, Waigani, Port Moresby.

Osborne, Lawrence. 2005. Letter from New Guinea: Strangers in the Forest: Contacting an Isolated People—On a Guided Tour. *The New Yorker*, April 18, 124–40.

Otto, Ton. 1997. After the "Tidal Wave": Bernard Narokobi and the Creation of a Melanesian Way. In *Narratives of Nation in the South Pacific*, ed. Ton Otto and Nicholas Thomas, 33–64. Amsterdam: Harwood Academic Publishers.

Pamba, Kevin. 1995. Students Vote to Boycott Classes. PNG *Post-Courier*, July 18, 2.

Papua New Guinea Institute of Applied Social and Economic Research. 1989. Socio-Economic Impact of Rural Credit (Final Report). Waigani, PNG: Institute of Applied Social and Economic Research.

Papua New Guinea National Statistical Office (NSO). 1993. 1990 National Population Census, Final Figures, Census Unit Populations, Northern Province. Port Moresby: National Statistical Office.

———. 1994a. Report on the 1990 National Population and Housing Census in Northern Province. Port Moresby: National Statistical Office.

———. 1994b. Report on the 1990 National Population and Housing Census in Papua New Guinea. Port Moresby: National Statistical Office.

Pattillo-McCoy, Mary. 1999. *Black Picket Fences: Privilege and Peril among the Black Middle Class*. Chicago: University of Chicago Press.

Pels, Peter, and Oscar Salemink, eds. 1999. *Colonial Subjects: Essays on the Practical History of Anthropology*. Ann Arbor: University of Michigan Press.

Perman, Sarah, with Laurent Duvillier, Natacha David, John Eden, and Samuel Grumiau. 2004. Behind the Brand Names: Working Conditions and Labour Rights in Export Processing Zones. Brussels: International Confederation of Free Trade Unions.

Pew Global Attitudes Project. 2005. Global Opinion: The Spread of Anti-Americanism. In *Trends 2005*, 105–22. Washington, DC: Pew Research Center.

Pierpont, Claudia Roth. 2004. The Measure of America: How a Rebel Anthropologist Waged War on Racism. *The New Yorker*, March 8, 48–63.

Pigg, Stacey Leigh. 1992. Inventing Social Categories through Place: Social Representations and Development in Nepal. *Comparative Studies in Society and History* 34:491–513.

Pike, Andrew, Hank Nelson, and Gavan Daws. 1982. *Angels of War: The People of Papua New Guinea and World War Two*. Documentary film. Port Moresby: Institute of PNG Studies.

Pilcher, Jeffrey. 1998. *¡Que vivan los tamales! Food and the Making of Mexican Identity*. Albuquerque: University of New Mexico Press.

Prados, John. 2002. Notes on the CIA's Secret War in Afghanistan. *Journal of American History* 89 (2): 485–97.

Prakash, Gyan. 1995. *After Colonialism: Imperial Histories and Postcolonial Displacements*. Princeton, NJ: Princeton University Press.

Prashad, Vijay. 2000. *The Karma of Brown Folk*. Minneapolis: University of Minnesota Press.

Proctor, Robert. 2003. Three Roots of Human Recency: Molecular Anthropology, the Refigured Acheulean, and the UNESCO Response to Auschwitz. *Current Anthropology* 44 (2): 213–40.

Rabinow, Paul. 1989. *French Modern: Norms and Forms of the Social Environment*. Cambridge, MA: MIT Press.

Rapport, Nigel, and Andrew Dawson, eds. 1998. *Migrants of Identity: Perceptions of "Home" in a World in Movement*. Oxford: Berg.

Rasmussen, Birgit Brander, Eric Klineberg, Irene J. Nexica, and Matt Wray. 2001. *The Making and Unmaking of Whiteness*. Durham, NC: Duke University Press.

Razack, Sherene. 1998. *Looking White People in the Eye: Gender, Race, and Culture in Courtrooms and Classrooms*. Toronto: University of Toronto Press.

Rebhun, Linda-Anne. 1999. *The Heart Is Unknown Country: Love in the Changing Economy of Northeast Brazil*. Stanford, CA: Stanford University Press.

Reed, Adam. 1999. Anticipating Individuals: Modes of Vision and their Social Consequence in a Papua New Guinea Prison. *Journal of the Royal Anthropological Institute* 5 (1): 43–56

———. 2003. *Papua New Guinea's Last Place: Experiences of Constraint in a Postcolonial Prison*. New York: Berghahn Books.

Reggio, Godfrey. 2002 [1983]. *Koyaanisqatsi: Life Out of Balance*. Film. Santa Monica, CA: MGM Home Entertainment.

Rew, Alan. 1974. *Social Images and Process in Urban New Guinea: A Study of Port Moresby*. St. Paul: West Publishing. American Ethnological Society Monograph, 57.

Rimoldi, Max. 1966. Land Tenure and Land Use among the Mount Lamington Orokaiva. Port Moresby: New Guinea Research Unit Bulletin No. 11.

Rinder, Lawrence. 2003. *The American Effect: Global Perspectives on the United States, 1990–2003*. New York: Whitney Museum of American Art.

Robbins, Joel. 1996. "Welcome to Big Bush Urapmin": Development, Labor, and the Construction of Nature in a Papua New Guinea Society. Paper presented at the American Anthropological Association Annual Meeting, San Francisco.

———. 1997a. 666, or Why is the Millennium on the Skin? Morality, the State, and Epistemology among the Urapmin of Papua New Guinea. In *Millennial Markers*, ed. P. J. Stewart and A. J. Strathern, 35–58. Townsville, Australia: James Cook University, Centre for Pacific Studies.

———. 1997b. "When Do You Think the World Will End?": Globalization, Apocalyptism, and the Moral Perils of Fieldwork in "Last New Guinea." *Anthropology and Humanism* 22:6–30.

———. 1998. On Reading "World News": Apocalyptic Narrative, Negative Nationalism, and Transnational Christianity in a Papua New Guinea Society. *Social Analysis* 42 (2): 103–30.

———. 2004a. *Becoming Sinners:* Christianity and Moral Torment in a Papua New Guinea Society. Berkeley: University of California Press.

———. 2004b. The Globalization of Pentecostal and Charismatic Christianity. *Annual Review of Anthropology* 33:117–43.

———. 2004c. Introduction: Global Religions, Pacific Island Transformations. *Journal of Ritual Studies* 15 (2): 7–12.

———. 2004d. Whatever Became of Revival? From Charismatic Movement to Charismatic Church in a Papua New Guinea Society. *Journal of Ritual Studies* 15 (2): 79–90.

Roberts, Byam. [ca. 1986]. Where the Good Boys Come From: The Story of Martyrs School. Popondetta: The Martyrs School.

Rockquemore, Kerry Ann, and David Brunsma. 2002. *Beyond Black: Biracial Identity in America.* Thousand Oaks, CA: Sage.

Rodrik, Dani. 1997. *Has Globalization Gone Too Far?* Washington, DC: Institute for International Economics.

Roediger, David. 1998. *Black on White: Black Writers on What It Means to be White.* New York: Schocken Books.

———. 1999. *The Wages of Whiteness: Race and the Making of the American Working Class.* Rev. ed. London: Verso.

———. 2002. *Colored White: Transcending the Racial Past.* Berkeley: University of California Press.

Rofel, Lisa. 1999. *Other Modernities: Gendered Yearnings in China after Socialism.* Berkeley: University of California Press.

Roger, Philippe. 2005. *The American Enemy: The History of French Anti-Americanism.* Trans. Sharon Bowman. Chicago: University of Chicago Press.

Rosaldo, Renato. 1989. *Culture and Truth: The Remaking of Social Analysis.* Boston: Beacon Press.

Roscoe, Paul. 1999. The Return of the Ambush: *"Raskolism"* in Rural Yangoru, East Sepik Province. *Oceania* 69:171–83.

Rosenblatt, Daniel. 1997. The Antisocial Skin: Structure, Resistance, and "Modern Primitive" Adornment in the United States. *Cultural Anthropology* 12:287–334.

———. 2004. An Anthropology Made Safe for Culture: Patterns of Practice and the Politics of Difference in Ruth Benedict. *American Anthropologist* 106 (3): 459–72.

Rosenstiel, Annette. 1983. *Red and White: Indian Views of the White Man, 1492–1982.* New York: Universe Books.

Ross, Andrew, and Kristin Ross, eds. 2004. *Anti-Americanism.* New York: New York University Press.

Rouse, Roger. 1995. Thinking through Transnationalism: Notes on the Cultural Politics of Class Relations in the Contemporary United States. *Public Culture* 7(2): 353-402.

Royster, Deidre. 2003. *Race and the Invisible Hand: How White Networks Exclude Black Men from Blue-Collar Jobs.* Berkeley: University of California Press.

Rubin, Barry, and Judith Colp Rubin. 2004. *Hating America: A History.* New York: Oxford University Press.

Rubinstein, Alvin, and Donald Smith, eds. 1985. *Anti-Americanism in the Third World: Implications for U.S. Foreign Policy.* New York: Praeger.

Rumsey, Alan. 1999. The White Man as Cannibal in the New Guinea Highlands. In *The Anthropology of Cannibalism,* ed. Lawrence Goldman, 105-21. Westport, CT: Bergin and Garvey.

Rural Industry Weekly. 2005. Oil Mill Upgrade Progressing Smoothly. PNG *Post-Courier,* March 31. Available online at http://www.postcourier.com.pg/20050331/rural07, accessed August 3, 2005.

Rutherford, Danilyn. 2003. *Raiding the Land of the Foreigners.* Princeton, NJ: Princeton University Press.

Sahlins, Marshall. 1976. *Culture and Practical Reason.* Chicago: University of Chicago Press.

———. 1992. The Economics of Develop-Man in the Pacific. *Res* 21:13-25.

———. 1993. "Cery Cery Fuckabede." *American Ethnologist* 20:848-67.

———. 1997. The Indigenization of Modernity. Paper presented at the American Anthropological Association Annual Meeting, Washington, DC, November 20.

———. 2000. *Culture in Practice: Selected Essays.* New York: Zone Books.

Said, Edward. 1978. *Orientalism.* New York: Vintage Books.

———. 1989. Representing the Colonized: Anthropology's Interlocutors. *Critical Inquiry* 15 (2): 205-25.

———. 1993. *Culture and Imperialism.* New York: Knopf.

Sapir, Edward. 1949 [1932]. Cultural Anthropology and Psychiatry. In *Selected Writings in Language, Culture, and Personality,* ed. David Mandlebaum, 509-21. Berkeley: University of California Press.

Sax, William. 1998. The Hall of Mirrors: Orientalism, Anthropology, and the Other. *American Anthropologist* 100 (2): 292-301.

Schieffelin, Bambi. 1990. *The Give and Take of Everyday Life: Language Socialization of Kaluli Children.* Cambridge: Cambridge University Press.

Schieffelin, Edward, and Robert Crittenden. 1991. *Like People You See in a Dream: First Contact in Six Papuan Societies.* Stanford, CA: Stanford University Press.

Schneider, David. 1984. *A Critique of the Study of Kinship.* Ann Arbor: University of Michigan Press.

Schor, Juliet. 1998. *The Overspent American: Upscaling, Downshifting, and the New Consumer.* New York: Basic Books.

Schumaker, Lyn. 2001. *Africanizing Anthropology: Fieldwork, Networks, and the Making of Cultural Knowledge in Central Africa.* Durham, NC: Duke University Press.

Schwimmer, Eric. 1969. Cultural Consequences of a Volcanic Eruption Experienced by the Mount Lamington Orokaiva. Eugene, Oregon: University of

Oregon Department of Anthropology, Comparative Study of Cultural Change and Stability in Displaced Communities in the Pacific, Report no. 9.

———. 1973. *Exchange in the Social Structure of the Orokaiva: Traditional and Emergent Ideologies in the Northern District of Papua.* New York: St. Martin's Press.

———. 1977. What Did the Eruption Mean? In *Exiles and Migrants in Oceania,* ed. Michael Lieber, 296-341. Honolulu: University of Hawai'i Press.

———. 1979. The Self and the Product: Concepts of Work in Comparative Perspective. In *Social Anthropology of Work,* ed. Sandra Wallman, 287-315. London: Academic Press. (ASA Monograph, 19.)

———. 1982. Betelnut: The Beer of the Orokaiva. In Marshall 1982, 319-23.

———. 1986. Le discours politique d'une communauté Papoue. *Anthropologie et Sociétés* 10:137-58.

———. 1987. Gramsci, History and the Future Economy. In *Beyond the New Economic Anthropology,* ed. John Clammer, 78-120. New York: St. Martin's.

Scott, David. 1999. *Refashioning Futures: Criticism after Postcoloniality.* Princeton, NJ: Princeton University Press.

Scott, James. 1998. *Seeing like a State: How Certain Schemes to Improve the Human Condition Have Failed.* New Haven, CT: Yale University Press.

Segal, Dan. 1993. "Race" and "Colour" in Pre-Independence Trinidad and Tobago. In *Trinidad Ethnicity,* ed. Kevin Yelvington, 81-115. Knoxville: University of Tennessee Press.

Seneviratne, H. L. 1992. Food Essence and the Essence of Experience. In *The Eternal Food,* ed. R. S. Khare, 179-200. Albany: State University of New York Press.

Shanklin, Eugenia. 1999. The Profession of the Color Blind: Sociocultural Anthropology and Racism in the 21st Century. *American Anthropologist* 100:669-79.

Sheriff, Robin. 2001. *Dreaming Equality: Color, Race, and Racism in Urban Brazil.* New Brunswick, NJ: Rutgers University Press.

Shiraev, Eric, and Vladislav Zubok. 2000. *Anti-Americanism in Russia: From Stalin to Putin.* New York: Palgrave.

Simmel, Georg. 1990 [1900]. *The Philosophy of Money.* Ed. David Frisby. Trans. Tom Bottomore and David Frisby. London: Routledge.

Sinduhije, Alexis. 1998. Welcome to America. *Transition,* no. 78: 4-23.

Sivaramakrishnan, K., and Arun Agrawal, eds. 2003. *Regional Modernities: The Cultural Politics of Development in India.* Stanford, CA: Stanford University Press.

Smedley, Audrey. 1999. *Race in North America: Origin and Evolution of a Worldview.* 2nd ed. Boulder, CO: Westview Press.

Smith, Michael French. 1994. *Hard Times on Kairiru Island: Poverty, Development, and Morality in a Papua New Guinea Village.* Honolulu: University of Hawai'i Press.

———. 1995. The Cultural Politics of Cooperation: An American Corporation and a Papua New Guinea Village. *Ethnology* 34:191-99.

———. 1996. The World Bank PNG Land Registration Scheme. Posting on ASAONET, Association for Social Anthropology Bulletin Board (asaonet@ listserv.uic.edu), accessed January 18. Ms. in files of author.

Smith, Samuel Stanhope. 1787. *An Essay on the Causes of the Variety of Complexion and Figure in the Human Species*. Philadelphia: Robert Aitken. Available online at http://opac.newsbank.com/select/evans/20712 (requires user name and password), accessed September 8, 2005.

Soueif, Ahdaf. 2002. Untitled. In Jack 2002, 78–81.

Spate, O. H. K. 1966. Education and Its Problems. In *New Guinea on the Threshold: Aspects of Social, Political, and Economic Development*, ed. E. K. Fisk, 117–34. Canberra: Australian National University Press.

Stasch, Rupert. 2001. Giving Up Homicide: Korowai Experience of Witches and Police (West Papua). *Oceania* 72 (1): 33–52.

Steinberg, Stephen. 1995. *Turning Back: The Retreat from Racial Justice in American Thought and Policy*. Boston: Beacon Press.

Stephan, Alexander, ed. 2005. *Americanization and Anti-Americanism: The German Encounter with American Culture after 1945*. New York: Berghahn Books.

Stephen, Michele. 1995. *A'aisa's Gifts: A Study of Magic and the Self*. Berkeley: University of California Press.

Stocking, George. 1968. *Race, Culture, and Evolution: Essays in the History of Anthropology*. Rev. ed. 1982. Chicago: University of Chicago Press.

———. 1974. *The Shaping of American Anthropology, 1883–1911: A Franz Boas Reader*. New York: Basic Books.

———. 1987. *Victorian Anthropology*. New York: Free Press.

———., ed. 1991. *Colonial Situations: Essays on the Contextualization of Ethnographic Knowledge*. Madison: University of Wisconsin Press.

———. 1992. *The Ethnographer's Magic and Other Essays in the History of Anthropology*. Madison: University of Wisconsin Press.

Stoler, Ann. 1995. *Race and the Education of Desire: Foucault's History of Sexuality and the Colonial Order of Things*. Durham, NC: Duke University Press.

———. 2002. *Carnal Knowledge and Imperial Power: Race and the Intimate in Colonial Rule*. Berkeley: University of California Press.

Strathern, Andrew. 1975. Veiled Speech in Mount Hagen. In *Political Language and Oratory in Traditional Society*, ed. Maurice Bloch, 185–203. London: Academic Press.

Strathern, Marilyn. 1975. No Money on Our Skins: Hagen Migrants in Port Moresby. Port Moresby: New Guinea Research Unit Bulletin No. 61.

———. 1981. Self-Interest and the Social Good: Some Implications of Hagen Gender Imagery. In *Sexual Meanings: The Cultural Construction of Gender and Sexuality*, edited by Sherry B. Ortner and Harriet Whitehead, 166–91. Cambridge: Cambridge University Press.

———. 1988. *The Gender of the Gift*. Berkeley: University of California Press.

———. 1990. Artefacts of History: Events and the Interpretation of Images. In *Culture and History in the Pacific*, ed. Jukka Siikala, 25–43. Helsinki: Finnish Anthropological Society Transactions, no. 27.

———. 1992. The Decomposition of an Event. *Cultural Anthropology* 7:244–54.

———. 2004. The Whole Person and Its Artifacts. *Annual Review of Anthropology* 33:1–19.

Sutton, David. 2001. *Remembrance of Repasts: An Anthropology of Food and Memory*. Oxford: Berg.

Swartz, Marc. 1961. Negative Ethnocentrism. *Journal of Conflict Resolution* 5 (1): 75–81.

Sykes, Karen. 1999. After the "Raskol" Feast: Youths' Alienation in New Ireland, Papua New Guinea. *Critique of Anthropology* 19 (2): 157–74.

Taaffe, Stephen. 1998. *MacArthur's Jungle War: The 1944 New Guinea Campaign*. Lawrence: University Press of Kansas.

Tai, Baeau. 2004. IRC [Internal Revenue Commission]: Sale of "777" Not Illegal: Tariff on Popular Mackerel Brand Cut to 20 Per Cent from 70 Per Cent. *The National* (PNG), January 12.

Táíwò, Olúfẹ́mi. 2003. This Prison Called My Skin: On Being Black in America. In *Problematizing Blackness: Self-Ethnographies by Black Immigrants to the United States*, ed. Percy Claude Hintzen and Jean Muteba Rahier, 35–51. New York: Routledge.

Tambiah, Stanley. 1985 [1969]. Animals Are Good to Think and Good to Prohibit. In *Culture, Thought, and Social Action: An Anthropological Perspective*, 169–211. Cambridge, MA: Harvard University Press.

Tannos, Jonathan. 1995a. Haiveta—Rescue Loans on the Way. PNG *Post-Courier*, July 17, 1–2.

———. 1995b. Proposed Plan Only an Option: Minister. PNG *Post-Courier*, July 18, 2.

Tararia, Almah. 2005. Land Registration Is Alienation. PNG *Post-Courier*, December 4, 11.

Taussig, Michael. 1993. *Mimesis and Alterity: A Particular History of the Senses*. New York: Routledge.

Tavakoli-Targhi, Mohamad. 2001. *Refashioning Iran: Orientalism, Occidentalism, and Historiography*. Houndmills, Basingstoke, Hampshire: Palgrave.

Tcherkézoff, Serge. 1997. Culture, nation, société: Changements secondaires et bouleversements fondamentaux au Samoa occidental. Vers un modèle pour l'étude des dynamiques culturelles. In Tcherkézoff and Douaire-Marsaudon 1997, 309–73.

Tcherkézoff, Serge, and Françoise Douaire-Marsaudon. *Le Pacifique-Sud aujourd'hui: Identités et transformations culturelles*. Paris: CNRS éditions, 1997.

Temane, Tande. 1995. Backing Grows for Protesters. *The National* (PNG), July 19, 3.

———. 1998. A Destiny Controlled by the Super Powers (on Bernard Narokobi press conference). PNG *Post-Courier*, May 26.

Thomas, Nicholas. 1992. The Inversion of Tradition. *American Ethnologist* 19:213–32.

———. 1997. Nations' Endings: From Citizenship to Shopping? In *Narratives of Nation in the South Pacific*, ed. Ton Otto and Nicholas Thomas, 211–19. Amsterdam: Harwood Academic Publishers.

———. 1999. Introduction. In *Double Vision: Art Histories and Colonial Histories in the Pacific*, ed. Nicholas Thomas and Diane Losche, 1–17. Cambridge: Cambridge University Press.

Todorov, Tzvetan. 1984. *The Conquest of America: The Question of the Other*. Trans. Richard Howard. New York: Harper and Row.

Torgovnick, Marianna. 1990. *Gone Primitive: Savage Intellects, Modern Lives*. Chicago: University of Chicago Press.

Turner, Mark. 1990. *Papua New Guinea: The Challenge of Independence*. Ringwood: Penguin Books Australia.

Tuzin, Donald. 1997. *The Cassowary's Revenge: The Life and Death of Masculinity in a New Guinea Society*. Chicago: University of Chicago Press.

Tvedt, Terje. 1998. *Angels of Mercy or Development Diplomats? NGOs and Foreign Aid*. Trenton, NJ: Africa World Press.

Tyrie, G., and P. Bleeker. 1990. The Popondetta Oil Palm Scheme: Soil and Management Factors in Relation to Yield Data. Konedobu, PNG: Department of Agriculture and Livestock Technical Report 90/2.

United Kingdom Parliament. 2004. House of Commons Hansard Written Answers for 16 Sept 2004 (pt. 17). Available online at http://www.parliament.the-stationery-office.co.uk/pa/cm200304/cmhansrd/vo040916/text/40916w17.htm, accessed September 17, 2005.

United Nations Food and Agriculture Organization (FAO). 1987. Papua New Guinea: Oro Province Nucleus Estate and Smallholder Project Identification Mission. Rome: FAO/World Bank Cooperative Programme Investment Centre Report No. 168/87.

United Nations Trusteeship Council. 1962. *Report of the United Nations Visiting Mission to the Trust Territory of New Guinea*. New York: United Nations. (The "Foot Report").

Van Ausdale, Debra, and Joe Feagin. 2001. *The First R: How Children Learn Race and Racism*. Lanham, MD: Rowman and Littlefield.

Voll, John. 2001. Bin Laden and the Logic of Power. In *CIAO Responds to the Terrorist Attacks against the United States: A Recruiting Tape of Osama bin Laden: Excerpts and Analyses*. Available at Columbia International Affairs Online (CIAO), http://www.ciaonet.org/cbr/cbr00/video/cbr_v/cbr_v_2c.html, accessed August 3, 2005.

Waddell, E. W., and P. A. Krinks. 1968. The Organization of Production and Distribution among the Orokaiva. Port Moresby: New Guinea Research Unit Bulletin No. 24.

Wagner, Roy. 1974. Are There Social Groups in the New Guinea Highlands? In *Frontiers of Anthropology*, ed. Murray Leaf, 95-122. New York: Van Nostrand.

———. 1975. *The Invention of Culture*. Chicago: University of Chicago Press.

Wagner, Venise. 1996. Crossover: The Rest of America Is Still Deeply Divided by Race, So How Come So Many White Suburban Youths Want to Be Black? A Special Report. *The Examiner* (San Francisco), November 10. Available online at http://www.sfgate.com/cgi-bin/article.cgi?file=/examiner/archive/1996/11/10/MAGAZINE6031.dtl, accessed August 2, 2005.

Waibauru, Jessie. 1995. Students on Rampage over World Bank Reforms. *Saturday Independent* (PNG), July 15, 1-2.

Waiko, John Douglas Dademo. 1970. A Payback Murder: The Green Bloodbath. *Journal of the Papua and New Guinea Society* 4 (2): 27-35.

———. 1972. Oro Oro: A History of the Binandere People. BA honors thesis, University of Papua and New Guinea Department of History, Port Moresby.

———. 1982. Be Jijimo: A History According to the Tradition of the Binandere People of Papua New Guinea. PhD diss., Australian National University, Canberra.

————. 1983. Na Binandere, Imo Averi? We Are Binandere, Who Are You? Paper presented at the Symposium on Mobility, Identity, and Policy in the Island Pacific, 15th Pacific Science Congress, Section C (Geography), Dunedin, New Zealand, February 2–8.

————. 1989. Australian Administration under the Binandere Thumb. In *Papua New Guinea: A Century of Colonial Impact, 1884–1984*, ed. Sione Latukefu, 75–108. Boroko, PNG: National Research Institute and the University of Papua New Guinea.

————. 1990. Binandere Forced Labour: Papua New Guinea. In *Labour in the South Pacific*, ed. C. Moore, J. Leckie, and D. Munro, 181–85. Townsville, Australia: James Cook University.

————. 1993. *A Short History of Papua New Guinea*. Melbourne: Oxford University Press.

Waram, Ruth. 1995. Land Law Overhaul Nearly Ready. PNG *Post-Courier*, June 23, 3.

Wardlow, Holly. 1998. Transformations of Desire: Jealousy and Resentment among the Huli of Papua New Guinea. Paper presented at the American Anthropological Association Annual Meeting, Philadelphia.

————. 2002a. Headless Ghosts and Roving Women: Specters of Modernity in Papua New Guinea. *American Ethnologist* 29 (1): 5–32.

————. 2002b. "Hands-Up"-ing Buses and Harvesting Cheese-Pops: Gendered Mediation of Modern Disjuncture in Melanesia. In Knauft 2002a, 144–72.

Ware, Vron, and Les Back. 2002. *Out of Whiteness: Color, Politics, and Culture*. Chicago: University of Chicago Press.

Watson, James, ed. 1997. *Golden Arches East: McDonald's in East Asia*. Stanford, CA: Stanford University Press.

Weisbuch, Robert. 2004. The Other Presidential Non-Issue. *Woodrow Wilson in Focus*, Fall, 1–2.

Weismantel, Mary. 1988. *Food, Gender, and Poverty in the Ecuadorian Andes*. Philadelphia: University of Pennsylvania Press.

————. 2001. *Cholas and Pishtacos: Stories of Race and Sex in the Andes*. Chicago: University of Chicago Press.

Wesch, Michael. 2006. Witchcraft, Statecraft, and the Challenge of "Community" in Central New Guinea. PhD diss., Anthropology, University of Virginia.

West, Francis. 1968. *Hubert Murray: The Australian Pro-Consul*. Melbourne: Oxford University Press.

Wetherell, David. 1977. *Reluctant Mission: The Anglican Church in Papua New Guinea, 1891–1942*. St. Lucia, Australia: University of Queensland Press.

White, Leslie. 2005. *Hii ni Dunia* "This Is the World": Youth Street Language on Poverty, Inequality, and Disease in Kigoma, Tanzania. BA honors thesis in Anthropology, University of Virginia. Charlottesville.

White, Shane. 1998. *Stylin': African American Expressive Culture from Its Beginnings to the Zoot Suit*. Ithaca, NY: Cornell University Press.

Whitten, Norman. 1996. Ethnogenesis. In *The Encyclopedia of Cultural Anthropology*, ed. D. Levinson and M. Ember. New York: Henry Holt.

Wilk, Richard. 1995a. The Local and the Global in the Political Economy of Beauty: From Miss Belize to Miss World. *Review of International Political Economy* 2 (1): 117–34.

————. 1995b. Learning to Be Local in Belize: Global Systems of Common Difference. In *Worlds Apart: Modernity through the Prism of the Local*, ed. Daniel Miller, 110-33. London: Routledge.

Williams, F. E. 1928. *Orokaiva Magic*. London: Oxford University Press.

————. 1930. *Orokaiva Society*. London: Oxford University Press.

Willie, Sarah Susannah. 2003. *Acting Black: College, Identity, and the Performance of Race*. New York: Routledge.

Willson, Margaret. 1989. The Generous Face Concepts of Trade and Personhood among the Papua New Guinea Chinese. PhD diss., Anthropology, University of London.

Wilson, Darryl. 1969. The Binandere Language Family. In *Papers in New Guinea Linguistics*, no. 9, 65-86. Canberra: Australian National University Pacific Linguistics Series A (Occasional Papers), no. 18.

————. 1974. Suena Grammar. Ukarumpa, Papua New Guinea: Summer Institute of Linguistics Workpapers in Papua New Guinea Languages, no. 8.

Wimsatt, William Upski. 1994. *Bomb the Suburbs*. 2nd ed. New York: Soft Skull Press.

Winant, Howard. 2001a. *The World Is a Ghetto: Race and Democracy since World War II*. New York: Basic Books.

————. 2001b. White Racial Projects. In *The Making and Unmaking of Whiteness*, ed. Birgit Brander Rasmussen, Eric Klineberg, Irene Nexica, and Matt Wray, 97-112. Durham, NC: Duke University Press.

Witt, Doris. 2004. *Black Hunger: Soul Food and America*. Minneapolis: University of Minnesota Press.

Wood, Mike. 1995. "White Skins," "Real People," and "Chinese" in Some Spatial Transformations of the Western Province, P.N.G. *Oceania* 66:23-50.

World Bank. 1965. *The Economic Development of the Territory of Papua and New Guinea: Report of a Mission Organized by the International Bank for Reconstruction and Development at the Request of the Government of the Commonwealth of Australia*. Baltimore: Johns Hopkins Press.

————. 1988. *Papua New Guinea: Policies and Prospects for Sustained and Broad-Based Growth*. 2 vols. Washington, DC: The World Bank.

————. 1999. Memorandum of the President of the International Bank for Reconstruction and Development to the Executive Directors on a Country Assistance Strategy of the World Bank Group for the Independent State of Papua New Guinea. Washington, DC: The World Bank Report, no. 19590-PNG.

Wormsley, William. 1993. *The White Man Will Eat You! An Anthropologist among the Imbonggu of New Guinea*. New York: Harcourt Brace.

Worsley, Peter. 1968 [1957]. *The Trumpet Shall Sound: A Study of "Cargo" Cults in Melanesia*. 2nd ed., augmented. New York: Schocken Books.

Wu, David. 1982. *The Chinese in Papua New Guinea, 1880-1980*. Hong Kong: Chinese University Press.

Wurm, Stephen. 1982. *Papuan Languages of Oceania*. Tübingen, Germany: Gunter Narr.

Yadi, Abby. 1995. World Bank Reforms Mean "New-Look" PNG. *Saturday Independent* (PNG), July 8, 1-2.

Yalu, Kemes. 1993. Oil Palm Growers Fleeing: Magistrate. PNG *Post-Courier*, January 21, 2.

Yokota, Kariann Akemi. 2004. Not Written in Black and White: American National Identity and the Curious Color Transformation of Henry Moss. *Common-Place: The Interactive Journal of Early American Life* 4 (2). Available online at http://www.common-place.org/vol-04/no-02/yokota/, accessed September 17, 2005.

Young, Michael. 1971. *Fighting with Food: Leadership, Values, and Social Control in a Massim Society.* Cambridge: Cambridge University Press.

Young, Robert C. 1995. *Colonial Desire: Hybridity in Theory, Culture, and Race.* London: Routledge.

Zimmer-Tamakoshi, Laura. 1996. Patterns of Culture in the Tower of Babel: Letters from Port Moresby, Papua New Guinea. *Journal de la Société des Océanistes* 103 (2): 163–71.

———, ed. 1998. *Modern Papua New Guinea.* Kirksville, MO: Thomas Jefferson University Press.

Index

Papua New Guinea, 2; 1890s to 1963, 42-46; 1963 to 1983, 46-48; 1983 to the present, 48-53; construction of whitemen as national phenomenon, 22-23, 220-34; corruption, 227-28, 230; expatriate population, 6, 48-51, 120-21, 216, 218, 266nn19, 20, 266-67n22, 273n16; government, 47, 51-52, 61; independence from Australia, 46; legal system, 229; Oro Province, 26-27; regional world, 32-37; segregation, 141-42; self-critique in, 14, 231-34, 257, 285n15; stereotype of insularity, 32-33; urban experience, 214-20; weak state, 48. *See also* land tenure

Papuan Infantry Battalion, 44

past, 97; continuity with in taro culture, 182-87; making things last in time, 67, 70-72. *See also* nostalgia for colonial era

paternalism, 42-44, 59, 228, 268n29

Patillo-McCoy, Mary, 251-52

patrilineal inheritance, 41, 268n29

patriotic public discourse (America), 23-24

Peace Corps, 49

Pels, Peter, 17

Pentecostal churches, 39, 52-53

Penunu, Augustine, 77-78

Penunu, Kingsford, 68-71, 74, 77-79, 82, 113, 242; on ancestors, 118; moon joke, 65-66, 87, 94, 178

performance of race, 250

Perman, Sarah, 257

person (*embo*), 21; *jo* (inside), 96-99, 116, 154. See also *hamo*

Phantom, the, 271n7

Pierpont, Claudia Roth, 247

Pigg, Stacey Leigh, 225

pigs, 130, 148. *See also* pork

Pike, Andrew, 44, 159

Pilcher, Jeffrey, 249

plantations, 43, 154-55. *See also* Higaturu Oil Palm Project

PNG Defense Force, 230

PNG Trade Union Congress, 230

policemen, 45

Police Motu, 5, 29, 60

political correctness, 253

pondo dopa feast, 84

Popondetta (town), 35-36, 48

pork, 22, 150-51. *See also* pigs

Portraits of the Whiteman (Basso), 269n7

postcolonial situation, 4-5, 7; crossover racial identities, 249-50; evaluation of whitemen in, 58-63; white flight, 20, 48-49, 60-61, 244

poverty, 3, 135-36, 141-42, 256-57, 275n24, 287n29

power, 17-18, 59

Prados, John, 257

Prakash, Gyan, 13

Prashad, Vijay, 248

primitivism. *See* orientalism/primitivism, discourses of

prison inmates, 274n19

Proctor, Robert, 247

projection, 143, 257-58

al-Qaeda, 258

questions asked of researcher, 15, 80-88, 106-7, 113, 142, 206-7

race: biologistic theories of, 246-48, 286n23; constructed in foods, 171-72, 204-8, 249; constructed in objects, 11-12, 204-8, 244-46, 248-49, 252, 286n22; hierarchical construction of, 251-52; modernity and, 9-15, 262n12; no-race posture, 247-48; not inherent in quality of persons, 204-5, 286n23; as performative, 250; simple dichotomous structure, 22, 61, 205-6, 225, 252; whiteness, 24, 122, 248, 261-62n9, 275-76n25. *See also* whitemen; whitemen, construction of

race cult, 251

racial categories, 6, 62, 120-22, 171-72, 205-6

racial coding, 253

racial stereotypes, 23; of African Americans, 12, 205; conventionalization of differences, 53-54, 55; debunking of ineffective, 246-47; as independent of actual persons, 7-8, 11-12, 245, 248-49, 252; robustness in the face of counterevidence, 12, 87-89, 112-13, 142, 146, 246, 248, 282n30. *See also* whitemen, construction of

racism, 11, 50, 240, 247, 253, 276n25

Rambo videos, 271n7

rapport, 16-17

Rapport, Nigel, 229

raskolism, 49, 135-37, 140-41, 232-33, 266n21, 276-77n27

reasoning backward, 166